Library of Congress Cataloging-in-Publication Data
Drew, Clifford J.
    Mental Retardation : a life cycle approach / Clifford J. Drew, Michael L. Hard-
man.—7th ed.
       p. cm.
    Includes bibliographical references and index.
    ISBN 0-13-010044-7 (case)
    1. Mentally handicapped. 2. Mental retardation. 3. Mentally handicapped—United
States.   I. Hardman, Michael L. II. Title
    HV3004.D72   2000
    362.3—dc21   99-18772
                                                         CIP

Cover art: David Shull, West Central School, Columbus, Ohio, Franklin County Board of
    Mental Retardation and Developmental Disabilities
Editor: Ann Castel Davis
Production Editor: Sheryl Glicker Langner
Design Coordinator: Diane C. Lorenzo
Text Designer: Pagination
Cover Designer: Tanya Burgess
Production Manager: Laura Messerly
Electronic Text Management: Marilyn Wilson Phelps, Karen L. Bretz, Melanie King
Director of Marketing: Kevin Flanagan
Marketing Manager: Meghan McCauley
Marketing Coordinator: Krista Groshong

This book was set in Baskerville by Prentice Hall, Inc. and was printed and bound by R.
R. Donnelley & Sons Company. The cover was printed by Phoenix Color Corp.

Photo credits: pp. 3, 53, 325, 379 by Prentice Hall College; p. 8 by Tom Watson/Merrill;
pp. 16, 19, 107, 139, 179, 268, 275, 307 by Anne Vega/Merrill; p. 21 by Gail Meese/Mer-
rill; pp. 31, 154 by Lloyd Lemmernan/Merrill; pp. 49, 69, 125, 133, 257, 273, 298, 313,
360, 370, 395, 401 by Scott Cunningham/Merrill; p. 80 by Photo Researchers; p. 95 by
Andy Brunk/Merrill; pp. 114, 189, 219, 228, 240, 349 by Todd Yarrington/Merrill; pp.
159, 204, 392 courtesy of Riverside Hospital; p. 168 by Ed Malitsky/Index Stock Imagery,
Inc.; p. 201 by George Dodson/Prentice Hall College; p. 289 by Larry Hammill/Merrill;
p. 331 by Jean-Claude Lejeune.

Printed in the United States of America

10 9 8 7 6 5 4 3

ISBN: 0-13-010044-7

Prentice-Hall International (UK) Limited, *London*
Prentice-Hall of Australia Pty. Limited, *Sydney*
Prentice-Hall of Canada, Inc., *Toronto*
Prentice-Hall Hispanoamericana, S. A., *Mexico*
Prentice-Hall of India Private Limited, *New Delhi*
Prentice-Hall of Japan, Inc., *Tokyo*
Prentice-Hall (Singapore) Pte. Ltd., *Singapore*
Editora Prentice-Hall do Brasil, Ltda., *Rio de Janeiro*

Mental Retardation

A Life Cycle Approach

Seventh Edition

Clifford J. Drew
University of Utah

Michael L. Hardman
University of Utah

Merrill
an imprint of Prentice Hall
Upper Saddle River, New Jersey
Columbus, Ohio

Preface

We are very pleased to present the seventh edition of *Mental Retardation: A Life Cycle Approach*. As you begin your study of mental retardation, we would like to give some perspective regarding what you will encounter. Our intent is to provide an introduction to mental retardation that is both readable and comprehensive. As suggested by the title, this volume is strongly based in human development. One of our earlier reviewers termed it "womb to tomb." You will follow the development of individuals with mental retardation from conception through birth, infancy, and early childhood, and then through the elementary school, adolescent, and adult years. You will also examine these people as they become old, facing many of the challenges that the general population does in aging and some that are unique. Mental retardation is a field in which this complete cycle of human life is important for a full understanding of the problems and issues involved.

We also discuss the field of mental retardation from the perspective of many disciplines, which is essential with this disability. A diagnosis of mental retardation and resulting treatment or intervention may come from any of several disciplines and often requires their united efforts. Therefore, it is important to examine interdisciplinary collaboration and its impact on the person with mental retardation to see how society and its various agencies respond to, interact with, and assist these people and their families.

This text is designed primarily for students in the social and behavioral sciences who are at the upper division undergraduate or beginning graduate level. Students in psychology, educational psychology, special education, sociology, education, rehabilitation, and social work will find the book particularly relevant to their preparation. Pre-med students and individuals anticipating professional work in nursing, law, and administration will also find a great deal that facilitates their careers.

Changes in This Edition

This edition includes many changes suggested by our reviewers and our students. We have combined some chapters and sections, reorganized others, and eliminated discussions of selected areas where students and reviewers thought such changes were important. This edition also has updated and expanded coverage of a number of growing areas related to mental retardation.

Our chapter on multicultural issues related to mental retardation continues to evolve as this broad area of concern matures in the field of mental retardation. In addition to material in this chapter, other topics relevant to multicultural issues, such as assessment bias, are integrated throughout the text.

Regarding the amount of material presented here, certain areas of discussion continue to mature in a manner that permits a more complete attainment of our original goals for the text. For example, the text is and has been focused on the full cycle of human development. Consequently, as the body of research on infants, toddlers, adults, and senior citizens with mental retardation has grown, our examination of these individuals has expanded. The commitment to analyzing mental retardation within the conceptual framework of human development remains and is much more complete in this edition than was possible when we wrote the first edition more than 25 years ago. Our purpose for this version is largely the same as it was with the release of the first edition. As authors, we hope that we have refined our skills and come closer to achieving the dream we had from the outset. In addition, the field has changed, and new topics have emerged as knowledge accumulated and societal emphases fluctuated. We have tried to reflect those changes while also retaining the fundamentals.

In addition to the basic information presented in the text are a number of pedagogical features to engage the reader actively, to facilitate a more complete understanding of the material and to provide instructors with a wider variety of teaching options. Each chapter begins with core concepts to be found in the text. Each core concept is repeated where it is discussed and finally is related to core questions designed to promote student comprehension. At the end of each chapter is a roundtable discussion section that presents an issue or a topic of interest in a format aimed at stimulating dialogue. All of these features have been incorporated to encourage active participation and interaction with the material.

Acknowledgments

The changes in this edition were made on the basis of suggestions from many sources and on our own observations of growth within the field. We are most appreciative for the guidance provided by our reviewers, colleagues, and students, who have contributed immensely to the development of this project. To those of you who gave so generously of your time reviewing earlier versions of this manuscript, we thank you. In particular, we appreciate the assistance of Michael Kallam, Fort Hays State University (KS); Tom Lombardi, West Virginia University; Peter R. Matthews, Lock Haven University (PA); Tes Mehring, Emporia State University (KS); and Carolyn Talbert-Johnson, University of Dayton. Their meticulous review of the manuscript and cogent comments helped greatly. We are grateful for the invaluable efforts of our able research assistant, Lesley Sebastian, who labored tirelessly to help assure the accuracy and comprehensive scope of our coverage. Finally, for the extra help in reading the manuscript when we couldn't find the time, for accepting our frequent complaints of fatigue, and for providing encouragement, support, and generally putting up with us, we once again thank our families. The type of suffering they put up with is truly cruel and unusual and should be discussed somewhere in our chapter on ethical concerns.

Clifford J. Drew
Michael L. Hardman

Contents

Chapter 6   Early Influences and Causation   159

Part 4   Mental Retardation: Preschool and School Years   187

Chapter 7   Infancy and Early Childhood   189

Chapter 11   The Older Person with Mental Retardation   325

Part 6 Family and Social Issues 347

Part 1

Introduction

Chapter 1 : Multidisciplinary Perspectives of Mental Retardation

Chapter 2 : Multicultural Issues

1

Multidisciplinary Perspectives of Mental Retardation

Core Concepts

- The concept of mental retardation is continually influenced by economic, societal, and situational factors.
- People with mental retardation often need more interaction with multiple disciplines and professions than those not considered to have retardation.
- No single discipline has the breadth and depth of expertise and resources necessary to fully provide for people who have mental retardation.
- The term *mental retardation* encompasses a wide range of behaviors; it is both a label of fact and a label of conjecture.
- The medical profession has a long history of involvement in the field of mental retardation.
- Many behavioral sciences, particularly psychology, have been concerned with mental retardation.
- Education probably has been the most involved with the challenges associated with mental retardation of any discipline or profession.
- To better serve and provide for individuals with mental retardation, professionals must continue to work toward overcoming friction among professions.
- The concept of mental retardation is made more complex because the varying professions that deal with it hold widely divergent viewpoints.
- The 1992 American Association on Mental Retardation (AAMR) definition employs measured intelligence, adaptive skills, and attempts to address the individual's environment, both present and optimal.
- It is important to distinguish between incidence and prevalence and to consider other factors, such as socioeconomic status (SES), severity, and age, when determining how frequently mental retardation occurs.
- Four dimensions are used in classification by the 1992 AAMR definition document covering (a) intellectual and adaptive functioning, (b) mental health, (c) physical health and etiology, and (d) environmental circumstances.
- Cross-categorical definition and classification models have emerged because conventional categories are not always effective and functional.
- The purposes and uses of definition and classification schemes must be considered and related to assessment procedures employed and to the impact of labels.
- A number of cultural changes between and within the professions are needed to enhance collaboration on challenges of those with disabilities.
- New issues and future directions in the definition and classification of mental retardation may include a better balance between individual and environmental factors.

People differ greatly in many ways, yet for the most part humans recognize a range of variability that they consider "normal." Behaviors and other characteristics in the normal range are not so extreme that they attract great attention. Outside this range, the differences are extreme enough to attract attention. People have been interested in individuals with physical, mental, and behavioral differences since the beginning of recorded history. The perspectives that religion, psychology, education, and various branches of medicine offer on such phenomena have been prominent throughout history, and perceptions of abnormality have varied widely over time and from one discipline to another. Definitions and concepts of abnormality still differ and probably will continue to change as knowledge expands and societal values shift. Like that of other disorders, the history of mental retardation has followed a changing path.

HISTORICAL PERSPECTIVES

It is important to briefly examine mental retardation's past in order to understand the forces affecting its present status. Without some historical perspective, what has succeeded and what has failed are soon forgotten. Without an understanding of the past, humans are temporally isolated and lack perspective on our present condition. Advances have been built on the accomplishments of a few insightful and caring people who could see beyond their daily tasks, dreaming and working for a better world for those with mental retardation. Such individuals had a compassionate desire to improve the condition of their fellow humans.

Core Concept

The concept of mental retardation is continually influenced by economic, societal, and situational factors.

Societies throughout all ages have been affected by mental retardation, although this does not mean that the way people have viewed those having this condition has been unchanging. Many diverse concepts and varying characteristics have played a part in different descriptions of people with mental retardation, depending on societal and situational influences during the given period. In fact, as one looks at the history of mental retardation, the picture is chameleon-like: Its appearance changes with the attitudes and convictions of the time. The concept of mental retardation has been elusive for a variety of reasons, not the least of which have been aspects of the economic, social, and political climates of various cultures throughout history. The following historical synopsis provides a brief accounting of attitudinal changes regarding mental retardation, based on the needs, ideas, and social conditions of the time. These shifting viewpoints had a significant impact on treatment approaches, just as they do in today's society (Berry & Hardman, 1998).

Before 1800, with a few notable exceptions, mental retardation was not considered an overriding social problem in any society because those with more severe retardation were either killed or died of natural causes at an early age. Those considered to have mild retardation could function fairly well in an agrarian society.

Although the earliest written reference to mental retardation is dated 1552 B.C., some anthropological studies have found evidence of mental retardation substantially predating that time. Severe head injuries were not uncommon during early times, and they most certainly resulted in behavioral irregularities. Human skulls dating to the Neolithic Age indicate that crude brain surgery had been performed. The surgical procedures apparently were intended to cure abnormal behavior. The methods used may have proceeded from the assumption that evil spirits caused strange behavior and that opening a hole in the skull permitted them to escape. Not all such operations were performed on people with mental retardation, but regardless of the reason for it, the treatment, at times, may have produced behavior resembling retardation.

Socioeconomic conditions have influenced human understanding and treatment of people with mental retardation considerably through the ages. Primitive tribes often looked on mental and physical defects with fear or as signs of disgrace, largely because of the stigma associated with such conditions. Superstitions and myths also bolstered this view. In a more pragmatic sense, those with disabilities often represented an economic drain on the tribe. In particular, nomadic tribes could ill afford to be burdened by nonproductive members who consumed limited food and water supplies but did not tangibly contribute to the common welfare. Individuals with retardation were frequently viewed as superfluous even when tribal civilization progressed and a less nomadic existence prevailed. The advent of farming and grazing could not dispel the threat of famine, which remained constantly on the horizon. The economic usefulness of people with disabilities was similar to what it had been during more nomadic times. Neither the religious nor the economic perspective was conducive to the care and maintenance of people with retardation; nonproductive citizens were expendable.

Throughout history, political authority has also been a potent force in determining the lot of those with mental retardation. Sometimes, authority supported harsh treatment of individuals with disabilities; at other times, more humane approaches were in favor. For example, in the sixth century, Pope Gregory I issued a decree instructing the faithful to assist those who were crippled. During this period, various types and degrees of care were provided for people with disabilities including those with retardation, who commonly were referred to as "idiots." England enacted legislation known as *de praerogative regis* (of the king's prerogative) under the rule of King Henry II in the 12th century. Individuals who were "natural fools" became wards of the king, and for the first time the law distinguished those whom society would now view as having mental retardation from those with mental illness. These were isolated efforts on behalf of people with mental retardation. Unfortunately, history is replete with examples of extremely discriminatory and repressive practices. Individuals with mental retardation, as well as those with other disability conditions, have long been at the mercy of the more able majority.

Although one may view the attitudes of earlier societies as primitive and uninformed, a serious examination of current thinking and practices results in a more balanced, less complacent perspective. Battles of advocacy groups in the courts and other arenas are public testimony that many challenges in the handling of people with mental retardation remain. Economic downturns and competition for funding place research and service support for mental retardation in jeopardy on a frequent basis. Future societies probably will think that the present efforts are nearly as primitive as we consider those of the past.

Reproductive sterilization has periodically been a prominent topic in the history of mental retardation. The sterilization issue has been entangled with a number of other questions: the nature-versus-nurture dispute, political and economic issues, and moral and social debates. Some early genealogical studies were very influential in generating the sterilization controversy in the United States. One such study by Henry Goddard (1913) received particularly widespread attention. Goddard traced the descendants of a Revolutionary War soldier to whom he gave the pseudonym Martin Kallikak. At one time in his life, Kallikak had sexual relations with a barmaid and fathered an illegitimate child. The descendants of this union were reported to be primarily thieves, prostitutes, and other social undesirables. Kallikak later married a "normal" woman; their descendants were purportedly normal and, in some cases, superior. The resulting conclusion was that because of genetics, one group was doomed to a life of degeneracy, whereas the other was almost certainly destined to be successful. Such reports fostered a sterilization movement in the early part of the twentieth century. Fear of mental retardation promoted widespread support for methods that would "control" it, among them sterilization and incarceration. The result was an almost immediate and complete destruction of special schools in some states. Institutions became custodial in order to "protect" society and to prevent reproduction. This was a considerable philosophical backlash because previously there had been at least guarded optimism that institutions would be able to provide education and training for those of their residents with mental retardation. Societal fears, therefore, have influenced the nature, role, and function of such institutions.

With the shift in purpose, people with mental retardation in institutions were viewed as permanent residents. They were not trained for any eventual return to society. Such actions represented the simplistic solution of preventing "problem" members of society from having children who, in turn, also might become "problem" citizens. With this solution, people could at once both deny responsibility for undesirable social conditions like retardation and allow expenditures for the care and well-being of those affected by it.

Although sterilization remains an issue, a fortunate reevaluation of the situation has been brought about by considerable expansion of the knowledge of heredity and advances in the social-skill training of those with mental retardation. Increased sophistication in research methodology has called studies like Goddard's into serious question. For example, professionals in the field are much less inclined to discount the effect of environmental influences on human development than was once the case. The descendants of Martin Kallikak and the barmaid were probably victims, at least in part, of their social situation. The descendants of Kallikak and his "normal" wife no doubt benefited from better educational and social conditions. A rational perspective requires consideration of both heredity and environment to avoid decisions and practices based on inadequate evidence.

MENTAL RETARDATION AND THE PROFESSIONS

Disciplinary Perspectives and Contributions

The question of what mental retardation is seems rather simple, yet it has plagued educators, psychologists, and other professionals for many years. Like questions in many areas of behavioral science, its simplicity is deceiving; any complete answer is highly complex. The literature about mental retardation shows that the response to this question has received considerable attention, particularly during the past 35 to 40 years.

Core Concept

People with mental retardation often need more interaction with multiple disciplines and professions than those not considered to have retardation.

In some senses, people with mental retardation are no different from the rest of the population. Their need for love, independence, support, and respect is the same as everyone else's. Everyone profits from the services and contributions of medicine, education, psychology, sociology, anthropology, social work, and religion, to name only a few areas. Individuals with mental retardation also may benefit from all these professions, but perhaps to an even greater degree. Here

Professionals from different disciplines need to work as team members to provide appropriate services for people with mental retardation.

our earlier claim that such people are no different from others becomes an obvious overstatement. During their lifetimes, citizens with mental retardation likely will receive services from a broader range of professions than their more mentally able counterparts. This probability dramatically highlights a need to consider the multiple professions involved in the field of mental retardation. The delivery of services and understanding of individuals with mental retardation are far beyond the scope of any single discipline (e.g., Pulcini & Howard, 1997). As a social phenomenon, mental retardation falls within the purview of a number of professions, and many are stakeholders in serving those with this condition (Chadsey-Rusch, Linneman, & Rylance, 1997).

Core Concept

No single discipline has the breadth and depth of expertise and resources necessary to fully provide for people who have mental retardation.

Professions are organized naturally around a circumscribed body of knowledge. However, their territories are somewhat arbitrary, and information often crosses disciplinary boundaries. Societal challenges do not readily align themselves according to the convenience of individual professions. Still, the academic model of establishing a disciplinary focus has been an effective method for directing intellectual efforts in particular areas. Before addressing the challenge of better interdisciplinary cooperation, we examine some linguistic considerations briefly and then explore the contributions of some broad areas of professions.

Terminology

Core Concept

The term **mental retardation** encompasses a wide range of behaviors; it is both a label of fact and a label of conjecture.

The term *mental retardation* has a ring of precision to many people; that is, one either has mental retardation or one does not. This perceived precision is due, in part, to the scientific orientation of western culture, in which constancy, regularity, and predictability are assumed. Past definitions of mental retardation show that perceptions of the phenomenon have changed over time. From characterizing mental retardation as a genetically determined and incurable condition, professionals have moved toward a more fluid conceptualization that includes not only biomedical causes but also environmental and social factors in determining whether someone has or does not have retardation at a given time (American Association of Mental Retardation, 1992). This change is the result of a number of factors, including advances in the natural and social sciences, economics, and the use of less pejorative terms.

As a concept, mental retardation shares with other phenomena the distinction of being linguistically influenced. The label of mental retardation is an encompassing one that includes a wide range of behavior. It shares with other such "people-labeling terms" the attribute of being a convenient, generalized expression about persons or groups (Hardman, Drew, & Egan, 1999). Mental retardation is both a label of fact and a label of conjecture. A label of fact must be quantifiable and verifiable, whereas a label of conjecture may include concepts that are as yet only hypothesized. As a label of fact, mental retardation must demonstrate observed characteristics that are verifiable and quantifiable, perhaps determined by biomedical diagnosis. Down syndrome, Tay-Sachs disease, and anencephaly are examples of conditions that can be verified through observation and medical techniques, although existing tests can quantify only approximate intelligence levels. Only about 20% of mental retardation is caused by biomedical factors, however. For the remaining 80%, the actual cause is uncertain. Therefore, mental retardation is also a label of conjecture. The influence of environment has been a major source for speculation because the incidence of milder forms of mental retardation is much higher in lower socioeconomic classes.

The framework within which a discipline views mental retardation affects societal perception of the nature and extent of the challenge. A technologically oriented society such as that in the United States responds to "breakthroughs," "cures," and "innovations" much more enthusiastically than it does to the social complexity and ambiguous nature of cultural challenges. The so-called natural sciences, on the one hand, tend to be more favored by people from such countries because the results seem more tangible and dramatic. Social sciences, on the other hand, are viewed with more suspicion because they work with the more fluid values, perceptions, and beliefs of society.

The orientation of a discipline affects its view of people with mental retardation. Differences in orientation result from the reasons individuals go into a particular discipline and from the training philosophy inherent in each discipline. It is not surprising, therefore, that physicians look for medical causes, psychologists seek psychological factors, and sociologists are interested in group influences on the behavior of individuals. Each discipline, at least initially, sees a person with mental retardation from its own perspective. Such a view should not, however, preclude different professions from at least being aware of and appreciating the contributions of their colleagues in related areas. Full and effective service delivery requires interdisciplinary and interagency collaboration (Elliott & Sheridan, 1992; McClelland & Sands, 1993; Randolph, Davis, & McKee, 1995; Sheridan, 1992; Welch & Sheridan, 1993, 1995).

Contributions of Biological and Medical Sciences

Mental retardation as a label of fact is best exemplified where there is an identifiable condition, and identifiable conditions are caused most frequently by a biomedical reason that results in structural damage. Even in this area, however, the cause of retardation is not always clear. Some chromosomal abnormalities are not always inherited (Down syndrome, microcephaly), and environmental factors such as lead poisoning and infection can contribute to or even cause structural damage.

Core Concept

The medical profession has a long history of involvement in the field of mental retardation.

Medical professionals have long been involved in mental retardation in a number of ways. A physician is frequently the first professional to identify, diagnose, and counsel parents of children with retardation. When mental retardation is evident at birth, as in the more severe cases caused by birth trauma or by a congenital condition, a physician is usually the first professional consulted. This precedence is because most parents have a family physician or pediatrician with whom they have had previous contact. At this point, if something appears to be amiss, parents most probably will turn to the professional they are accustomed to consulting.

It is not unusual for physicians to view mental retardation as a physiological problem. Although changes in this viewpoint are evident in the medical field, physicians frequently have not had sufficient background to understand the nonmedical ramifications of mental retardation. This lack may limit their effectiveness in working with the family as a unit. It certainly deters them from providing maximally effective parent counseling, which often has been one of their tasks. Changes in medical training, however, promise considerable improvement in the physician's knowledge.

Medical research is another important area of medicine that warrants mention. Advances in medical research have had a dramatic impact on certain types of mental retardation (e.g., Hagerman, 1996; Wong, Kenwick, Willems, & Lemmon, 1995). Because of intense efforts in investigating some of the clinical syndromes, such as phenylketonuria (PKU) and hypoparathyroidism, it has become possible and even common to implement procedures that prevent some forms of mental retardation. To reach this point, however, interdisciplinary collaboration was required. Once medical research had located the causal factor, it became necessary to turn to those skilled in chemistry and nutrition to implement preventive measures. Thus, even in what appears to be a very limited area—preventing a few selected types of mental retardation—the importance of interdisciplinary effort is evident.

Advances in genetics have opened avenues that should allow professionals to prevent some forms of mental retardation. Present research in genetic engineering gives promise of the future elimination of many more extreme deviations. Both positive and negative outcomes of such progress must be considered; such a process calls for input from multiple professions. At present some forms of mental retardation are preventable before conception. Prospective parents who may be carriers of defective genes can undergo genetic screening and receive counseling regarding the likelihood of their having offspring with the defect. Parents at risk then are faced with the decision of whether or not to have children. Similar options are currently available to parents who have conceived but face the probability of giving birth to an infant with the defect. Many moral and social issues surrounding such decisions currently are being debated nationally in legal and ethical forums, as well as in the basic sciences.

Psychiatry has a very lengthy history of dealing with mental retardation. When the American Association on Mental Deficiency (AAMD—now the AAMR) was organized in 1876, it began with eight charter members, all psychiatrists. Psychiatrists, when they have dealt with mental retardation, have focused primarily on the more severely involved. This practice has resulted in an inaccurate view of the broad spectrum of mental retardation. Past approaches also have tended to operate from a curative, traditional medical model. In view of such a posture, it is little wonder that the psychiatric profession in general has become somewhat discouraged and uninterested in mental retardation. Leaders and progressive thinkers in psychiatry, however, have advocated a shift away from the microscopic approaches of the past. Within the discipline is considerable hope that territories will become less rigidly marked, which would be a potentially positive shift for more adequate delivery of services to those with mental retardation.

Contributions to the Behavioral Sciences

Core Concept

Many behavioral sciences, particularly psychology, have been concerned with mental retardation.

Because mental retardation is partially a social phenomenon, one would expect that the academic fields concerned with behavior would have expressed interest in it. Behavioral sciences have made many important contributions to the understanding and treatment of mental retardation (Rojahn, Tasse, & Sturmey, 1997). Most, however, have dealt with it in only a limited fashion. Each field generally has operated independently and within the confines of its own terminology and parameters. The consequent reduction in effective contributions to education about and treatment of mental retardation exemplifies the importance of interdisciplinary collaboration. Still, each of the behavioral fields has added to the store of knowledge about mental retardation.

Psychology has been the behavioral science most directly involved in the study of mental retardation. Three important areas to which psychology has contributed are (a) intelligence theory and testing, (b) learning theory research, and (c) interpersonal social aspects (e.g., Bihm, Sigelman, & Westbrook, 1997; Campo, Sharpton, Thompson, & Sexton, 1997; Sternberg & Grigorenko, 1997). Knowledge about mental retardation would not have progressed as far as it has without the data and knowledge generated by experimental psychology. Likewise, the testing and evaluation provided by psychometric researchers and school psychologists have long been a part of the overall picture in providing programs for children with mental retardation and other disabilities (Hoy & Gregg, 1994; Kamphaus & Frick, 1996). This discipline, however, like others, frequently has operated independently, within the confines of its own terminology and perspective.

Historically, anthropology has focused relatively little attention on mental retardation, and yet it has offered some extremely important insights into the broader perspective of the condition. Early work by Edgerton (1968) described the anthropological study of mental retardation as nonexistent and argued for drastically expanded efforts. Edgerton's work (e.g., 1986, 1988) represents important anthropological contributions and has added considerable information about the adaptation of people with retardation to their environments. Although the limited data provided by anthropology are important in and of themselves, the research approach has far-reaching implications in other ways and for other professions (Edgerton, 1984a, 1984b; Espe-Sherwindt & Crable, 1993).

Anthropology offers some intriguing possibilities from the standpoint of research methodology. The major anthropological approach to research represents qualitative research methods, emphasizing the observation and recording information about people in their natural environment (Drew, Hardman, & Hart, 1996). This is a substantially different approach from that historically used in the study of mental retardation. More often than not, mental retardation researchers have elected the research method of experimental psychology, which studies the person with mental retardation in terms of performance or reaction to some artificially imposed treatment or situation. Consequently, relatively little is known about the performance or adaptation of the individuals with retardation in a variety of natural environments. Anthropological research using qualitative methodology provides useful information to complement the existing knowledge base. Educational planning in particular might profit substantially from qualitative research generating knowledge about how people with retardation operate in a natural setting (Best & Kahn, 1998; Miles & Huberman, 1994; Stainback & Stainback, 1989). Thus, anthropology is a discipline that has not been broadly involved in mental retardation to date, but one that may make substantial contributions in an interdisciplinary effort.

Sociology has been investigating mental retardation, at least tangentially, for a number of years. A number of authors have examined disabilities from sociological perspectives and concepts of social competence and deviance (Espe-Sherwindt & Crable, 1993; Guralnick, 1997; Hardman et al., 1999; Tossebro, 1995). In many cases, these authors discuss the need to view disabilities from a sociological perspective, rather than from the traditional clinical model. Such issues should become increasingly important in the years ahead as the United States and other countries continue to face the complex challenges of mental retardation. But the full contribution of sociology to the understanding of retardation in a larger societal framework remains untapped.

The law periodically has been an important force in the area of mental retardation. Unfortunately, the legal profession, as opposed to other professions, tends to operate in an adversarial role. The case of *Covarrubias v. San Diego Unified School District* (1971), which challenged special class placements, offers an example of the usual legal role. In it an injunction negated further placements until procedural changes had been made. Only recently have collaborative alliances been formed between the legal and other professions (Conley, Luckasson, & Bouthilet, 1992).

The preceding discussion of selected professions has both given examples of disciplinary perspectives and stressed the absence of interaction between professions. We could easily have selected other areas for inclusion because of their attention (or lack of it) to mental retardation.

Contributions of Education

Core Concept

Education probably has been the most involved with the challenges associated with mental retardation of any discipline or profession.

Many areas have contact, as need or interest arises, with individuals who have mental retardation. However, education—specifically, special education—is involved perhaps more comprehensively by virtue of its nature and delegated role in society. Educators do not have the luxury of viewing the world from a restricted framework or retreating behind disciplinary fences when faced with the multidisciplinary needs of those with mental retardation (Phillips-Hershey & Ridley, 1996). The role of education in mental retardation has been primarily one of instruction and research relating to instructional effectiveness (e.g., McDonnell, Thorson, McQuivey, & Kiefer-O'Donnell, 1997; Scruggs, Mastropieri, & Wolfe, 1995). In a comprehensive service-delivery model, however, the idea of instruction is an oversimplification. People do not exist in isolation or learn in a vacuum. The real contribution of education in aiding the understanding of mental retardation has been to (a) identify needs, (b) stimulate research and theory, and (c) coordinate a host of services.

Identifying children with mental retardation was one of the earliest efforts of education. The first intelligence test worthy of the name was developed by Alfred Binet at the behest of the French minister of public education. The task was to develop a way to determine which children are likely to fail in school programs and, thus, need special help; so the measurement of intelligence, therefore, has been influenced largely by educational needs, rather than by the interests of the discipline. Over the years, first educators and then theorists and test makers recognized that personality factors were also important in determining a child's present and future performance levels. Professionals have since been introduced to the concepts of adaptive behavior and social intelligence. The involvement of education in mental retardation greatly facilitated the development of these and other constructs. In other areas, the great strides in differential diagnosis, individualization of instruction, task analysis, and contingency management techniques were enhanced by educators and their interest in providing better services for youngsters with mental retardation. For example, the need to understand mild mental retardation has influenced research efforts to increase knowledge about the importance of environmental influences on intelligence. The development of secondary school programs has created a need for appropriate curricula and has prompted research on the sociological factors that relate to community placement for adolescents and young adults with mental retardation.

Without proactive recognition of the needs of those with mental retardation, educators would not be where they are today in either understanding or providing services for this group of people. We do not wish to disparage the academic disciplines and their contributions, but only to place their relative contributions into proper perspective. Educators often have been a catalyst core, stimulating the efforts of the disciplines and then using their findings for the betterment of society.

Disciplinary Factionalism

Core Concept

To better serve and provide for individuals with mental retardation, professionals must continue to work toward overcoming friction among professions.

The discussion thus far outlined a number of different disciplinary perspectives. As one examines disciplinary contributions, it becomes evident that efforts within a profession, when isolated from substantive interdisciplinary collaboration, often result in less effective delivery of services to people with mental retardation. Although change has been slow, the different professions are making progress toward bridging the gaps among their perspectives and diminishing disciplinary friction. At least two factors have prompted this progress. First, experience has shown that persons with mental retardation being served are the ultimate victims of inadequate cooperation. This victimization has provided a considerable impetus toward increasing cooperation. A second factor promoting change is the realization that something can actually be done to promote interdisciplinary collaboration (Welch & Sheridan, 1995). When knowledge is limited to a single field, differences in perspective and disciplinary friction result. The acquisition of enough information to understand another perspective reduces friction. Occasionally, a broader knowledge base may bring about the realization that apparent differences in perspective are actually not so divergent as first thought.

Beyond the challenges resulting from different perspectives, professional jealousy and territorialism often generate additional differences to a point where openly antagonistic factionalism exists between people in different professions and agencies (Hermary & Rempel, 1990). Such factionalism manifests itself in ways as diverse as published criticism and daily interaction between practitioners working—in theory, together—in the field of mental retardation. To some

Overcoming friction between disciplines is important to enhancing service to people with mental retardation.

degree, examination of roles and issues in the public forum, such as published articles, is healthier than other forms of factionalism; it may often be constructive.

Professions within an organization or agency frequently disagree (Siperstein, Wolraich, & Reed, 1994). One has only to attend regional or national conventions to hear derogatory comments about "the medical contingent," "those educators," "this division," or "that psychology group." Such an atmosphere of dissension results more in political conflict than in constructive improvement and hinders interdisciplinary collaboration substantially. We have made these comments in all editions of this text. It is fortunate that advances are being made in collaboration, but much remains to be accomplished (Welch & Sheridan, 1995).

Beyond the professional organizational level, similar factionalism exists openly in state service and political arenas. Agencies frequently compete for limited funds to operate their programs, and lobbying techniques may aim to improve the lot of one group by making another appear inadequate. When they use such tactics to preserve an agency or a discipline, people often lose sight of the real reason for cooperation, that is, to serve those citizens with mental retardation.

Because factionalism exists at various levels, it is not surprising that some friction also occurs at the practitioner level—the contact point between the service-delivery system and the client. The same professional jealousies and perceived territorial rights are found in daily interactions between professionals in contact with clients who have mental retardation. A teacher may become angry because the school psychologist does not provide information that is helpful for instruction. The psychologist may deride the teacher for being unable to understand a psychological report and to make an intuitive leap from it to instructional activities. Beyond differences in the way an individual with retardation is viewed—whether from the standpoint of instruction or of test performance—professional antagonism aggravates the problem of inadequate cooperation.

Factionalism becomes unacceptable when it interferes with the work of the practitioner. Here it becomes most obvious who suffers as a result of an inability to cooperate; fortunately, improvement seems to be greatest at this level. Practitioners have more opportunities to see the unfortunate results of inadequate service than do professionals working less closely with clients who have mental retardation. It is therefore much more difficult for them to ignore or remain unaware of the crucial necessity for interdisciplinary cooperation and mutual effort.

The advent of the idea of inclusion or least restrictive placement for all children with disabilities has led to the placing of a number of children in general education classrooms. Special education personnel, it was promised, would support the general education teacher. Although in some instances this has been successful, frequently special education personnel have not been able to provide the degree of service needed. In today's schools, many regular teachers have students with mental retardation mainstreamed in their classes. In some cases, these teachers are only superficially or not at all familiar with the characteristics of mental retardation.

CONCEPTS, DEFINITIONS, AND CLASSIFICATION

The remainder of this chapter examines the concepts, definitions, and classification systems of mental retardation. By reviewing the material in this and the following chapters, the reader will have a good overview of mental retardation. Mental retardation is a multifaceted phenomenon. It challenges education, medicine, psychology, law, society in general, and always the family involved. In this volume, we have attempted to place mental retardation in its broadest perspective—squarely in the center of human existence—because, above all, mental retardation is a human challenge. It cannot be viewed from a narrow focus if one wishes to obtain an accurate and comprehensive perspective.

MENTAL RETARDATION AS A CONCEPT

Core Concept

The concept of mental retardation is made more complex because the varying professions that deal with it hold widely divergent viewpoints.

The literature on mental retardation suggests strongly that conceptual issues are complex and somewhat unclear (Einfeld & Aman, 1995; Gresham, MacMillan, & Siperstein, 1995; Hodapp, 1995; Smith, 1997). Definitions over the years have encountered difficulties trying to incorporate advances in conceptual understanding and social progress while attempting to maintain psychometric or measurement precision. Clarifying the concept of mental retardation has become increasingly complex as many previously unknown factors are taken into account.

Earlier in this chapter we sketched the long historical interest in mental retardation. References to people with such a condition are found in the ancient history of various civilizations, which raises some interesting questions about definitional processes (Berry & Hardman, 1998). If people have been paying attention to it for so long, why do confusion and vagueness about the classification and definition of mental retardation still remain?

Many factors contribute to this lack of precision and definition. Mental retardation always implies a reduced level of intelligence, and the concept of intelligence has played a central role in the definition of mental retardation (Jarman & Das, 1996). Every controversy about the nature of intelligence has a direct impact on the field of mental retardation, so part of the difficulty in defining mental retardation relates to the notion of permanence and measurement of intelligence. Social competence has also been an important element of most recent definitions of mental retardation. The relationships between intelligence and social competence have varied considerably across different definition and classification schemes (MacMillan & Reschly, 1997).

Mental retardation has always been an area of interest and study for many professions, a fact that has contributed significantly to the challenges of definitional and conceptual clarity. There has never been a legitimate science of mental retardation independent of other disciplines. Psychiatrists, sociologists, psychologists, educators, anthropologists, and many others—each with a different perspective and language—have all addressed the challenge of mental retardation. The many different definitions and classification systems of these disciplines tend to focus on the constructs of a particular profession, rather than on the affected individual. Sociologists set out to study mental retardation as a social challenge, psychologists examine it as a psychological condition, physicians treat it as a medical condition, and so on. Even wide variations are evident within professional areas, such as clinical, developmental, and experimental psychology. We do not intend to deny the value of a multidisciplinary approach to any condition; in fact, we strongly subscribe to its worth. We do wish, however, to highlight the fact that the central conceptual focus—the individual with mental retardation—is in danger of being ignored. We intend to present mental retardation from a multidisciplinary perspective while maintaining a focus on the concept of the individual affected.

The absence of a single core conceptualization of mental retardation that is both logically and theoretically sound and still functional has seriously detracted from the preparation of professionals who work with those with mental retardation. Although a high degree of sophistication has been developed in certain technical aspects of programming for children (e.g., diagnosis, behavioral control), the lack of an effective generic concept of mental retardation has impeded the overall

Mental retardation is a human problem that affects this child and all of us.

progress of service delivery to these people. Professional expertise often consists of a great deal of technical skill in certain areas but a limited amount of knowledge about individuals with mental retardation in their total environment. Efforts are now underway to formulate conceptual frameworks that will facilitate more effective professional preparation. Individuals with mental retardation must be viewed as developing human beings with varying needs and characteristics, living in a society with fluid and complex performance standards.

From our viewpoint, human development is a cornerstone that facilitates the exacting task of viewing mental retardation across disciplines, causes, and the full range of human life. This book rests on this conceptual cornerstone, and its subtitle—*A Life Cycle Approach*—derives from it. As you read this volume you will find that its overall structure is the life cycle, from conception through old age. Certain topics tend to stand somewhat alone, and in most cases you will find mini-discussions of those topics in the context of development. We hope that the perspective of human development will be as useful and interesting to you as you examine the complex and fascinating study of mental retardation as it has been to us.

MENTAL RETARDATION: A DEFINITION IN TRANSITION

Core Concept

The 1992 AAMR definition employs measured intelligence, adaptive skills, and attempts to address the individual's environment, both present and optimal.

Definitions of mental retardation have varied widely over the years and from discipline to discipline. As suggested in the title of this section, mental retardation's definition is currently in a transition period. In the previous edition of this text, we noted considerable agreement among the general definitions in use at that time. These included definitions by the AAMR; the American Psychiatric Association (APA) (1987); and Public Law 101–476, the Education of the Handicapped Act Amendments of 1990. Revised definitions subsequently have been published by the AAMR (1992) and the APA (*DSM-IV,* 1994). These two sources remain very similar in their views of mental retardation, with a nearly verbatim correspondence in their basic definitions.

The AAMR definition of mental retardation states that

> *mental retardation* refers to substantial limitations in present functioning. It is characterized by significantly subaverage intellectual functioning, existing concurrently with related limitations in two or more of the following applicable adaptive skill areas: communication, self-care, home living, social skills, community use, self-direction, health

and safety, functional academics, leisure, and work. Mental retardation manifests before age 18. (AAMR, 1992, p. 1)

Add to this definition four assumptions that are essential considerations in applying the definition:

1. Valid assessment considers cultural and linguistic diversity as well as differences in communication and behavioral factors;
2. The existence of limitations in adaptive skills occurs within the context of community environments typical of the individual's age peers and is indexed to the person's individualized needs for supports;
3. Specific adaptive limitations often coexist with strengths in other adaptive skills or other personal capabilities; and
4. With appropriate supports over a sustained period, the life functioning of the person with mental retardation will generally improve. (AAMR, 1992, p. 1)

As with past definitions, the AAMR document provides explanations to amplify concepts and clarify meaning for those professionals in the field of mental retardation. For convenience, portions of this material have been excerpted and presented in the text that follows.

Social skill adaptation is an important element in the definition of mental retardation.

Explanation of the Definition of Mental Retardation

Mental retardation refers to substantial limitations in present functioning ... Mental retardation is defined as a fundamental difficulty in learning and performing certain daily life skills. The personal capabilities in which there must be a substantial limitation are conceptual, practical, and social intelligence. These three areas are specifically affected in mental retardation whereas other personal capabilities (e.g., health and temperament) may not be.

It is characterized by significantly subaverage intellectual functioning ... This is defined as an IQ standard score of approximately 70 to 75 or below, based on assessment that includes one or more individually administered general intelligence tests developed for the purpose of assessing intellectual functioning. These data should be reviewed by a multidisciplinary team and validated with additional test scores or evaluative information.

Existing concurrently ... The intellectual limitations occur at the same time as the limitations in adaptive skills.

With related limitations ... The limitations in adaptive skills are more closely related to the intellectual limitation than to some other circumstances such as cultural or linguistic diversity or sensory limitation.

In two or more of the following applicable adaptive skill areas ... Evidence of adaptive skill limitations is necessary because intellectual functioning alone is insufficient for a diagnosis of mental retardation. The impact on functioning of these limitations must be sufficiently comprehensive to encompass at least two adaptive skill areas, thus showing a generalized limitation and reducing the probability of measurement error.

Communication, self-care, home living, social skills, community use, self-direction, health and safety, functional academics, leisure, and work ... These skill areas are central to successful life functioning and are frequently related to the need for supports for persons with mental retardation. Because the relevant skills within each adaptive skill area may vary with chronological age, assessment of functioning must be referenced to the person's chronological age.

Mental retardation manifests before age 18 ... The 18th birthday approximates the age when individuals in this society typically assume adult roles. In other societies, a different age criterion might be determined to be more appropriate.

The following four assumptions are essential to the application of this definition ... These statements are essential to the meaning of the definition and cannot be conceptually separated from the definition. Applications of the definition should include these statements. Each statement has clear implications for subsequent assessment and intervention.

1. **Valid assessment considers cultural and linguistic diversity as well as differences in communication and behavioral factors ...**

Failure to consider factors such as the individual's culture, language, communication, and behaviors may cause an assessment to be invalid. Sound professional judgment and the use of a multidisciplinary team appropriate to the individual and his or her particular needs and circumstances should enhance the validity of assessments.

2. **The existence of limitations in adaptive skills occurs within the context of community environments typical of the individual's age peers and is indexed to the person's individualized needs for support . . .** Community environments typical of the individual's age peers refer to homes, neighborhoods, schools, businesses, and other environments in which persons of the individual's age ordinarily live, learn, work, and interact. The concept of age peers should also include consideration of individuals of the same cultural or linguistic background. The determination of the limitations in adaptive skills goes together with an analysis of supports that can include services that the individual needs and supports in the environments.

3. **Specific adaptive limitations often coexist with strengths in other adaptive skills or personal capabilities . . .** Individuals frequently have strengths in personal capabilities independent of mental retardation. Examples include: (a) an individual may have strengths in physical or social capabilities that exist independently of the adaptive skill limitations related to mental retardation (e.g., good health); (b) an individual may have a strength in a particular adaptive skill area (e.g., social skills) while having difficulty in another skill area (e.g., communication); and (c) an individual may possess certain strengths within a particular specific adaptive skill while at the same time having limitations within the same area (e.g., functional math and functional reading, respectively). Some of a person's strengths may be relative rather than absolute; thus, the strengths may be best understood when compared to the limitations in other skill areas.

4. **With appropriate supports over a sustained period, the life functioning of the person with mental retardation will generally improve . . .** *Appropriate supports* refer to an array of services, individuals, and settings that match the person's needs. Although mental retardation may not be of lifelong duration, it is likely that supports will be needed over an extended period of time. Thus, for many individuals, the need for supports will be life long. For other individuals, however, the need for supports may be intermittent. Virtually all persons with mental retardation will improve in their functioning as a result of effective supports and services. This improvement will enable them to be more independent, productive, and integrated into their community. In addition, if individu-

als are not improving significantly, this relative lack of improvement should be the basis for determining whether the current supports are effective and whether changes are necessary. Finally, in rare circumstances, the major objective should be to maintain current level of functioning or to slow regression over time.

Source: *Mental Retardation: Definition, Classification, and Systems of Supports* (9th ed.) (pp. 5–7). Washington, DC: American Association on Mental Retardation. Copyright 1992 by the American Association on Mental Retardation. Reprinted by permission.

Although the importance of adaptive behavior and community integration (with supports) has been evident in the mental retardation literature for some time, **measurement** of adaptive behavior has not achieved the desired precision despite great efforts in this area (e.g., Jacobson & Mulick, 1992; Storey, 1997; Wilson, Seaman, & Nettelbeck, 1996). Adaptive behavior remains a very important concept in the most recent AAMR definition (1992), although the assessment concerns continue, as well as other apprehensions regarding implementation and the possibility of magnifying difficulties with overrepresented ethnic minorities (Gresham et al., 1995; MacMillan, Gresham, & Siperstein, 1993).

Including adaptive behavior in definitions of mental retardation first occurred during the early 1960s and represented a rather dramatic broadening of formally stated criteria. Professionals had largely ignored adaptive behavior in framing definitions previously, depending almost exclusively on measured intelligence as the defining characteristic of mental retardation. Individuals' behaviors are considered adaptive by the degree to which they manage their personal needs, display social competence, and avoid problem behaviors (Bruininks & McGrew, 1987). Use of the term *adaptive skills* in the 1992 AAMR definition reflects an attempt to provide an array of competency areas, rather than relying on a more generic concept of adaptive behavior. As indicated in the definition, 10 adaptive skill areas are considered. Table 1–1 presents a summary of these areas and examples of how they might be portrayed.

One perspective of a person with mental retardation is an individual who relies on some type of action on the part of the family or community for protection or support. Two factors usually enter into this perception: (a) the deficits or level of functioning of the individual with mental retardation and (b) the threshold of community tolerance. The kind of action taken depends on the degree to which an individual deviates significantly from community norms—from those zones of behavior or performance society deems acceptable. The 1992 AAMR definition conceptualizes mental retardation in this manner—in the context of his or her environment. Figure 1–1 captures the framework graphically.

People who have mental retardation often come to the attention of someone in their community because their behavior deviates (or is thought likely to deviate) enough from the norm to be noticeable. This is true regardless of the degree of retardation. Identification of the individual who has more severe retardation may occur at birth or very early in life. This identification usually

TABLE 1–1
1992 AAMR Adaptive Skill Area

Skill area	Portrayal
Communication	The ability to understand and communicate information by speaking or writing, through symbols, sign language, or nonsymbolic behaviors, such as facial expressions, touch, or gestures.
Self-care	Skills in such areas as toileting, eating, dressing, hygiene, and grooming.
Home living	Functioning in the home, including clothing care, house-keeping, property maintenance, cooking, shopping, home safety, and daily scheduling.
Social	Social interchange with others, including initiating and terminating interactions, responding to social cues, recognizing feelings, regulating own behavior, assisting others, and fostering friendships.
Community use	Appropriate use of community resources, including travel in the community; shopping at stores; obtaining services such as at gas stations and medical and dental offices; and using public transportation and facilities.
Self-direction	Making choices, following a schedule, initiating contextually appropriate activities, completing required tasks, seeking assistance, resolving problems, and demonstrating appropriate self-advocacy.
Health and safety	Maintaining own health, including eating; identifying, treating, and preventing illness; basic first aid; sexuality; physical fitness; and basic safety.
Functional academics	Abilities and skills related to learning in school that also have direct application in life.
Leisure	Developing a variety of leisure and recreational interests that are age- and culture-appropriate.
Work	Ability that pertains to maintaining part- or full-time employment in the community, including appropriate social and related work skills.

Adapted from Mental Retardation: Definition, Classification, and Systems of Supports *(9th ed.) (pp. 40–41). Washington, DC: American Association on Mental Retardation. Copyright 1992 by the American Association on Mental Retardation, by permission.*

happens because some anomaly, either physical or behavioral, is already observable at this stage of development. For those who deviate less obviously from the norm, identification may not occur until much later, as they begin to develop language or enter school. Initial suspicions may then be investigated further through formal diagnostic evaluation and clinical observation by professional personnel. Details about diagnosis and evaluation are given later in this volume.

FIGURE 1–1
Graphic Conceptualization of the
1992 AAMR Definition of Mental
Retardation

From Mental Retardation: Definition,
Classification, and Systems of Sup-
ports *(9th ed.) (p. 10). Washington,
DC: American Association on Mental
Retardation. Copyright 1992 by the
American Association on Mental
Retardation, by permission.*

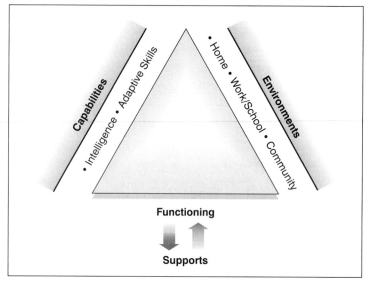

General Structure of the Definition of Mental Retardation

INCIDENCE AND PREVALENCE

Core Concept

It is important to distinguish between incidence and prevalence and to
consider other factors, such as socioeconomic status (SES), severity, and
age, when determining how frequently mental retardation occurs.

Two terms frequently have been confused in the field of mental retardation—*incidence* and *prevalence*. **Incidence** refers to the number of new cases identified during a given time period (often 1 year). Tabulating incidence involves a count of all
individuals newly identified as having retardation during that period, whether
newborns or youngsters diagnosed in school. **Prevalence** refers to all cases existing at a given time, including both newly identified cases and cases still labeled as
having mental retardation from some earlier diagnosis. Figure 1–2 illustrates
how incidence and prevalence differ and how they relate to each other. Obviously, these two kinds of counting do not result in the same number. But the
terms have often been used rather loosely, sometimes interchangeably, in the literature. Wherever possible, we examine incidence and prevalence separately.

How frequently do individuals evidence sufficient deviancy to be considered
to have mental retardation? A precise answer to this question is difficult to obtain.
Accurate accounting is neither easy nor economically feasible. Inconsistent definition and classification schemes over the years have made the problems of determining frequency of retardation even more formidable, particularly from a cross-
cultural perspective (Feldman & Walton-Allen, 1997; Fujiura & Yamaki, 1997).

Estimates of the prevalence of mental retardation in the United States historically have ranged from about 1% to 3% of the general population, with the 3% figure being most consistently cited. In its 16th Annual Report to Congress (1994), the U.S. Department of Education estimated that 12% of the children with disabilities (ages 6 to 21) in U.S. public schools have mental retardation.

Translating estimated U.S. percentages into numbers of individuals with retardation is interesting, albeit difficult. Although some estimates are dated, the epidemiology of mental retardation has not changed fundamentally in more than 30 years (Fryers, 1987). According to the U.S. Department of Education (1994), 532,427 youngsters ages 6 to 21 with mental retardation were served under the Individuals with Disabilities Education Act (IDEA) and Chapter 1 during 1992–1993. Beyond the school years covered by specific federal laws, however, such figures become much more difficult to determine and are based on population projections. The President's Task Force on the Mentally Handicapped (1970) estimated that 6 million Americans had mental retardation. More recent estimates based on the 3% prevalence figure place the numbers in excess of 7 million (Hardman et al., 1999). Which figures are accurate? We cannot choose with any degree of confidence. Figures like these defy confirmation because of the astronomical cost of a complete census of those with retardation.

Those with more mild retardation represent by far the largest proportion of the mental retardation population (Murphy, Yeargin-Allsopp, Decoufle, & Drews, 1995). Hardman et al. (1999) estimated that about 2.5% of the total population

FIGURE 1–2
Incidence and Prevalence of
Mental Retardation

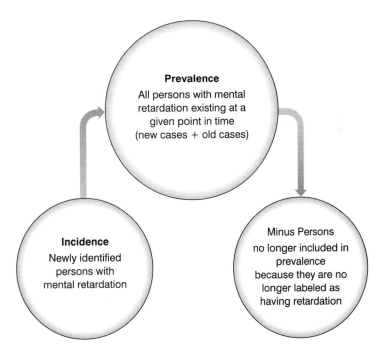

Prevalence
All persons with mental retardation existing at a given point in time (new cases + old cases)

Incidence
Newly identified persons with mental retardation

Minus Persons no longer included in prevalence because they are no longer labeled as having retardation were mildly affected. The moderate level of mental retardation is generally thought to involve about 0.3% of the total population, and the severe and profound levels combined account for approximately 0.1%. These figures do not total exactly 3%, although they are close. Recent estimates suggest that about 90% of people with mental retardation function at the mild level (U.S. Department of Education, 1994). It should be noted that the 1992 AAMR definition does not employ a classification system regarding degree of retardation (mild, moderate, severe/profound); a person either has mental retardation or does not. The approach taken in this most recent document is to suggest varying levels of intensity for the supports needed by an individual with retardation. Four intensity levels of supports are outlined in the following manner: (a) **intermittent**—the supports are provided as needed, which is characteristically periodic and for short durations; (b) **limited**—supports are provided more consistently (not intermittently), but they are not typically intense; (c) **extensive**—regular assistance, perhaps daily, is provided in some environments, such as at work; and (d) **pervasive**—supports are of high intensity, constant, and needed across environments. As noted in the definition document, the level of support required tends to parallel the person's limitations (AAMR, 1992). It is likely that the prevalence of mental retardation is highest at the intermittent support level and progressively less as one moves toward the pervasive level. However, this definition document has not been available long enough for implementation to provide such information.

Variation is found in the incidence of mental retardation at different chronological ages. Research has indicated consistently that the incidence of mental retardation is highest during the school years, approximately 5 to 18 years of age, with much lower numbers both at preschool and at postschool levels. This distribution relates both to the level of retardation and to the tasks presented to the individual at different ages. Before children enter the formal school environment, all but the more severely affected can perform as expected. Youngsters identified as having retardation before about age 6 are often more seriously involved, reflecting levels of disability that constitute only a small percentage of all individuals with mental retardation. As children enter school, they encounter a concentrated emphasis on abstract learning, such as the acquisition of academic skills. In such an environment, children with mental retardation become highly visible because abstract skills are their area of greatest difficulty. The majority of youngsters identified as having mental retardation at this stage function in the mild range of intellectual deficit. The identification of cases of mental retardation decreases dramatically in people whose formal schooling has ended. The majority of individuals with mental retardation have been identified by the time they leave school. If no one has so identified an individual during the school years, when tasks emphasize abstraction, identification is unlikely to occur in the less demanding postschool environment.

The prevalence of mental retardation also varies a great deal as a function of age. Across all levels of IQ, the highest prevalence occurs in the 6 to 19 age range (nearly 70% of the population with mental retardation). The pattern of prevalence is similar for those with mental retardation but who have IQs of 50 and above, except that an even higher percentage falls in the 6 to 19 age range (80%) and smaller percentages in the preschool and postschool ranges. Several factors contribute to this pattern. The years of formal schooling are particularly taxing for those with mental retardation because the tasks require conceptual performance in areas in which they are most deficient. The drop in prevalence after school years is interesting and occurs for reasons related to but somewhat different from incidence influences. After formal education, many individuals with retardation (particularly those in the 50+ IQ range) are placed back in an environment where the demands focus less on their areas of greatest difficulty. They seem more able to adapt in the postschool environment. In addition to a lower incidence during postschool years, prevalence also is reduced because some individuals may no longer be functioning as retarded and are thus "declassified." This reduction in prevalence has often been referred to as the phenomenon of "disappearing" or "6-hour" retardation (referring to the time spent in school each day). This may indicate that the school curriculum is out of phase with later life and may not represent effective education, at least for these people. The prevalence patterns also differ as a function of age for the lower IQ ranges. A much lower rate of prevalence occurs in children between the ages of 6 and 19. This pattern is influenced by a higher incidence during the early years of life and a higher mortality rate among more severely affected individuals when they are young.

Finally, mental retardation prevalence also varies across different levels of SES. Various estimates have suggested considerable prevalence differences as a function of SES and degree of impairment. Table 1–2 presents a summary of approximate prevalence rates of retardation per 1,000 school-age children by SES level and IQ level. As indicated in Table 1–2, no difference appears in prevalence as a function of SES level at the two lower levels of functioning (IQ 20 to 50 and below 20). The two higher levels of functioning (IQ 50 to 75 or 80 and IQ 75 or 80 to 90), however, show an increasing prevalence as SES decreases. These figures suggest that in the lower levels of mental retardation, where greater central nervous system damage pervades, different SES levels are equally vulnerable. The prevalence of milder impairments seems more sensitive to environmental influences. Because the majority of individuals with retardation are mildly impaired, the social dimensions of mental retardation stand out.

MENTAL RETARDATION CLASSIFICATION

Core Concept

Four dimensions are used in classification by the 1992 AAMR definition document covering (a) intellectual and adaptive functioning, (b) mental health, (c) physical health and etiology, and (d) environmental circumstances.

TABLE 1–2
Retardation Prevalence per
1,000 School-Age Children by
SES and IQ Level

Degree of impairment	Socioeconomic status		
	High	Middle	Low
IQ below 20	1	1	1
IQ 20 to 50	4	4	4
IQ 50 to 75 or 80	10	25	50
IQ 75 or 80 to 90	50	170	300

Note: IQ ranges are given for the convenience of the reader. They represent ranges that vary to some degree, depending on the source of data.

Classification schemes for mental retardation have varied over the years in much the same fashion that definitions have. Prior to publication of the 1992 AAMR manual, classification focused primarily on two major parameters: (a) severity of the disability and (b) causation or etiology. Terminology such as *mild, moderate,* and *severe* or *profound mental retardation* related primarily to disability severity with respect to both measured intelligence and adaptive behavior. Etiology classification was based predominately on the biomedical causes of mental retardation (e.g., infection, trauma, metabolism, nutrition). The two parameters of severity and etiology have been so prominent in the field of mental retardation that some have claimed they have actually generated two distinct research cultures—one focusing on etiology and one on severity of impairment (Baumeister, 1997; Hodapp & Dykens, 1994).

The *DSM-IV* classification system continues to describe those with mental retardation in terms of degrees of severity that reflect the measured level of intellectual functioning (APA, 1994). Four degrees of severity are employed, with a fifth category reflecting situations in which the person's intelligence is untestable. As outlined in *DSM-IV,* these severity classifications are as follows: (a) **mild mental retardation,** with IQ levels of 50–55 to approximately 70, (b) **moderate mental retardation,** with IQ levels of 35–40 to 50–55, (c) **severe mental retardation,** with IQ levels of 20–25 to 35–40, (d) **profound mental retardation,** with IQ levels below 20 or 25, and (e) **mental retardation,** severity unspecified, for which a strong presumption of mental retardation exists but the individual's intelligence is not testable by use of standard instruments. This latter category exists for circumstances in which the person functions at a level too low for testing, is uncooperative, or is too young for reliable assessment (e.g., infants) (APA, 1994, p. 40). This classification varies from that of the AAMR (1992). AAMR does not employ such terms as *mild, moderate, severe,* and *profound* to suggest degree of intellectual impairment. A measured IQ of 70 to 75 is set as the ceiling, and AAMR then turns to other classification factors. Both AAMR (1992) and the APA (1994) clearly acknowledge the measurement error potential involved in assessing intelligence.

With the publication of its 1992 manual, AAMR challenged the field to view mental retardation in a manner different from that used before. Four dimensions are outlined and intended for use in the processes of diagnosis, classification, and determining what support is needed for an individual: (a) Dimension I—intellectual functioning and adaptive behavior, (b) Dimension II—psychological/emotional considerations, (c) Dimension III—physical/health/etiology considerations, and (d) Dimension IV—environmental considerations. These dimensions provide the overall organizing concept for examining someone suspected of having mental retardation.

Diagnosis of mental retardation focuses on Dimension I, the intellectual functioning and adaptive skills. Essentially, three criteria are used in the process of determining a diagnosis of mental retardation. The *first criterion* relates to an intellectual functioning level with an IQ of 70 to 75 or below as measured on an appropriately standardized intelligence test. The term *appropriate* requires attention to the person's cultural, social, and linguistic background. The *second criterion* for diagnosis requires that the intellectual functioning deficit must coexist with significant disabilities in at least two of the adaptive skill areas outlined in Table 1–1. The *third criterion* dictates that the mental retardation must be evident before the age of 18. For a person having met these three criteria, the AAMR considers that a diagnosis of mental retardation is legitimate, and classification is undertaken by identifying the person's strengths, limitations, and needs for supports.

The AAMR classification process involves all four dimensions. In Dimension I (intellectual functioning and adaptive skills), the individual's strengths and limitations are described in the context of the 10 adaptive skill areas (e.g., communication, self-care, home living). Although intellectual functioning is a part of Dimension I, once the diagnosis is completed, it does not enter into clas-

Effective assessment must use a variety of types of measurement, often including direct observation of specific skills, to develop a useful and accurate evaluation.

sification. Under Dimension II, the psychological/emotional strengths and limitations based on clinical assessments, behavioral observations, or formal diagnosis of some other source are described. This clinical assessment of the person's mental health should involve multiple sources of data (e.g., interviews, psychometric instruments, observations), and those sources are included in the description. For Dimension III, the general physical health is described, and the etiology or cause of the mental retardation is indicated if known. The person's general health status is an important consideration because it relates to his or her overall vitality and, therefore, to the treatment plan. Knowledge about etiology is of interest under this dimension because of its presumed utility in prevention or minimization of effect in some cases. Although for many cases of mental retardation the cause still remains unknown, in some situations, prevention is possible (e.g., preventing maternal alcohol or drug abuse). Likewise, some conditions may be treated early to prevent central nervous system damage (e.g., dietary control for those with phenylketonuria) or to limit detrimental effects through special programs of rehabilitation or education. The classification attention to Dimension IV involves a description of environmental circumstances for the person with mental retardation. This description includes a report on the individual's current environment, as well as what would maximally promote growth and functioning.

The final step in AAMR's diagnosis, classification, and program planning process focuses on development of a profile of the support needed by the person with mental retardation. As mentioned earlier, AAMR suggests four levels of supports: (a) intermittent (episodic as needed), (b) limited (not episodically related but of a limited time), (c) extensive (regularly in some environments), and (d) pervasive (constant and intense). In developing a profile of supports, these levels are considered across Dimension I (focusing on the 10 adaptive skill areas), Dimension II (mental health or psychological/emotional factors), Dimension III (physical/health), and Dimension IV (environmental considerations, such as living, work, and education settings). Throughout the diagnosis, classification, and program planning process, it is assumed that an interdisciplinary team is employed to provide the most comprehensive and appropriate analysis of the person's status. Figure 1–3 graphically presents a summary of the diagnosis, classification, and program planning process with the AAMR system.

CROSS-CATEGORICAL ISSUES

Core Concept

Cross-categorical definition and classification models have emerged because conventional categories are not always effective and functional.

Mental retardation is one category among several that refer to atypical conditions involving ability or behavior. Others include such examples as learning dis-

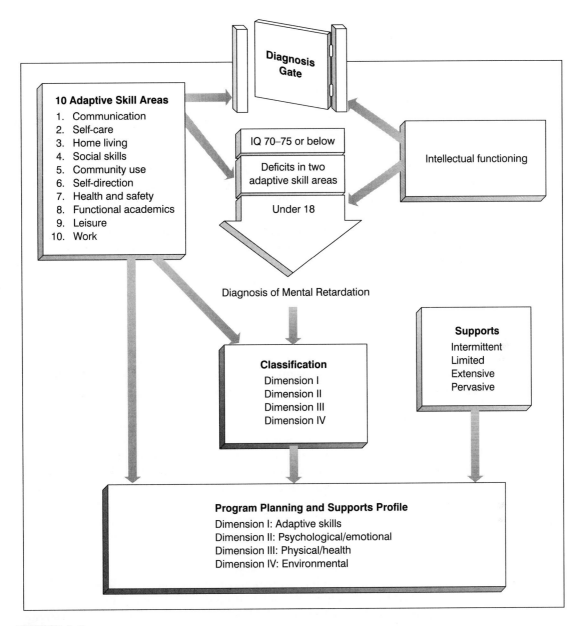

FIGURE 1–3
Diagnosis, Classification, and Program Planning Using the 1992 AAMR Definition

abilities and behavioral disorders or emotional disturbance, among many more. The use of such categories has had a long history among professionals working in the various fields of disabilities. Considerable interest has emerged in the literature regarding perspectives on disabilities that cross traditional categorical boundaries—often called "cross-categorical views." Some authors contend that traditional categories do not adequately distinguish between different disability conditions and do not serve the needs of individuals from a service-delivery standpoint. Not surprisingly, some believe that cross-categorical views are not functional and see the traditional categories as being more appropriate. The issues involved in categorical and cross-categorical approaches to defining disabilities have received substantial attention and continue to be controversial (Halgren & Clarizio, 1993; Langford, Boas, Garner, & Strohmer, 1994; Lipsky & Gartner, 1989; Stainback, Stainback, & Forest, 1989).

Interest in cross-categorical definitions arose primarily because, in certain circumstances, the traditional categories did not clearly distinguish between people with disorders carrying different labels (Epstein, Polloway, Foley, & Patton, 1990). In some instances, those with disparate categorical labels did not appear all that different; they seemed to have a number of characteristics in common. Additionally, treatment or interventions for some individuals with different labels appeared to be quite similar, or at least to have a number of similar elements. What has become evident is that categorical terminology is functional for some purposes with some conditions but that for other circumstances it does not serve well (Hardman et al., 1999; Millington, Szymanski, & Hanley-Maxwell, 1994). It is important to give consideration to the purposes and uses of definition and classification schemes.

Cross-categorical models have often been based on the concept of symptom severity with terminology such as *mild learning and behavior disorders, moderate learning and behavior disorders,* and *severe and profound/multiple disorders.* Definitions for such broad categories include a range of ability and behavioral deficits and a variety of assessment approaches. Although any framework of this nature is necessarily general, the focus of this scheme is on functional and behavioral specificity, articulated and evaluated for intervention purposes on an individualized basis (Hardman et al., 1999). It is also clear that cross-categorical models do not supplant conventional categories totally. But where categories do not serve well, cross-categorical models are worthy of consideration.

Cross-categorical models appear most applicable to individuals who are mildly affected by a disability. People with mild mental retardation, mild behavioral disorders, and mild learning disabilities have many shared characteristics. Youngsters at the mild disability level of functioning have a great deal of performance and skill overlap in the classroom, regardless of their specific labels (Hardman et al., 1999). Service delivery from a cross-categorical model, based on functional skills, may be most reasonable for these individuals (Epstein et al., 1990; Langford et al., 1994).

More severely involved disabilities have greater distinctiveness, and conventional categories are more relevant. Individuals with moderate to severe disabilities have fewer shared characteristics, although some remain, and these are typically acknowledged by cross-categorical models. Primary disabling conditions are more easily identified as impairment severity increases. People with more severe mental retardation are also more likely to be affected by multiple challenges. This likelihood is particularly true for those at the lowest level of functioning. Those with profound mental retardation have a relatively high incidence of congenital heart disease, epilepsy, respiratory distress, sensory impairments, and poor muscle tone. From a definition or classification standpoint, these are often viewed as associated conditions and would require pervasive supports using the AAMR model (1992). From the perspective of intervention or treatment, each must be addressed on a case-by-case basis. Treatment is the ultimate outcome of any diagnosis and therefore of any definition or classification, irrespective of whether a conventional categorical or cross-categorical approach is used. An appropriate choice of classification scheme depends on the context of use.

PURPOSES AND USES OF DEFINITIONS AND CLASSIFICATIONS

Core Concept

The purposes and uses of definition and classification schemes must be considered and related to assessment procedures employed and to the impact of labels.

There are a variety of reasons for development of definitions and classifications. At times they provide a conceptual picture of the entity being defined or classified and facilitate communication between professionals. Beyond these roles, however, remains the vital reason for defining and classifying: the translation of statements into action and, in the case of mental retardation, delivery of appropriate service (Smith, 1997).

The adequacy with which a classification scheme translates into practice is the acid test of the system. A number of factors influence the ease with which this translation can occur; two are particularly evident from the preceding discussion of definitions and classification. The first is how faithfully a scheme reflects reality; the second relates to how well the purposes or objectives of the group using a definition or classification are served. If a classification or definition system is out of touch with actual circumstances, it is of questionable value and probably will fall into disuse.

One also must consider the second factor: How well served are the purposes or objectives of the group using a scheme? Purposes and objectives have been nearly as numerous and diverse as the professions involved with mental retardation. Many years ago, Heber (1962) noted that mental retardation has not historically been treated as a scientific concept, but rather as one with primary relationships to social, administrative, and legal matters. Current literature supports this statement, and the absence of discussions of mental retardation with clearly stated intervention purposes is striking.

Many past attempts at defining and classifying individuals with mental retardation have approached this process with grouping as a principal goal. Grouping, or placing like individuals together on some dimension, serves certain types of purposes well; yet, others are addressed only minimally or not at all. For example, grouping may serve administrative convenience quite efficiently. It makes individuals easy to count, funds easy to allocate by type of individual, and services easy to justify to legislatures. Grouping also serves legal purposes well. Placing an individual in a particular category facilitates decisions about legal responsibility for action or guardianship. The reader should realize that we are writing from the perspective of a service professional or agency. In both cases, a certain degree of impersonality is involved in decision making. Administrative personnel, legislators, and staff at legal agencies are often working with numbers and names, rather than with the individuals the numbers and names represent. We are not addressing the question of how well the individual is served by such decisions. For the individual, service or justice may be marginal or absent.

We do not intend to detract from the value of grouping or the progress that the field of mental retardation has made because of it. In fact, the impetus from legislation and administration of funds at local, state, and federal levels has permitted dramatic service improvements over the years. The issue is that one classification framework may be effective in one sector but serve poorly another sector whose purposes are different.

Educational classifications of retardation have most often followed the grouping approach. Unfortunately, such an approach may not be effective for purposes of instruction, particularly with at-risk learners. The evidence consistently indicates this, and educators of youngsters with mental retardation are recognizing the challenges of group classification for instructional purposes. Problems arise when educational programs focus on grouping, rather than on specifying purposes, objectives, and resulting classificatory schemes more in harmony with the instructional process. The literature demonstrates a long-standing awareness of such problems. Concern has arisen when evaluation indicates that the curriculum for individuals with retardation reflects convenience in administrative arrangement as much as consideration for the student's needs.

An interesting phenomenon begins to emerge when one reviews a number of sources discussing mental retardation. Because classification and definition are related to diagnosis and evaluation, one serious deficit is evident with respect to both assessment and conceptualization. The conceptual weakness revolves around the relationship of evaluative assessment, classification, and, ultimately, programming. We have evaluated; this is the classification; now what? Early approaches to this topic often suggested that nature should be allowed to take its course, that one can "predict a typical course and outcome with a fair degree of confidence." Diagnostic purposes are adequately served here if the only inclination is a passive response; no active education or instruction is implied. Current trends in instructional philosophy and technique do not support a passive predictive approach but dictate active intervention with specific behavioral objectives. A logical and functional link must exist between assessment and intervention (Gregory, 1996; Kamphaus & Frick, 1996).

Criterion-Referenced Versus Norm-Referenced Measurement

Definitions are not always precise; definitions of mental retardation have suffered difficulties compounded by the demand for measurement. This imprecision is one facet of the AAMR definition that has had questions raised about it: How are the conceptualizations going to be translated into practical measurement (Greenspan, 1997; Gresham et al., 1995)? Placing individuals into groups—often IQ groupings in the field of mental retardation—has been predominant in definition and classification for years. The measurement approach most often used for this scheme is known as **norm-referenced assessment.** Norm-referenced evaluation has not historically been of much value for educational programming. More conceptually sound and pragmatically oriented evaluation approaches have been developed in areas other than mental retardation. It is necessary to explore these approaches' ideas about instruction for persons with retardation in order to make educational programming more effective.

Norm-referenced evaluation is the single type of psychological testing with which most people are familiar. Probably the best-known assessment of this nature is the intelligence test. The goal of norm-referenced evaluation is to measure an individual's functioning in comparison with some standard or group norm. A test score indicates whether the person stands above or below another student or some hypothetical average student. This type of evaluation is of value for purposes of grouping and, beyond that, has relevance for certain educational decisions. But the approach has limitations for overall instructional programming, and it cannot be expected to yield all of the information necessary for the actual teaching process. Global acceptance of the norm measure in the past has led to diminished educational effectiveness for those with mental retardation and much frustration with psychometric information in general.

During the past 25 years, a counterpart evaluation concept has developed to meet a variety of needs not addressed by norm-referenced assessment. This concept, known as criterion-referenced evaluation, does not place the individual's performance in comparative context with either other students or a normative standard. **Criterion-referenced assessment** often focuses on specific skills and looks at absolute level of performance. It attends to the actual level of mastery that an individual exhibits or, from a different perspective, the level at which a student becomes unable to perform a given task. This type of information is more useful to a teacher because it indicates the level at which to begin instruction. Criterion-referenced evaluation has become very popular in recent years, but despite its obvious usefulness for instruction, it does not by itself provide all of the information needed for a well-reasoned total educational effort. The development of effective total evaluation models related to learning has become a high priority. Such models are discussed in detail in Chapter 3.

Labeling

In examining classification, it is important also to consider labeling. Labeling has been a source of controversy and concern for many years. For example, over 50 years ago Maslow (1948) examined the potential problems of labeling, and interest in possible difficulties associated with such designations has continued (see Hastings, 1994; Millington et al., 1994; Somogyi, 1995). Classification and labeling are not necessarily synonymous. Many years ago Hobbs noted that "by *classifying* we mean the act of assigning a child or a condition to a general category or to a particular position in a classification system. . . . By *labeling* we mean to imply more than the assignment of a child to a category. We intend to include the notion of public communication of the way the child is categorized" (1975, p. 43). This distinction is logical and important as research on labeling continues. Under current classification schemes, however, it may have limited practical significance for those working as care providers. It is difficult to imagine a case in which an individual would be referred, evaluated, and classified without having some label attached. The nature of human communication involves giving names to phenomena we observe. To speak about something causes us to label it, whether by a given name, a type name, or an impression that the phenomenon gives to the speaker (and we typically have names or labels for such impressions). Labeling occurs more commonly than most of us consciously realize. There are many labels, types of labels, and sources of labeling (e.g., societal, official, and unofficial labeling). What a label is intended to signify may differ from the meanings associated with the term. It is clear that terms evoke a variety of responses from different individuals (Hardman et al., 1999) and result in many types of services for those labeled. This set of circumstances is certainly the case for labels of deviance, illustrating the complexity of the relationship between labeling and other factors related to categorization and treatment, as well as part of the difficulty in determining the effects of labeling.

For many it has become fashionable to denounce labels and labeling with strong statements regarding their detrimental effects or lack of usefulness. Many have rallied to the cause of eliminating labels. The idea behind most of these efforts is that labeling has a negative impact on those labeled. This belief has great emotional appeal. But empirical evidence of the effects of labeling is difficult to obtain because of the complex interrelationship of labeling with other factors. If we are to continue and progress in research on the effects of labeling, we must be able either to isolate the effects or to study the problem in the context of its complexities.

One of the most frequently discussed issues is that of the impact of a label on the individual who bears it, even though definitive evidence about this influence is much less available than folklore would suggest. But the topic certainly warrants discussion because it is so central to the controversy.

The idea of the self-fulfilling prophecy has played a prominent role in controversies related to labeling impact. This notion springs from an assumption that expectations and the treatment of the labeled individual resulting from those expectations largely determine the individual's behavior. The label, it is assumed, substantially influences expectations. This perspective came to popularity because of the widely cited work by Rosenthal and Jacobson (1966, 1968), although the idea had been presented long before (Merton, 1948). Despite its intuitive appeal, solid empirical evidence supporting the notion of the self-fulfilling prophecy has been limited. The Rosenthal and Jacobson (1966, 1968) work has been severely criticized for serious methodological flaws, and the controversy continues unresolved (Gelfand, Jenson, & Drew, 1997).

Considerable research has been unable to replicate Rosenthal and Jacobson's findings, likely due to the serious flaws in their research methods (Gelfand et al., 1977). Such evidence seems to question the self-fulfilling prophecy notion. It is important to emphasize, however, that these studies were only unable to replicate the findings of Rosenthal and Jacobson. It is most unfortunate that such an important problem was studied with such flawed methodology, particularly when it drew so much attention. There is little question that people form certain expectations of students with retardation and such expectations affect their perceptions and assessment of competence (Caplan, 1995). Evidence supports this assertion (Millington et al., 1994; Langford et al., 1994). Yet it remains unclear what information people use in forming their expectations, and the precise effect that expectations (and labels) have is uncertain (Merton, 1987). Personal impressions that trigger biases may be formed on the basis of very little information (sometimes a single cue), even in the face of evidence to the contrary (Skowronski & Carlston, 1989). Attention to this area and its broad impact in several contexts continues (Bihm et al., 1997; Madon, Jussim, & Eccles, 1997; Perske, 1997; Somogyi, 1995).

NEW ISSUES AND FUTURE DIRECTIONS

Core Concept

A number of cultural changes between and within professions are needed to enhance collaboration on challenges of those with disabilities.

Two broad considerations about cooperation among professions must be examined. One is the knowledge base; the other is the service base. We can best approach the accumulation of data through both multidisciplinary and interdisciplinary models. **Multidisciplinary** models are those in which various professions approach a particular condition from their own focus (e.g., psychological aspects of mental retardation or medical aspects of mental retardation). Each discipline's database grows, but frequently little of the information is of help in crossing disciplinary boundaries. Unlike the multidisciplinary method, the **interdisciplinary** model attempts to develop "knowledge bridges" among professions. From these efforts, subdisciplinary areas such as social psychology, sociolinguistics, and neuropsychology have developed.

A serious movement has gained considerable momentum in special education to refrain from labeling handicapping conditions. Such terms as *mental retardation, behavior disorders,* and *learning disabilities,* although convenient for communication, often tell little about a person's characteristics or skill level. Likewise, these terms, when used in social contexts, often create flawed perceptions, imprecise applications, and inaccurate generalizations. Tradition also has designated professions by labels—psychology, education, psychiatry—that are extremely convenient for communication. In fact, society could not operate without terminology and classifications. Disciplinary labels, however, do generate certain difficulties. Although they may help communicate in restricted settings, they also generate myriad connotations for each discipline. As a result, the same type of stereotyping that disability labels produce also emerges from the use of disciplinary labels. The labels all too frequently serve primarily to specify and promote boundaries—to assert territorial rights. And territorialism is a strong deterrent to effective interdisciplinary collaboration.

We suggested earlier that a broader knowledge base appears to facilitate interdisciplinary collaboration. In retrospect this seems logical—perhaps simplistic. Without at least some information about another person's profession, it is extremely difficult even to communicate, much less to collaborate. Professionals are all quite experienced at obtaining information by reading journals and books. In many cases, however, such approaches are not enough to break down interdisciplinary barriers. Frequent personal contact with individuals from other professions is more valuable. In fact, some would maintain that such contact is not only helpful but also prerequisite to facilitating interdisciplinary efforts.

When the topic of interdisciplinary collaboration is raised, people often indicate that attitudes must change before it can occur. Although most would agree with such a statement, few would be able to specify how to accomplish this. Attitude is an extremely elusive concept, and it is far from easy to tell how one knows when an attitude has changed. It is somewhat easier, however, to speak in terms of altering certain behaviors.

One important behavioral change for interdisciplinary collaboration involves reaction to terminology differences. Frequently dramatic differences in terminology are found among professions. A person's use of a different terminology often generates negative reactions, sometimes even openly derogatory remarks, from individuals with different disciplinary perspectives. It is easy to see how such reactions lend themselves to friction and antagonism, rather than to cooperation. Individuals working in an interdisciplinary setting must minimize their negative reactions to differences in terms. This does not mean adopting another's terms, concepts, and approaches, but it does imply that value judgments about the approach of the other discipline should be set aside. For example, Person A may not choose to incorporate the term *ego strength* into his or her vocabulary or conceptualization. If that is an important term in Person B's disciplinary perspective, however, Person A can understand its meaning and judge it as different—but not inappropriate—terminology. Certainly, the acceptance of "differentness" is a goal of people working for the benefit of individuals with mental retardation, and improvements in interactions among professionals can reduce friction and ultimately promote greater effectiveness in terms of interdisciplinary collaboration.

A second major behavioral change relates to the delivery of services to those with mental retardation. We have discussed how the various professions, operating through their applied branches, work independently of one another. Educators often have been left with a series of tests and reports that are mostly meaningless for planning a given child's educational program. In an interdisciplinary service approach model, although assessments are derived independently, the program parameters are decided on in collaboration. This approach, however, also has some drawbacks. Hardman et al. (1999) pointed out that, too often, professional cooperation diminishes after initial program development, and efforts at coordinating services often are limited.

A third approach, called the **transdisciplinary** model, has emerged as an effort to overcome some of the problems of the other two models. The approach emphasizes the role of a primary therapist, who acts as the contact person for service provisions, so the number of professionals with direct child contact is minimal. In a transdisciplinary plan, no discipline is dominant; all should support each other and make their own contributions. This approach requires a mature professional attitude that recognizes and allows for relevant disciplinary contributions. The emphasis is on the person with mental retardation and that person's needs, rather than on the professions working independently or without coordination. The role of the teacher (whether regular or special) in this method becomes predominant because the teacher sees the children on a daily basis and is most conversant with their skills, aptitudes, and needs. The teacher, then, would be the primary therapist and the focal point for diagnoses and direct service to the child.

One of the crucial points of a chapter on disciplinary collaboration involves the purpose of the professional effort. Often, people in the various professions working in mental retardation lost sight of the reason for their effort—the citizen with retardation. Too much time and attention are devoted to professional self-preservation, sometimes to the detriment of the individuals being served. People in the fields frequently focus more on professional image than on the needs of those with mental retardation. Whether the perspective is primarily medical, educational, psychological, or based on some other discipline, it is essential that the focus be maintained on serving the total individual.

Core Concept

New issues and future directions in the definition and classification of mental retardation may include a better balance between individual and environmental factors.

Mental retardation, like most other phenomena associated with human development and performance, is an enormously complex condition. It is not a unidimensional disorder; to capture the vital elements and contributors adequately in a single definition or classification system is far from simple. In this chapter, we have examined some of the issues pertaining to mental retardation definitions. Many changes have occurred over the years as theories have been discarded and weak logic strengthened. In 1987 Baumeister noted, "The dominant systems of definition and classification have not changed radically over the past two decades. The focus continues to be on subaverage general intelligence and deficits in adaptive behavior" (p. 799). The foundation remains a concept centered on individual people almost to the exclusion of the world around them. It was his concern that a more balanced view was important, focusing on "both the individual and the demands and constraints of specific environments" (Baumeister, 1987, p. 800).

The 1992 AAMR definition has presented such a perspective. It is not a definition that will simplify matters, but a person's functioning in his or her environment is not a simple matter. We know that people do not function in a vacuum and that environment significantly influences their performance. Throughout this volume are references to the vital influence of environmental circumstances on the development of abilities, performance, and behavior. One of the major challenges at this point is to determine how well the AAMR scheme can be translated into practice. Such concerns have emerged, and the field now must undertake this most difficult task (Greenspan, 1997; Jacobson, 1994; Smith, 1997; Storey, 1997; Wilson et al., 1996), including refinement of policies, procedures, and related assessment.

One of the major elements of mental retardation—intelligence—has been reformulated in a manner that considers environmental factors (Sternberg, 1985). This concept also has been placed in the context of mental retardation, although prior to the publication of the most recent AAMR definition (Sternberg & Spear, 1985). Theoretical and empirical research must explore the extension of such thinking to issues of definition and classification.

One of the foremost questions confronting the AAMR (1992) definition is utility in the field. Definition and classification must translate into practical applications of diagnosis and treatment. Such conceptions do little if they are no more than theories in the pages of scientific journals. Diagnosis and treatment, to be widely accepted, must not become so burdensome that they are not used. Experience with well-conceived assessment systems, which are complex and time consuming, has suggested that lack of convenience is a deterrent to broad usage. Utility must receive attention in reconceptualization efforts that translate into field application. Additionally, some evidence suggests that an overwhelming number of minority children are classified as having mental retardation even under assessment systems designed to be pluralistic (Heflinger, Cook, & Thackery, 1987). This concern also emerges in the early examinations of the AAMR definition (Gresham et al., 1995; MacMillan et al., 1993).

Core Questions

1. How did politics, economics, and basic lifestyles affect the lives of persons with mental retardation before 1900?
2. What were some of the factors that influenced the development of institutions in the United States for persons with mental retardation?
3. Why is the term *mental retardation* considered to be linguistically influenced?

4. Why is mental retardation both a label of fact and a label of conjecture?
5. What are three areas in which psychology has contributed to the understanding of those with mental retardation?
6. What are the primary contributions of education in helping the understanding of the phenomenon of mental retardation?
7. What are some of the reasons that disciplinary factionalism has arisen and continues to exist?
8. What can be done to reduce friction between disciplines and professions involved with persons with mental retardation?
9. How has the concept of mental retardation differed among professions, and how might this difference affect an individual with retardation?
10. What four assumptions are essential in applying the 1992 AAMR definition of mental retardation?
11. What is the difference between incidence and prevalence?
12. When considering the question of how frequently mental retardation occurs, how do SES, age, and severity affect the answer?
13. How has the involvement of many disciplines studying mental retardation been both an advantage and a disadvantage?
14. How do the 10 skill areas identified in the 1992 AAMR definition document enter into diagnosis, classification, and program planning?
15. How can definition and classification systems serve some purposes well and yet be inappropriate for others?
16. Why is it important that a relationship exist between definitions, classifications, assessment, and programming?
17. What difficulties may be encountered when using a grouping-oriented classification system and criterion-referenced assessment?
18. What difficulties may be encountered when using norm-referenced assessment in conjunction with a definition that does not focus on grouping but that instead emphasizes functional skill levels?

Roundtable Discussion

1. As a concept, mental retardation has been known throughout recorded history. The perception of what is and what is not deemed mental retardation has changed continually. With the development of scientific approaches to the study of human behavior, many disciplines and professions emerged and began to identify areas of primary investigation, concern, and service.
   In a discussion group, consider the societal influences on mental retardation and how present-day attitudes toward persons with mental retardation may or may not reflect them. What would be some realistic approaches to overcoming disciplinary and professional friction?
2. When discussing or otherwise considering any phenomenon, the definition of what is being addressed is the foundation upon which discussion is based. Communication between you and your student colleagues would be difficult indeed if some of you were talking about automobile transportation and

others were considering air travel while you all were using the same term, say, mustifig. You would encounter difficulty agreeing on cost per mile, miles easily traveled in an hour, and many other factors. This is an exaggerated illustration, but in some ways it is not all that different from mental retardation as it is defined, categorized, counted, and served.

In your study group or on your own, examine mental retardation from the perspective of sociology, medicine, psychology, education, and politics (for example). Describe the phenomenon, discuss service, and address various aspects of how it should be conceptualized. Examine parameters of classification, labeling, and assessment. After completing this exercise, determine how you will conceptualize the phenomenon of mental retardation to best learn all that must be known about it and how those affected can best be served. Reflect on the information in this chapter and consider the task facing early professionals working in mental retardation. They did (and do) not have a simple assignment. We hope you will do better.

References

American Association on Mental Retardation (AAMR). (1992). *Mental retardation: Definition, classification, and systems of supports* (9th ed.). Washington, DC: Author.

American Psychiatric Association (APA). (1987). *Diagnostic and statistical manual of mental disorders* (3rd rev. ed.). Washington, DC: Author.

American Psychiatric Association (APA). (1994). *Diagnostic and statistical manual of mental disorders* (4th ed.). Washington, DC: Author.

Baumeister, A. A. (1987). Mental retardation: Some conceptions and dilemmas. *American Psychologist, 42,* 796–800.

Baumeister, A. A. (1997). Behavioral research: Boom or bust? In W. E. MacLean, Jr. (Ed.), *Ellis' handbook of mental deficiency, psychological theory, and research* (3rd ed., pp. 3–45). Mahwah, NJ: Erlbaum.

Berry, J., & Harman, M. (1998). *Lifespan perspectives on the family and disability.* Boston: Allyn & Bacon.

Best, J. W., & Kahn, J. V. (1998). *Research in education* (8th ed.). Boston: Allyn & Bacon.

Bihm, E. M., Sigelman, C. K., & Westbrook, J.P. (1997). Social implications of behavioral interventions for persons with mental retardation. *American Journal on Mental Retardation, 101,* 567–578.

Bruininks, R. H., & McGrew, K. (1987). *Exploring the structure of adaptive behavior.* Minneapolis: University of Minnesota, University Affiliated Program on Developmental Disabilities.

Campo, S. F., Sharpton, W. R., Thompson, B., & Sexton, D. (1997). Correlates of the quality of life of adults with severe or profound mental retardation. *Mental Retardation, 35,* 329–337.

Caplan, P. J. (1995). *They say you're crazy: How the world's most powerful psychiatrists decide who is normal.* Reading, MA: Addison-Wesley.

Chadsey-Rusch, J. Linneman, D., & Rylance, B. J. (1997). Beliefs about social integration from the perspectives of persons with mental retardation, job coaches, and employers. *American Journal on Mental Retardation, 102,* 1–12.

Conley, R. W., Luckasson, R., & Bouthilet, G. N. (Eds.). (1992). *The criminal justice systems and mental retardation: Defendants and victims.* Baltimore: Paul H. Brookes.

Covarrubias v. San Diego Unified School District, 7-394, Tex. Rptr. 1971.

Drew, C. J., Hardman, M. L., & Hart, A. W. (1996). *Designing and conducting research: Inquiry into education and social science* (2nd ed.). Boston: Allyn & Bacon.

Edgerton, R. B. (1968). Anthropology and mental retardation: A plea for the comparative study of incompetence. In H. J. Prehm, L. A. Hamerlynck, & J. E. Crosson (Eds.), *Behavioral research in mental retardation* (pp. 75–87). Eugene, OR: Rehabilitation Research and Training Center in Mental Retardation.

Edgerton, R. B. (1984a). Anthropology and mental retardation: Research approaches and opportunities. *Culture, Medicine, & Psychiatry, 8,* 25–48.

Edgerton, R. B. (1984b). The participant observer approach to research in mental retardation. *American Journal of Mental Deficiency, 88,* 498–505.

Edgerton, R. B. (1986). Alcohol and drug use by mentally retarded adults. *American Journal of Mental Deficiency, 90,* 602–609.

Edgerton, R. B. (1988). Aging in the community: A matter of choice. *American Journal of Mental Retardation, 92,* 331–335.

Einfeld, S. L., & Aman, M. (1995). Issues in the taxonomy of psychopathology in mental retardation. *Journal of Autism and Developmental Disorders, 24*(2), 143–147.

Elliott, S. N., & Sheridan, S. M. (1992). Consultation and teaming: A review of problem-solving interactions among educators, parents, and support personnel. *Elementary School Journal, 92,* 315–338.

Epstein, M. H., Polloway, E. A., Foley, R. M., & Patton, J. R. (1990). Comparisons of performance on academic probes by students with mild retardation, learning disabilities and behavior disorders. *Special Services in the Schools, 6,* 121–134.

Espe-Sherwindt, M., & Crable, S. (1993). Parents with mental retardation: Moving beyond the myths. *Topics in Early Childhood Special Education, 13,* 154–174.

Feldman, M. A., & Walton-Allen, N. (1997). Effects of maternal mental retardation and poverty on intellectual, academic, and behavioral status of school-age children. *American Journal on Mental Retardation, 101,* 352–364.

Fryers, T. (1987). Epidemiological issues in mental retardation. *Journal of Mental Deficiency Research, 31,* 365–384.

Fujiura, G. T., & Yamaki, K. (1997). Analysis of ethnic variations in developmental disability prevalence and household economic status. *Mental Retardation, 35,* 286–294.

Gelfand, D. M., Jenson, W. R., & Drew, C. J. (1997). *Understanding child behavior disorders* (3rd ed.). Fort Worth: Harcourt Brace.

Goddard, H. H. (1913). *The Kallikak family.* New York: Macmillan.

Greenspan, S. (1997). Dead manual walking? Why the 1992 AAMR definition needs redoing. *Education and Training in Mental Retardation and Developmental Disabilities, 32,* 179–193.

Gregory, R. J. (1996). *Psychological testing: History, principles, and applications* (2nd ed.). Boston: Allyn & Bacon.

Gresham, F. M., MacMillan, D. L., & Siperstein, G. N. (1995). Critical analysis of the 1992 AAMR definition: Implications for school psychology. *School Psychology Quarterly, 10,* 1–19.

Guralnick, M. J. (1997). Peer social networks of young boys with developmental delays. *American Journal on Mental Retardation, 101,* 595–612.

Hagerman, R. J. (1996). Biomedical advances in developmental psychology: The case for Fragile X syndrome. *Developmental Psychology, 32,* 416–424.

Halgren, D. W., & Clarizio, H. F. (1993). Categorical and programming changes in special education services. *Exceptional Children, 59,* 547–555.

Hardman, M. L., Drew, C. J., & Egan, M. W. (1999). *Human exceptionality: Society, school, and family* (6th ed.). Needham Heights, MA: Allyn & Bacon.

Hastings, R. P. (1994). On "good" terms: Labeling people with mental retardation. *Mental Retardation, 32,* 363–365.

Heber, R. (1962). Mental retardation: Concept and classification. In E. P. Trapp & P. Himelstein (Eds.), *Readings on the exceptional child: Research and theory* (pp. 69–81). New York: Appleton-Century-Crofts.

Heflinger, C. A., Cook, V. J., & Thackery, M. (1987). Identification of mental retardation by the System of Multicultural Pluralistic Assessment: Nondiscriminatory or nonexistent? *Journal of School Psychology, 25,* 177–183.

Hermary, M. E., & Rempel, J. (1990). Parental and staff perceptions of individual programming teams: Collaboration in and beyond the conference. *Education and Training in Mental Retardation, 25,* 25–32.

Hobbs, N. (1975). *The futures of children.* San Francisco: Jossey-Bass.

Hodapp, R. M., & Dykens, E. M. (1994). Mental retardation's two cultures of behavioral research. *American Journal on Mental Retardation, 98,* 675–687.

Hoy, C., & Gregg, N. (1994). *Assessment: The special educator's role.* Pacific Grove, CA: Brooks/Cole.

Jacobson, J. W. (1994). Review of *Mental retardation: Definition, classification, and systems of support.* *American Journal on Mental Retardation, 98,* 539–541.

Jacobson, J. W., & Mulick, J. A. (1992). A new definition of mentally retarded or a new definition of practice. *Psychology in Mental Retardation and Developmental Disabilities, 18*(2), 9–14.

Jarman, R. F., & Das, J. P. (1996). A new look at intelligence and mental retardation. *Developmental Disabilities Bulletin, 24,* 3–17.

Kamphaus, R. W., & Frick, P. J. (1996). *Clinical assessment of child and adolescent personality and behavior.* Boston: Allyn & Bacon.

Langford, C. A., Boas, G. J., Garner, W. E., & Strohmer, D. C. (1994). Selecting clients for supported employment: Functional criteria or categorical labels? *Journal of Applied Rehabilitation Counseling, 25*(3), 37–41.

Lipsky, D. K., & Gartner, A. (Eds.). (1989). *Beyond separate education: Quality education for all.* Baltimore: Paul H. Brookes.

MacMillan, D. L., Gresham, F. M., & Siperstein, G. N. (1993). Conceptual and psychometric concerns about the 1992 AAMR definition of mental retardation. *American Journal on Mental Retardation, 98,* 325–335.

MacMillan, D. L., & Reschly, D. J. (1997). Issues of definition and classification. In W. E. MacLean, Jr. (Ed.), *Ellis' handbook of mental deficiency, psychological theory, and research* (3rd ed., pp. 47–74). Mahwah, NJ: Erlbaum.

Madon, S., Jussim, L., & Eccles, J. (1997). In search of the powerful self-fulfilling prophecy. *Journal of Personality and Social Psychology, 72,* 791–809.

Maslow, A. (1948). Cognition of the particular and of the generic. *Psychological Review, 55,* 22–40.

McClelland, M., & Sands, R. G. (1993). The missing voice in interdisciplinary communication. *Qualitative Health Research, 3*(1), 74–90.

McDonnell, J., Thorson, N., McQuivey, C., & Kiefer-O'Donnell, R. (1997). Academic engaged time of students with low-incidence disabilities in general education classes. *Mental Retardation, 35,* 18–26.

Merton, R. K. (1948). The self-fulfilling prophecy. *Antioch Review, 8,* 193–210.

Merton, R. K. (1987). Three fragments from a sociologist's notebooks: Establishing the phenomenon, specified ignorance, and strategic research materials. *Annual Review of Sociology, 13,* 1–28.

Miles, M. B., & Huberman, A. M. (1994). *Qualitative data analysis: An expanded sourcebook* (2nd ed.). Thousand Oaks, CA: Sage.

Millington, M. J., Szymanski, E. M., & Hanley-Maxwell, C. (1994). Effect of the label of mental retardation on employer concerns and selection. *Rehabilitation Counseling Bulletin, 38,* 27–43.

Murphy, C. C., Yeargin-Allsopp, M., Decoufle, P., & Drews, C. D. (1995). The administrative prevalence of mental retardation in 10-year-old children in metropolitan Atlanta, 1985 through 1987. *American Journal of Public Health, 85,* 319–323.

Perske, R. (1997). Prisoners with mental disabilities in 1692 Salem and today. *Mental Retardation, 35,* 315–317.

Phillips-Hershey, E. H., & Ridley, L. (1996). Strategies for acceptance of diversity of students with mental retardation. *Elementary School Guidance and Counseling, 30,* 282–291.

President's Task Force on the Mentally Handicapped. (1970). *Action against mental disability.* Washington, DC: Government Printing Office.

Pulcini, J., & Howard, A. M. (1997). Framework for analyzing health care models serving adults with mental retardation and other developmental disabilities. *Mental Retardation, 35,* 209–217.

Randolph, D. L., Davis, S. E., & McKee, P. D. (1995). A multidisciplinary approach to graduate and undergraduate internships: A national directory. *Psychology: A Journal of Human Behavior, 32,* 1–7.

Rojahn, J., Tasse, M. J., & Sturmey, P. (1997). The stereotyped behavior scale for adolescents and adults with mental retardation. *American Journal on Mental Retardation, 102,* 137–146.

Rosenthal, R., & Jacobson, L. (1966). Teacher expectancies: Determinants of pupils' IQ gains. *Psychological Reports, 19,* 115–118.

Rosenthal, R., & Jacobson, L. (1968). *Pygmalion in the classroom.* New York: Holt, Rinehart & Winston.

Scruggs, T. E., Mastropieri, M. A., & Wolfe, S. (1995). Scientific reasoning of students with mild mental retardation: Investigating preconceptions and conceptual change. *Exceptionality, 5,* 223–244.

Sheridan, S. M. (1992). What do we mean when we say "collaboration"? *Journal of Educational and Psychological Consultation, 3,* 89–92.

Siperstein, G. N., Wolraich, M. L., & Reed, D. (1994). Professionals' prognoses for individuals with mental retardation: Search for consensus within interdisciplinary settings. *American Journal on Mental Retardation, 98,* 519–526.

Skowronski, J. J., & Carlston, D. E. (1989). Negativity and extremity biases in impression formation: A review of explanations. *Psychological Bulletin, 105,* 131–142.

Smith, J. D. (1997). Mental retardation as an educational construct: Time for a new shared view? *Education and Training in Mental Retardation and Developmental disabilities, 32,* 167–173.

Somogyi, K. M. M. (1995). "On 'good' terms: Labeling people with mental retardation": Response. *Mental Retardation, 33,* 63.

Stainback, S., Stainback, W., & Forest, M. (Eds.). (1989). *Educating all students in the mainstream of regular education.* Baltimore: Paul H. Brookes.

Stainback, W., & Stainback, S. (1989). Using qualitative data collection procedures to investigate supported education issues. *Journal of the Association for Persons with Severe Handicaps, 14,* 271–277.

Sternberg, R. J. (1985). *Beyond IQ: A triarchic theory of human intelligence.* London: Cambridge University Press.

Sternberg, R. J., & Grigorenko, E. L. (1997). Are cognitive styles still in style? *American Psychologist, 52,* 700–712.

Sternberg, R. J., & Spear, L. C. (1985). A triarchic theory of mental retardation. In N. R. Ellis & N. W. Bray (Eds.), *International review of research in mental retardation* (Vol. 13, pp. 301–326). New York: Academic Press.

Storey, K. (1997). Quality of life issues in social skills assessment of persons with disabilities. *Education and Training in Mental Retardation and Developmental Disabilities, 32,* 197–200.

Tossebro, J. (1995). Impact of size revisited: Relation of number of residents to self-determination and deprivatization. *American Journal on Mental Retardation, 100,* 59–67.

U.S. Department of Education. (1994). To assure the free appropriate public education of all children with disabilities. *16th Annual Report to Congress on the Implementation of the Individuals with Disabilities Education Act.* Washington, DC: Government Printing Office.

Welch, M., & Sheridan, S. M. (1993). Educational Partnerships in teacher education: Reconceptualizing how teacher candidates are preparing for teaching students with disabilities. *Teacher-in-Action, 15*(3), 35–46.

Welch, M., & Sheridan, S. M. (1995). *Educational Partnerships: An ecological approach to serving students at risk.* Orlando, FL: Harcourt Brace Jovanovich.

Wilson, C., Seaman, L., & Nettelbeck, T. (1996). Vulnerability to criminal exploitation: Influence of interpersonal differences among people with mental retardation. *Journal of Intellectual Disability Research, 40,* 8–16.

Wong, E. V., Kenwick, S., Willems, P., & Lemmon, V. (1995). Mutations in the cell adhesion molecule L1 cause mental retardation. *Trends in Neurosciences, 18,* 168–172.

Chapter **2**

Multicultural
Issues

Core Concepts

- Cultural diversity involves critically important differences that require attention as one examines mental retardation both as a concept and in the context of individual diagnosis.
- Poverty exists at a rather high level among many culturally different groups and creates a number of environmental disadvantages that may impair a child's mental development.
- Social values that differ from culture to culture may result in behavioral or performance deviation from the cultural majority, which some might view as reflecting mental retardation.
- Language differences that create academic difficulties for some culturally different children may place them in jeopardy of being considered as having mental retardation.
- Personnel and procedures involved in the assessment, diagnosis, and intervention process may all contribute to a biased overrepresentation of culturally different children as having mental retardation.
- Cultural diversity may result in some influences that generate actual developmental disadvantages, as well as differences.
- Professionals in the field of mental retardation must change basic models of research on mental retardation so that the influences of cultural diversity on human development can be more fully understood.

As evident from the material in Chapter 1, departures from normal functioning are part of the nature of mental retardation. People with mental retardation exhibit lower intellectual performance, accompanied by reduced functioning in social skills. The perspective and expectations for intellectual and social functioning emanate from the context of society, and definitions of mental retardation emerge from societal expectations (AAMR, 1992; APA, 1994). Standards of performance are broadly defined by the social majority. The source of these general performance standards gives rise to several concerns related to ethnic and cultural diversity that have existed for years and that continue to present potential problems (Greenspan, 1997; Gresham, MacMillan, & Siperstein, 1995; MacMillan, Gresham, & Siperstein, 1993; Smith, 1997).

Core Concept

Cultural diversity involves critically important differences that require attention as one examines mental retardation both as a concept and in the context of individual diagnosis. ☼

Countries with multiple cultures, such as the United States, are always faced with circumstances in which definitions of acceptable behavior differ among various groups. Yet, broad and general standards that cross cultural boundaries also operate and must be determined in some way. Typically, such definitions emanate from sources and institutions that primarily represent the views of the cultural majority (Spina & Tai, 1998). Scientists, public officials, and others in positions of authority more often reflect the perspectives of the cultural majority than those of smaller groups or population segments (O'Connor, 1997; Lillard, 1998; Gauvain, 1998; Suarez-Orozco, 1996).

Issues related to cultural diversity are integrated into topical discussions in this volume, where they play a major role. These issues pervade many aspects of mental retardation, such as causation, assessment, prevention, and placement and treatment. In this chapter, however, we examine certain subjects separately. One serious problem is that of misdiagnosis and classification of individuals as having mental retardation when, in fact, their behavior or performance is related to cultural difference, rather than to significantly reduced functioning. The concept of the self-fulfilling prophecy (the idea that one becomes what one is labeled) is prominent in this area. The self-fulfilling prophecy suggests that if a person is labeled as having mental retardation, over time he or she will begin to function as a person who has mental retardation—even if the initial diagnosis was inaccurate.

The self-fulfilling prophecy was first discussed in print over 50 years ago by Merton (1948), although it did not become well known until publication of the work of Rosenthal and Jacobson on teacher expectations (1968a, 1968b). Rosenthal and Jacobson's results suggest that children's performance levels reflect their teachers' expectations to a substantial degree. This research generated a great deal of controversy, and the topic remains one of considerable interest in a number of areas (Dvir, Eden, & Banjo, 1995; Madon, Jussim, & Eccles, 1997). We as professionals still have much to learn before the effects of expectation are fully understood. It is clear, however, that the self-fulfilling prophecy represents an area of concern, particularly for youngsters who may be identified as having mental retardation more on the basis of cultural background than on performance level. Evidence continues to emerge suggesting that matters such as ethnicity have an influence on youngsters being identified as having a disability and receiving special education (Satcher, 1995; Yeargin-Allsopp, Drews, & Decoufle, 1995).

ASSOCIATED INFLUENCES

Many factors contribute to what we are and how we function in the world around us. We inherited certain material from our parents that affects how we look and act. We also are greatly influenced by both our current environment and the one in which we grew up. All of these contributions come together in a complex, interactive manner to affect the person that each of us is now.

Certain influences contributing to lowered intellectual functioning are related to culturally different populations in this country. They are associated with mental retardation by virtue of environmental conditions beyond the control of the people shaped by them—for example, poor health care and poverty. Other influences are inherent where there is cultural and ethnic diversity, such as social customs or mores and language differences. These are more purely cultural influences and come into play with respect to a literal perspective of the term *differences* in the sense that behavior and performance that are predominant in one culture may not play the same role in another. All of these factors concern workers in the area of mental retardation.

Poverty

Core Concept

Poverty exists at a rather high level among many culturally different groups and creates a number of environmental disadvantages that may impair a child's mental development.

Poverty is one of the strongest influences on sociocultural environment today, and impoverished economic circumstances are found more often among ethnic minorities than among their White counterparts (Wohl & Aponte, 1995). Lamison-White (1997), reporting for the U.S. Bureau of the Census, indicated that 8.6% of the non-Hispanic White population live below the poverty level. The proportions of African American and Hispanic populations in this economic condition, however, are much higher—28.4% and 29.4%, respectively (see Figure 2–1). This situation places many members of ethnic minorities at a considerable disadvantage from several standpoints, with the impoverished circumstances playing a significant role. For example, minority children from poor environments tend to have lower educational and occupational expectations than their Caucasian counterparts from more advantaged neighborhoods (Cook, Church, Ajanaku, & Shadish, 1996). Some researchers even assert that poverty is a threat to scholastic functioning and that it is clear that there is a strong relationship between poverty and poor school performance (Bryant & Maxwell, 1997). Despite this strong relationship, it is important to note that poverty does not exert a simple, singular influence. The effects of poverty represent a complex interaction of factors, including such matters as detrimental physical components of the environment (e.g., poor health care, increased health and development risks), the children's self-perception of competence, teachers' assessment of their effort, and other influences within the environment (Barnett, Vondra, & Shonk, 1996; Masten & Coatsworth, 1998). Poverty emerges as a significant topic of concern in many discussions of educational problems, educational and social reform, and early intervention efforts. Poverty increases the probability of childhood malnutrition, as well as the risk of detrimental exposure to such toxic agents as lead and other harmful environmental substances. Extreme poverty may also lead to homelessness, which contributes to irregular school attendance, chronic health problems, and a number of developmental delays (Cheng Gorman & Balter, 1997; Guralnick, 1998). These same factors are also interrelated with each other, and with migrancy and homelessness, which emphasizes the difficulty of isolating the impact of single variables in

Severe malnutrition and poor health care resulting from impoverished living conditions occurs more frequently among culturally diverse populations and may lead to mental retardation.

the area of cultural diversity (Feldman & Walton-Allen, 1997; Fujiura & Yamaki, 1997; Milburn & Curry, 1995; Wilson, 1996).

Poverty affects the type and level of health care that people receive as youngsters and the nutrition that builds their physical systems during important developmental periods, both before birth and during the first few years of life. Evidence suggests that during these periods ethnic minorities suffer from more health complications than their White counterparts. Gelfand, Jenson, and Drew (1997) examined these issues and noted that "only 5 percent of white upper-class infants have some complications at birth, compared with 15 percent of low SES whites and *51 percent of all nonwhites*, who have very low incomes as a group" (p. 92, emphasis in the original). Ethnic and cultural background substantially influences nutritional intake of young children, which is likely to affect their health status (Cheng Gorman & Balter, 1997). Children who begin their developmental years in unfavorable circumstances have a substantial probability of continued slower or abnormal development and of being labeled as having mental retardation. The environment continues to present a context of health risk, health risk

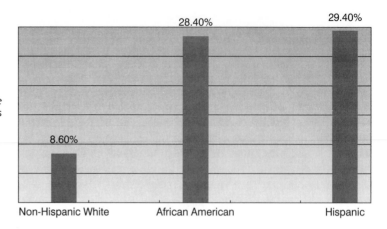

behaviors, and increased jeopardy for "premature morbidity or mortality" for adolescents from some racial backgrounds (Pack, Wallander, & Browne, 1998, p. 409). And finally, poor adults from racial minority backgrounds also show evidence of significant chronic stress, perhaps suffering the cumulative effects of such influences over a long period of time (Tran & Dhooper, 1997). Symptoms of chronic stress and elevated depression appear in minority parents of children with mental retardation (Blacher, Shapiro, Lopez, Diaz, & Fusco, 1997; Chen & Tang, 1997). While such effects are not necessarily surprising, they present a serious risk because many of these parents do not have health-care resources that are often available to other populations and are important to help buffer the negative effects of such conditions (Blacher et al., 1997).

Cultural-Social Mores

Core Concept

Social values that differ from culture to culture may result in behavioral or performance deviation from the cultural majority, which some might view as reflecting mental retardation.

Certainly, social and cultural mores do not contribute to a person's mental retardation in the same way as genetic abnormality. They do, however, play a significant role in how others view the person's performance in particular areas and in the person's demeanor (Rivers & Morrow, 1995). And these matters influence the overall view of a person's level of functioning, making a direct impact on whether that individual is seen as having mental retardation.

Different cultures view education and formal schooling quite differently. The U.S. educational system follows the value system of the White cultural majority. It does not equally reflect the beliefs of the members of various subcultures who spend time in U.S. schools (Spina & Tai, 1998). Belief structures are very different in American subcultures, and sources of knowledge, values, expectations, wisdom, and attitudes toward achievement are quite diverse (Aponte & Barnes, 1995; Cummings & DeHart, 1995; Ramirez, Nguyen, & Kratochwill, 1998). Such belief systems are also extremely potent, and understanding them may be a key factor in the success or failure of an intervention (Cheng Gorman & Balter, 1997). The impact of deep-seated cultural beliefs is understandable, particularly when one considers that these ideas have permeated children's early developmental years and have shaped their views of the world. This type of culture-specific value system can and often does substantially control how a youngster approaches, acts, and performs in school. It takes little imagination to see how a child with different cultural priorities might do poorly and be considered eligible for a diagnosis of mental retardation.

Cultural and social mores may also significantly influence the treatment of individuals with health problems and disabilities, and the services sought by their families (Blanche, 1996; Brown & Segal, 1996). Mental retardation is a disorder that many cultures recognize, but how it is conceptualized, how it is treated, and its social interpretation are as diverse as the cultures. Accepting certain handicapping conditions is very difficult for some groups. Culturally related beliefs and superstitions often play a significant role in the way people view abnormality and have a considerable impact on acceptance (Blacher et al., 1997; Rivers & Morrow, 1995). And for the different family structures of various cultural subgroups, caregiving for family members with disability conditions varies. For example, the extended families common to some cultural groups affect beliefs about where care for such individuals should come from and may result in anxiety or even suspicion regarding special services from outside the family. This presents an interesting challenge as educators and other professionals attempt to engage parents in planning for their child's education as required by federal laws such as IDEA. Parents from some cultural minority groups may be reluctant to join with school personnel in such planning because they do not trust such government organizations or have other views that impede such collaboration (Hardman, Drew, & Egan, 1999). Parents of youngsters with disabilities may feel great shame, may be unwilling to seek or accept outside assistance, or may have actually been left behind during clandestine emigration. Thus, interacting with the educational system is not an easy matter for parents of children from other cultures. Such difficulties are compounded in some circumstances in which the parents' communication with the system is further inhibited by language differences (Wohl & Aponte, 1995).

Cultural and social mores clearly affect how individuals approach and interact with institutions that represent authority and reflect the belief systems of the cultural majority (Cheng Gorman & Balter, 1997). Because of this diversity, different demeanors and behaviors have different meanings in various population subgroups. Behavior that is highly regarded, seen as reflecting intelligence, or viewed as reflecting an attitude that is positively valued by one culture may be viewed as offensive, unwise, or even unintelligent in another. The magnitude of such differences is highlighted in the context of achievement goals and intrinsic achievement motivation often associated with success in our educational system (Harackiewicz, Barron, & Elliot, 1998). The meanings of facial expressions, emotional expressions, and proper behavior have definite culturally related ties (Ekman, 1993; Russell, 1994). Including information on these complex cultural influences is vital when one considers the overall phenomenon of mental retardation. Cultural influences are of great practical impact as children from cultural minority groups are educated. They also challenge professionals to prove the conceptual soundness and utility of mental retardation definitions.

Language

Core Concept

Language differences that create academic difficulties for some culturally different children may place them in jeopardy of being considered as having mental retardation.

Cultural diversity also results in a number of language differences that often contribute to academic difficulties in a school system designed and operated by the cultural majority (Perez, 1997). Academic problems stemming from language differences may result in referral, assessment, and inappropriate labeling of a child as having mental retardation if consideration is not given to cultural factors. Language differences may be absolute, as when a youngster's family speaks a language other than English. Additional differences may be found when the youngster's linguistic patterns represent what is known as nonstandard language or nonstandard English. **Nonstandard language** is evident in the communication patterns of some cultural or racial subgroups and may result in biased perceptions and assessment (Jussim, Fleming, Coleman, & Kohberger, 1996).

Language patterns emerging from the speech configurations in nonstandard English are sufficiently different from those of the cultural majority to cause considerable academic difficulty for a youngster in the school system. It is easy to see how a teacher from the dominant culture might find it difficult to understand the child. It is also easy to see how teachers and others might think that the child had a language deficiency or disorder and might therefore refer the child for testing for mental retardation. Once into the referral-assessment cycle, the child using nonstandard language could be diagnosed and placed into special education service patterns that could label that individual for life. This is a particularly unfortunate outcome if the diagnosis of mental retardation is erroneous and due to a cultural difference, rather than to actual intellectual status. Consideration of cultural background in communication disorder diagnosis is complex, differing in some significant ways among cultural groups (Battle, 1997). Such consideration, however, grows increasingly essential by educators at all levels as school populations become more culturally diverse (Lamison-White, 1997; Wald, 1996).

Misdiagnosis based on language differences places assessment in a critical position. Language differences and inaccurate or biased diagnostic assessment have received considerable attention in the literature (e.g., Campbell, Dollaghan, Needleman, & Janosky, 1997; Stuart-Smith & Martin, 1997). Issues pertaining to the fairness of assessment for children with language and cultural differences continue to perplex evaluation specialists and are not easily resolved (Diaz-Rico & Weed, 1995; McMillan, 1997; Tavern & Sheridan, 1995). Minimizing assessment error and interpretation bias appears to be the most satisfactory approach in order to provide the most effective instruction possible to all children.

ISSUES OF ASSESSMENT AND INTERVENTION

Core Concept

Personnel and procedures involved in the assessment, diagnosis, and intervention process may all contribute to a biased overrepresentation of culturally different children as having mental retardation.

Assessment has played a central role in dealing with culturally different people and mental retardation (deValenzuela & Cervantes, 1998). Diagnostic testing for deficiencies or differences is at the core of the process by which one determines whether an individual has mental retardation. If this process is unfavorably biased against cultural differences, then the likelihood increases that a child who actually reflects diversity, rather than deficiency, will be labeled with mental retardation. Youngsters from minority backgrounds do appear more frequently in disability categories than would be expected on the basis of the proportion of culturally different people in the population. This disproportionately high rate of identification frequently involves deficiencies diagnosed through psychoeducational assessment, which suggests that the evaluation process and the uses of assessment information may include serious bias (Aiken, 1997; Gregory, 1996; Lyman, 1998). It should also be noted that there are concerns regarding the AAMR (1992) definition with respect to the possibility that the definition itself may magnify the problem of minority overrepresentation (Greenspan, 1997; Gresham et al., 1995; Smith, 1997).

Measurement bias can occur in many fashions. Cultural bias in assessment leads to inaccurate results based on cultural background. Such results are testing artifacts—conclusions from an evaluation that reveal cultural background, rather than actual mental abilities or skills (Hopkins, 1998; McMillan, 1997). This type of error in psychological assessment has been of concern to professionals for many decades (e.g., Burt, 1921), and arguments about the causes of such bias, its effects, and resolutions of it continue in the scientific literature (Robinson, 1997; Saccuzzo & Johnson, 1995)

Norm-referenced measurement procedures, which often employ normative data, language patterns, and knowledge or content based on the cultural majority, are highly vulnerable to assessment bias. Under the conditions presumed by norm-referenced tests, individuals from minority and culturally different backgrounds may have a built-in performance disadvantage (Gronlund, 1998; Hopkins, 1998). Such a disadvantage may occur because their performance scores are compared with those of a large group of individuals who are tested as a part of instrument development (the norm group). The norm group may not include an appropriate number of minority individuals and therefore not be adequately representative. Further, the conditions of testing may reflect procedures more comfortable for those of the cultural majority. This type of inequitable assessment has played a dominant role in widely publicized court cases involving Hispanic and African American students (*Diana v. State Board of Education,* 1970; *Larry P. v. Riles,* 1972, 1979). Such cases have had a major impact on the manner in which testing is viewed.

Attempts to design culturally fair test instruments have been made for many years but have met with little success. Certain improvements were achieved with respect to minimizing conspicuous culture-specific components and developing complex systems of assessment that attempt to consider cultural background through multiple measures (Hopkins, 1998; Janda, 1998). Difficulties remain, however, and concerns regarding minority children's disadvantage continue to appear in the literature (e.g., Mayfield & Reynolds, 1997; Losey, 1995; Paolo, Ryan, Ward, & Hilmer, 1997).

Attention to the instruments of assessment *without concern for the people and processes involved in evaluation* leaves room for considerable cultural bias in psychological assessment. People often make diagnostic and classification decisions based on specific data and form impressions from scant information. Efforts must be undertaken to minimize the personal bias of professionals involved in psychological assessment. These efforts will require additional training or different preparation specifically incorporating information about cultural factors, language background, and curriculum or intervention plans into the evaluation (Aponte & Clifford, 1995; Lyman, 1998). Some would even argue that additional professionals must be trained who are themselves of diverse ethnic backgrounds (Ewing, 1995; Wald, 1996).

Earlier, we examined the influences associated with minority and culturally different status. Knowledge of such information about each individual child is extremely important in any assessment and often must be obtained through interviews with parents and other significant people in the youngster's environment. Determining such matters as the language spoken in the home, who the child's caretakers are, and what activities are undertaken all add to the picture of the world the child lives in. Professionals must obtain this background information in a manner sensitive to differences in cultural attitudes and mores, or it, too, has the potential for being inaccurate or biased (Gergen, Gulerce, Lock, & Misra, 1996). An accurate understanding of the child requires contextual understanding of that youngster in the family (Speight, Thomas, Kennel, & Anderson, 1995; Szapocznik & Kurtines, 1993). Table 2–1 summarizes important points of consideration during the assessment process with children from diverse backgrounds.

Psychological assessment plays a vital role in assessing mental retardation. It is an important component in the process of identifying and serving those

TABLE 2–1
Process Checklist for Serving Children from Diverse Backgrounds

This checklist provides professionals with points to consider in the process of educating children from culturally diverse backgrounds. These matters should be considered during each of the following: Referral and testing or diagnostic assessment; classification, labeling, or class assignment change; teacher conferences or home communication.

PROCESS	ISSUE(S)	QUESTIONS TO BE ASKED
Referral, Testing, or Diagnostic Assessment	Language Issues	Is the native language different than that in which the child is being taught and should this be considered in the assessment process? What is the home language? What is the normal conversational language? What language can the student be successfully taught or assessed in—academic language?
	Cultural Issues	What are the views of the culture from which the child comes toward schooling? Are there differences in expectations between the school and family for the child's schooling goals? What are the cultural views toward illness or disability?
	Home Issues	What is the family constellation and who are the family members? What is the family economic status?
Classification, Labeling, or Class Assignment Change	Language Issues	Does the proposed placement change account for any language differences that are relevant, particularly academic language?
	Cultural Issues	Does the proposed placement change consider any unique cultural views regarding schooling?
	Home Issues	Does the proposed change consider pertinent family matters?
Teacher Conferences or Home Communication	Language Issues	Is the communication to parents or other family members in a language that is understood?
	Cultural Issues	Are there cultural views that influence communication between family members and the schools as a formal governmental organization? Is there a cultural reluctance of family members to come to the school? Are home visits a desirable alternative? Is communication from teachers viewed positively?
	Home Issues	Is the family constellation such that communication with the schools is possible and positive? Are family members positioned economically and otherwise to respond to communication from the schools in a productive manner? If the family is low SES, is transportation a problem for conferences?

From Human Exceptionality: Society, School, and Family *(6th ed., p. 64) by M. L. Hardman, C. J. Drew, and M. W. Egan, 1999, Needham Heights, MA: Allyn & Bacon.*

who need specialized treatment (deValenzuela & Cervantes, 1998). Assessment must not, however, become a mechanism for discrimination or an expression of cultural prejudice. To allow such misuse runs counter to the basic purpose of intervention to help those who need treatment. Chapters 3 and 4 are devoted solely to assessment. As you read and study these chapters, it is important to keep multicultural issues firmly in mind.

HUMAN DEVELOPMENT AND MULTICULTURAL ISSUES

Core Concept

Cultural diversity may result in some influences that generate actual developmental disadvantages, as well as differences.

A wide variety of factors as diverse as inherited genetic material and environmental influences such as nutrition, disease, and toxic substances affect the course of human development. All of these factors may have favorable or unfavorable consequences on the rate and quality of a young person's developing abilities, depending on how they come in contact with the individual and when the contact occurs. Many of these factors are discussed in more detail in later chapters as we address the developmental abnormalities resulting in mental retardation. In this section, we address how some of these influences are associated with cultural diversity and how they may, in this context, have an impact on the development of children and youths from minority cultures.

Earlier in this chapter, we discussed impoverished economic circumstances as a condition often associated with ethnic minority status in this country. For example, poverty occurs much more frequently among African American and Hispanic populations than it does in those of the cultural majority (Fujiura & Yamaki, 1997). More than three times as many members of these groups live in conditions below the poverty level as do members of the dominant culture (Lamison-White, 1997). Such circumstances severely limit accessibility to quality health care, adequate nutrition, early stimulation, and a variety of other environmental features that promote favorable growth and development in youngsters. These matters dramatically influence maturation both prenatally and during the important growth periods after birth. During these times in the life cycle, crucial physical, neurological, and cognitive structures undergo their most rapid growth. The foundations of a person's development are laid at this point and play a very strong role in determining how later maturation proceeds. To the degree that inadequate health care, nutrition, and other circumstances exist in culturally diverse populations, children in these groups are placed at risk for delayed or otherwise abnormal development that may result in mental retardation (Masten & Coatsworth, 1998). Chapters 6 and 7, in particular, discuss such unfavorable developmental circumstances and their potential outcomes.

The influences just mentioned may generate serious developmental disadvantages for culturally different youngsters, adversely affecting basic neurological and cognitive structures. In addition to these factors, what is learned during the formative years plays a pivotal role in later behavior. The content of what is learned may produce sociocultural differences that set minority youngsters apart from their peers in the cultural majority (Spina & Tai, 1998). Earlier, we noted that cultural and social mores influence the view of education and formal schooling. Different cultures display divergent belief structures, with varying opinions about the sources of wisdom and knowledge and attitudes toward achievement. Certain Native American cultures view group cooperation for excellence more favorably than individual striving or competition for achievement. This perspective has a significant impact on school performance where the dominant culture places a high value on individual achievement and behavior. These and other types of social values are learned very early in the developmental life cycle and have a powerful influence on how children approach and engage the world around them. Their impact on how youngsters from culturally different populations perform in institutions designed and operated by the cultural majority should not be underestimated. Such early learning is extremely durable and often creates serious conflict as youngsters encounter varying belief systems in the world beyond their cultural background.

Society's role in changing the circumstances of human development is not clear. Few would argue that it is important to alter the contingencies that present developmental disadvantages to children. To do otherwise runs counter to the basic philosophy of a society that explicitly promotes the well-being of its entire people. Serious philosophical questions arise, however, about the degree of conformity society should require. Most would not subscribe to a basic doctrine that requires culturally diverse belief systems to be brought into conformity with those of the cultural majority. The dimension of developmental differences presents a complicated challenge, one that is not easily solved.

NEW ISSUES AND FUTURE DIRECTIONS

Core Concept

Professionals in the field of mental retardation must change basic models of research on mental retardation so that the influences of cultural diversity on human development can be more fully understood.

The face of behavioral science is undergoing tremendous changes in its basic research models. Quantitatively oriented experimental and clinical psychology have formed the foundations of traditional research methodologies used in the study of mental retardation. These methodologies usually have had a quantitative, norm-referenced framework as their context. The largest body of research in mental retardation reflects investigation of the phenomenon as a concept of performance or ability deficit predominantly viewed in relation to normative abilities derived from the cultural majority. Historically, only isolated researchers have pursued investigations of mental retardation emphasizing the study of individuals in the context of their environment (see Edgerton, 1967, 1988; Edgerton, Bollinger, & Herr, 1984).

Professionals' understanding of mental retardation is only as adequate as the research models. It is important to realize that mental retardation does not occur in the laboratory, but in the context of the broader society. Although the laboratory has provided considerable information, that information must be placed in context to achieve understanding, which, from the perspective of this chapter, means consideration of cultural diversity issues. Social and cultural environments must become integral in the study of child development both generally and with regard to developmental deviations such as mental retardation (Baumeister, 1997; Drew, Hardman, & Hart, 1996; Gelfand et al., 1997).

The study of mental retardation as a part of the social and cultural environment is gaining considerable momentum. Qualitative research models, like those of ethnography, hold great promise for future understanding of this multidimensional problem. As Stainback and Stainback (1989) noted, "There is growing interest in the potential contributions of qualitative research to scholarly inquiry, and what was a quiet and perhaps peripheral aspect of educational research has been moving rapidly toward center stage in recent years" (p. 271). Where once little was written about methodology, now volumes are beginning to rival those available in quantitative research (Bogdan & Biklen, 1998; Lancy, 1993; Miles & Huberman, 1994; Patton, 1990).

As these changes are occurring, it is important to realize that the choice of methods is expanding, not that one is supplanting another. There is little reason to think that the future will involve discarding the strengths of quantitative investigation. What will be needed is the strength of multiple methods studying the same questions with the same populations. Future research will require investigators to be thoughtful eclectics, incorporating the necessary rigor while shedding the narrow perspective of a single model (Drew et al., 1996). Such an approach holds great promise for improving the understanding of the complex interactions of cultural diversity and mental retardation.

Core Questions

1. How does cultural diversity result in differences that one must address when considering mental retardation conceptually?
2. How does cultural diversity result in differences that one must consider when diagnosing an individual as having mental retardation?
3. How does poverty create environmental circumstances that might impair a child's mental development?
4. How might social values emerge in the behavior or performance of a culturally different individual and suggest a diagnosis of mental retardation?
5. How might language differences place a child in jeopardy of being diagnosed as having mental retardation?
6. How do assessment procedures potentially place a culturally different individual at an unfair disadvantage, with the possible result of a label of mental retardation?

7. How might assessment personnel influence diagnostic evaluation in a manner that inaccurately identifies a culturally different individual as having mental retardation?

8. How might the environmental circumstances of cultural diversity have such an adverse influence on human development that they help cause mental retardation?

9. How have traditional research models in mental retardation failed to account for the influences of cultural diversity in human development?

Roundtable Discussion

Mental retardation is a problem that by definition involves differences from normal functioning. Individuals with mental retardation perform poorly from both intellectual and social perspectives. In examining mental retardation, it is important to consider who sets the norms of behavior and performance. For the most part, society shapes these norms on the basis of the views of the cultural majority, without much reflection of the belief structures of ethnic minority populations.

In your study or discussion group, examine the potential effects of having one segment of the population set the standards for another group; focus on a subgroup that does not share the belief systems of the majority. Remember that ethnic minorities represent a greater proportion of those labeled handicapped than would be expected. Does this fact represent discrimination? How do you separate discrimination from actual disadvantages associated with cultural diversity? Should performance or behavior reflecting cultural differences be considered in applying the label of mental retardation?

References

Aiken, L. R. (1997). *Psychological testing and assessment* (9th ed.). Boston: Allyn & Bacon.

American Association on Mental Retardation (AAMR). (1992). *Mental retardation: Definition, classification, and systems of supports* (9th ed.). Washington, DC: Author.

American Psychiatric Association (APA). (1994). *Diagnostic and statistical manual of mental disorders* (4th ed.). Washington, DC: Author.

Aponte, J. F., & Barnes, J. M. (1995). Impact of acculturation and moderator variables on the intervention and treatment of ethnic groups. In J. F. Aponte, R. Y. Rivers., & J. Wohl (Eds.), *Psychological interventions and cultural diversity* (pp. 19–39). Boston: Allyn & Bacon.

Aponte, J. F., & Clifford, J. (1995). Education and training issues for intervention with ethnic groups. In J. F. Aponte, R. Y. Rivers., & J. Wohl (Eds.), *Psychological interventions and cultural diversity* (pp. 283–300). Boston: Allyn & Bacon.

Barnett, D., Vondra, J. I., & Shonk, S. M. (1996). Self-perceptions, motivation, and school functioning of low-income maltreated and comparison children. *Child Abuse and Neglect, 20*(5), 397–410.

Battle, D. E. (1997). Language and communication disorders in culturally and linguistically diverse children. In D. K. Bernstein & E. Tiegerman-Farber (Eds.), *Language and communication disorders in children* (pp. 382–410). Boston: Allyn & Bacon.

Baumeister, A. A. (1997). Behavioral research: Boom or bust? In W. E. MacLean, Jr. (Ed.), *Ellis' handbook of mental deficiency, psychological theory, and research* (3rd ed., pp. 3–45). Mahwah, NJ: Erlbaum.

Blacher, J., Shapiro, J., Lopez, S., Diaz, L., & Fusco, J. (1997). Depression in Latina mothers of children with mental retardation: A neglected concern. *American Journal on Mental Retardation, 101,* 483–496.

Blanche, E. I. (1996). Alma: Coping with culture, poverty, and disability. *American Journal of Occupational Therapy, 50*(4), 265–276.

Bogdan, R. C., & Biklen, S. K. (1998). *Qualitative research for education* (3rd ed.). Boston: Allyn & Bacon.

Brown, C. M., & Segal, R. (1996). The effects of health and treatment perceptions on the use of prescribed medication and home remedies among African American and White American hypertensives. *Social Science and Medicine, 43,* 903–917.

Bryant, D., & Maxwell, K. (1997). The effectiveness of early intervention for disadvantaged children. In M. J. Guralnick (Ed.), *The effectiveness of early intervention* (pp. 23–46). Baltimore: Paul H. Brookes.

Burt, C. (1921). *Mental and scholastic tests.* London: King.

Campbell, T., Dollaghan, C., Needleman, H., & Janosky, J. (1997). Reducing bias in language assessment: Processing-dependent measures. *Journal of Speech and Hearing Research, 40,* 519–525.

Chen, T. Y., & Tang, C. S. (1997). Stress appraisal and social support of Chinese mothers of adult children with mental retardation. *American Journal on Mental Retardation, 101,* 473–482.

Cheng Gorman, J. C., & Balter, L. (1997). Culturally sensitive parent education: A critical review of quantitative research. *Review of Educational Research, 67,* 339–369.

Cook, T. D., Church, M. B., Ajanaku, S., & Shadish, W. R., Jr., (1996). The development of occupational aspirations and expectations among inner-city boys. *Child Development, 67,* 3368–3385.

Cummings, C. M., & DeHart, D. D. (1995). Ethnic minority physical health: Issues and interventions. In J. F. Aponte, R. Y. Rivers, & J. Wohl (Eds.), *Psychological interventions and cultural diversity* (pp. 234–249). Boston: Allyn & Bacon.

DeValenzuela, J. S., & Cervantes, H. (1998). Issues and theoretical considerations in the assessment of bilingual children. In L. M. Baca & H. T. Cervantes (Eds.), *The bilingual special education interface* (3rd ed., pp. 144–166). Upper Saddle River, NJ: Merrill/Prentice Hall.

Diana v. State Board of Education, C-70-37 R.F.P. (N.D. California, Jan. 7, 1970).

Diaz-Rico, L. T., & Weed, K. Z. (1995). *The crosscultural, language, and academic development handbook.* Boston: Allyn & Bacon.

Drew, C. J., Hardman, M. L., & Hart, A. W. (1996). *Designing and conducting research: Inquiry in education and social science* (2nd ed.). Boston: Allyn & Bacon.

Dvir, T., Eden, D., & Banjo, M. L. (1995). Self-fulfilling prophecy and gender: Can women be Pygmalion and Galatea? *Journal of Applied Psychology, 80,* 253–270.

Edgerton, R. B. (1967). *The cloak of competence: Stigma in the lives of the mentally retarded.* Berkeley: University of California Press.

Edgerton, R. B. (1988). Aging in the community: A matter of choice. *American Journal of Mental Retardation, 92,* 331–335.

Edgerton, R. B., Bollinger, M., & Herr, B. (1984). The cloak of competence: After two decades. *American Journal of Mental Deficiency, 88,* 345–351.

Ekman, P. (1993). Facial expression and emotion. *American Psychologist, 48,* 384–392.

Ewing, N. (1995). Restructured teacher education for inclusiveness: A dream deferred for African American children. In B. A. Ford, F. E. Obiakor, & J. Patton, (Eds.), *Effective education of African American exceptional learners* (pp. 189–208). Austin, TX: Pro-Ed.

Feldman, M. A., & Walton-Allen, A. N. (1997). Effects of maternal mental retardation and poverty on intellectual, academic, and behavioral status of school-age children. *American Journal on mental retardation, 101,* 352–364.

Fujiura, G. T., & Yamaki, K. (1997). Analysis of ethnic variations in developmental disability prevalence and household economic status. *Mental Retardation, 35,* 286–294.

Gauvain, M. (1998). Culture, development, and theory of mind: Comment on Lillard (1998). *Psychological Bulletin, 123,* 37–42.

Gelfand, D. M., Jenson, W. R., & Drew, C. J. (1997). *Understanding child behavior disorders* (3rd ed.). Fort Worth: Harcourt Brace.

Gergen, K. J., Gulerce, A., Lock, A., & Misra, G. (1996). Psychological science in cultural context. *American Psychologist, 51,* 496–503.

Greenspan, S. (1997). Dead manual walking? Why the 1992 AAMR definition needs redoing. *Education and Training in Mental Retardation and Developmental Disabilities, 32,* 179–193.

Gregory, R. J. (1996). *Psychological testing: History, principles, and applications* (2nd ed.). Boston: Allyn & Bacon.

Gresham, F. M., MacMillan, D. L., & Siperstein, G. N. (1995). Critical analysis of the 1992 AAMR definition: Implications for school psychology. *School Psychology Quarterly, 10,* 1–19.

Gronlund, N. E. (1998). *Assessment of student achievement* (6th ed.). Boston: Allyn & Bacon.

Guralnick, M. J. (1998). Effectiveness of early intervention for vulnerable children: A developmental perspective. *American Journal on Mental Retardation, 102,* 319–345.

Harackiewicz, J. M., Barron, K. E., & Elliot, A. J. (1998). Rethinking achievement goals: When are they adaptive for college students and why? *Educational Psychologist, 33*(1), 1–21.

Hardman, M. L., Drew, C. J., & **Egan, M. W.,** (1999). *Human exceptionality: Society, school, and family* (6th ed.). Needham Heights, MA: Allyn & Bacon.

Hopkins, K. D. (1998). *Educational and psychological measurement and evaluation* (8th ed.). Boston: Allyn & Bacon.

Janda, L. (1998). *Psychological testing, theory, and applications.* Boston: Allyn & Bacon.

Jussim, L., Fleming, C. J., Coleman, L., & Kohberger, C. (1996). The nature of stereotypes: II. A multiple-process model of evaluations. *Journal of Applied Social Psychology, 26,* 283–312.

Lamison-White, L. (1997). *Poverty in the United States: 1996,* U. S. Bureau of the Census, *Current Population Reports* (Ser. P60-198), U.S. Government Printing Office, Washington, DC.

Lancy, D. F. (1993). *Qualitative research in education: An introduction to the major traditions.* White Plains, NY: Longman.

Larry P. v. Riles, 343 F. Supp. 1306 (N.D. California 1972); 343 F. Supp. 1306, 502 F. 2d 963 (N.D. California 1979).

Lillard, A. (1998). Ethnopsychologies: Cultural variations in theories of mind. *Psychological Bulletin, 123,* 3–32.

Losey, K. M. (1995). Mexican American students and classroom interaction: An overview and critique. *Review of Educational Research, 65,* 283–318.

Lyman, H. B. (1998). *Test scores and what they mean* (6th ed.). Boston: Allyn & Bacon.

MacMillan, D. L., Gresham, F. M., & Siperstein, G. N. (1993). Conceptual and psychometric concerns about the 1992 AAMR definition of mental retardation. *American Journal on Mental Retardation, 98,* 325–335.

Madon, S., Jussim, L., & Eccles, J. (1997). In search of the powerful self-fulfilling prophecy. *Journal of Personality and Social Psychology, 72,* 791–809.

Masten, A. S., & Coatsworth, J. D. (1998). The development of competence in favorable and unfavorable environments. *American Psychologist, 53,* 205–220.

Mayfield, J. W., & Reynolds, C. R. (1997). Black-White differences in memory test performance among children and adolescents. *Archives of Clinical Neuropsychology, 12,* 111–122.

McMillan, J. H. (1997). *Classroom assessment: Principles and practice for effective instruction.* Boston: Allyn & Bacon.

Merton, R. K. (1948). The self-fulfilling prophecy. *Antioch Review, 8,* 193–210.

Milburn, N. G., & Curry, T. L. (1995). Intervention and treatment for ethnic homeless adults. In J. F. Aponte, R. Y. Rivers, & J. Wohl (Eds.), *Psychological interventions and cultural diversity* (pp. 250–265). Boston: Allyn & Bacon.

Miles, M. B., & Huberman, A. M. (1994). *Qualitative data analysis: An expanded sourcebook* (2nd ed.). Thousand Oaks, CA: Sage.

O'Connor, C. (1997). Dispositions toward (collective) struggle and educational resilience in the inner city: A case analysis of six African-American high school students. *American Educational Research Journal, 34,* 593–629.

Pack, R. P., Wallander, J. L., & Browne, D. (1998). Health risk behaviors of African American adolescents with mild mental retardation: Prevalence depends on measurement method. *American Journal on Mental Retardation, 102,* 409–420.

Paolo, A. M., Ryan, J. J., Ward, L. C., & Hilmer, C. D. (1997). Different WAIS-R short forms and their relation to ethnicity. *Personality and Individual Differences, 21,* 851–856.

Patton, M. Q. (1990). *Qualitative evaluation and research methods* (2nd ed.). Newbury Park, CA: Sage.

Perez, B. (1997). *Sociocultural contexts of language and literacy.* Mahwah, NJ: Erlbaum.

Ramirez, S. Z., Nguyen, T., & Kratochwill, T. R. (1998). Self-reported fears in Hispanic youth with mental retardation: A preliminary study. *Mental Retardation, 36,* 145–156.

Rivers, R. Y., & Morrow, C. A. (1995). Understanding and treating ethnic minority youth. In J. F. Aponte, R. Y. Rivers., & J. Wohl (Eds.), *Psychological interventions and cultural diversity* (pp. 164–180). Boston: Allyn & Bacon.

Robinson, E. G. (1997). Systematic distortion of statistics as a result of racism and its effect on the human services system. *Mental Retardation, 35,* 221–223.

Rosenthal, R., & Jacobson, L. (1968a). *Pygmalion in the classroom: Teacher expectation and pupils' intellectual development.* New York: Holt, Rinehart & Winston.

Rosenthal, R., & Jacobson, L. (1968b). Self-fulfilling prophecies in the classroom: Teachers' expectations as unintended determinants of pupils' intellectual competence. In M. Deutsch, I. Katz, & A. R. Jensen (Eds.), *Social class, race, and psychological development* (pp. 219–253). New York: Holt, Rinehart & Winston.

Russell, J. A. (1994). Is there universal recognition of emotion from facial expression? A review of the cross-cultural studies. *Psychological Bulletin, 115,* 102–141.

Saccuzzo, D. P., & Johnson, N. E. (1995). Traditional psychometric tests and proportionate representation: An intervention and program evaluation study. *Psychological Assessment, 7(2),* 183–194.

Satcher, D. (1995). The sociodemographic correlates of mental retardation. *American Journal of Public Health, 85,* 304–306.

Smith, J. D. (1997). Mental retardation as an educational construct: Time for a new shared view? *Education and Training in Mental Retardation and Developmental Disabilities, 32,* 167–173.

Speight, S. L., Thomas, A. J., Kennel, R. G., & Anderson, M. E. (1995). Operationalizing multicultural training in doctoral programs and internships. *Professional Psychology: Research and Practice, 26,* 401–406.

Spina, S. U., & Tai, R. H. (1998). The politics of racial identity: A pedagogy of invisibility. *Educational Researcher, 27(1),* 36–40, 48.

Stainback, W., & Stainback, S. (1989). Using qualitative data collection procedures to investigate supported education issues. *Journal of the Association for Persons with Severe Handicaps, 14,* 271–277.

Stuart-Smith, J., & Martin, D. (1997). Investigating literacy and pre-literacy skills in Panjabi/English schoolchildren. *Educational Review, 49,* 181–197.

Suarez-Orozco, M. M. (1996). California dreaming: Proposition 187 and the cultural psychology of racial and ethnic exclusion. *Anthropology and Education Quarterly, 27,* 151–167.

Szapocznik, J., & Kurtines, W. M. (1993). Family psychology and cultural diversity. *American Psychologist, 48,* 400–407.

Tavern, A., & Sheridan, S. (1995). Parent training in interactive book reading: An investigation of its effects with families at risk. *School Psychology Quarterly, 10,* 41–64.

Tran, T. V., & Dhooper, S. S. (1997). Poverty, chronic stress, ethnicity and psychological distress among elderly Hispanics. *Journal of Gerontological Social Work, 27(4),* 3–19.

Wald, J. L. (1996). *Culturally and linguistically diverse professionals in special education: A demographic analysis.* Reston, VA: Council for Exceptional Children.

Wilson, G. (1996). Toward a revised framework for examining beliefs about the causes of poverty. *Sociological Quarterly, 37,* 413–428.

Wohl, J., & Aponte, J. F. (1995). Common themes and future prospects. In J. F. Aponte, R. Y. Rivers., & J. Wohl (Eds.), *Psychological interventions and cultural diversity* (pp. 301–316). Boston: Allyn & Bacon.

Yeargin-Allsopp, M., Drews, C. D., & Decoufle, P. (1995). Mild mental retardation in Black and White children in metropolitan Atlanta: A case-control study. *American Journal of Public Health, 85,* 324–328.

Part 2

Identifying People with Mental Retardation

Chapter 3 : Assessment Issues and Procedures

Chapter 4 : Understanding Intelligence and Adaptive Skills

Chapter **3**

Assessment Issues and Procedures

Core Concepts

- Careful attention to the proper use of assessment instruments has a great impact on the results of measurement.
- The purpose of any assessment greatly influences the procedure(s) employed and the way data are interpreted. Recognition of this has led to the articulation of such important concepts as norm and criterion referencing and formative and summative evaluation.
- Assessment procedures are quite different, depending on the age of the person and the performance area being evaluated.
- Screening assessment is very important throughout a person's life span, but it is crucial in early life.
- Prenatal evaluation can provide extremely important information about the fetus.
- Assessment of the newborn can identify problems and prompt immediate intervention to prevent mental retardation.
- Evaluation beyond the newborn stage includes many assessment areas not previously amenable to measurement.
- Functioning in intellectual, language, perceptual-motor, and social/adaptive behavior is important in evaluating the status of preschool youngsters. Proper assessment must employ procedures appropriate for this age range.
- Multiple areas of functioning must be evaluated during the elementary years. Proper evaluation uses technically and conceptually sound procedures appropriate for this age range.
- Assessment during adolescent and adult years involves use of age- or functioning-level–appropriate procedures. Attention must be given also to the changing purposes of evaluation in these years.

Viewed broadly, psychological assessment has a lengthy history when compared with other areas of behavioral science. Within the specialty of psychological assessment, the measurement of intelligence has received a great deal of attention over the years. Work in the measurement of intelligence has been a major force in all psychological assessment, and the roots of psychological assessment go deep into the field of mental retardation. Alfred Binet began the serious efforts to measure intelligence in 1904. Binet was commissioned by school officials in Paris to develop a means by which those children who were "truly dull" could be identified. Although interest had been expressed in psychological measurement before this, Binet's assignment generally is viewed as an important beginning.

The influence of development in psychological assessment is evident far beyond the area of mental retardation, and its methodology has become increasingly complex, sophisticated, and, some would say, elegant. In certain areas, however, its sophistication may be no more than superficial. This chapter discusses assessment issues, frameworks, and procedures from the perspective of mental retardation and in terms of the various phases of the human life cycle.

ISSUES AND CONCEPTS

Research on the measurement of intelligence has a very long history. Likewise, efforts to evaluate other areas of functioning—personality, language, and social development—also have been under way for a long time. Although significant effort has been directed at such measurement, much of the work has not been undertaken in as thoughtful a manner as might be appropriate or desirable. In some cases the development of assessment instruments has been driven by commercial motives rather than the cautious and systematic investigations of science.

Assessment Use

Core Concept

Careful attention to the proper use of assessment instruments has a great impact on the results of measurement.

One difficulty plaguing behavioral evaluation over the years has been the misuse of assessment procedures. Instrument development has occurred at a very rapid rate, often at the expense of careful and deliberate thought about the purposes and uses of the tests. Assessment literature reflects serious concern about usage over many years (e.g., Aiken, 1997; Camara, 1997; Gronlund, 1998; Lyman, 1998; Merenda, 1997). Much of this concern emerged because over the years, many practitioners seemed to have a fixation on instruments of assessment with much less attention to questions of why the testing was being done. Because this was a driving force for the commercial market of testing materials, technical precision in psychological assessment seemed always to be ahead of conceptual considerations for practical assessment. Technical precision in this context relates to instrument construction; conceptual considerations relate to the underlying purposes for assessment and the use of the resulting information. Some questions also have been raised about how much technical precision generally has been achieved, but the use problem is fundamental and even may be more serious because, logically, concepts need to be in place before an evaluation can take place. Evidence regarding the relationship between assessment data and decisions made by placement teams raises serious questions. In some cases, concerns have been raised about limited relationships between assessment information and the instructional prescriptions of individualized education programs (IEPs) designed for children (Hoy & Gregg, 1994). These concerns raise the very crucial question, Why should one test if the information is not directly used for instruction or other intervention? The conceptual problems related to purpose and usage may be reflected also in the practical applications of assessment.

There has been a significant proliferation of psychoeducational instruments during the past 25 years. In today's market there is most likely an instrument available that purports to measure every facet of human behavior that one would want to evaluate. Further, new instrumentation is being developed and placed on the market continually (and at what seems to be an accelerating rate). Yet questions arise about the degree of technical precision of much psychoeducational assessment. This concern is an appropriate one. But the problems related to technical precision are not the result of insufficient knowledge or theory about instrument development and measurement. Measurement theory has become a rather highly developed area in behavioral science and has been studied for many years (e.g., Aiken, 1997; Hopkins, 1998; Janda, 1998). Unfortunately, many instruments on the market do not give adequate attention to sound measurement practices. The great demand from the field appears to have resulted in inadequate instruments.

Assessment Referencing

Core Concept

The purpose of any assessment greatly influences the procedure(s) employed and the way data are interpreted. Recognition of this has led to the articulation of such important concepts as norm and criterion referencing and formative and summative evaluation.

Development and articulation of measurement concepts regarding the reference used for data interpretation represents one of the more important developments in the field of assessment. Practically speaking this refers to what standards or comparisons are used for a child's performance. Is his or her performance compared to those of others or is it compared to some specified learning or skill goal that might be set? Most prominent in this work is the distinction between norm- and criterion-referenced evaluation. Clarification of these concepts forced the field to be clear about at least one dimension of how test information is to be used. It should also be noted that different referents or performance standards might be employed for the same data. That is, a child's score on a ten-item test might be compared with the scores of others or it simply might represent an important instructional goal to be reached. Using different referents does not necessarily mean that different test items are employed, just that the performance data are compared with a different standard.

Norm Referencing.   Early assessment developments focused on how an individual performed, compared with others, particularly in the area of intelligence. A child's test score was viewed in relation to his or her age-mates or some standard norm. Research and repeated testing of individuals at various ages usually establish norms or databases for comparison. Similar procedures are used in assessment of factors other than intelligence. Personality measures usually compare one person's response to certain questions with those of other people who have particular personality descriptions. Educational achievement often is measured by the amount of information a child has accumulated, as demonstrated by correct responses on a variety of test questions. The child's performance then is compared with that of other children who are about the same age or grade level.

Assessment in which the performance of an individual is compared with that of others is known as **norm-referenced evaluation.** The term is self-explanatory; how well an individual performs is compared or referenced to the scores of others by using established norms. Mental age (MA) is a concept that is norm-referenced, and Binet and Simon (1908) intended it to be so when they first defined MA. Many other areas of assessment, particularly those using standardized tests, are also norm-referenced.

The norm-referenced approach has been predominant for many years. For the most part, professionals involved in all types of assessment (e.g., developmental status, intelligence, personality) have interpreted performance relative to norms. Norm referencing has served some purposes well. During the development of assessment as a science, it was the foundation for both researchers and practitioners working in all areas of human behavior. But gradually some serious problems emerged.

As the science of human behavior progressed, measurement problems that obviously needed attention developed. Standardized tests provided information that was useful for some purposes but not for others. Educators, for example, frequently found that scores from norm-referenced evaluation did not translate easily into teaching plans. A single score often was used for decisions about educational placement, with little or no additional information about the child. Such single scores gave the teacher, at best, meager guidance concerning activities and specific areas to target in instruction. A global score or a psychologist's report did not indicate where to begin in teaching specific mathematics or reading skills. This lack left teachers with many practical problems to solve in trying to teach the child. No logical link connected evaluation and instruction.

Similar problems emerged in working with individuals with mental retardation and other disabilities in social-vocational efforts and other aspects of the adult world. Norm-referenced assessment information did little to facilitate placement, planning, and programming. Professionals working in such social agencies as welfare and employment departments and sheltered workshops soon found that they had to augment such information with their own, more specific evaluations. Sheltered workshop directors, for example, had to determine what specific skills a client with retardation already had and which needed to be taught for the individual to perform productively. The difficulties with norm-referenced assessment described here do not mean that it is of no value. To suggest that would be inaccurate and add fuel to a debate that has continued for some time. The examples noted above reflect purposes for which norm-referenced assessment is ill suited.

Criterion Referencing.   **Criterion-referenced evaluation** is nearly synonymous with what norm-referenced evaluation is not. Individual performance is not compared with some norm. Criterion-referenced evaluation assesses specific skill areas individually, rather than generates a score based on a composite of several skills.

Criterion-referenced evaluation does not compare an individual's performance with that of others. Assessment tasks or test items are usually arranged in a sequence of increasing difficulty, and a person's functioning is viewed in terms of absolute performance level or the actual number of operations completed. If a child being tested on counting skills is able to progress successfully through counting by twos but no farther, that is his or her absolute performance. The child counts by twos with 100% accuracy, but by threes with 0% accuracy. This level of performance may be referenced in one or both of two ways. The first way involves the evaluator and the teacher (frequently the same person) asking, Is this level of proficiency adequate for this child at this time? The level of proficiency necessary for the child is the criterion (hence the term *criterion-referenced evaluation*). If a child needs to be able to count by threes, the teacher knows exactly what instruction to give. As the child progresses, he or she may need to perform at a more advanced skill level, depending on environmental requirements, and the criterion for this skill will change accordingly.

The second way that performance or skill level is referenced involves comparison of the individual's performance in one area with performance in others; for example, a child may perform well in letter recognition but poorly in sound blending. The evaluator examines performances in various skill areas, frequently constructs a profile of the child's strengths and weaknesses, and pinpoints instructional effort from the profile. The referent for evaluation data is still in one individual's performance, but now between skill areas. Usually the measurement involves performance on specific tasks. The evaluator draws no inferences about such abstract concepts as intelligence, instead relating performance measurement directly to instruction. Criterion-referenced evaluation has improved the relationship between evaluation and teaching, changing the way education is conceived and executed.

Past years have witnessed a theoretical difference of opinion in child assessment. Obviously, norm- and criterion-referenced evaluations operate from different approaches. Proponents of each viewpoint have spent much time and effort defending their positions, often without careful examination of what the other approach has to offer. This is unfortunate; such professional wrangling has little positive result. Although arguments continue to some extent, attention to basic measurement principles and reasoned applications have begun to replace rhetoric (Hopkins, 1998; McCauley, 1996).

Criterion-referenced evaluation has been applied in a wide variety of settings, one of the most pertinent applications being the direct linkage between assessment and classroom instruction. This use has evolved into an application that has received considerable attention in the field—curriculum-based assessment. **Curriculum-based assessment** uses the sequential objectives of the student's curriculum as the referent or criterion for evaluating progress. Consequently the curriculum that a student is being taught is the referent for evaluation. The objectives associated with the curricular activities represent the standard for success as the youngster's performance is assessed. This approach emphasizes the link between instructional objectives and assessment, improving the potential for instructional decision making (Eckert, Shapiro, & Lutz, 1995; Gronlund, 1998). Curriculum-based assessment also provides a natural and efficient process for screening assessment, a topic examined later in this chapter. Curriculum-based assessment is a specific application of referencing evaluation for a particular purpose. In some cases, other terms, such as ***objectives-referenced measurement,*** have been used, although distinctions are less crucial once the more general concept of assessment referencing is understood (Eckert et al., 1995).

Analysis of the usefulness of criterion- and norm-referenced assessment over time has led many to conclude that neither approach in isolation results in a totally effective evaluation process. Criterion-referenced evaluation is useful for specific instructional programming, a need not served well by norm-referenced evaluation. Many children with mental retardation, however, ultimately must function in a larger world, perhaps in a regular educational setting on a partial basis. This broader world usually operates on a competitive basis, with children's performances compared with each other, so it is largely a norm-referenced world. To maximize a child's chances for success, information that will indicate how the child's performance compares with others in the larger world must be obtained. It would be disastrous to bring a child's skill level from Point A to Point B (criterion-referenced evaluation) and find that Point C was necessary for success in a regular educational setting. Those working with individuals who have mental retardation cannot afford to be rigid in using only some of the tools available to them. Because they serve different purposes, both norm- and criterion-referenced evaluation must be used. Referencing of assessment information clearly depends on the use or application intended.

Formative and Summative Evaluation

Other conceptual developments look directly to the purposes of evaluation and have led to the articulation of two broad categories: formative and summative. **Formative evaluation** in this framework is assessment that focuses not on a desired ultimate behavior but rather on the next step in an instructional program. Formative evaluation is frequently an integral part of the instructional program. **Summative evaluation** is quite different. It involves assessment of terminal behaviors and evaluates a child's performance at the end of a given program. These conceptualizations also have been combined with norm- and criterion-referenced evaluation and other measurement models to develop functional and comprehensive views of assessment that have been applied in a broad range of settings (e.g., Fuchs, Fuchs, Hamlett, & Walz, 1993; Ornstein & Cienkus, 1995; Osborne & House, 1995; Richey, 1995). Myopic views of evaluation and psychological assessment seem to be giving way to more thoughtful approaches to the broad field. This change is promising because it means that workers in the field are being more thorough and reasoned in their consideration of assessment.

Assessment Bias

Discriminatory testing is another concern in the assessment field, an issue examined in the context of multicultural issues in Chapter 2. Questions about discriminatory assessment surface particularly often with respect to the standardized, norm-referenced testing of minority group children. African Americans, Hispanics, and Native Americans, as well as others, have legitimately claimed that evaluation instruments contain cultural bias and prejudice. Likewise, they have raised serious concerns regarding the absence of assessment specialists with appropriate training and background (Aponte & Clifford, 1995; Ewing, 1995; Lyman, 1998). Assessment bias, whether due to instrumentation or administration, generates inaccurate results that are at least partially due to cultural background, rather than to actual mental abilities or skills (Aiken, 1997; deValenzuela & Cervantes, 1998; Gregory, 1996). Because psychoeducational assessment instruments usually are devised by individuals from the cultural majority, test items are probably more representative of that group than others. Likewise, norms and the scientists who develop them are more frequently reflecting the cultural majority than the minority subgroups (Wood, Lundgren, Ouellette, Busceme, & Blackstone, 1994). When minority children's scores are compared with norms established on other populations, the children are often at a disadvantage because of cultural differences. Such bias in psychological assessment has been evident for many years, although only in recent decades have significant efforts begun to address the problem (Hopkins, 1998; Janda, 1998; Mayfield & Reynolds, 1997).

Attempts to construct unbiased instruments have been largely disappointing. Widespread concerns regarding the disadvantage of minority children in testing continue to appear on a regular basis (e.g., Battle, 1997; Gresham, MacMillan, & Siperstein, 1995; Smith, 1997). Some of the efforts undertaken, however, are beginning to place the assessment of minority children on firmer ground. In part, this bolstering has meant more appropriate applications of norm- and criterion-referenced assessment procedures, as well as formative and summative evaluation models for instruction (Gronlund, 1998; Hopkins, 1998; Lowenthal, 1994). Much research remains to be done in this area, however, because a full understanding of bias, its effects on assessment outcomes, and a resolution of the problem remain elusive (deValenzuela & Cervantes, 1998; Robinson, 1997; Saccuzzo & Johnson, 1995).

Evidence continues to indicate that factors such as ethnicity influence a youngster's likelihood of being diagnosed as disabled, and minority children still represent a disproportionately large segment of the population identified as having mental retardation (Greenspan, 1997; Gresham et al., 1995; Smith, 1997). Some authors claim that basic reform in educational purpose is needed in addition to work in assessment development (Hardman, Drew, & Egan, 1999). The problem of cultural unfairness remains, whether the problem is one of assessment bias or one of prejudice in the educational system. The reader can find a more complete examination of the range of environmental and cultural factors associated with minority status in Chapter 2. From the discussion there, it is clear that some factors, such as poverty, are broad societal problems far beyond the scope of psychoeducational assessment.

Although the issues in the preceding discussion have been articulated in the past, the reader should not assume that these problems have evaporated with the passage of time. The problems of educational uses and misuses of norm-referenced assessment have been addressed only in a limited fashion and, some believe, inappropriately (Aponte & Clifford, 1995; Janda, 1998). Issues arising from the use of criterion-referenced assessment have yet to be broadly explored and merit much more attention. Further, professional training in diagnostic assessment remains limited and needs to be reformed (Ewing, 1995; Lyman, 1998). The need for basic reform in professional training is crucial in view of how information goes into forming impressions (Gergen, Gulerce, Lock, & Misra, 1996). Ordinary human frailty leaves plenty of room for racial and cultural bias on the part of psychodiagnosticians. The work in assessment has scarcely begun.

EARLY LIFE

Core Concept

Assessment procedures are quite different, depending on the age of the person and the performance area being evaluated.

Assessment procedures are necessarily quite different at various stages in the life of a child. This section examines approaches to evaluation during the early years of life, from birth to about 2 years of age. Evaluation at this point in the life of children is conducted for at least two related purposes: (a) identification of children who already show mental retardation in their development and (b) identification of children who have a high probability of showing developmental retardation later. These purposes are two essential components of early screening assessment. In the discussion that follows, we first examine the idea of screening, then look at reasons for identification, and finally explore potential results. Identification cannot stand alone, or else it would be merely an exercise.

Screening Concepts

Core Concept

Screening assessment is very important throughout a person's life span, but it is crucial in early life.

Screening is somewhat like sorting sizes for things like fruit. For example, oranges might be rolled across a screen with certain-sized holes. These holes would permit oranges of an acceptable size or smaller to fall through. Those that are larger than the acceptable marketable size will not fall through the screen and will be sorted out for other purposes (special gift packages). Those that fall through would include oranges of marketable size plus those that are much smaller. A second screening process might then be used. This second phase would involve a screen with holes that were much smaller than the first screen's. The only oranges that would fall through the second screen are those that are unmarketable because they are too small (these could be used for frozen orange juice). This process leaves only those oranges that are in the size range that the buying public prefers. Screening for mental retardation is somewhat like this. Only those who now have developmental retardation or exhibit behaviors that suggest that they will later have mental retardation are sorted out by early screening.

High risk situations like those noted above may trigger assessment and actual intervention aimed at prevention. Prevention in this circumstance may involve pregnancy prevention if genetic screening of the parents indicates a problem or pregnancy termination if screening information indicates the unborn fetus is negatively affected. Genetic counseling may be employed in a wide range of circumstances where developmental abnormalities are probable and may result in advice that a pregnancy should be avoided or closely monitored if the potential parents decide to proceed (Simonoff, Bolton, & Rutter, 1996). Matters such as genetic counseling, prenatal assessment, and selective abortion have long been controversial and continue to raise many questions regarding ethics and moral beliefs (Blumberg, 1994).

For some children, the possibility of preventing mental retardation or lessening the impact may be minimal. These are the children who have severe mental retardation, frequently because of a birth defect or congenital malformation. Such conditions make identification easier, but because of the severity of the problems, positive action is more difficult. Even in these situations, early identification plays a vital role in terms of planning for the future of the child and the family (Crnic & Stormshak, 1997). Certain problems persist in accomplishing early screening assessment for mental retardation. One serious difficulty in assessing young children is accuracy of prediction (Molfese & Acheson, 1997). The behavioral repertoire of the infant is much different from that of the child at age 6 or 10 years. The infant is functioning primarily in a motor-skill world. Grasping, rolling over, sitting, and crawling are a few of the baby's behaviors. Infant vocalizations are quite limited and frequently focus on such physiological factors as hunger, pain, and fatigue. Early screening tries to predict later behaviors that are very different. Because the best predictor of performance on a given task is performance on a sample of that task or a similar one—in most cases, impossible with an infant—prediction is not so accurate as one would like.

However, this does not mean that prediction is impossible. If this were so, there would be little reason even to consider early screening. Fortunately for child-care workers, developmental status and progress in the psychomotor areas that dominate the world of the infant do predict, though grossly, later levels of functioning (Wildin, Smith, Anderson, & Swank, 1997). Accuracy of prediction is much greater with the infant who has a severe disability and exhibits clearer signs of impairment earlier. The mild disability presents the greatest challenges to early screening.

Another concern in early screening assessment involves the factors evaluated. Recent research and thinking in this area have made some changes in the indicators that early screening assesses. Valuable predictive information may be obtained by evaluating environmental factors in addition to examining the child's developmental status directly. Professionals traditionally have used such indicators as socioeconomic status and parental education and occupation to differentiate between environments, but now other factors have been shown to be more important influences on a child's development. Some of these are parents' language style, their attitudes about achievement, and general involvement with the young child. Research is beginning to study these areas, which promise to become even more important in the future (Barnard, 1997).

Genetics, Other Assessment, and Prevention Issues. The early identification of disability conditions is very important and, in many cases, enhances the probability of a more favorable outcome than in circumstances where later identification and intervention occurs (Bryant & Maxwell, 1997; Wildin et al., 1997). In certain cases the ultimate impact of a disability condition can be reduced substantially with early treatment or intervention. Certain disabilities even may be prevented if action is taken early enough.

The idea of prevention focuses particularly on pregnancies, anticipated pregnancies, or newborn children who are thought to be at risk for developmental retardation. Certain pregnancy situations are at greater risk for developmental accidents or disruption of the normal developmental processes than others. Such circumstances involve trauma to the fetus that might come from environmental circumstances, such as high levels of environmental toxins like drugs, alcohol, radiation, and others (Jansson, Svikis, Lee, & Paluzzi, 1996; Hannigan, Martier, & Naber, 1995). Other risk circumstances might emerge from known genetic conditions that have some probability of being transmitted to the child and that cause some level of developmental retardation. Genetic conditions such as phenylketonuria represent this type of abnormality and represent a circumstance that is amenable to prenatal screening and intervention. Finally, high-risk circumstances may also occur that seem to be related to parental status such as age. In some cases, such as certain types of Down syndrome, actual genetic anomalies occur in the developing fetus that appear to be related to matters like maternal age.

Early screening generally has been discussed in terms of its positive value for the child faced with the possibility of mental retardation and for the child's parents. In a broader societal context, certain ethical issues arise. One of the negative outcomes of early assessment is labeling. Labels and their impact on children have been a serious concern in special education for some time. The potential for harm is even greater if a label is attached to a youngster in infancy. To avoid labeling, child-care workers must move to behavior- and skill-oriented descriptions. And here we should say once more that assessment, evaluation, or early screening cannot be justified if its only purpose is identification. During the school years, evaluation and education must be linked. Purposive evaluation is even more crucial in the early years. The negative effect of assessing a young child, stigmatizing the child with a label, and doing nothing in the form of positive action beyond that is unimaginable. We do not support evaluation at any time in the life of an individual if it is only for categorization.

Earlier, we mentioned the problems involved in evaluation of minority groups. These problems are of even greater concern in early assessment, for issues of poverty, race, and environment play a large role in early screening (Landry, Denson, & Swank, 1997; Molfese, DiLalla, & Lovelace, 1996). As professionals gain skill in dealing with these issues not only early childhood assessment but also early childhood education should become increasingly important in treating mental retardation.

Early Life Assessment

Core Concept

Prenatal evaluation can provide extremely important information about the fetus. ☼

Prenatal.   Advances in medical science and health-care techniques during the past decade have had a significant impact on the field of mental retardation. One area in which dramatic developments have occurred involves prenatal assessment and detection of mental retardation.

During pregnancy the most common assessment involves routine monitoring of the physical condition of mother and fetus by the obstetrician or other trained health-care personnel. Part of this assessment process includes a detailed record of the mother's family and medical history. In addition to the history, the mother's blood pressure, uterus size, urine status, and other indicators are monitored throughout the pregnancy to ensure that no symptoms are present that would signal danger for the fetus, as well as for the mother. At this level of examination, the mother's physical condition is the primary source of information for

Prenatal assessment of this young fetus is important since this represents a vulnerable period.

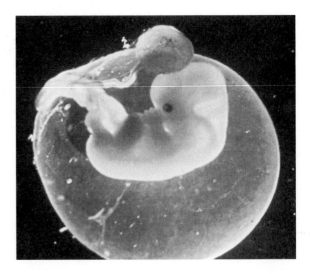

assessment. The obstetrician also examines the fetus by various means as the pregnancy proceeds. This ongoing monitoring is crucial to maximize the probability of a healthy baby being born. The mother's diet frequently is altered, and occasionally medication is administered to correct minor deviations from the optimum situation for fetal development. Women who do not have access to good health care run a much higher risk of giving birth to a child with a defect. High-risk pregnancies are more frequent among women who cannot afford adequate health care or who for some other reason do not have adequate medical resources available to them (e.g., Bryant & Maxwell, 1997; Gelfand, Jenson, & Drew, 1997).

Routine, ongoing prenatal assessment is generally adequate as long as a healthy mother and fetus are involved. Certain danger signs, however, prompt more extensive evaluation. If the family or medical history suggests that a particular problem may occur (e.g., an inheritable disorder), routine monitoring is not sufficient. If the mother's or fetus's physical condition is deviant, more extensive evaluation and action are in order. In such cases, evaluation becomes diagnosis aimed at the prenatal assessment of fetal status. Certain biological and chemical characteristics of the fetus can be measured. Diagnostic analyses of this type are not possible with every type of retardation, and work has focused on clinical syndromes that involve genetic metabolic disorders resulting in severe mental retardation.

Accurate diagnosis is possible for a variety of hereditary disorders, and the list expands continually (e.g., Down syndrome, galactosemia, Gaucher's disease, maple syrup urine disease, PKU, Tay-Sachs disease) (e.g., Kelly, Wathen, Rice, & Iles, 1997; Simonoff et al., 1996). Some of these disorders are rare, but in an entire society, the ability to detect and take action is a major contribution to the field of mental retardation. Even more significant is the ability to prevent the personal tragedies resulting from the birth of children with such devastating disorders and to provide intervention and support for parents (Helm, Miranda, & Chedd, 1998). In most cases, parents of these children are forced to watch a progressive deterioration from what appeared to be a healthy normal baby to a child destined for a passive existence or premature death.

Much of this kind of prenatal assessment is not yet routine (e.g., Carmichael Olson & Burgess, 1997). For the most part, the general obstetric monitoring mentioned suffices for a first level of screening, like the first screening in our orange-sorting analogy. In certain cases, however, metabolic or genetic disorders have a higher probability of occurrence, and in these cases current thinking recommends routine diagnostic prenatal evaluation. Tay-Sachs disease, for example, is a disorder transmitted genetically and found primarily in individuals of Ashkenazi Jewish origin. When two individuals with this background plan to have children, it is wise to always evaluate fetal status from a prenatal diagnostic standpoint. Strong arguments also can be made for evaluation of all pregnant women over 40 years of age. Maternal age is important in the birth of children with Down syndrome. The detection process for prenatal identification of Down syndrome is still being refined (Simonoff et al., 1996). As this work progresses, it is quite possible that such diagnostic screening will be recommended even for others younger than 40 years.

Core Concept

Assessment of the newborn can identify problems and prompt immediate intervention to prevent mental retardation.

Newborn.   A variety of assessment techniques is used with the newborn (Als, 1997; Wildin et al., 1997). Clinical assessment at this time is vital. Immediately after a birth, several factors are noted and rated by using what is known as the Apgar score. This procedure generally is completed by delivery room staff at 1 and 5 minutes after birth and may be repeated, if needed, until the infant's condition has stabilized. Five factors are included in the Apgar scoring: heart rate, respiratory effort, muscle tone, reflex irritability, and color. Each is rated by giving a score of 0, 1, or 2 (0 indicating low or weak, 2 indicating high or strong). The separate scores are added together. Extremely low Apgar scores at the 5-minute measure suggest a potential problem (Messinger, Dolcourt, King, & Bodnar, 1996). Newborns with a 5-minute score of 3 or below have three times as many neurological problems at age 1 as babies of similar birth weights with Apgar scores of 7 to 10. Apgar scores of 6 or lower are viewed with concern. Infants with such scores usually are monitored closely for the first several days, with interventions as necessary.

Other assessment procedures can be conducted during the very early part of a child's life. Some evaluate neurological status and reflex behaviors such as their sucking responses (Anderson, Wilding, Woodside, & Swank, 1996; Medoff-Cooper & Gennaro, 1996). Other procedures attempt to detect inherited or congenitally present abnormalities (they overlap with some of the procedures discussed above in the section on prenatal assessments). As with the prenatal evaluation process, biological-chemical analysis is frequently the means for newborn screening. Table 3–1 lists a number of inherited abnormalities that are identifiable through the analysis of blood specimens alone.

As indicated in Table 3–1, a number of these anomalies are treatable conditions. Treatment can prevent or substantially diminish the developmental problem that would result if the condition were unknown or ignored. These treatable disorders make up most of those we have listed, a fact that seems to support neonatal screening. Yet such assessment is not necessarily routine. Diagnosis of these disorders can be made from analysis of a dried blood spot, and in each case completely or partially automated analysis is possible, which streamlines the process and permits cost-effective mass screening. It is hoped that health-care services in the future will routinely include biological-chemical analysis.

Certain other abnormalities are detectable from clinical observation at the newborn stage. Medical examination of conditions such as Down syndrome and cranial anomalies can indicate with considerable accuracy the existence of a problem. Such effective evaluation, however, involves only conditions that are present and observable either at birth or in the first few days of the infant's life.

TABLE 3–1
Inherited Abnormalities Identifiable Through Blood Analysis

Phenylketonuria (PKU)*
Maple syrup urine disease*
Tyrosinemia*
Homocystinuria*
Histidinemia*
Valinemia*
Galactosemia transferase deficiency*
Argininosuccinic aciduria*
Orotic aciduria*
Hereditary angioneurotic edema
Galactosemia transferase or kinase deficiency*
Emphysema (adult)
Liver disease (infant)
Sickle cell anemia
*Items marked with an asterisk are treatable conditions.

Core Concept

Evaluation beyond the newborn stage includes many assessment areas not previously amenable to measurement.

Beyond the Newborn Stage.   Certainly, no widespread agreement can be reached concerning when one stage of development ends and another begins. In fact, it is misleading even to suggest that a "stage" is an identifiable and discrete entity. Stage theories of development have been somewhat controversial and continue to kindle interest and debate (Berk, 1997; Schickedanz, Schickedanz, Forsyth, & Forsyth, 1998). Usage of terms like *newborn, infant,* and *early childhood* is fluid, at best. In the previous section, the term *newborn* meant the time shortly after birth. The use of this term was not intended to suggest that the term covered a "stage"; it was used for convenience. Henceforward, we place evaluation in an age context instead of using terms that connote stages.

Certain measurements are difficult to make from birth through the first few years of life. This is particularly true when attempting to predict later intelligence. Before the child acquires language, his or her sensorimotor development is necessarily the basis for evaluation. Because later intelligence measures are heavily weighted according to verbal performance, prediction difficulty is natural. Progress in this area of assessment has been made, however.

Intellectual. A number of instruments and evaluation procedures attempt to assess intellectual functioning in young children. The revised Bayley Scales of Infant Development represent one such instrument. The Bayley scales have certain strengths that should not be overlooked as one considers alternatives for assessing very young children (Messinger et al., 1996; Wildin et al., 1997). The Bayley scales include test items for the first 2 months after birth; the items may be useful in situations where assessment of the very young or of older individuals functioning at a very low level is required. Further, the subscales for mental and motor performance have clinical appeal, although they may be misleading because they are only partial measures. The Mental subscale includes items assessing perception, memory, learning, problem solving, vocalization, preliminary verbal communication, and the very beginning of abstract thinking. The Motor subscale includes items assessing gross motor skills and the development of hand and finger manipulation. The Bayley scales rely heavily on the assessment of sensorimotor performance because there are few other means of performance evaluation at this age. The Bayley scales are accurate for certain high-risk populations such as premature babies. Although predictive validity evidence is scarce on the Bayley scales, reliability is high (Worthen, Borg, & White, 1993).

Other techniques have been developed and are used by many professionals for early assessment of a child's intellectual functioning. Most of these are not widely known because of the difficulty involved in assessing intelligence in the very early years. Instruments that have been employed at this age include the Kuhlmann-Binet Scale (birth through 30 months), the Griffiths Scale (birth through 4 years), and the Revised Gesell Scale (birth through 5 years). We return to intellectual assessment at the preschool level.

Language. Although closely related to cognitive development, some distinct efforts have focused on early language assessment. The assessment of language at this very early age is challenging, and much of the work has been of an experimental nature. In certain cases, the experimental assessment procedures developed for research purposes have not been developed further and therefore have not been brought to the broader marketplace. We examine a few of these evaluation techniques and how they fit within broader models of assessment in order to provide the reader with some concept of the approaches involved and the difficulties encountered.

Robinson and Robb (1997) note that two broad models are prominent in the literature on language assessment for very young children. One model promotes an evaluation that is generally called naturalistic assessment, where the child's language status is observed and evaluated in natural settings. These circumstances might be situations such as play in routine settings wherein the child's language facility is evaluated as he or she participates in natural environments. Such observation requires a period of time during which the evaluator collects data that, it is hoped, represents the child's language status in a natural setting. This type of information is viewed quite favorably by professionals in the field of language development but is also costly in terms of the time necessary to gather assessment information and also requires considerable training of observers who represent the language assessment mechanism (Crais, 1995; Owens, 1996).

An alternative model to naturalistic assessment is one where an instrument is employed to assess language development status. Such an instrument might be a language test or a time-limited standardized protocol for evaluating language development status of the child. Selected language assessment instruments that are commercially available are listed in Table 3–2.

The trade-off between naturalistic assessment and evaluation instruments developed for determining language status are fairly clear. Criticism of the instrument administration approach is often directed at the limited scope of evaluation that is imposed, and also at the circumstances for assessment, which do not indicate language status in natural circumstances (which has much greater flexibility and therefore increased ecological validity and utility) (Robinson & Robb, 1997). On the other front, using instruments to assess language status often does not involve as much time for the evaluation as the more lengthy naturalistic assessment approach. Language assessment during the very early years is a significant challenge. Often it must include consideration of other matters in the child's life as well, such as his or her physical status and socioeconomic circumstances (Silliman & James, 1997).

Evaluation of language development is an increasingly important area of interest in terms of early assessment, particularly with respect to developmental mental retardation. As professionals continue to refine skill description, specific areas of performance level will become more important. Language assessment may represent only language skill, rather than measure the abstract concept of

TABLE 3–2
Language Assessment Instruments Used with Infants

Instrument	Authors
Preschool Language Scale–3	Zimmerman, Steinger, & Pond (1992)
Infant-Toddler Language Scale	Rossetti (1990)
Receptive-Expressive-Emergent Language Scale–Revised	Bzoch & League (1991)
Birth to Three Developmental Scales	Bangs & Dodson (1986)
MacArthur Communicative Development Inventories	Fenson et al. (1993)
Sequenced Inventory of Communicative Development–Revised	Hedrick et al. (1984)
Early Language Milestone Scale	Coplan (1993)
Assessing Linguistic Behavior	Olswang et al. (1987)
Neonatal Behavioral Assessment Scale	Brazelton (1973)
Communication and Symbolic Behavior Scales	Wetherby & Prizant (1993)
Mother/Infant Communication Screening	Raack (1989)
Parent-Child Interaction Assessment	Comfort & Farran (1994)

From "Early Communication Assessment and Intervention: An Interactive Process" by N. B. Robinson and M. P. Robb, 1997, in D. K. Bernstein and E. Tiegerman-Farber (Eds.), Language and Communication Disorders in Children *(4th ed., p. 163), Boston: Allyn & Bacon.*

mental development. It is already clear that an area like language will be broken down further into component behaviors. As this occurs, efforts in evaluation, screening, and diagnosis probably will take on a very different description, increase professionals' predictive ability, and certainly lead more directly to intervention and modification.

Social/Adaptive Behavior.   Evaluation of social-emotional development presents a challenge to those working with young children. All of the instruments that try to assess this area of behavior have a common problem: the reliability of the assessment itself. In terms of standardized instrumentation, we limit examination in this section to the Vineland Adaptive Behavior Scale. Although it suffers from some mixed reliability results, it is one of the few instruments useful at this young age.

The Vineland Adaptive Behavior Scales (VABS) represent a revision of the original Vineland Social Maturity Scale, which was used in the mental retardation field for many years. Standardization information about the revision is still emerging from field applications and research. Early results are promising, although caution is always warranted as new instrumentation matures. The VABS is administered individually by a person who is very familiar with the person being evaluated. Three forms are available; two are interview editions, and the third is a classroom edition. The four domains of assessment are communication, daily living skills, socialization, and motor skills. This instrument is norm-referenced, based on national samples of subjects (ages newborn to 18 years 11 months for the interview editions; 3 to 12 years 11 months for the classroom edition). Although the norming appears good and validity is termed adequate, reliability varies considerably (Salvia & Ysseldyke, 1995). The various forms of the Vineland are used in a variety of settings with a broad range of children including those with autism, mental retardation, low birth weight status at birth, and youngsters at risk because of prenatal drug exposure (Carpentieri & Morgan, 1996; Collacott & Cooper, 1995; Phelps, Wallace, & Bontrager, 1997). Although all instrumentation is subject to limitations, the VABS appear to be a useful assessment of a child's developmental status in the targeted areas of functioning (Rosenbaum, Saigal, Szatmari, & Hoult, 1995).

Assessment during the very early part of life is also accomplished by observational protocols that do not represent standardized instrumentation. These procedures, for want of a better term, have been labeled the "functional analysis approach." This work rests on the basic principles of applied behavior analysis and is highly relevant to issues of early childhood assessment. The functional analysis approach to assessment requires direct observation of the child, rather than reliance on behavioral description reported by an informant. Observation is conducted of children who are referred for behavioral or developmental problems; it takes place in the setting in which the problem occurs. Data typically are divided into three categories: behavioral deficits, behavioral excesses, and inappropriate stimulus control. Within these general categories, the behavioral description of the child's functioning is very specific, permitting precise intervention, rather than a broad spectrum or "shotgun treatment" approach. Its specificity is a definite strength of the functional analysis assessment framework, but observation requires substantial training in applied behavior analysis. Either professional or paraprofessional staff members with the proper preparation can conduct the evaluation. A second strength of functional analysis assessment is its use of direct observation, rather than such indirect methods as interviews. Interviews have long been viewed as problematic and have added substantially to the difficulties of reliability and validity of assessment.

Multiple Domain Assessment.   Thus far, our discussion has focused on instruments and techniques that assess a child's developmental status in a limited area (e.g., language). Although the boundaries of performance areas are far from distinct, many professionals have attempted to assess intellectual development, language development, and social-emotional development discretely, as well as to consider the early health status and possible presence of inheritable disorders. Assessment from a somewhat broader framework, including infant-environment interactions, has attracted some attention in recent years, and developmental screening techniques that evaluate several factors simultaneously while still providing specific information in each area have been designed. These techniques have become popular for several reasons, one certainly being the greater efficiency of using a single instrument to assess several performance areas.

One rather well-known multifactor instrument is the Revised Denver Developmental Screening Test. This instrument is useful from birth to 6 years of age and scores a child's status in four areas of development: gross-motor, fine-motor, language, and personal-social. It is easily administered in about 20 minutes (including scoring and interpretation), requires no special training, and is available in Spanish. Considerable research has been conducted on the Denver scale's standardization and prescreening procedures. Results generally report adequate reliability and validity for screening purposes, although questions have been raised regarding the full Denver norms (Salvia & Ysseldyke, 1995). The Denver is used in a broad range of circumstances despite the fact that it is not always precise in identifying children who later develop poorly (Boivin, Green, Davies, & Giordani, 1995; Fowler, Glinski, Reiser, & Horton, 1997; Wagner, Menke, & Ciccone, 1995). This instrument is intended to provide a preliminary estimate of developmental delay that should lead to a more thorough diagnosis if results warrant.

Another developmental battery used in the early years is the Battelle Developmental Inventory. This procedure evaluates developmental skills from birth to age 8, is individually administered, and is intended for use by those who teach young children from the infant level through preschool. Five domains are assessed: personal-social, adaptive, motor skills, communication, and cognitive. The evaluation includes observations of the child, parental interviews, and administering standardized items to the child. The Battelle can be administered quickly—10 to 30 minutes for screening and 10 to 15 minutes for children under 3 years of age. Like other multiple domain assessment techniques, the Battelle is used in a wide range of settings, although some have noted that the validity evidence is limited (Cohen & Mannarino, 1996; Salvia & Ysseldyke, 1995; Sayers, Cowden, Newton, & Warren, 1996).

PRESCHOOL YEARS

Core Concept

Functioning in intellectual, language, perceptual-motor, and social/adaptive behavior is important in evaluating the status of preschool youngsters. Proper assessment must employ procedures appropriate for this age range.

From the discussion above, it is obvious that there is no clear-cut age at which certain instruments stop being used altogether and others become appropriate. Some assessment techniques discussed in the preceding section can be used during the preschool years, whereas others cannot. Likewise, certain evaluation procedures discussed in this section extend down to the early years. This section examines selected evaluation procedures used primarily during the years immediately preceding a child's school enrollment.

Intellectual Functioning

One assessment most frequently associated with developmental mental retardation is the measurement of intelligence. Although many people think of intelligence as a concrete entity, it is really an abstraction, something inferred to exist to a greater or lesser degree, depending on an individual's performance on selected tasks. Continuing developments in evaluation have prompted the conceptual clarification that a particular score on an intelligence test is representative of various performances and that the concept of intelligence, as a general ability, is an inferred, rather than a known, observable entity.

Part of the conceptualization of intelligence results from the framework of early instrumentation. Binet's early work was based on the idea that intelligence was a general ability factor. Consequently, his approach involved a mixture of items and aimed at an assessment that represented a composite measure, presumably including performances related to the notion of general intelligence. The fourth edition of the Stanford-Binet test still generates a composite measure, although some uses in clinical and diagnostic settings have resulted in attempts to isolate various performances.

The Stanford-Binet test is recommended as appropriate for ages 2 through 23 years of age. Frequently, however, other instruments are used for individuals over 12 years of age because of the longer administration time required for older people. The Stanford-Binet frequently has been viewed as the standard against which intelligence measurement is compared. Its norms, validity, and reliability appear good, and the new edition is seen as an improvement over its predecessor (Salvia & Ysseldyke, 1995; Worthen et al., 1993).

Another instrument frequently used with preschool children to assess intelligence is the Wechsler Preschool and Primary Scale of Intelligence-Revised (WPPSI–R). The WPPSI–R is recommended for use with children from 3 through 7 years of age. Designed somewhat differently from the Binet test, the WPPSI–R organizes items into 13 subtests (Information, Comprehension, Similarities, Arithmetic, Vocabulary, Sentences, Picture Completion, Picture Arrangement, Block Design, Object Assembly, Animal Pegs, Mazes, and Geometric Designs). This organization encourages the use of the instrument as a measure of more specific skill areas, although it should be noted that reliabilities on the subtests are much lower than for the full-scale scores. The WPPSI–R is being used increasingly with the preschool child for whom evaluation of intellectual performance is required. Restandardized in 1989 (with 50% new items from the WPPSI), a more complete picture of field use is continuing to emerge.

A rather widely used approach to assessing children's intelligence involves picture vocabulary tests. Although often used in this fashion, it is important to emphasize that picture vocabulary tests are not measures of intelligence in the same manner as those discussed above. They tend to assess receptive vocabulary, which generally is considered to be only one dimension of intelligence. Salvia and Ysseldyke (1995) noted that picture vocabulary tests may be useful as screening instruments but that placement decisions should not be made on the basis of their scores. Although some picture vocabulary tests have certain elements that are technically sound, it is not unusual for other elements (e.g., validity) to be completely ignored.

Language Functioning

As the child grows older, the distinction between assessing language development and assessing intellectual functioning becomes increasingly blurred, to the point of imperceptibility. This results from several factors. First, at least in terms of normal language development, the child's language structure rapidly grows more sophisticated. By the time normal children reach 3 or 4 years of age, they can typically use all of the basic syntactic structures in language (Bochner, Price, & Jones, 1997). A different response mode becomes possible from when the very young child was operating almost totally as a sensorimotor organism. Test developers working with children of this age range are quick to take advantage of this new response mode. The assessment of intellectual status includes a much heavier verbal component as the child gets older, so the relationship between language and intellectual assessment grows closer.

Evidence of this close link is found in the Peabody Picture Vocabulary Test–Revised (PPVT–R), which is used by some as an estimate of intelligence. Although the PPVT–R occasionally is described as an intelligence test, many professionals view it more as a receptive language measure. In fact, some characterize it primarily as such a measure (Lerner, 1997; Salvia & Ysseldyke, 1995). Because of the way the items are presented, the view of the PPVT–R as measuring receptive language is more plausible. However, caution should be exercised in most interpretation of assessment results that attempt to infer extensively regarding subdomains. As noted earlier, picture vocabulary tests as presently constructed probably should be viewed only as preliminary screening procedures.

The Illinois Test of Psycholinguistic Abilities (ITPA) is also frequently viewed as assessing language. The ITPA was developed for use with children from 2 years 4 months to 10 years 3 months of age. It is a highly complicated instrument that provides a profile of the child's performance in 12 subtest areas (10 are regularly administered, 2 are optional). Initially, the ITPA was used primarily with children who had learning disabilities. As concepts of prescriptive education have grown in popularity, however, application of the ITPA has spread to other populations, including those with developmental retardation. Although the ITPA is a useful instrument, it is not without problems. First, it is cumbersome to use (at least for some subjects) and requires considerable examiner training. Second, some of the subtests are far from pure in their measurement of a specific skill, and depending on the setting, they may or may not yield relevant instructional information. Third, a problem arises with its standardization population. Only children with IQ scores between 84 and 116 were included in the normative group, so a large database does not exist for many children with mental retardation (the norm sample was also only 4% African American). This problem does not altogether preclude its use, but the existence of such data would offer a clearer picture of the ITPA's measurement properties when used with children who have mental retardation and represent a broader diversity. It appears that the norms of the ITPA are restricted, suggesting caution in applications with populations often of interest in the field of mental retardation. These criticisms may surprise many who have used the ITPA extensively, but it emphasizes the importance of examining assessment devices before use.

The ITPA perhaps has been more useful as a conceptual framework than as an assessment instrument. It changed the way many professionals view a child, moving many toward the functional analysis of skill level as a way of thinking. This has long been the position of those skilled in applied behavior analysis, but a gap remains. Proponents of applied behavior analysis want much more precision in skill definition than the ITPA makes possible. The conceptual change is significant, however, when viewed from the broader perspective of the purposes of evaluation.

Various other instruments provide language assessment procedures with differing degrees of precision and standardization. Instead of describing such instruments, however, we wish to discuss the larger question of evaluation approach. Many professionals concerned with practical application have viewed assessment as important only in its relation to intervention or instruction. Such a perspective does not place much value on scores unless they represent performance precisely related to specific instructional activities that will result in skill change. Such an approach tends to discount issues such as cause (except in the rare cases that can be rectified by surgery). Evaluation in this framework often reflects ongoing monitoring built into the instructional program or designed specifically for a given instructional program. This kind of assessment is in line with the concepts of prescriptive education (in fact, it represents a potent force in the development of those concepts) and is precise in pinpointing where instructional effort is most needed.

Perceptual-Motor Functioning

Assessment of perceptual-motor skills is more commonly conducted with children suspected of having learning disabilities than with those thought to have developmental retardation. Yet perceptual-motor functioning is a crucial skill area in instruction for children with mental retardation. Without the requisite visual-motor skills, a child can scarcely perform the basic tasks demanded in many instructional settings, let alone succeed from an academic standpoint. A child experiencing difficulty in these areas should be assessed for specific level of functioning and have instructional activities specifically designed to match these skills.

The Developmental Test of Visual Perception (DTVP) is one of the better known assessment techniques in the perceptual-motor area. This instrument was designed for use with children from about 4 to 8 years of age, but one can extend this age range for children who exhibit developmental retardation to a significant degree. The DTVP can be administered either individually or to groups and requires about 40 minutes to complete. It assesses five areas: eye-hand coordination, figure-ground perception, form constancy, position in space, and spatial relations. From a technical soundness standpoint, the DTVP has a number of problems. The subtests are not independent, and reliability and validity are not satisfactory for diagnostic prescriptive teaching (Salvia & Ysseldyke, 1995). Although the overall perceptual score is fairly reliable, this instrument is best used as a research tool, rather than for instructional purposes.

The Developmental Test of Visual-Motor Integration (VMI) also measures perceptual-motor skills but has a much more solid technical soundness. This instrument involves a paper and pencil performance by the child, to whom geometric forms are presented as stimuli to be copied. Although the VMI was designed primarily for use at the preschool and early primary levels, it can be administered to students from 2 to 19 years of age. The VMI was devised to assess how well motor behavior and visual perception are integrated. Like other perceptual-motor evaluations, it tries to identify fundamental skill deficits related to academic tasks. Such skills are pinpointed for remedial instruction. In reaching the final form for the 1989 edition, large standardization samples were used from a broad cross section of subjects. Although these norms were developed on a large cross-sectional sample, the makeup of the norm groups remains unclear. This vagueness causes some serious difficulty in using the test in a norm-referenced framework. Among the perceptual-motor instruments, the VMI stands out with fairly high reliability and validity.

Social/Adaptive Behavior

Evaluation approaches for assessing social skills were discussed in the section on very young children. In many cases, the upper age range of the measures extends far beyond the young child into preschool and elementary school years and even beyond. As the child progresses, judgments or ratings by others—caretakers, teachers, and parents—are often part of social skill assessment. It is important to remember that their ratings are not always reliable and in agreement. Such information sources are very important, however, and continued research is needed to resolve or minimize these difficulties.

Adaptive behavior is a concept involving skills that may be viewed generically as part of social competence. As mentioned in Chapter 1, adaptive skill areas are a major element in the 1992 AAMR definition of mental retardation. One of the major challenges now facing this definition is assessment—particularly in the area of adaptive skills (Jacobson & Mulick, 1992; Storey, 1997; Wilson, Seaman, & Nettelbeck, 1996). Earlier development of an adaptive behavior scale by the AAMR (then the AAMD) led to a number of disappointments. Standardization, validity, and reliability (basically the general technical soundness) for both versions were found deficient (AAMD Adaptive Behavior Scale for Children and Adults; AAMD Adaptive Behavior Scale, School Edition) (Salvia & Ysseldyke, 1995). Although the 1992 AAMR definition makes specific reference to these instruments, it is clear that they are currently inadequate and that a great deal of work is needed to make them serviceable.

Also mentioned in the AAMR definition are the Scales of Independent Behavior (SIB), which fares somewhat better from a technical soundness standpoint. The SIB may be used to assess adaptive functioning in individuals from infancy to adulthood. It is administered individually, and items generate four clusters or areas of functioning: (a) motor skills (gross and fine motor), (b) social interaction and communications (including social interaction, language comprehension, and language expression), (c) personal living skills (with five subscales pertaining to meal preparation and eating, dressing, toileting, self-care, and domestic skills), and (d) community living skills (time, money, work skills, home, and community). The SIB also includes maladaptive behavior indicators. Although there are some differences, the functioning clusters and subscales could serve the adaptive skill areas defined by AAMR (1992). Validity evidence for the SIB appears to be excellent, although the reliability of the subscales is variable and may cause some problems, depending on how they are used (Sylvia & Ysseldyke, 1995).

Another instrument for assessing adaptive functioning is the Adaptive Behavior Inventory (ABI). The ABI is one of those procedures that blurs the age categories used here in that it is primarily for use with students from 6 to nearly 19 years of age. Agewise, it is more appropriate for the "Elementary School Years" section that immediately follows. It is presented here, however, to examine this instrument and the SIB in the context of the AAMR adaptive skill areas. The AAMR delineated 10 adaptive skill areas as outlined in Table 3–3 (see Chapter 1 for details). The ABI includes five subtests that can be administered independently and with little time investment: Self-Care Skills, Communication Skills, Social Skills, Academic Skills, and Occupational Skills. From a technical soundness standpoint, the norms, reliability, and validity appear to be adequate (Salvia & Ysseldyke, 1995).

TABLE 3–3
AAMR Adaptive Skill Areas and Assessment Domains of Two Instruments

AAMR Skill Area	Scales of Independent Behavior (SIB)	Adaptive Behavior Inventory (ABI)
Communication	Part of social interaction and communication	Communication
Self-care	Part of personal living skills	Self-care
Home living	Part of personal living skills	
Social	Social interaction and communication	Social skills
Community use	Community living skills	Some of self-care items
Self-direction	Some in community living skills	
Health and safety	Some in personal living skills	
Functional academics		Academic skills
Leisure		
Work	Part of community living skills	Occupational

Table 3–3 presents a quick summary of the AAMR adaptive skill areas and the assessment domains of the last two adaptive behavior instruments discussed—the SIB and the ABI. Gaps are clearly evident, but in a number of areas, measurement domains or scales appear to address or at least partially attend to these areas. It should be noted as well that these two instruments appear to have relatively sound psychometric properties when compared with others in the adaptive behavior area. The SIB and the ABI may play significant roles in assessing adaptive skills as defined by the AAMR.

ELEMENTARY SCHOOL YEARS

Core Concept

Multiple areas of functioning must be evaluated during the elementary years. Proper evaluation uses technically and conceptually sound procedures appropriate for this age range.

The elementary school child who has developmental retardation may be somewhat out of phase with the usual chronological age-formal education sequence. We use the phrase *elementary years* here only as a guideline. The overlap in age ranges for assessment approaches has already become obvious. Only techniques that become appropriate for this age range receive primary attention in this section. We also devote separate attention to emerging systems of assessment.

Intellectual Functioning

Several previously mentioned intellectual assessment instruments reached into the 5-to-12-year age range. In addition to these techniques, one of the best-known intelligence tests becomes age appropriate in this range: the Wechsler Intelligence Scale for Children–III (WISC–III). An updated version of the WISC–R, its recent release precludes much accumulation of field information, although it appears comparable to its predecessor (Worthen et al., 1993). Designed in a somewhat similar fashion as the WPPSI, it is recommended for use with children between the ages of 5 and 15 years. The WISC has 12 subtests divided into two general areas: verbal and performance. Like most standardized instruments, the WISC is basically a norm-referenced instrument. Its score gives a composite IQ that indicates general ability. The instrument also provides for a profile of the child's performance in individual subtest areas, which generates more specific information than the composite IQ. Data from further field applications of the WISC–III will determine how it compares with previous editions, from a practical standpoint.

Although the recommended age range extends from about 5 to 15 years, the WISC–III may not be the preferred instrument in this range. For general assessment of mental retardation, the Stanford-Binet was viewed as stronger than the WISC–R up to age 8, mostly because of its standardization and clinical use. As data accumulate on the WISC–III, this preference may no longer hold. Certainly, the WISC–III is more appropriate for children from about 8 to 15 years of age.

Achievement

Many of the specific areas of assessment discussed for earlier age levels continue to be important during the elementary years. Determination of which areas require evaluation is based on a critical analysis of the areas in which a child has difficulty. One assessment area, however, becomes more important to evaluate than before: achievement. Many procedures assess academic achievement during the elementary years, including formal standardized instruments, as well as teacher-made assessment techniques for daily monitoring (Gronlund, 1998). Both norm- and criterion-referenced applications are used widely, as are individually and group-administered procedures. Each approach has its strengths, depending on the purpose of the evaluation. The following discussion is necessarily selective in those examined. Additional information regarding a more complete selection of instruments may be found in a number of sources devoted to this purpose (e.g., Salvia & Ysseldyke, 1995).

The revised edition of the Peabody Individual Achievement Test (PIAT–R) is an individually administered achievement test that assesses six content areas: mathematics, reading recognition, reading comprehension, spelling, general information, and written expression. The PIAT–R is designed for use from kindergarten through the 12th grade. Although the PIAT–R is a general achievement measure, it also may be used for instructional purposes. Easily administered, the PIAT–R results in a profile of the child's performance in the areas tested. The scores are presented in a variety of forms, including percentile ranks, age and grade equivalents, stanines, and normal curve equivalents. (Written Expression, a new subtest in this version, is scored differently by using scoring criteria provided in the manual.) Depending on the specific evaluation purpose, an examiner may select from these score formats as reporting dictates. Reliability is high for the objectively scored subtests. The manual provides information regarding reliability on the Written Language subtest, which is lower. Validity, of course, is based on the correspondence of the items with the curriculum being used. Although developed as a norm-referenced instrument, skilled teachers may find criterion-referenced applications useful.

The seventh edition of the Metropolitan Achievement Test battery (MAT7) is an achievement battery that is group administered. The MAT7 is divided into two groups of tests: the Survey and Diagnostic batteries. The Survey battery assesses students' general achievement in reading, mathematics, language, social studies, and science. The Diagnostic battery addresses the three areas of reading, mathematics, and language. Both batteries are designed for students from about kindergarten through 12th grade (Diagnostic begins at K.5). By design, both the Survey and Diagnostic batteries may be used in norm- and criterion-referenced application. The Metropolitan is an example of how standardized instrumentation can be designed and used in a meaningful fashion for multiple purposes. Although the normed areas of evaluation are important, equally significant is what can be done with them. When analyzed in terms of the skills

Certain paper and pencil assessments are still used to evaluate functioning.

required by each item, the MAT7 can provide a vast amount of information about a child's functioning. This information then can be coordinated for specific determination of discrete activities for the child's instructional program. This kind of analysis demands considerable information and teacher training in task analysis and precision teaching. When such educational expertise is brought to the teaching task, instruments like the MAT7 are highly relevant for the education of both children with mental retardation and others.

The achievement instruments discussed thus far have been general achievement measures, with some providing specific skill information. On certain occasions, it is necessary to use an instrument that focuses specifically on one content area and provides an in-depth assessment of subskills in that area. Such an instrument is the revised Keymath Diagnostic Arithmetic Test (Keymath–R). Keymath–R was developed for use with children as young as the kindergarten level and ranging upward through Grade 8. Two forms (A and B) of Keymath–R are provided. Math performance is assessed in terms of three areas: basic concepts, operations, and applications. Scores create a profile of specific skills, although Keymath-R also may be scored on the basis of percentiles and standard scores.

Achievement assessment that results in only grade- or age-equivalency scores (as well as percentiles and standard scores) is norm-referenced information. In many cases, these same tests may be used in ways that make them criterion-referenced, if the child's performance is not compared with other children's or with some norm. The more discrete and specific an assessment is, the greater its potential for drawing specific inferences for instruction. The highest relevance for instruction comes from assessment that is an integral part of the instructional program. Ideally, this type of achievement assessment continuously monitors a child's progress in specific skills. Instruction is aimed precisely at the child's level of functioning, permitting a highly efficient interface between evaluation and instruction. There is much in favor of such an approach for educating those who have developmental retardation.

Assessment Systems

Assessment procedures examined thus far have often had one area as their primary focus. Clinicians have often found it necessary to use several instruments to obtain a complete picture of an individual's capabilities. But some assessment development efforts evaluate a number of different attributes.

The System of Multicultural Pluralistic Assessment (SOMPA) evaluates a variety of attribute areas and is an attempt to provide for comprehensive, nondiscriminatory assessment. It is designed to be used with children from 5 to 11 years of age. Assessment is extremely comprehensive and views the individual in terms of three broad perspectives: the medical model, the social system model, and the pluralistic model. The SOMPA provides for an estimated learning potential (ELP) that strives to provide balance for social and ethnic groups on WISC instrumentation. It also includes an adaptive behavior measure called the Adaptive Behavior Inventory for Children (ABIC). Scoring for all measures is converted to percentiles and placed in a profile. The SOMPA is different in approach and addresses child functioning in a manner that has not been undertaken previously on any widespread basis. The complicated and massive nature of the evaluation and some resulting questions about its clinical usefulness have deterred from widespread utilization of the SOMPA. Public school students in California were used for norming, and caution should be exercised regarding applications in other circumstances. Longitudinal research suggests that the SOMPA has some validity for predicting school achievement for ethnic minority students (Figueroa & Sassenrath, 1989). SOMPA has been used in a variety of earlier research settings, although it has not surfaced as a system with widespread adoption (Barona & Pfeiffer, 1992; Matthew, Golin, Moore, & Baker, 1992).

A second, larger evaluation system is the revised Woodcock-Johnson Tests of Cognitive Ability-Revised (WJTCA–R). This system covers an unusually wide age span (preschool to adult) and is designed to evaluate both academic achievement and cognitive ability (Laurent, 1997). Academic achievement is assessed by using 14 subtests, and the Cognitive Ability battery includes 21 subtests (some of each group are standard; others are supplementary). Administration of the entire battery is very time consuming, and scoring is complicated. A relatively high level of skill is required for administration (Mather & Jaffe, 1992). The WJTCA–R is adequately standardized, with a much broader sample than described for the SOMPA. The WJTCA–R is still a maturing instrument, and as noted with others, field applications will provide useful information.

ADOLESCENT AND ADULT YEARS

Core Concept

Assessment during adolescent and adult years involves use of age- or functioning-level–appropriate procedures. Attention also must be given to the changing purposes of evaluation in these years.

As we indicated at the beginning of each section, the age categories used must be viewed as guideposts. Consequently, the phrase *adolescent and adult years* is only a general reference that is used in this section to mean 13 years of age and older. Many of the evaluation techniques previously examined extend well into this age range.

Intellectual Functioning

The instrument frequently used in the middle adolescent and older years is the Wechsler Adult Intelligence Scale–Revised (WAIS–R). This is a revised version of the earlier WAIS and has content similar to the WISC–II and WPPSI–R (although age appropriate). The WISC–III, discussed earlier, extends into the early adolescent years (5 to 15 years). The WAIS–R is appropriate for assessing the intellectual functioning of people older than 15. The WAIS-R includes 11 subscales divided into verbal and performance categories. The technical soundness of the WAIS–R essentially echoes what was noted earlier for the versions used with younger individuals.

Vocational Functioning

One area that becomes increasingly relevant as the person with mental retardation grows older is his or her skill level for vocational training and placement. During adolescence and adulthood, the individual who has mental retardation usually encounters vocational training as a part of formal education. In fact, the design of the vocational training received should be considered in detail both in the individualized educational plan (IEP) and the individualized transition plan (ITP) (AAMR, 1992; Hardman et al., 1999). The nature of this training (as well as later placement) varies considerably, depending on the degree of impairment.

Assessment of vocational functioning, like other areas previously discussed, must be considered in the light of its purpose. One purpose of vocational assessment has nearly always been the prediction of vocational success. A second purpose involves determination of what skills are needed by the individual as the transition planners consider potential placements. And a third purpose is the evaluation of that training and placement success. Vocational assessment varies perhaps more than any other measurement area. There is an extremely broad range of potential placements (e.g., jobs, tasks) and an equally diverse range of individual skills.

Work samples seem to function very effectively for evaluating vocational functioning. Sometimes called "career simulation," work-sample observations have a very direct relationship to both job performance and the skills that need attention in preparing for the job (Hoy & Gregg, 1994). Work-sample assessment is analogous to evaluation that uses applied behavior analysis techniques of observation and recording performance. This type of precise skill analysis has provided the most practically oriented information in other areas, and its utility in vocational assessment is not surprising. Evaluation takes place in a setting that is as nearly natural as possible. The close link between the assessment procedure and its purpose or referent setting provides the most useful and accurate data.

In addition to observing the individual's task performance, it is also important to evaluate other matters related to job success. Individuals with mental retardation often exhibit different social interactions from their counterparts without retardation (Braitman, Counts, Davenport, & Zurlinden, 1995; Ferguson, McDonnell, & Drew, 1993; Myers & Dagley, 1996). Such behaviors, plus other "nonwork" factors, often contribute to vocational failure as much as actual job performance. They are a part of the broader picture relating to overall success in a vocational setting. These factors require assessment just as the actual skill in performing job tasks do. Once again, behavioral observations in circumstances similar to that of the vocational setting are helpful. To the degree that the people and other stimuli can simulate an actual workplace, the utility of the evaluation data will be enhanced.

Perhaps the strongest deterrent to more widespread acceptance of direct observation and work-sample assessment is convenience. Work sampling and direct observation as assessment procedures tend to be cumbersome in terms of development and administration. Considerable time and effort are involved, to say nothing of the training of observers and evaluators. However, the alternatives for vocational assessment of those with mental retardation are limited. A variety of standardized vocational-type assessments are available as diverse as testing for graduate school and general aptitude and finger dexterity (Hoy & Gregg, 1994; Worthen et al., 1993). It is clear in many cases, however, that these have limited relevance for adolescents and adults with mental retardation. It is also important to note that work-sample and observational assessment techniques are not nearly so inconvenient when they are designed as an integral part of a training program. Many successes in vocational assessment remain somewhat unknown because they are an integrated part of training, rather than a separate published test on the market.

NEW ISSUES AND FUTURE DIRECTIONS

Many of the issues raised in assessment have historically paralleled prevailing debates and issues in mental retardation. This was illustrated by the early nature-versus-nurture controversy on the source of intelligent behavior and continues today in more abstract questions about fundamental conceptions of mental retardation (e.g., AAMR, 1992; Polloway, 1997; Switzky, 1997). Assessment in mental retardation is moving from its position as a somewhat isolated, almost laboratory-based activity into the center of culture, society, and environment. It is no longer acceptable merely to test people's ability in a "stimulus-free environment" to determine how they will adapt and function in the broader world in which they live. Assessment and program planning and implementation are rapidly becoming matters of serious collaboration between disciplines that scarcely interacted a decade ago (Elliott & Sheridan, 1992; Sheridan, 1992; Welch & Sheridan, 1995). Additionally, emerging qualitative research methodology tries to study people in the context of their environment more than ever before (deMarrais, 1998; Drew, Hardman, & Hart, 1996; Miles & Huberman, 1994; Stringer, 1997). Social and cultural environments will become integral in the study and assessment of mental retardation.

Such changes serve some very important purposes in the field of psychoeducational measurement. From one standpoint, they should present a more accurate view of how an individual functions and what his or her ability is in the relevant environmental context. We hope that such an assessment will also have greater utility than previously has been the case (e.g., ability testing that has little usefulness for instruction). Often called "authentic" or "alternative" assessment in current terminology, the field is moving away from sterile test scores to information that has the most likelihood of relating to the task (Gronlund, 1998; Worthen et al., 1993). Some work is beginning to view assessment as more than a static evaluation, with more of a view of what is being termed dynamic testing

(Grigorenko & Sternberg, 1998). From another perspective, assessment in context also may hold promise for alleviating some of the problems of evaluating individuals from minority subgroups. Integrating information about family stress, environmental circumstances, culture, language, and other pertinent factors into a child's evaluation has considerable potential for producing more appropriate assessment (Szapocznik & Kurtines, 1993).

Better methods, however, will not solve certain assessment difficulties. Designing environmentally contexted measurement will not do away with prejudice. Improvement will not be so great that assessment inaccuracies are solely the result of racial bias on the part of the examiner. This is a problem of professional ethics. Additionally, placing assessment in environmental context is not simple. It is likely to be both difficult and cumbersome. This result must be of concern to those working in the area of measurement, for if assessment is not user friendly, it will not be used.

Core Questions

1. Why are the uses of assessment procedures so important in the outcome of evaluation?
2. Why is it essential to clarify the purposes involved in assessment before one embarks on a testing effort?
3. Many conceptual developments have been important in the field of assessment during the past years. Among them have been the notions of formative and summative evaluation and the distinctions between norm- and criterion-referenced assessment. How do these concepts fit into the evaluation picture, and why were they important?
4. What are some difficulties encountered in predicting later functioning from infant assessment procedures?
5. Outline potential assessment instruments or procedures that you would find important during the prenatal period. Describe conditions that would prompt such assessment.
6. Describe assessment procedures you might employ for early life (neonatal) and preschool years. Discuss conditions that would prompt you to undertake such assessment.
7. How might you prepare an appropriate evaluation plan for children during the elementary school years? What considerations would come into play in your assessment plan?
8. Outline relevant assessment considerations for the adolescent and adult years. How are these different from earlier considerations?
9. In reviewing the life-span perspective, how do purposes change, and what considerations must be given to selection of an assessment approach?

Roundtable Discussion

Assessment is much more complex than merely picking up a test and administering it to a child. Careful consideration must be given from the outset to why one is evaluating and what is to be the result. Throughout the assessment process, one must exercise care in the choice of techniques, in how to undertake procedures, and in how to interpret data. Proper assessment must also consider the age of the individual being evaluated because different domains become relevant at different ages and because techniques diverge widely.

In your study group or on your own, design an evaluation plan that will attend to the considerations raised in this chapter. If you are working with others, have each person be responsible for a different age level and one or two individuals attend to the conceptual issues related to assessment. Compare your final plan with an existing one that you are aware of, such as that used in a school district. Full consideration of the life span must extend beyond the school years to health and social services agencies.

References

Aiken, L. R. (1997). *Psychological testing and assessment* (9th ed.). Boston: Allyn & Bacon.

Als, H. (1997). Earliest intervention for preterm infants in the newborn intensive care unit. In M. J. Guralnick (Ed.), *The effectiveness of early intervention* (pp. 47–76). Baltimore: Paul H. Brookes.

American Association on Mental Retardation (AAMR). (1992). *Mental retardation: Definition, classification, and systems of supports* (9th ed.). Washington, DC: Author.

Anderson, A. E., Wilding, S. R., Woodside, M., & Swank, P. R. (1996). Severity of medical and neurologic complications as a determinant of neurodevelopmental outcome at 6 and 12 months in very low birth weight infants. *Journal of Child Neurology, 11,* 215–219.

Aponte, J. F., & Clifford, J. (1995). Education and training issues for intervention with ethnic groups. In J. F. Aponte, R. Y. Rivers., & J. Wohl (Eds.), *Psychological interventions and cultural diversity* (pp. 283–300). Boston: Allyn & Bacon.

Bangs, T., & Dodson, S. (1986). *Birth to Three Developmental Scales.* Allen, TX: DLM Teaching Resources.

Barnard, K. E. (1997). Influencing parent-child interactions for children at risk. In M. J. Guralnick (Ed.), *The effectiveness of early intervention* (pp. 249–268). Baltimore: Paul H. Brookes.

Barona, A., & Pfeiffer, S. I. (1992). Effects of test administration procedures and acculturation level on achievement scores. *Journal of Psychoeducational Assessment, 10,* 124–132.

Battle, D. E. (1997). Language and communication disorders in culturally and linguistically diverse children. In D. K. Bernstein & E. Tiegerman-Farber (Eds.), *Language and communication disorders in children* (pp. 382–410). Boston: Allyn & Bacon.

Berk, L. E. (1997). *Child development* (4th ed.). Boston: Allyn & Bacon.

Binet, A., & Simon, T. (1908). Le développement de l'intelligence chez les enfants. *L'Année Psychologique, 14,* 1–94.

Blumberg, L. (1994). The politics of prenatal testing and selective abortion. Special Issue: Women with disabilities: Reproduction and motherhood. *Sexuality-and-Disability, 12*(2), 135–153.

Bochner, S., Price, P., & Jones, J. (1997). *Child language development.* San Diego: Singular Publishing.

Boivin, M. J., Green, S. D. R., Davies, A. G., & Giordani, B. (1995). A preliminary evaluation of the cognitive and motor effects on pediatric HIV infection in Zairian children. *Health Psychology, 14,* 13–21.

Braitman, A., Counts, P., Davenport, R., & Zurlinden, B., (1995). Comparison of barriers to employment for unemployed and employed clients in a case management program: An exploratory study. *Psychiatric' Rehabilitation Journal, 19,* 3–8.

Brazelton, T. (1973). *Neonatal Behavioral Assessment Scale.* Philadelphia: Lippincott.

Bryant, D., & Maxwell, K. (1997). The effectiveness of early intervention for disadvantaged children. In M. J. Guralnick (Ed.), *The effectiveness of early intervention* (pp. 23–46). Baltimore: Paul H. Brookes.

Bzoch, K., & League, R. (1991). *Receptive-Expressive-Emergent-Language Test (REEL-2).* Los Angeles: Western Psychological Services.

Camara, W. J. (1997). Use and consequences of assessments in the USA: Professional, ethical, and legal issues. *European Journal of Psychological Assessment, 13*(2), 140–142.

Carmichael Olson, H., & Burgess, D. M. (1997). Early intervention for children prenatally exposed to alcohol and other drugs. In M. J. Guralnick (Ed.), *The effectiveness of early intervention* (pp. 109–145). Baltimore: Paul H. Brookes.

Carpentieri, S., & Morgan, S. B. (1996). Adaptive and intellectual functioning in autistic and nonautistic retarded children. *Journal of Autism and Developmental Disorders, 26*(1), 611–620.

Cohen, J. A., & Mannarino, A. P. (1996). Factors that mediate treatment outcome of sexually abused preschool children. *Journal of the American Academy of Child and Adolescent Psychiatry, 35,* 1402–1410.

Collacott, R. A., & Cooper, S. A. (1995). Urine fetish in a man with learning disabilities. *Journal of Intellectual Disability Research, 39,* 145–147.

Comfort, M., & Farran, D. C. (1994). Parent-child interaction assessment in family-centered intervention. *Infants and Young Children, 6,* 33–45.

Coplan, J. (1993). *Early Language Milestone Scale* (2nd ed.). Austin, TX: Pro-Ed.

Crais, E. (1995). Expanding the repertoire of tools and techniques for assessing the communication skills of infants and toddlers. *American Journal of Speech-Language Pathology, 4*(3), 47–59.

Crnic, K., & Stormshak, E. (1997). The effectiveness of providing social support for families of children at risk. In M. J. Guralnick (Ed.), *The effectiveness of early intervention* (pp. 209–225). Baltimore: Paul H. Brookes.

DeMarrais, K. B. (1998). *Inside stories: Qualitative research reflections.* Mahwah, NJ: Erlbaum.

DeValenzuela, J. S., & Cervantes, H. (1998). Issues and theoretical considerations in the assessment of bilingual children. In L. M. Baca and H. T. Cervantes (Eds.), *The bilingual special education interface* (3rd ed., pp. 144–166). Upper Saddle River, NJ: Merrill/Prentice Hall.

Drew, C. J., Hardman, M. L., & Hart, A. W. (1996). *Designing and conducting research: Inquiry in education and social science* (2nd ed.). Boston: Allyn & Bacon.

Eckert, T. L., Shapiro, E. S., & Lutz, J. G. (1995). Teachers' ratings of the acceptability of curriculum-based assessment methods. *School Psychology Review, 24,* 497–511.

Elliott, S. N., & Sheridan, S. M. (1992). Consultation and teaming: A review of problem-solving interactions among educators, parents, and support personnel. *Elementary School Journal, 92,* 315–338.

Ewing, N. (1995). Restructured teacher education for inclusiveness: A dream deferred for African American children. In B. A. Ford, F. E. Obiakor, & J. Patton, (Eds.), *Effective education of African American exceptional learners* (pp. 189–208). Austin, TX: Pro-Ed.

Fenson, L., Dale, P., Reznick, S., Thal, D., Bates, E., Hartung, J., Pethick, S., & Reilly, J. (1993). *MacArthur Communicative Development Inventories.* San Diego: Singular Publishing.

Ferguson, B., McDonnell, J., & Drew, C. (1993). Type and frequency of social interaction among workers with and without mental retardation. *American Journal on Mental Retardation, 97,* 530–540.

Figueroa, R. A., & Sassenrath, J. M. (1989). A longitudinal study of the predictive validity of the System of Multicultural Pluralistic Assessment (SOMPA). *Psychology in the Schools, 26,* 5–19.

Fowler, E. S., Glinski, L. P., Reiser, Catherine, A., & Horton, V. K. (1997). Biophysical bases for delayed and aberrant motor development in young children' with achondroplasia. *Journal of Developmental and Behavioral Pediatrics, 18*(3), 143-149.

Fuchs, L. S., Fuchs, D., Hamlett, C. L., & Walz, L. (1993). Formative evaluation of academic progress: How much growth can we expect? *School Psychology Review, 22,* 27–48.

Gelfand, D. M., Jenson, W. R., & Drew, C. J. (1997). *Understanding child behavior disorders* (3rd ed.). Fort Worth: Harcourt Brace.

Gergen, K. J., Gulerce, A., Lock, A., & Misra, G. (1996). Psychological science in cultural context. *American Psychologist, 51,* 496–503.

Greenspan, S. (1997). Dead manual walking? Why the 1992 AAMR definition needs redoing. *Education and Training in Mental Retardation and Developmental Disabilities, 32,* 179–193.

Gregory, R. J. (1996). *Psychological testing: History, principles, and applications* (2nd ed.). Boston: Allyn & Bacon.

Gresham, F. M., MacMillan, D. L., & Siperstein, G. N. (1995). Critical analysis of the 1992 AAMR definition: Implications for school psychology. *School Psychology Quarterly, 10,* 1–19.

Grigorenko, E. L., & Sternberg, R. J. (1998). Dynamic testing. *Psychological Bulletin, 124,* 75–111.

Gronlund, N. E. (1998). *Assessment of student achievement* (6th ed.). Boston: Allyn & Bacon.

Hannigan, J. H., Martier, S. S., & Naber, J. M. (1995). Independent associations among maternal alcohol consumption and infant thyroxine levels and pregnancy outcome. *Alcoholism Clinical and Experimental Research, 19,* 135–141.

Hardman, M. L., Drew, C. J., & Egan, M. W., (1999). *Human exceptionality: Society, school, and family* (6th ed.). Needham Heights, MA: Allyn & Bacon.

Helm, D. T., Miranda, S., & Chedd, N. A. (1998). Prenatal diagnosis of Down syndrome: Mothers' reflections on supports needed from diagnosis to birth. *Mental Retardation, 36,* 55–61.

Hedrick, D., Prather, E., & Tobin, A. (1984). *Sequenced Inventory of Communication Development* (Revised). Los Angeles: Western Psychological Services.

Hopkins, K. D. (1998). *Educational and psychological measurement and evaluation* (8th ed.). Boston: Allyn & Bacon.

Hoy, C., & Gregg, N. (1994). *Assessment: The special educator's role.* Pacific Grove, CA: Brooks/Cole.

Jacobson, J. W., & Mulick, J. A. (1992). A new definition of mentally retarded or a new definition of practice. *Psychology in Mental Retardation and Developmental Disabilities, 18*(2), 9–14.

Janda, L. (1998). *Psychological testing, theory, and applications.* Boston: Allyn & Bacon.

Jansson, L. M., Svikis, D., Lee, J., & Paluzzi, P. (1996). Pregnancy and addiction: A comprehensive care model. *Journal of Substance Abuse Treatment, 13,* 321–329.

Kelly, A. J., Wathen, N. C., Rice, A., & Iles, R. K. (1997). Low levels of amniotic fluid pregnancy specific b-1-glycoprotein in Down's syndrome. *Early Human Development, 37,* 175–178.

Landry, S. H., Denson, S. E., & Swank, P. R. (1997). Effects of medical risk and socioeconomic status on the rate of change in cognitive and social development for low birth weight children. *Journal of Clinical and Experimental Neuropsychology, 19,* 261–274.

Laurent, J. (1997). Characteristics of the standard and supplemental batteries of the Woodcock-Johnson Tests of Cognitive Ability Revised with a college sample. *Journal of School Psychology, 35,* 403–416.

Lerner, J. W. (1997). *Learning disabilities: Theories, diagnosis, and teaching strategies* (7th ed.). Boston: Houghton Mifflin.

Lowenthal, B. (1994). Types of assessment for young children with special needs. *Early Child Development and Care, 104,* 53–59.

Lyman, H. B. (1998). *Test scores and what they mean* (6th ed.). Boston: Allyn & Bacon.

Mather, N., & Jaffe, L. E. (1992). *Woodcock-Johnson Psycho-Educational Battery: Recommendations and reports* (rev. ed.). Brandon, VT: Clinical Psychology.

Matthew, J. L., Golin, A. K., Moore, M. W., & Baker, C. (1992). Use of SOMPA in identification of gifted African-American children. *Journal for the Education of the Gifted, 15,* 344–356.

Mayfield, J. W., & Reynolds, C. R. (1997). Black-White differences in memory test performance among children and adolescents. *Archives of Clinical Neuropsychology, 12,* 111–122.

McCauley, R. J. (1996). Familiar strangers: Criterion-referenced measures in communication disorders. *Language, Speech, and Hearing Services in Schools, 27,* 122–131.

Medoff-Cooper, B., & Gennaro, S. (1996). The correlation of sucking behaviors and Bayley Scales of Infant Development at six months of age in VLBW infants. *Nursing Research, 45,* 291–296.

Merenda, P. F. (1997). Update on the battle for psychological testing rights, 1997. *Psychological Reports, 80*(3, Pt 1), 1019–1026.

Messinger, D., Dolcourt, J., King, J., & Bodnar, A. (1996). The survival and developmental outcome of extremely low birth weight infants. *Infant Mental Health Journal, 17,* 375–385.

Miles, M. B., & Huberman, A. M. (1994). *Qualitative data analysis: An expanded sourcebook* (2nd ed.). Thousand Oaks, CA: Sage.

Molfese, V. J., & Acheson, S. (1997). Infant and preschool mental and verbal abilities: How are infant scores related to preschool scores? *International Journal of Behavioral Development, 20,* 595–607.

Molfese, V. J., DiLalla, L. F., & Lovelace, L. (1996). Perinatal, home environment, and infant measures as successful predictors of preschool cognitive and verbal abilities. *International Journal of Behavioral Development, 19,* 101–119.

Myers, L. L., & Dagley, J. C. (1996). Vocational assessment and work behavior evaluation: Predicting rehabilitation outcome. *Vocational Evaluation and Work Adjustment Bulletin, 29,* 9–13.

Olswang, L., Stoel-Gammon, C., Coggins, T., & Carpenter, R. (1987). *Assessing Linguistic Behavior.* Seattle: University of Washington Press.

Ornstein, A. C., & Cienkus, R. (1995). Evaluation of students: A practitioner's perspective. *High School Journal, 79,* 65–71.

Osborne, J. L., & House, R. M. (1995). Evaluation of counselor education programs: A proposed plan. *Counselor Education and Supervision, 34,* 253–269.

Owens, R. E., Jr. (1996). *Language development* (4th ed.). Boston: Allyn & Bacon.

Phelps, L., Wallace, N. V., & Bontrager, A. (1997). Risk factors in early child development: Is prenatal cocaine/polydrug exposure a key variable? *Psychology in the Schools, 34,* 245–252.

Polloway, E. A. (1997). Developmental principles of the Luckasson et al. (1992) AAMR definition of mental retardation: A retrospective. *Education and Training in Mental Retardation and Developmental Disabilities, 32,* 174–178.

Raack, C. (1989). *Mother/Infant Communication Screening.* Schaumburg, IL: Community Therapy Services.

Richey, R. C. (1995). Trends in instructional design: Emerging theory-based models. *Performance Improvement Quarterly, 8*(3), 96–110.

Robinson, E. G. (1997). Systematic distortion of statistics as a result of racism and its effect on the human services system. *Mental Retardation, 35,* 221–223.

Robinson, N. B., & Robb, M. P. (1997). Early communication assessment and intervention: An interactive process. In D. K. Bernstein & E. Tiegerman-Farber (Eds.), *Language and communication disorders in children* (4th ed., pp. 155–196). Boston: Allyn & Bacon.

Rosenbaum, P., Saigal, S., Szatmari, P., & Hoult, L. (1995). Vineland Adaptive Behavior Scales as a summary of functional outcomes of extremely low-birthweight children. *Developmental Medicine and child Neurology, 37,* 577–586.

Rossetti, L. (1990). *The Rossetti Infant-Toddler Language Scale.* Moline, IL: Lingua Systems.

Saccuzzo, D. P., & Johnson, N. E. (1995). Traditional psychometric tests and proportionate representation: An intervention and program evaluation study. *Psychological Assessment, 7*(2), 183–194.

Salvia, J., & Ysseldyke, J. E. (1995). *Assessment* (6th ed.). Boston: Houghton Mifflin.

Sayers, L., K., Cowden, J. E., Newton, M., & Warren, B. (1996). Qualitative analysis of a pediatric strength intervention on the developmental stepping movements of infants with down syndrome. *Adapted Physical Activity Quarterly, 13,* 247–268.

Schickedanz, J. A., Schickedanz, D., Forsyth, P., & Forsyth, G. A. (1998). *Understanding children and adolescents* (3rd ed.). Boston: Allyn & Bacon.

Sheridan, S. M. (1992). What do we mean when we say "collaboration"? *Journal of Educational and Psychological Consultation, 3,* 89–92.

Silliman, E. R., & James, S. (1997). Assessing children with language disorders. In D. K. Bernstein & E. Tiegerman-Farber (Eds.), *Language and communication disorders in children* (4th ed., pp. 197–271). Boston: Allyn & Bacon.

Simonoff, E., Bolton, P., & Rutter, M. (1996). Mental retardation: Genetic findings, clinical implications and research agenda. *Journal of Child Psychology and Psychiatry and Allied Disciplines, 37,* 259–280.

Smith, J. D. (1997). Mental retardation as an educational construct: Time for a new shared view? *Education and Training in Mental Retardation and Developmental Disabilities, 32,* 167–173.

Storey, K. (1997). Quality of life issues in social skills assessment of persons with disabilities. *Education and Training in Mental Retardation and Developmental Disabilities, 32,* 197–200.

Stringer, E. T. (1997). *Community-based ethnography: Breaking traditional boundaries of research, teaching, and learning.* Mahwah, NJ: Erlbaum.

Switzky, H. N. (1997). Mental retardation and the neglected construct of motivation. *Education and Training in Mental Retardation and Developmental Disabilities, 32,* 194–196.

Szapocznik, J., & Kurtines, W. M. (1993). Family psychology and cultural diversity. *American Psychologist, 48,* 400–407.

Wagner, J. D., Menke, E. M., & Ciccone, J. K. (1995). What is known about the health of rural homeless families? *Public Health Nursing, 12,* 400–408.

Welch, M., & Sheridan, S. M. (1995). *Educational partnerships: An ecological approach to serving students at risk.* Orlando, FL: Harcourt Brace Jovanovich.

Wetherby, A., & Prizant, B. (1993). *Communication and Symbolic Behavior Scales*. Chicago: Riverside.

Wildin, S. R., Smith, K., Anderson, A., & Swank, P. (1997). Prediction of developmental patterns through 40 months from 6- and 12-month neurologic examinations in very low birth weight infants. *Journal of Developmental and Behavioral Pediatrics, 18,* 215–221.

Wilson, C., Seaman, L., & Nettelbeck, T. (1996). Vulnerability to criminal exploitation: Influence of interpersonal differences among people with mental retardation. *Journal of Intellectual Disability Research, 40,* 8–16.

Wood, W., Lundgren, S., Ouellette, J., Busceme, S., & Blackstone, T. (1994). Minority influence: A meta-analytic review of social influence processes. *Psychological Bulletin, 115,* 323–345.

Worthen, B. R., Borg, W. R., & White, K. R. (1993). *Measurement and evaluation in the schools*. White Plains, NY: Longman.

Zimmerman, I., Steinger, V., & Pond, R. (1992). *Preschool language Scale-3*. San Antonio, TX: Psychological Corporation.

Chapter 4

Understanding Intelligence and Adaptive Skills

Core Concepts

- Of all the ways people differ, none have generated as much continuing interest and speculation as has intelligence.
- Interest in the development of intelligence increased as people moved from primarily hunting, gathering, and agrarian societies.
- Intelligence has too frequently been conceived in a linear fashion because of the development of quantitative measures; qualitative factors also must be considered.
- Discussion regarding the causes of mental retardation stimulated debates about whether intelligence is primarily genetically determined or environmentally influenced.
- The need to know about the influence of a person's expectations, motivations, and social intelligence has stimulated research on the relationship between sociopersonal factors and intelligence.
- Attempts to measure it have generated considerable controversy about definitions of intelligence.
- Guilford and Piaget presented two different approaches to the complex task of understanding the nature of intelligence.
- Mental age and IQ historically have been central in assessment of mental retardation, although many other factors are emerging as important for full evaluation.
- The trend toward a reconceptualization of intelligence includes a renewed interest in affect, achievement, and qualitative factors.

Core Concept

Of all the ways people differ, none have generated as much continuing interest and speculation as has intelligence. ☀

Physical differences in humans are easily seen through variation in height, weight, skin and hair coloring, physical coordination, gender, and many other distinctive attributes that make individuals recognizable. One can also differentiate people in more subtle ways about their creativity, personality, and intelligence, to name a few of the more abstract human traits. All of these traits are of interest, but none have been so controversial as intelligence. Intelligence has been an intriguing subject for philosophers, psychologists, and laypeople for a variety of reasons. In Western culture, few concepts have been studied as avidly as that of intelligence, both in definition and in measurement. At times, scientists and test developers have been so caught up in quantifying intelligence that we have experienced difficulty keeping the concept in focus. It is important to keep a firm grasp on the conceptual identity of what is being measured as one collects data on a trait or characteristic. Otherwise, it may be difficult to assign meaning to the data or information obtained (Campbell & McCord, 1996; Janda, 1998).

At least two factors have contributed to the problem: (a) a tendency to rush the development and marketing of instruments that purport to measure intelligence and (b) a simplistic notion that test performance is valid and reliable regardless of cultural or motivational influences. There certainly has been no lack of awareness about these influences. Investigators in all behavioral sciences have pointed out definitional problems and the impact of behaviors that are not easily quantified, subject to situational influences and short-term changes (e.g., Aiken, 1997; Gronlund, 1998; Wood & Brown, 1994). Psychologists' "success" in developing tests actually presents a significant problem, particularly if the instruments neglect other relevant aspects of intelligent behavior, such as the influence of social and cultural mores, language, early environmental influences, physical development, and sex role expectations.

Core Concept

Interest in the development of intelligence increased as people moved from primarily hunting, gathering, and agrarian societies.

The phenomenon of intelligence has been of interest for centuries. As humans formed social groupings the need to specify skills and competencies of group members became necessary to facilitate the efficient division of labor. The need to prepare individuals for group membership emerged when people saw that some were more skilled in certain areas than others. As societies developed and became more complex, the need to explain individual differences also increased in importance. The development of theories of intelligence parallels society's progress from hunting groups through agrarian communities, the industrial age, and into the atomic, space, and information ages. The rapid progress in this information-oriented society, with ever-expanding computerization of activities, has placed a renewed emphasis on the importance of intelligence.

The advent of the space and computer ages and the development of world markets made the need to identify those with high intellectual ability more pronounced. Governments of industrial nations have undertaken searches and provided rewards for the intellectually capable through grants for higher education, merit scholarships, and the promise of exciting, well-paid positions in a variety of areas. Conversely, this emphasis also has brought increased attention to those whose intellectual capabilities are limited. Such individuals constitute a concern in technologically advanced societies because they frequently become social liabilities. In less mechanized times, individuals with limited intellectual ability often could make significant contributions to society by performing work that did not require a high level of skill. As technology has advanced and influenced the entire spectrum of society, the need for unskilled and semiskilled individuals has diminished. Machines now more efficiently perform the work formerly done by individuals with little formal education. This change has not been a great problem for those who have the requisite intellectual ability but simply lack the necessary training to undertake more skilled labor. But for those who cannot profit educationally to the same extent as their more intelligent peers, opportunities for high status and a fulfilling life have decreased sharply. Any humane society must explore ways to reduce the social and economic liability of all of its less gifted citizens, including those with mental retardation, while also providing educational opportunities appropriate to their intellectual abilities. Individual self-respect often depends on developing resources through education. A society that does less than it is able degrades and demeans both its citizens and the society itself.

In these circumstances, the need to identify and isolate particular characteristics associated with limited mental ability, both from biological and environmental causes, becomes paramount. Much of the public controversy surrounding intelligence pertains to its measurement or the manner in which the assessment of intelligence has been implemented. Major difficulties relate to intellectual assessment in the context of our culturally diverse society, as outlined in Chapter 2. In some areas, such as California, the issues of discrimination in assessing intelligence and other psychoeducational factors have resulted in legal intervention regarding assessment (see discussion in Chapter 2). In these cases the implementation experience in measuring intelligence will significantly impact the overall view and conceptualization of a major human performance area, heretofore termed intelligence (deValenzuela & Cervantes, 1998). Mental retardation clearly involves matters other than measured intelligence (AAMR, 1992). Limited intellectual ability is central, however, and intelligence is a topic that warrants examination. The need to understand, define, and measure this phenomenon remains an important task as attempts are made to provide better care for those with mental retardation in this society.

THE CONCEPT OF INTELLIGENCE

Core Concept

Intelligence has too frequently been conceived in a linear fashion because of the development of quantitative measures; qualitative factors also must be considered.

There are about as many ways to define intelligence as there are people interested and motivated enough to try. Over 40 years ago, Abraham (1958) noted that 113 different definitions of "the gifted" were being used at that time, and interest in this area continues, although the concepts of giftedness have taken a variety of twists and turns (Friedman & Rogers, 1998; Roets, 1998; Smutny, 1997). Likewise, mental retardation, at the other end of the intellectual spectrum, has produced a plethora of definitions. The number of definitions for these two intellectual extremes has led many people to think of intelligence in a quantitative sense. Intelligence, however, cannot be considered solely as a simple linear phenomenon ranging from more to less or from bright to mental retardation. The complexity of human intelligence dictates that its qualitative aspects must also be considered. An appreciation of the many determinants affecting intelligence is necessary if professionals are ever fully to understand and appreciate the phenomenon. From genetic selection at conception through the adult and advanced years, an almost infinite number of variables exists that can affect intellectual abilities of the developing human organism (Lamb, 1998; Ross, 1998; Schickedanz, Schickedanz, Forsyth, & Forsyth, 1998). As scientists continue to grapple with the concept of intelligence two questions consistently stand out: How is intelligence developed? and How can scientists gain some understanding of its composition in order to make predictions about future behavior? Neither question has been completely answered.

DEVELOPMENT OF INTELLIGENCE

Core Concept

Discussion regarding the causes of mental retardation stimulated debates about whether intelligence is primarily genetically determined or environmentally influenced.

Questions about how intelligence develops contributed to what is commonly known as the nature-versus-nurture controversy, which was directly stimulated by the phenomenon of mental retardation. Is intelligence genetically determined with little or no contribution from later environmental conditions and influences, or is it primarily dependent on environmental factors, with only a limited genetic contribution? Advocates of both positions have, at times, been very vocal in championing their view and claiming the naïveté of their opponents. The controversy has persisted in this country since the turn of the century, with varying social and economic factors affecting the way society views and provides for people with mental retardation. A more reasoned approach, one that attempts to establish the interrelatedness and interaction of heredity and environment, has emerged from this controversy (Gordon & Lemmons, 1997; Plomin & Petrill, 1997; Scarr, 1997). This attempt signals a certain level of theoretical maturity, with a trend away from extreme perspectives toward a middle position that recognizes and draws on the facts established by both sides.

The question that spurs such heated debates is not really whether hereditary factors or environmental conditions play the major role in mental retardation but their presumed effect. It is well established that some conditions are caused by hereditary factors—for example, microcephaly, neurofibromatosis, and Tay-Sachs disease. Similarly, it has been shown that environmental conditions can affect the level of mental functioning. It is therefore no longer a matter of debate whether genetics affects human intelligence or whether environmental factors play a part in the dynamics of intelligence. Both play a role in which each depends on the other for intelligence to be manifested. The contributions of heredity in setting the limits of intelligence are recognized, and the influence of environmental factors is accounted for in determining the range of intelligence. Figure 4–1 illustrates this interaction, showing that the inherited genetic material (genotype) of particular individuals or groups, when affected by environmental factors, produces an observable result (phenotype) that is directly proportional to how favorable the environment is.

Although the concept of interaction between heredity and environment is acceptable to almost all scientists, a controversy remains about how much each aspect contributes. Scientists presently are unable to accurately partition genetic and environmental contributions into percentages to indicate the precise amount that each contributes to individual performance (Blinkhorn, 1997). Attempts to ascertain the relative contributions of each continue, ranging from "best guesses" to stringently controlled research. Studies using twins have generally found that identical twins, whether raised together or apart, are more similar than random pairs of non-related persons (e.g., Cannon, Kaprio, Loennqvist, Huttunen, & Koskenvuo, 1998; Teachman, 1997; True et al., 1998). Problems arise, however, even with this research methodology because all variables cannot be controlled and because twins often are placed in similar environments when raised apart (Gelfand, Jenson, & Drew, 1997).

The nature-nurture debate has persisted for many years (e.g., Jensen, 1969, 1994; Bickerton, 1998). Periodically these arguments and related social issues surface in the public's eye, often contributing more to controversy than to scientific solution of the questions (Herrnstein & Murray, 1994). The contexts for the nature-nurture discussion cover many areas beyond the development of intelligence as scientists seek explanations of how various human conditions

FIGURE 4–1
Scheme of the Reaction Range Concept for Four Hypothesized Genotypes

From "Genetic Aspects of Intelligent Behavior" by I. Gottesman, 1963, in N. R. Ellis (Ed.), Handbook of Mental Deficiency, New York: McGraw-Hill. Copyright 1963 by McGraw-Hill Co. Printed by permission of Norman R. Ellis.

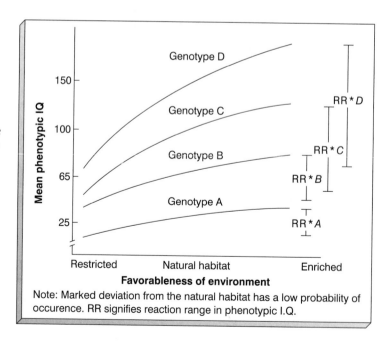

Note: Marked deviation from the natural habitat has a low probability of occurence. RR signifies reaction range in phenotypic I.Q.

evolve. Research continues to explore such topics as schizophrenia, alcohol and drug abuse, a variety of gender differences, and even the ability to form close relationships in the context of genetic and environmental influences (Cannon et al., 1998; Jang, Livesley, & Vernon, 1997; Pike & Plomin, 1997).

Core Concept

The need to know about the influence of a person's expectations, motivations, and social intelligence has stimulated research on the relationship between sociopersonal factors and intelligence.

A variety of factors influence intelligence, or performances that most people would agree contribute to the measurement of intelligence. Certainly, intelligent behavior in people's daily lives is not pure, without other sources having some impact (Hayman, 1998). In fact, most initial concerns about schoolchildren have to do with inappropriate behavior, not a perceived lack of intelligence. The AAMR definition of mental retardation (see Chapter 1) focuses significantly on adaptive skill areas, which attempt to address these important influences on personal and social success. Behaviors generally associated with the social aspect of intelligence have often been the focus of research and scientific literature in mental retardation and many other fields of study (e.g., Dykens, Hodapp, & Evans, 1994; Lubinski & Humphreys, 1997; Scheier & Botvin, 1998). A wide variety of behaviors is involved in the performance area broadly termed **social intelligence** and **social competence** or **personal competence.** For example, interpersonal interaction and forming relationships, communication, and self-regulation and reacting appropriately to the subtle cues in one's environment fit into such areas of performance (Masten & Coatsworth, 1998). Although measurement presents some challenges, many of these behaviors reliably appear as limitations in the behavioral repertoire of those with mental retardation (e.g., Guralnick, 1997; Lachiewicz, Spiridigliozzi, Gullion, Ransford, & Rao, 1994; McCurry et al., 1998).

Expectation of an event or expectancy has a considerable effect on how a person behaves. **Expectancies** are simply attitudes or one's outlook that prompts a person to decide whether something may or may not occur. They are related to previous experiences. A person with an expectancy of failure in a certain situation, for example, cannot be expected to enter the same or similar situations with a positive expectation of success. Those with mental retardation often have a lifetime of experiences that shape their expectations toward failure and success in a wide variety of circumstances. Motivation is related to expectancies, as well as to competence and anxiety. A person who expects to fail and who does not feel competent generally has little motivation to engage in new or different tasks. Low motivation can influence test results by preventing the test taker from diligently trying to perform the tasks.

Social intelligence reflects a person's ability to understand and engage effectively in social situations. Adaptive behavior is a corollary of social competence. Professionals have recognized for some time that social behavior is one of

Social interaction and experience may have a significant influence on a youngster's performance.

the primary factors in determining whether a person is viewed as having mental retardation or not. Virtually everyone is familiar with people who, despite a low IQ, are socially aware enough to function adequately in society. A number of attributes (subcomponents) of social intelligence have been identified and continue to be studied (e.g., Lubinski & Humphreys, 1997; Scheier & Botvin, 1998).

MEASUREMENT OF INTELLIGENCE

Core Concept

Attempts to measure it have generated considerable controversy about definitions of intelligence.

Questions about the measurement of intelligence elicit controversy over definition. The manner in which intelligence is defined influences the methods used to determine relative degrees of intelligence for prediction purposes (Cooper, 1998; Lubinski & Humphreys, 1997). Basically, there are two extremes in how people think about intelligence. Some people take a factorial approach, attempting to isolate and identify the component parts of the intelligence concept. Others conceptualize intelligence as a holistic construct that is either hypothetical or so intermingled with total personality that it cannot be conceived of as a separate and distinct entity. Most definitions fall between these two extremes.

It is one thing to theorize about the nature of intelligence and another to attempt to measure its parts. First, one must make a decision about the essential components of the phenomenon. If, for example, prospective test makers believe that intelligence cannot be understood apart from personality, then their test will likely include measures of emotions, experiences, physical condition, age, and other factors involved in personality development. The obvious difficulty with this approach is that it is difficult to construct tests to include all of the factors that might be required. Because of this, intelligence tests can measure only limited samples of behavior at a given time in a given place.

The best tests of intelligence presently available cannot and should not be considered the right way or the only way of measuring intellectual ability. Intelligence cannot be measured directly. As with any other concept, its primary components must be identified before any inferences can be made. The measurable attributes must be isolated, evaluated, and subjected to experimental analysis. This analysis is what early test constructors did, for example, in deciding that judgment was involved in intellectual functioning. Successful test development occurs to the degree that a test maker effectively identifies **measurable attributes** (often referred to as **subtests**), standardizes them, and provides validity and reliability data. Current intelligence tests include attributes that test makers believe are the best of the measurable aspects of intelligence now available. How well a person performs on the components of a test (e.g., vocabulary, judgment, analogies) determines how much one can infer about the individual's relative intelligence. The question of how far a test of intelligence can measure attributes of intelligence adequately is a source of continuing debate. Such matters as a child's persistence and attention definitely have an impact on test score.

As the use of intelligence tests with different groups increased over the years, it became clear that many factors argue against the indiscriminate use of tests and quick stereotyping of a person by IQ. We hope that a renewed call for consideration of the rights of others has raised a new consciousness. Many of the early psychologists and educators in the mental-testing movement in the United States warned against indiscriminate use of intelligence and IQ tests and against belief in their sanctity.

At the beginning of the 21st century, those in the field of intelligence testing find themselves in a position of having promised too much; slighted some important aspects of the intelligence puzzle, such as social and motivational aspects; and allowed practical considerations to outdistance sound theoretical development. There is a need to reconsider the development of theory and its relationship to the testing movement.

Most tests have emanated from the factorialists, rather than from those who have taken the holistic approach toward intelligence. Charles Spearman (1863–1945) initiated the factorial approach and believed that intelligence could best be expressed through two factors: (a) a general or "g" factor and (b) a specific or "s" factor. Spearman (1904) assumed that the g factor represented "true intelligence" in that the various tests of intelligence were consistently interrelated. He then hypothesized that a g factor was present in all valid tests of intelligence because it appeared to be a constantly recurring entity. But because the correlations were not perfect among tests, Spearman further hypothesized that an s factor was also present—though to a lesser degree than the g factor—and that the s factor resulted from those activities that could be associated with particular situations.

A contemporary of Spearman, Edward L. Thorndike (1874–1949), took a broader view in developing a multifactor theory. He believed that intellectual functioning could be divided into three overall factors: (a) abstract intelligence, in which a facility for dealing with verbal and mathematical symbols is manifested; (b) mechanical or concrete intelligence, in which the ability to use objects in a meaningful way is stressed; and (c) social intelligence, in which the capacity to deal with other persons is paramount. Thorndike took issue with Spearman's two-factor theory, maintaining that the correlations among tests, although demonstrably high, were not necessarily attributable only to a g factor. Further, Thorndike believed that neural interconnections in the brain influence intelligence and that whether the number of these interconnections is high or low can be inferred from a person's performance capabilities.

Core Concept

Guilford and Piaget presented two different approaches to the complex task of understanding the nature of intelligence. ✹

A considerable amount of debate arose as a result of the apparent disagreement between Spearman and Thorndike. Research during the next 40 years showed that much of the presumed difference between their data was due to divergent research techniques, rather than to substantive differences between their theories. But the debate remains unresolved. Proponents of the multiple-factor theory versus the single-factor theory are still at odds; the issue is still important. The work of J. P. Guilford and Jean Piaget, two theorists who have approached the problem from different theoretical frameworks, offers a perspective on the complex task of defining intelligence.

Guilford and his associates at the University of Southern California developed a program of research on the factorial approach to identifying the primary elements of intelligence. Guilford (1982) proposed a three-dimensional theoretical model that specifies parameters (content, products, and operations), incorporates previously identified primary factors, and assumes the existence of yet unidentified factors. This model (Figure 4–2) postulates the existence of 150 possible primary intellectual abilities. In Guilford's structure of intelligence (SOI), the intent is to identify discrete factors and to distinguish them from one another. Guilford indicated that the model should not be seen as a collection of independent factors but as a model to stimulate thinking about intelligence.

Guilford's model viewed human thought processes as involving five major categories in the **content** dimension: (a) visual (having a visual or tactile form, e.g., books, trees, houses, clouds); (b) auditory (involving the processing of sounds into meaningful symbols); (c) symbolic (possessing a summarizing quality, e.g., numbers, musical notes, codes); (d) semantic (requiring that meanings be attached to intangibles, e.g., the word *pencil* refers to object); and (e) behavioral (involving nonverbal qualities, e.g., perceptions, desires, moods).

The **product** aspect of Guilford's intelligence model includes six major types or categories that serve to organize figural, symbolic, and semantic con-

FIGURE 4–2
The Structure-of-Intellect Model
with Three Parameters

Adapted from The Nature of
Human Intelligence *by J. P. Guil-
ford, 1967, New York: McGraw-
Hill. Copyright 1967 by McGraw-
Hill Book Co. Adapted by
permission.*

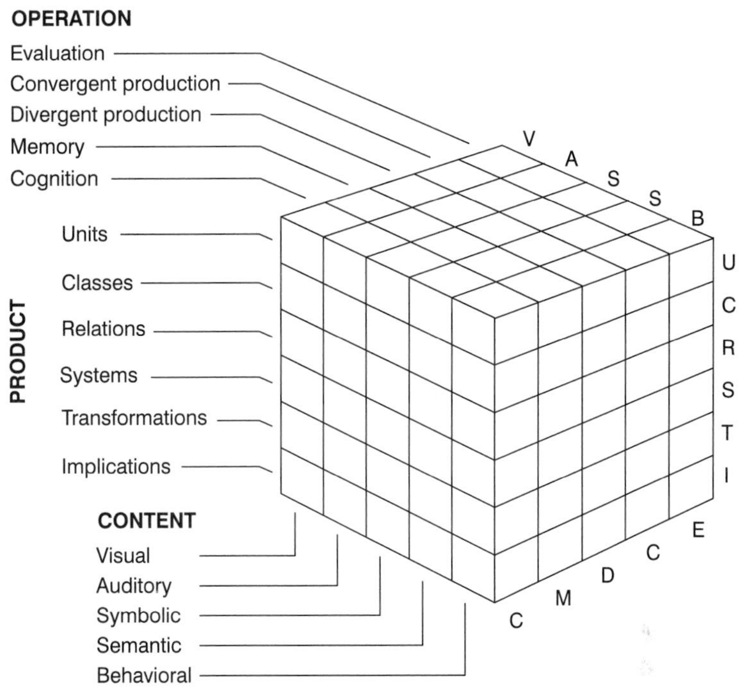

OPERATION
Evaluation
Convergent production
Divergent production
Memory
Cognition

Units
Classes
Relations
Systems
Transformations
Implications

PRODUCT

CONTENT
Visual
Auditory
Symbolic
Semantic
Behavioral

tent. The subdivisions are (a) units (the processing of a single item, e.g., a number, a letter, a word); (b) classes (the classification of sets of items or information
by common properties, e.g., figure symbols); (c) relations (the activity of developing relationships between a product subdivision and a content subdivision or
even relationships between relations); (d) systems (an aggregate of interacting
parts, e.g., in sentence diagramming, numerical operations, social situations); (e)
transformations (the more abstract and creative activity of transforming material
into results, conclusions, or physical configurations different from those anticipated); and (f) implications (the most abstract of the product subdivisions, one
that involves anticipation and making predictions).

The third aspect of Guilford's model—**intellectual operation**—includes the
mental processes involved in using the information or content with which it
works. Guilford defined five types of operations: (a) cognition (the process of
comprehension, knowing, understanding, familiarity; the comprehension of
interesting material in a nonthreatening atmosphere, e.g., games, television); (b)
memory (the ability to recall specific information, e.g., arithmetical steps, telephone numbers; both short- and long-term memory are included in this subdivision); (c) divergent production or thinking (the process of being able to generalize and produce alternatives based on information possessed or provided); (d)
convergent production or thinking (the process of being able to produce an
acceptable response derived, it is assumed, from a large quantity of material);
and (e) evaluation (mental activities, e.g., judging, comparing, contrasting, mak-

ing decisions). Guilford's model continues to receive some attention in the literature (e.g., Bogoyavlenskaya, 1995; Busato, Prins, Hamaker, & Visser, 1995)

Jean Piaget (1896–1980) is unique among theorists in that he approached the problem of understanding intellectual functioning from an entirely different framework. Instead of developing various tasks and then evaluating the correctness of the response, Piaget focused on the psychological process that led to the response. He was concerned primarily with interpreting the development of behavior.

Whereas Guilford was influenced by early work in factorial statistical analysis, Piaget's early preparation was in biology and zoology. His approaches have evolved over more than 50 years. During this time, his work has gone through three distinct phases. In the first phase, he investigated children's language and thought, judgment and reasoning, conception of the world, conception of physical causality, and moral judgments. During this phase, Piaget questioned the view that child development resulted completely from either environmental or genetic influences. His concepts suggested that mental growth was influenced neither entirely by nature nor solely by nurture, but rather by the continuous interaction of both aspects (Gardner, Kornhaber, & Wake, 1996). In the second phase, Piaget attempted to observe intelligence and development of the idea of reality in his three children by observing their behavior in situations involving objects and persons. Piaget demonstrated a genius for observation that was continually guided by his theoretical formulations, and in his observations he accumulated evidence to support his theories on the development of cognitive structures. In the third phase of Piaget's research, he and his associates investigated a number of issues that had arisen in his early theories: concrete operations, conservation, relations, preconceptual symbolization, formal operations, sensorimotor stages, probability, perceptions, illusions, and logical operations.

Piaget postulated a series of intellectual developments. The order of their appearance is important but not the age at which they appear. He believed that intelligence is an adaptive process and is only one aspect of all biological functioning. The environment places an individual simultaneously in the position of adapting to it and modifying it. The term *accommodation* was used by Piaget to describe the adaptation of an individual to the environment; he used the term *assimilation* to describe an individual's modification of the environment to fit his or her perceptions. An organism is considered to have adapted when equilibrium (balance) is reached between accommodation and assimilation. Piaget used this biological concept of equilibrium in describing learning activities. A child at play uses assimilation: The stick becomes a fishing pole, a rifle, or a baton; the shoe becomes a car or a boat. When the child is playacting, however, accommodation becomes predominant: The youngster becomes an astronaut, a rock star, a movie star, or a champion tennis player in an attempt to imitate the desired model through accommodating ephemeral perceptions. Assimilation and accommodation are complementary and antagonistic functions. Each creates alternate states of disequilibrium until the two are gradually resolved into a state of equilibrium.

Piaget postulated a sequence of developmental periods and substages that he believed to be generally the same for everyone. According to Piaget (1960), maturation and experience influence a child's rate of progress through the following sequences. The four main periods and their substages are as follows:

1. *Sensorimotor* **period.** This period is from birth to about 1½ to 2 years of age. In this period, the child is involved in a number of behavioral activities leading to a stable imagery.
2. *Preoperational* **period.** This period is divided into two substages: preconceptual and intuitive.
    a. *Preconceptual* **substage.** This substage occurs from about 1½ to about 4 years of age. Symbolic thought and language manifest themselves, indicating the child's awareness of objects and realization of his or her relation to and interrelation with them. The child is now able to initiate actions.
    b. *Intuitive* **substage.** From about 3 to 7 years of age, the child's thought is restricted to what is directly perceived. The child enters this stage unable to understand constancy, believing that, for example, the amount of liquid is less and not the same in a bowl than in a narrow cylinder. By the end of this stage, the child is able to recognize other points of view but is not able to transfer generalizations to other situations.
3. *Concrete* **operations period.** This period falls roughly between 7 and 11 years of age. During this stage, the child moves toward the ability to understand the conservation of quantity, length, and number. The youngster now understands, for example, the constancy of the amount of liquid regardless of the size or shape of the container and is able to generalize about other situations.
4. *Formal* **operations period.** From approximately 11 years of age onward, the child is involved in a continuous refinement of approaches to complex problems. The child engages in reasoning activities that are beyond a concrete operational approach. Children are now hypothesizing and making correct deductions. Words, which provide the developing human being with increasingly abstract concepts to manipulate, are now a primary tool used to solve problems.

Piaget advanced a developmental theory of intelligence. He envisioned both qualitative and quantitative differences as the person develops. His orientation differed from that of other theorists engaged in studying intelligence and represented a different way of looking at children's intellectual growth.

Mental Age and Intelligence

Core Concept

Mental age and IQ historically have been central in assessment of mental retardation, although many other factors are emerging as important for full evaluation. ✵

Two additional concepts require brief attention. Neither is new to the field of psychological assessment or mental retardation. In fact, both have great historical significance and have been particularly prominent in the assessment of intelligence. These are the ideas of mental age (MA) and intelligence quotient (IQ). They serve as convenient summaries of an individual's performance on tasks that presumably tap behavior representing intelligence. Both have caused difficulties, however, primarily from the ways people have used them.

Mental Age.   The concept of **mental age (MA)** was developed by Binet and Simon (1908) as a means of expressing a child's intellectual development. An MA score represents the average performance of children with chronological age (CA) equal to that score. For example, a child who obtains an MA of 5 years 6 months has performed in a manner similar to the average performances of children whose CA is 5 years 6 months. MA has been a useful concept, especially in mental retardation, because it is norm-referenced to average intellectual development at various CA levels. The general idea of mental development expressed by MA is easy to grasp. MA provides a convenient means of communication with parents and others about children with mental retardation. Most parents and other laypeople have had opportunities to observe children at various ages, so they have behavioral reference points that help them generally understand the abilities of individuals with mental retardation.

The MA concept has been less useful in other contexts. Because it is a summary score derived from performance on various types of test items, it is a composite measure. The single score provides little information about specific skill levels. Two children may obtain the same MA and have very different patterns of skill strengths and deficits. For example, an MA of 7 years might be attained by a child who is chronologically age 5 years and by another who is chronologically age 9 years. These children might be labeled as being "bright," having "mental retardation," or a number of other terms. The same MA may have been obtained from very different specific performances. The developmentally advanced child (CA 5) more frequently succeeds in verbal reasoning and abstract items. The slower child (CA 9) more frequently responds correctly on performance items or those for which previous learning was highly repetitive. Equivalent MAs do not indicate similar skill capabilities; the usefulness of the concept is limited in terms of teaching, particularly when instruction is pinpointed to skill deficits. Analysis of mental age remains of interest to researchers despite limitations in the way it may have been used or misused in the past (Lavergne & Vigneau, 1997; Moore, Hobson, & Anderson, 1995).

Intelligence Quotient.   The **intelligence quotient (IQ)** came into use somewhat later than MA. Originally, IQ was derived by dividing an individual's MA by his or her CA and multiplying the result by 100. Thus, a child 6 years old who obtained an MA of 6 would have an IQ of 100 ($6/6 = 1 \times 100 = 100$). This approach to IQ calculation was known as **ratio IQ.** Certain difficulties developed in the use of the ratio IQ, prompting its decline beginning about the mid-1940s. Since that time, the deviation IQ has been used as an alternative to the ratio calculation. This approach uses a statistical computation known as the **standard**

deviation to derive the IQ. The deviation approach to determining IQ offered several advantages. The ratio calculation was quite unstable from age level to age level, making IQ comparison between ages difficult. The deviation approach for deriving IQ is a standard score with much more stability along the age continuum. The ratio calculation also became problematic as the individual approached adulthood. As CA increased, an apparent leveling or even a decline occurred in measured intelligence, even when more items were answered correctly. The ratio IQ thus was less viable for assessing individuals other than developing children. Because deviation IQ is referenced to a standard score, it circumvents these difficulties and is more consistent at all ages. The boxed material below summarizes how standard deviation is used, particularly in psychoeducational assessment in the context of measured intelligence. This box illustrates how different levels of performance results in varying individual perspectives.

Like MA, IQ is a composite measure derived by performance in several skill areas. The problems noted for MA and IQ are similar in this regard. The global score, though providing an overall assessment of performance, does not indicate specific skill strengths and deficits, a problem that may have been more acute with IQ than with MA. Because of its single score and apparent simplicity, users of IQ have tended to forget the component performance of the score and have treated it instead as a unitary concept. Also, people began to look on the score as sacred and permanent, rather than as a reflection of performance on a variety of tasks. This misconception led to considerable misuse and eventual disenchantment with the concept.

IQ remains in use today, and in many cases the abuses continue. We hope, however, that people using IQ now have a better perspective on what it actually assesses and less often see it as a permanent status marker resulting in labels that themselves become entities. Modification of the IQ concept, plus expansion of evaluation concepts in general, appears to have prompted movement in the direction of more realistic use of the IQ score. Research aimed at refining its assessment, analyzing its various components, and examining how the concept emerges in various disability conditions continues (McCurry et al., 1998; Rourke, 1997; van den Broek, Golden, Loonstraa, Ghinglia, & Goldstein, 1998).

One final point needs mention in this section. A very important link exists between assessment and treatment (Bolen, 1998). In some situations, it has seemed that testing was being conducted with no clear notion of possibilities or plans for intervention. Such assessment is, at best, illogical. A second issue related to the assessment-treatment link is this: Some practitioners claim that the amount of testing required detracts significantly from instructional time. This is a serious problem, particularly when the time available is limited (the school year). A balance clearly is needed because assessment is ancillary to the primary goal of effective intervention. If assessment and intervention are not in balance, service-delivery needs are not being met.

Our discussion has explored certain issues and conceptual developments in psychological assessment. The examination was by no means exhaustive, but it does provide a backdrop for the study of assessment procedures.

The Bell Curve:

Everything You Ever Wanted to Know About a Standard Deviation

Standard deviation is a *measure* of the amount that an individual score differs from the average. Put another way, standard deviation gives us a way to measure the difference between the average score of a group of people and how well a given individual performed in comparison to that average.

Let's take, for example, an intelligence test. Questions are put together by a group of researchers that, for the sake of our discussion, measure the construct known as *intelligence*. Once the questions have been developed, this test is administered to a group of people to see how well they do on each of the questions. When all the scores are added up and divided by the number of people who have taken the exam, the average scores turns out to be 100. This certainly doesn't mean that everyone scored 100; it is merely a mathematical way of establishing what is average.

When we look at individual scores on the intelligence test, we find that some people actually do score 100, whereas others score either higher or lower. Johnny, for example, has a score of 83. So just what does the score of 83 mean in comparison to the scores of the rest of the people who have taken this test?

We can now use a mathematical procedure to determine the extent to which Johnny's score differs from the average score of 100. The measurement is called a standard deviation from the average. Again, for the sake of discussion, we find that, on this intelligence test, each standard deviation is

continues on next page

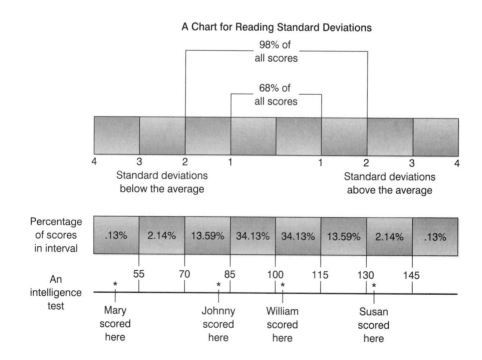

A Chart for Reading Standard Deviations

Experience with telephones helps children develop social skills.

abilities, then there is little reason to believe that that person cannot function at an acceptable level.

The triarchic theory is a much broader theory of intelligence than many previously proposed. The theory goes beyond intelligence—as exemplified by the ability to perform scholarly work—to extend the horizons of the concept of intelligence. It runs counter to the "g" conception of intelligence and has been examined in a number of contexts as diverse as aging, giftedness, "common sense," and a practical educational standpoint (Sternberg, 1997b; Sternberg, Ferrari, & Clinkenbeard, & Grigorenko, 1996; Sternberg, Wagner, Williams, & Horvath, 1997). Although Sternberg discussed a number of measurement and "intelligence testing" issues (Torf & Sternberg, 1998; Sternberg et al., 1997), a great deal of work remains before his theories are given the acid test of application.

Howard Gardner's multiple intelligence theory is another broad-based concept that focuses on varying areas of competence, rather than on the general factor approach. Gardner became dissatisfied with both Piagetian intelligence theory and the orientation of schools toward linguistic and logicomathematical symbolization (Gardner, 1993; Gardner et al., 1996). His research convinced him that the mind is modular and capable of working with many symbolic systems (numerical, linguistic, spatial) independently. A person may be particularly adept at one symbolic system (say, music) without having concomitant skills in other systems. By measuring only one or two aspects of intelligence (linguistic and logical), existing tests define intelligent behavior very narrowly. Gardner defined intelligence very broadly to include solving problems and creating products that have value in at least one cultural setting. As a result of extensive research and analysis of the work of others, Gardner developed a list of seven types of intelligence. He believes that everyone possesses all seven cognitive elements but does not display them uniformly because of both hereditary and environmental influences. The types of skills that people possess direct their future endeavors as long as the culture accepts and is responsive to the importance of that skill. For example, a person with excellent linguistic aptitude may flourish in a society that values such abilities but be frustrated in developing these skills in a culture that is more logicomathematically oriented.

Gardner and his colleagues have proposed seven intelligences. Each is distinct from the others, although they are related and complementary.

1. *Logicomathematical* intelligence relates to the ability to carry out numerical and reasoning tasks and is a critical skill for mathematicians and scientists.
2. *Linguistic* intelligence focuses on language and its uses. Writers and poets have high skill levels in this domain.
3. *Musical* intelligence is associated with the composition and performance of music. Composers and performers exhibit a high degree of ability in this area.
4. *Spatial* intelligence relates to the ability to see objects clearly in a visual-spatial sense and to manipulate them on the basis of dimensional perceptions. Artists (particularly sculptors), astronauts, pilots, and others demonstrate a high degree of this type of intelligence.
5. *Bodily-kinesthetic* intelligence is translated into bodily movement, both fine- and gross-motor ability. Examples of individuals with high levels of this skill are dancers, athletes, and surgeons.
6. *Interpersonal* intelligence includes the ability to perceive the feelings and attitudes of others. Individuals who successfully interact with others are skilled in this area—for example, politicians, therapists, salespeople.
7. *Intrapersonal* intelligence can be summarized as the ability to know oneself. Persons in touch with their feelings, strengths, and weaknesses demonstrate a high capacity in this area. Psychiatrists and clinical psychologists are expected to possess this skill to a high degree.

Gardner's work has been examined in a number of contexts, including school curriculum and the nurturing of talent, as well as the providing of students with more than one performance alternative (Chen & Gardner, 1997). Some attention also has been given to Gardner's theory with respect to assessment (e.g., Flanagan, Genshaft, & Harrison, 1997), although additional effort is clearly needed in order to move toward an application level (Klein, 1997).

Considerable movement is occurring in the areas of theory and testing at the present time. The recognition that affect is important and that different intelligences are possible is producing a renewed vigor in the area of cognition and learning (Wilkens, 1997). The next decade should see advances in the field of theory and testing. Some believe that by the early part of the 21st century, the field of psychometrics (psychoeducational assessment) will address the measurement of intelligence in vastly different ways than has been the case in past history (deValenzuela & Cervantes, 1998). Professionals must proceed with caution, however, in order not to embrace every new theory or test without thoughtful analysis. We should learn at least that much from past errors. The broadening of intelligence theory to include such things as culture and experience follows closely on calls for reconceptualizing mental retardation, perhaps as what we have seen in the AAMR definition (1992). Rethinking the concepts of mental retardation has been encountered in nearly every facet of what we have discussed thus far and is likely to emerge again as we proceed.

Core Questions

1. How have societal changes affected the concepts of intelligence?
2. What is meant by the nature-versus-nurture controversy, and why is it important?
3. Why is social intelligence an important aspect of intelligence?
4. Why can't intelligence be measured directly?
5. What is the orientation of factorialists toward understanding intelligence?
6. What approach did Piaget take in his study of intellectual development? How does it differ from the factorial approach?
7. In what ways are the theories of Sternberg and Gardner similar to and different from earlier theories of intelligence?
8. What next steps remain as acid tests for the theoretical work of both Sternberg and Gardner?

Roundtable Discussion

Humankind's search for the critical aspects of and keys to the development of intelligence has been carried out rigorously by many scientists. Scientists have moved from simplistic views of what intelligence is to complex theories about its characteristics. In doing so, we have identified both quantitative and qualitative aspects of intelligence. For those interested in the study of mental retardation, an understanding of past history, present formulations, and future considerations about intelligence is both important and necessary.

In a study group, discuss the development of knowledge about intelligence to the present day. As a part of the discussion, members should relate what they believe were important developments and what they were surprised to learn. Further discussion should focus on what individuals believe about the different approaches and how their perception of persons with mental retardation has been influenced by using one or another approach.

References

Abraham, W. (1958). *Common sense about gifted children.* New York: Harper & Row.

Aiken, L. R. (1997). *Psychological testing and assessment* (9th ed.). Needham Heights, MA: Allyn & Bacon.

American Association on Mental Retardation (AAMR). (1992). *Mental retardation: Definition, classification, and systems of supports* (9th ed.). Washington, DC: Author.

Berthoud-Papandropoulou, J. & Kilcher, H. (1996). Relationships between the clinical method and the zone of proximal development in a constructivist approach to language acquisition. In A. Tryphon & J. Voneche (Eds.), *Piaget-Vygotsky: The social genesis of thought* (pp. 171–187). Hove, England, UK: Taylor & Francis Ltd.

Bickerton, D. (1998). The creation and re-creation of language. In C. B. Crawford & D. L. Krebs (Eds.), *Handbook of evolutionary psychology: Ideas, issues, and applications* (pp. 613–634). Mahwah, NJ: Erlbaum.

Binet, A., & Simon, T. (1908). Le développement de l'intelligence chez les enfants. *L'Année Psychologique, 14,* 1–94.

Blinkhorn, S. (1997). Symmetry as destiny: Taking a balanced view of IQ. *Nature, 387,* 849–850.

Bogoyavlenskaya, D. B. (1995). About the nature and method of creative abilities investigation. *Psikhologicheskiy Zhurnal, 16,* 49–58.

Bolen, L. M. (1998). Assessing intelligence using the WISC—III. In H. Booney (Ed.), *Psychological assessment of children: Best practices for school and clinical settings* (2nd ed., pp. 197–245). New York: Wiley.

Busato, V. V., Prins, F. J., Hamaker, C., & Visser, K. H. (1995). A replicated learning-style study: The relationship between learning style and intelligence. *Tijdschrift voor Onderwijsresearch, 20,* 332–340.

Butterworth, G. (1996). Infant intelligence. In Khalfa, J. (Ed.), *What is intelligence? The Darwin College lecture series* (pp. 49–71). Cambridge, England, UK: Cambridge University Press.

Campbell, J. M., & McCord, D. M. (1996). The WAIS-R comprehension and picture arrangement subtests as measures of social intelligence: Testing traditional interpretations. *Journal of Psychoeducational Assessment, 14,* 240–249.

Cannon, T. D., Kaprio, J., Loennqvist, J., Huttunen, M., & Koskenvuo, M. (1998). The genetic epidemiology of schizophrenia in a Finnish twin cohort: A population-based modeling study. *Archives of General Psychiatry, 55,* 67–74.

Chen, J. Q., & Gardner, H. (1997). Alternative assessment from a multiple intelligences theoretical perspective. In D. P. Flanagan, J. L. Genshaft, & P. L. Harrison (Eds.), *Contemporary intellectual assessment: Theories, tests, and issues* (pp. 105–121). New York: Guilford Press.

Cooper, C. (1998). *Individual differences.* London: Arnold.

DeValenzuela, J. S., & Cervantes, H. (1998). Issues and theoretical considerations in the assessment of bilingual children. In L. M. Baca & H. T. Cervantes (Eds.), *The bilingual special education interface* (3rd ed.). Upper Saddle River, NJ: Merrill/Prentice Hall.

Dykens, E. M., Hodapp, R. M., & Evans, D. W. (1994). Profiles and development of adaptive behavior in children with Down syndrome. *American Journal on Mental Retardation, 98,* 580–587.

Flanagan, D. P., Genshaft, J. L., & Harrison, P. L. (1997). *Contemporary intellectual assessment: Theories, tests, and issues.* New York: Guilford Press.

Friedman, R., & Rogers, K. B. (1998). *Talent in context: Historical and social perspectives on giftedness.* Washington, DC: American Psychological Association.

Gardner, H. (1993). *Multiple intelligences: The theory in practice.* New York: Basic Books.

Gardner, H., Kornhaber, M. L., & Wake, W. K. (1996). *Intelligence: Multiple perspectives.* Ft. Worth, TX: Harcourt Brace.

Gelfand, D. M., Jenson, W. R., & Drew, C. J. (1997). *Understanding child behavior disorders* (3rd ed.). Fort Worth: Harcourt Brace.

Gordon, E. W., & Lemons, M. P. (1997). An interactionist perspective on the genesis of intelligence. In R. J. Sternberg & E. L. Grigorenko (Eds.), *Intelligence, heredity, and environment* (pp. 323–340). New York: Cambridge University Press.

Gottesman, I. (1963). Genetic aspects of intelligent behavior. In N. R. Ellis (Ed.), *Handbook of mental deficiency* (pp. 253–296). New York: McGraw-Hill.

Gronlund, N. E. (1998). *Assessment of student achievement* (6th ed.). Boston: Allyn & Bacon.

Guilford, J. P. (1967). *The nature of human intelligence.* New York: McGraw-Hill.

Guilford, J. P. (1982). Cognitive psychology's ambiguities: Some suggested remedies. *Psychological Review, 89*, 48–59.

Guralnick, M. J. (1997). Peer social networks of young boys with developmental delays. *American Journal on Mental Retardation, 101*, 595–612.

Hardman, M. L., Drew, C. J., & Egan, M. W. (1999). *Human exceptionality: Society, school, and family* (6th ed.). Needham Heights, MA: Allyn & Bacon.

Hayman, R. L. (1998). *The smart culture: Society, intelligence, and law.* New York: New York University Press.

Herrnstein, R. J., & Murray, C. (1994). *The bell curve: Intelligence and class structure in American life.* New York: The Free Press.

Janda, L. (1998). *Psychological testing, theory, and applications.* Boston: Allyn & Bacon.

Jang, K. L., Livesley, W. J., & Vernon, P. A. (1997). Gender-specific etiological differences in alcohol and drug problems: A behavioural genetic analysis. *Addiction, 92*, 1265–1276.

Jensen, A. (1969). How much can we boost IQ and scholastic achievement? [Review of *Intelligence*]. *Harvard Educational Review, 39*, 1–123.

Jensen, A. (1994). [Review of *Intelligence* (2nd ed.)]. *American Journal on Mental Retardation, 98*, 663–667.

Klein, P. D. (1997). Multiplying the problems of intelligence by eight: A critique of Gardner's theory. *Canadian Journal of Education, 22*, 377–394.

Lachiewicz, A. M., Spiridigliozzi, G. A., Gullion, C. M., Ransford, S. N., & Rao, K. (1994). Aberrant behaviors of young boys with fragile X syndrome. *American Journal on Mental Retardation, 98*, 567–579.

Lamb, M. E. (1998). *Non-traditional and traditionally understudied families: Parenting and child development.* Mahwah, NJ: Erlbaum.

Lavergne, C., & Vigneau, F. (1997). Response speed on aptitude tests as an index of intellectual performance: A developmental perspective. *Personality and Individual Differences, 23*, 283–290.

Lubinski, D., & Humphreys, L. G. (1997). Incorporating general intelligence into epidemiology and the social sciences. *Intelligence, 24*, 159–201.

Mann, L., & Sabatino, D. A. (1994). *Foundations of cognitive process in remedial and special education.* Austin, TX: Pro-Ed.

Masten, A. S., & Coatsworth, J. D. (1998). The development of competence in favorable and unfavorable environments: Lessons from research on successful children. *American Psychologist, 53*, 205–220.

McCurry, C., McClellan, J., Adams, J., Norrei, M., Storck, M., Eisner, A., & Breiger, D. (1998). Sexual behavior associated with low verbal IQ in youth who have severe mental illness. *Mental Retardation, 36*, 23–30.

Moore, D. G., Hobson, R. P., & Anderson, M. (1995). Person perception: Does it involve IQ-independent processing? *Intelligence, 20*, 65–86.

Piaget, J. (1960). The general problems of the psychobiological development of the child. In J. M. Tanner & B. Inhelder (Eds.), *Discussions on child development* (pp. 3–27). London: Tavistock.

Pike, A., & Plomin, R. (1997). A behavioural genetic perspective on close relationships. *International Journal of Behavioral Development, 21*, 647–667.

Plomin, R., & Petrill, S. A. (1997). Genetics and intelligence: What's new? *Intelligence, 24*, 53–77.

Raijmakers, M. E. J., van Koten, S., Molenaar, P. C. M. (1996). On the validity of simulating stagewise development by means of PDP networks: Application of catastrophe analysis and an experimental test of rule-like network performance. *Cognitive Science, 20*, 101–136.

Roets, L. F. (1998). *Standards and benchmarks for education of gifted and talented.* Des Moines: Leadership Publisher.

Ross, V. (1998). *The annuals of child development* (Vol. 13). Bristol: Taylor & Francis.

Rourke, B. P. (1997). Significance of verbal-performance discrepancies for subtypes of children with learning disabilities: Opportunities for the WISC—III. In A. Prifitera & D. H. Saklofske (Eds.), *WISC—III clinical use and interpretation: Scientist-practitioner perspectives* (pp. 139–156). San Diego: Academic Press.

Scarr, S. (1997). Behavior, genetic, and socialization theories of intelligence: Truce and reconciliation. In R. J. Sternberg & E. L. Grigorenko (Eds.), *Intelligence, heredity, and environment* (pp. 3–41). New York: Cambridge University Press.

Scheier, L. M., & Botvin, G. J. (1998). Relations of social skills, personal competence, and adolescent alcohol use: A developmental exploratory study. *Journal of Early Adolescence, 18*, 77–114.

Schickedanz, J. A., Schickedanz, D., Forsyth, P., & Forsyth, G. A. (1998). *Understanding children and adolescents* (3rd ed.). Boston: Allyn & Bacon.

Smutny, J. F. (1997). *The young gifted child: Potential and promise, an anthology.* Cresskill: Hampton Press.

Spearman, C. E. (1904). General intelligence: Objectivity determined and measured. *American Journal of Psychology, 15,* 201–293.

Sternberg, R. J. (1997a). The triarchic theory of intelligence. In D. P. Flanagan & J. L. Genshaft (Eds.), *Contemporary intellectual Assessment: Theories, tests, and issues* (pp. 92–104). New York: Guilford Press.

Sternberg, R. J. (1997b). Educating intelligence: Infusing the triarchic theory into school instruction. In R. J. Sternberg & E. L. Grigorenko (Eds.), *Intelligence, heredity, and environment* (pp. 343–362). New York: Cambridge University Press.

Sternberg, R. J., Ferrari, M., Clinkenbeard, P., & Grigorenko, E. L. (1996). Identification, instruction, and assessment of gifted children: A construct validation of a triarchic model. *Gifted Child Quarterly, 40,* 129–137.

Sternberg, R. J., Wagner, R. K., Williams, W. M., & Horvath, J. A. (1997). Testing Common Sense. In D. F. Russ-Eft & H. S. Preskill (Eds.), *Human resource development review: Research implications* (pp. 102–132). Thousand Oaks, CA: Sage Publications.

Strage. A. (1997). Agency, communion, and achievement motivation. *Adolescence, 32,* 299–312.

Taj, H. (1997). Achievement motivation in relation to cognitive and affective variables. *Indian Journal of Psychometry and Education, 28,* 131–136.

Teachman, J. (1997). Gender of siblings, cognitive achievement, and academic performance: Familial and nonfamilial influences on children. *Journal of Marriage and the Family, 59,* 363–374.

Torf, B., & Sternberg, R. J. (1998). Changing mind, changing world: Practical intelligence and tacit knowledge in adult learning. In C. M. Smith & T. Pourchot (Eds.), *Adult learning and development: Perspectives from educational psychology* (pp. 109–126). Mahwah, NJ: Erlbaum.

True, W. R., Heath, A. C., Scherrer, J. F., Waterman, B., Goldberg, J., Lin, N., Eisen, S. A., Lyons, M. J., Tsuange, M. T. (1998). Genetic and environmental contributions to smoking. *Addiction, 92,* 1277–1287.

Van den Broek, A., Golden, C. J., Loonstraa, A., Ghinglia, K., & Goldstein, D. (1998). Short forms of the Wechsler Memory Scale—Revised: Cross-validation and derivation of a two-subtest form. *Psychological Assessment, 10,* 38–40.

Wilkens, D. (1997). *Multiple intelligence.* Westminster: Teacher Created Materials.

Wood, P., & Brown, D. (1994). The study of intraindividual differences by means of dynamic factor models: Rationale, implementation, and interpretation. *Psychological Bulletin, 116,* 166–186.

Part **3**

Development and Causation

Chapter 5

Basic Principles of Early Development

Core Concepts

- *Genotype, phenotype, growth matrix,* and *maturation* are terms for important concepts in human development.
- Theories of human development have differed dramatically about the importance of influences, ranging from prepotency of genetic material to total environmental shaping.
- The human developmental process has been characterized by some as one of continuous growth, whereas others have viewed it as a series of abrupt, discontinuous stages.
- Certain periods of development are critical both for growth and because of the organism's vulnerability to injury and developmental risk during them.
- Cephalocaudal and proximodistal growth trends begin very early in prenatal development and also can be observed during the first few years of life.
- Prenatal fetal development during weeks 10 through 12 is particularly important because of the tissues being formed at that time.
- The birth process represents another important time when potential risk to the child is high.
- Many consider the time immediately following birth as the most dangerous period of human life.
- The knowledge gained from scientific advances both holds great promise for improving the early developmental fortunes of children and raises serious social questions.

This chapter examines certain human development concepts that form the basis for the book's organization as a whole. The developmental life cycle is our fundamental perspective of mental retardation. The reader already has seen that mental retardation is a multidimensional condition. Myriad factors contribute to its occurrence and have been studied and treated by many disciplines, as discussed earlier in Chapter 1. We believe that a unifying conceptual framework is vital to understanding mental retardation. It is our view that human development is a better conceptual vehicle than any other. We examine the biological, psychological, and educational dimensions of mental retardation from a developmental perspective and explore the complex interactions of these seemingly disparate topics from a developmental approach.

Developmental pathology is a relatively recent area of study that has evolved into the investigation of problems and detrimental events that emerge in human development. Developmental psychopathology represents the productive combination of methods and content from multiple fields, brought together to focus on a variety of human disabilities and disorders that have their roots in the errors occurring in human developmental processes (Albano & Morris, 1998; Sonuga-Barke, 1998). Although developmental psychopathology is relatively new, child development traditionally has held a very prominent position in psychology and education and has employed the rigors of the scientific method only during the last century (Berger & Thompson, 1998; Burack & Enns, 1997). Above all, studying the course of human development is a quest for understanding human behavior, a conceptual organizer through which explanations are sought to comprehend why people behave as they do. Developmental psychology is a way of looking at things and an extremely useful means of examining such abnormalities as mental retardation. Developmental psychopathology—the developmental study of psychological deviance—has become increasingly visible in recent years. But as a field of study, it is still maturing with respect both to its knowledge base and to its research methodology.

This chapter introduces principles of early development that have particular relevance to mental retardation. It is not a substitute for a basic course in human growth and development, which we highly recommend. Applying the basic concepts of child development to the study of mental retardation is important for a number of reasons. For many subgroups of the population with mental retardation, developmental factors are central to intellectual, physical, and psychological status. From a basic biological standpoint, many of the clinical syndromes are integrally related to human development. Beyond biology, the broad psychological view of the population having the mildest form of mental retardation has long spotlighted child development within the nature-versus-nurture controversy (Leonard, 1998; Rutter, Simonoff, & Plomin, 1996), and this group represents the largest proportion of people with retardation. Acquaintance with the concepts of child development is essential for the student of mental retardation.

HUMAN DEVELOPMENT: TERMINOLOGY, CONCEPTS, AND THEORY

Core Concept

Genotype, phenotype, growth matrix, *and* maturation *are terms for important concepts in human development.*

Human growth and development has become a more complex field as research and technology in all of its contributing sciences have advanced. The information base has expanded dramatically because of additions from biology, embryology, genetics, psychology, and many other areas, all of which have been molded into a body of highly technical knowledge with unique properties beyond those of the contributing areas. Background information about developmental terminology, concepts, and theoretical perspectives is important to an understanding of the human development field.

Concepts and Terms

Many different factors influence a person's life status at any given time. As used here, **life status** refers broadly to one's physical, psychological, and behavioral attributes, as well as to talents and abilities. All of these personal elements are influenced by genetic material inherited from parents plus environmental circumstances that have nourished or impeded development. These components combine and interact in a unique fashion to produce the person one sees at a particular point. As we begin this discussion of early development it is important that the reader become acquainted with certain terms and concepts pertaining to the elements in this complex human equation.

Parents transmit genetic material to their offspring that strongly influences what the offspring become. This genetic material can be likened to a computer chip that encodes a number of messages. These messages are activated to influence many aspects of physical and psychological growth. Geneticists use the term **genotype** to refer to the genetic message makeup of an individual. Established at conception by the combining of sperm and ovum, the genotype is usually constant. Only rarely does this constancy fail, as when a mutation or other error in cell division alters subsequent cell divisions. The human genotype is not readily accessible for actual inspection, but the **phenotype,** a term that refers to observable physical traits, may be used to draw inferences about the genotype. The phenotype is the observable result of interaction between the genotype and the environment.

Another related term in child development is **growth matrix**. The growth matrix is also the result of interactions between heredity and environment. Although partially observable (because it includes the phenotype), the growth matrix also includes all of the internal aspects of a child that generate a given response in a particular situation. The growth matrix is more than a simple combination of phenotype and genotype, however. One distinction is that whereas genetic concepts are relatively constant, the growth matrix changes as interactions occur between the organism and its environment. The growth matrix is a product of that interaction and at the same time determines or regulates individual response patterns.

Maturation is a term also used in child development in a way that requires definition. Although some difference in usage exists, maturation generally signifies any development or change in the status or underlying process of a behavioral trait that takes place in the demonstrable absence of specific practical experience. In the present context, one additional restriction is added: the absence of specific instruction. Thus, in this context, maturation is distinguishable from **learning,** which refers to changes associated with specific practice or instruction. In many situations, it is difficult to discriminate between changes resulting from maturation and changes resulting from learning. A history of maturation and of learning and a combination of the two are involved in any child's current developmental status. This developmental status and its components are related to the notion of readiness.

Readiness exists when the child is at a point in development (including previous maturation and learning) where he or she might be expected to profit from a particular situation. A familiar example is "reading readiness." From the present standpoint, reading readiness refers to the point in a child's development at which one could expect progress as a result of exposure to reading experience or instruction. Of course, if the status from either a maturational or previous learning standpoint were deficient (inadequate to establish readiness), the child is not expected to progress as a result of a given stimulation. There is no magic formula "X amount of maturation plus Y amount of previous learning equals readiness." Although developmental readiness includes both, widely varying amounts and types of each may exist in different children who have reached readiness for an experience.

Developmental Theories

Core Concept

Theories of human development have differed dramatically about the importance of influences, ranging from prepotency of genetic material to total environmental shaping.

The complexities of human development have been of interest since the beginning of recorded history. Some of the most common theoretical positions have an extremely long history. Certain prescientific explanations of human growth and development, although amusing in retrospect, were quite popular in the past.

Preformationist Perspective.   The preformationist theory of human growth and development had a substantial early following. According to preformationism, the human organism is preformed before birth; this theory proposed that the foundation elements of human behavior are intact from the beginning and do not qualitatively develop or change during life. The preformationists thus denied the importance of growth and development except in the sense of quantity, or growing larger. The early homuncular theory of human reproduction exemplified the preformationist position. This theory held that a completely formed, tiny person existed in the sperm. This tiny person, called a **homunculus,** began to grow in size at conception but did not change in the sense that tissue changes occurred qualitatively, such as in the formation of various organs.

Environmental effects on human development were largely discounted by the preformationist position. Prenatal as well as postnatal environment was of little consequence as far as development went from this viewpoint. The concessions usually made to environmental effects involved only expansion of existing abilities, drives, and behaviors. Preformationists thought that neither new growth nor directional influence of development did much to change the preformed organism.

Predeterministic Perspective.   Predeterministic theorists' assumptions appear similar to that of the preformationists, at first glance. Although their outcome is much the same, some significant differences are discernible between the two theoretical positions. Predeterministic positions did not view human development as a simple accentuation of a preformed organism. Qualitative growth and tissue differentiation played a substantial role in most theories of predeterminism. An example of this is found in the doctrine of recapitulation, which was described in great detail by G. Stanley Hall (1904). Recapitulation hypothesized that the development of the child from conception to maturity progressed through all of the evolutionary phases of the human race. Although quite popular for a period around the turn of the century, this theory fell into disfavor primarily because of the absence of objective or observable data to support its sweeping hypotheses (Notterman, 1997).

The outcome of predeterministic theories was essentially the same as preformationism in that environmental influence was thought to be minimal, perhaps limited to restricting development. Growth patterns were viewed as innate or internally regulated. More recently, the disciplines of biology, genetics, and embryology have provided factual knowledge supporting the notion that certain development is regulated primarily internally (e.g., prenatal growth and certain infantile behavioral development). Former predeterministic contentions of innate control, however, involved broad applications that have received no scientific support.

Tabula Rasa Perspective. In the context of human development, **tabula rasa** refers to approaches that emphasize the prepotency of environmental influences. The term means "blank slate" and was popularized by John Locke in the 17th century. For purposes of this discussion, *tabula rasa* is used generically to represent positions emphasizing extreme environmental impact.

Tabula rasa theories differed substantially from the approaches of preformationism and predeterminism. Tabula rasa positions minimized the influence of internal factors (e.g., heredity) on human development. Environment was seen as playing a predominant role in nearly all aspects of development. Tabula rasa theorists considered the human organism plastic and infinitely amenable to molding by external influences. Thus, an individual's ability was dependent on what was "written" on the blank slate through experience. The weakness of this framework, like that of preformationism and predeterminism, was the extreme to which proponents of the position went.

Neither tabula rasa nor predeterministic approaches to child development were satisfactory. Belief in preformed human functioning at birth has little logical or empirical support. With the exception of very simple reflex responses, few human behavioral dimensions are not influenced by environment. The fundamental error of predeterministic proponents was their disregard for the impact of experience. Tabula rasa theorists caught the pendulum at the opposite end of its swing. The assumption that environmental impact is a significant contributor to human growth and development does represent reality, but tabula rasa theorists emphasized the impact of this factor far too strongly.

Interactional Perspectives. Human development specialists now generally subscribe to the notion of an interaction between heredity and environ-

The interaction of young children with others in their environment is very important to their early development.

ment (Berger & Thompson, 1998; Halpern, 1997; Rutter et al., 1996). Both genetic and environmental factors set limits for growth, as well as selectively influence each other. Genetic material determines limits even under the most favorable environment conceivable. Likewise, environment limits the fulfillment of genetic potential. Genetic material determines which factors in the environment are more potent by rendering the organism more sensitive to some than to others. Similarly, environmental factors such as culture and ecology operate on genetic expression by providing selective influences on ability development.

The interactional approach to human growth and development emphasizes analysis of relationships between heredity and environment (Parisi, 1997). This emphasis represents a substantial difference from earlier positions, which assumed the prepotence of one over the other. Although other approaches may be conceptually simpler, the interactional position seems to represent reality better.

THE DEVELOPMENTAL PROCESS

The emergence of an interactional view of human development generated a more intense focus on developmental processes. Researchers and theoreticians began to ask questions that were more amenable to study than were the philosophical positions exemplified by former views. A number of interesting questions have focused on the nature of the developmental process and have become rather controversial. This section presents an examination of some of these questions.

Continuity Versus Discontinuity of Growth

Core Concept

The human developmental process has been characterized by some as one of continuous growth, whereas others have viewed it as a series of abrupt, discontinuous stages.

One area that has generated substantial discussion involves the continuity or discontinuity of human growth. The question is, Does development proceed by gradual continuous quantitative change or in stages typified by abrupt discontinuous changes in quality?

Theories emphasizing stages encouraged the discontinuity view of human development. Early developmental stage theories implied little or no process overlap from one stage to the next. Each developmental stage was specifically and qualitatively different from the others. The first developmental theorist to dismiss the notion of discontinuity was Piaget (1926). From his background in biology and zoology, Piaget formulated a theory of stages of cognitive development that incorporated the occurrence of immature and mature responses at all developmental levels. His concept of intelligence included three global developmental periods: (a) the period of sensorimotor intelligence, (b) the period of preparation for and organization of concrete operations, and (c) the period of formal operations. Sensorimotor intelligence development, he thought, began at birth and continued for about the first 2 years of life. Piaget viewed the development of intelligence in the second period, from about 2 to 11 years of age, as involving the essential formation of a conceptual framework that the child uses in interaction with the environment. The third period, from 11 years of age on, is the time, Piaget contended, during which an individual works with abstract thought. During this period (formal operations), the person begins to think of hypothetical possibilities instead of relying exclusively on concrete operations, in which cognition depends on a concrete or real object as a basis. Piaget conceived the total developmental picture as one of a dynamic interaction, with the organism operating on the environment, as well as being molded by it. His theory has come under heavy fire, and issues involving the plasticity of human growth and critical periods continue to be debated in the literature (e.g., Serbin, 1997).

The continuity position contends that growth is a gradual process, rather than a series of abrupt changes followed by periods of less rapid change (plateaus). A variety of factors can be mentioned in support of the theory of growth continuity. First, it is well known that both mature and immature responses are made by children at all levels of development. Second, theories of continuity test hypotheses generated from general behavior theories more effectively than do discontinuous stage theories.

Both continuity and discontinuity theories of development have had strong proponents. Growth and development specialists, however, have largely progressed beyond the point where polarized thinking prevails. No one believes that theoretically formulated stages are precise definitions involving exact ages, behaviors, and response levels. They are convenient approximations based on averages and are useful in conceptualizing developmental processes and suggesting directions for research, although methodologically sound research is very difficult to conduct on critical periods in human development (Berger & Thompson, 1998; Serbin, 1997).

Critical Periods and Developmental Vulnerability

Core Concept

Certain periods of development are critical both for growth and because of the organism's vulnerability to injury and developmental risk during them.

Developmental deviancy is a central concern in the field of mental retardation, as it is in other disability areas. The concept of developmental vulnerability is related to developmental deviance and is of vital importance to those studying mental retardation. Here we use **vulnerability** to refer to how susceptible the organism is to being injured or altered by a traumatic incident. **Traumatic incident** is defined broadly to include such occurrences as exposure to toxic agents (poisons) and cell division mutations, as well as other deviations from the usual sequence of development.

Biology and embryology have provided a great deal of information about how human growth occurs (Moore & Persaud, 1998). From the time of conception, a series of complex cell divisions occurs that ultimately results in the entity called a human being. During the early part of this developmental process, the original fertilized cell divides repeatedly to form a mass no larger than the point of a sharp pencil (at about 14 days) and eventually (at about 9 months) to the size of a newborn child. Obviously, this implies a very dramatic growth process. Cell division occurs extremely rapidly in the first few days after the ovum is fertilized by a sperm. The mass that is to become the fetus does not actually become implanted or attached to the mother's uterus until about 2 weeks after fertilization. In this short period, cell division has progressed with considerable speed and has begun the process of tissue differentiation. Both the speed of cell division and the process of tissue differentiation are important with regard to the vulnerability to trauma.

After cell division begins, chemical reactions occur that generate new cells of different types (tissue differentiation). These cells multiply, forming three different layers of tissue: the ectoderm, the mesoderm, and the endoderm. Figure 5–1 pictorially represents the three cell tissue layers. Although the tissue layers are named because of their early developmental position (ectoderm, outer layer; mesoderm, middle layer; endoderm, inner layer), they eventually form different parts of the organism. Parts of the ectoderm become nervous tissue, various types of muscle come from the mesoderm, and so on. During the time that a

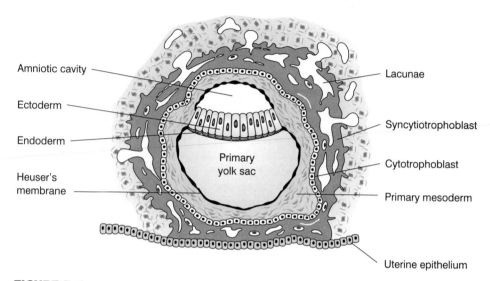

FIGURE 5–1

Conceptus at About 12 Days, Showing Cell Tissue Layers

From Synopsis of Anatomy *by L. J. A. Didio, 1970, St. Louis: Mosby. Copyright 1970 by C. V. Mosby Co. Reprinted by permission.*

particular organ or system is being formed, the cells generating that system divide very rapidly. During specific periods, for instance, the central nervous system is the primary part of the organism that is developing. During that time, the cells that constitute the central nervous system divide more rapidly than other types of cells, and at this time the central nervous system is most vulnerable to trauma. If a toxic agent or infection occurs in the mother at this time, the developing central nervous system (or some particular part of it) probably will be the most affected.

Other critical periods occur during prenatal development. These periods are biologically important for the healthy growth of the fetus. Some professionals have long suspected that critical periods also exist after birth. Hypotheses regarding postnatal critical periods and vulnerability have varied considerably. In some cases, the "critical periods" of early childhood have been viewed as those times that are optimal for the child to learn or experience certain things. Others have conceived the critical-period idea in terms of irreversibility, holding that if a child does not acquire certain skills or does not experience certain stimuli at the appropriate time, development will be altered in some way that is not reversible. Under some circumstances, the theoretical outcome of either viewpoint is the same. The child, if not taught at the critical time, may not learn given material as well as might be possible. The critical-period concept has had considerable effect in both research about and education of very young children. Educational programs like Montessori have flourished because of the intuitive appeal of the critical-period concept. Firm research evidence supporting the importance/irreversibility view, however, has been fragmentary in certain areas and remains difficult to investigate (Serbin, 1997).

PRENATAL DEVELOPMENT

The prenatal period of human development has long been recognized as highly important. Very early explanations of prenatal development tended to be more philosophical and metaphysical than scientific in orientation, illustrated by the prescientific homunculus notion. Contemporary advances in research methods have permitted at least limited glimpses of this previously unexplored region. Although much of our information about prenatal development has come from studies with animals, direct knowledge about the human organism is continually increasing. This section surveys the sequence of prenatal development. Information about this subject facilitates a broader understanding of developmental deviations as they relate to mental retardation.

Core Concept

Cephalocaudal and proximodistal growth trends begin very early in prenatal development and also can be observed during the first few years of life.

Early cell division occurs at different rates, depending on which portion of the organism is mainly being formed at that time. Additionally, two important general growth trends warrant mention. The first is known as the **cephalocaudal developmental trend,** or **growth gradient.** As the term suggests, the fetus develops more rapidly in the head area (*cephalo-*) first, with maturation in the lower extremities (*caudal*) or "tail" following. At almost all stages of a young child's development, the upper regions (and behaviors associated with these regions) are more nearly complete than the lower regions. Dramatically evident prenatally, the cephalocaudal trend also is present after birth. A young child is skilled in a behavior involving the arms before developing a similar skill in the legs. The second general developmental trend is the **proximodistal gradient.** This term refers to the fact that more rapid growth and development occur near the center of the organism (*proximo-*), with extremities (*distal*) maturing later. This trend is also present both prenatally and during the first few years of infant life.

Very soon after fertilization occurs, the cell division process commences that ultimately results in a fully formed human. As noted earlier, it takes about 2 weeks for the dividing cell mass to become attached to the uterus. Even before this implantation occurs, the cells begin to differentiate. As the ectoderm, mesoderm, and endoderm are initially formed, considerable flexibility remains in what individual cells within those layers can become. Thus, at the 14-day stage, a given cell within the mesoderm still could grow into something besides the parts of the body usually formed from the mesoderm. Determination of resulting organs at this point is more a function of layer position than of the composition of the cell.

Cell flexibility disappears, however, as growth proceeds. The layers themselves become increasingly differentiated; as this occurs, individual cells become more specialized (Larsen, 1997). Table 5–1 is a summary of some types of structures associated with each tissue layer.

The embryo is still very small at the time of implantation. Despite all that has gone on, the mass is little larger than a dot made by a sharp pencil. The estimated size is about that of a ball 2 millimeters in diameter, and the weight cannot even be estimated. It is difficult to conceive that such a tiny piece of matter not only is living but also has already begun to differentiate in anticipation of forming such structures as eyes, a brain, and muscles. After implantation (14 days), activity continues at an extremely rapid pace. By about the 18-to-24-day point (from the time of fertilization = fertilization age), weight is still undeterminable; size is portrayed in Figure 5–2. At this point, blood cells much like those that will serve in later life (Moore & Persaud, 1998) have begun to form.

Several developments have occurred by the time the embryo has reached the 4-week point (fertilization age). Weight is detectable, at about 0.4 g. Figure 5–2 portrays the embryo's approximate size and shape at this point. A primitive circulatory system has developed, and the heart structure has begun pulsation (Larsen, 1997; Moore & Persaud, 1998). The initial formative stages of other systems, such as trunk muscles and muscles necessary for respiratory and intestinal functions, also occur in the 4th week. Limb buds appear at this time, and the nervous system reaches a point that is crucial for development of both the sense organs and the area that later will become the spinal cord. Figure 5–2 illustrates that the tiny embryo already has assumed the curved shape of the unborn human. This shape is generated primarily at the 4-week period by a very rapid lengthening of the neural tube (spinal area), which is not matched by growth on the front (ventral) side.

TABLE 5–1
Cell Tissue Layers of the Embryo

Endoderm	Mesoderm	Ectoderm
Epithelium of pharynx, tongue, root, auditory tube, tonsils, thyroid	Muscles (all types)	Epidermis, including cutaneous glands, hair, nails, lens
	Cartilage, bone	
	Blood, bone marrow	Epithelium of sense organs, nasal cavity, sinuses
Larynx, trachea, lungs	Lymphoid tissue	
Digestive tube	Epithelium of blood vessels, body cavities	Mouth, including oral glands, enamel
Bladder		
Vagina	Kidney, ureter, gonads, genital ducts	Anal canal
Urethra		Nervous tissue
	Suprarenal cortex	
	Joint cavities	

Adapted from Developmental Anatomy *(7th ed.) by L. B. Arey, 1974, Philadelphia: W. B. Saunders Co. Copyright 1974 by W. B. Saunders Co. Reprinted by permission.*

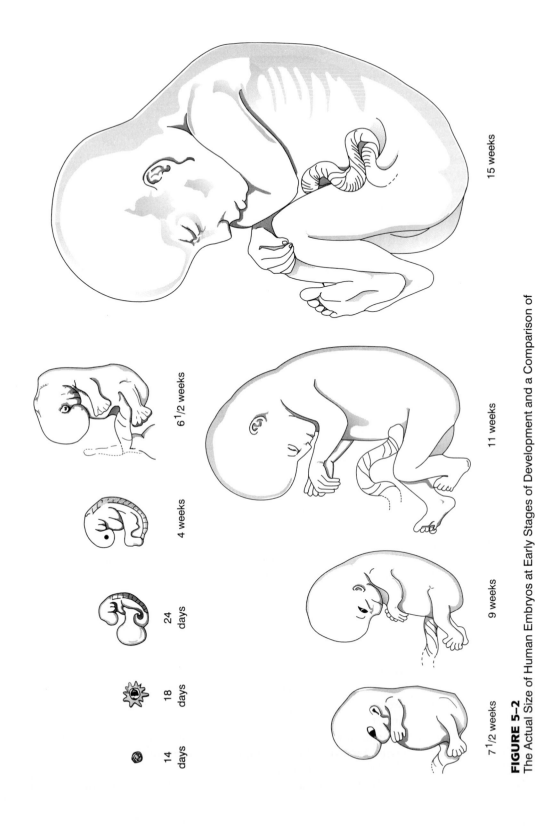

FIGURE 5–2
The Actual Size of Human Embryos at Early Stages of Development and a Comparison of
the Relative Stages of External Development

*From Child Health Maintenance: Concepts in Family Centered Care (2nd ed., p. 105) by P. L.
Chinn, 1979. St. Louis: Mosby. Copyright 1979 by C. V. Mosby Co. Reprinted by permission.*

14
days

18
days

24
days

4 weeks

6¹/₂ weeks

7¹/₂ weeks

9 weeks

11 weeks

15 weeks

The embryo has grown and developed to a considerable extent at 6½ weeks fertilization age. Figure 5–2 illustrates the approximate embryonic size and shape at this time. The circulatory system and heart are now more nearly complete. You can also see the positioning of the eyes on either side of the head area. Later, these will assume the more frontal position characteristic of the human infant. Lungs and intestinal system are more complete, and for the first time a primitive form of the gonad is observable. Differentiation of this tissue has not occurred yet with respect to gender (Larsen, 1997). Figure 5–2 also portrays the embryo at about 7½ weeks fertilization age. The embryo begins to develop openings for waste systems at this point (both urethral and anal). The circulatory system reaches a stage at which heart valves develop, and sensory nerve tissue in the upper region progresses.

The embryo is essentially complete as the fertilization age reaches the 8th week. Beyond this point, it commonly is referred to as a fetus. There is some difference with regard to when this term is applied. Although most use it in the 9th week (Larsen, 1997), some consider the fetal period to begin earlier (Moore & Persaud, 1998), and others define it somewhat later. Figure 5–2 also illustrates the size and shape of a fetus at about the 9th week. The eyes have begun to assume frontal position. The fetus has noticeably changed its posture. The head region at this point constitutes nearly half the total mass, and the cerebral cortex has formed.

Core Concept

Prenatal fetal development during weeks 10 through 12 is particularly important because of the tissues being formed at that time.

Particularly crucial growth occurs in the head region during weeks 10 through 12. From about this time through the 13th week, the palate completes fusion. The forehead is somewhat outsized in comparison with the rest of the head (see Figure 5–2) and at this point contains a brain that is essentially complete in configuration. Inspection of the external organs permits determination of the gender of the fetus. The skeleton begins the process of becoming bone matter (ossification), and the vital structures of the eyes are nearly formed (Larsen, 1997).

At 12 weeks, a fetus has completed one of the most crucial periods in its developmental life span. By no means is the tiny fetus ready to take on the outside world, but the primary body structures are formed (Thibodeau & Patton, 1997). In Chapter 6, we refer repeatedly to the first trimester of prenatal life. From our discussion of vulnerability and its relationship to tissue growth, it is very easy to see why this period is so vital. Trauma occurring during these first weeks is most likely to injure the essential body structure being formed at this time. The fetus at 12 weeks has a weight of about 19 grams. It has a long way to go but has made a lot of progress since the mass was so tiny that it could not be weighed.

The fetus reaches a weight of approximately 600 grams during the second trimester of prenatal life (weeks 12 through 24). At this point, appearance leaves no doubt that the fetus is a tiny human. The second trimester is also the time when the mother first experiences fetal movement. Fetal bodily proportions change, as illustrated in Figure 5–2 (15 weeks). Several important internal developments occur during the second trimester. Various glands mature to the point that metabolic functions can begin. The lungs become complete, although not until the third trimester are they adequate to sustain life. The extremely important function of myelinization also begins during the second trimester. **Myelinization** refers to the development of a sheathlike material that covers and protects the nervous system. During the second trimester, development of the myelin covering begins in the spinal cord area. This process continues during the third trimester, when the myelinization of higher cortical matter begins. Completion of the myelin covering of the cerebral cortex is accomplished primarily after birth (Moore & Persaud, 1998). The progression of the myelin covering also relates to the child's vulnerability to trauma (see Chapter 7).

Development that occurs during the final trimester of prenatal life is essential for sustaining life outside the mother's body. One vital change involves the final development of the lung structures. Changes continue right up to the last month of gestation. The fetus is also growing larger and stronger at a rapid rate. By the time term is reached, at about 40 weeks gestational age, the average fetus weighs somewhere around 3,200 grams. Brain and sensory organs continue to develop, reaching functional stage at birth (Thibodeau & Patton, 1997). Thus, although the basic structural components have long since been formed, the third trimester of gestation involves developments that are crucial for survival.

BIRTH

After about 280 days of gestation, the fetus leaves the intrauterine environment of the mother's body and begins its life in the outside world. Despite the vast improvements in delivery techniques that have occurred over the years, many facets of childbirth are still not well understood. This section presents a survey of the salient aspects of this dramatic event.

Core Concept

The birth process represents another important time when potential risk to the child is high.

Preparation for childbirth does not occur at the last moment. Certain changes in the mother's anatomy that are necessary for birth to proceed smoothly have been under way since about midpregnancy. The muscle structure of the uterus has been rearranged substantially to facilitate fetal expulsion. Another change that is essential to permit passage of the fetus through the birth canal has occurred in the cervical area. Figure 5-3 illustrates an advanced fetus in the uterine environment. In the latter days of pregnancy and during the onset of labor, expansion occurs in the upper part of the cervical area. By the time the fetus is moving down the birth canal, the cervical muscle structure has expanded to the point where the tubelike structure shown at the bottom of Figure 5-3 no longer exists.

FIGURE 5–3
Advanced Fetus in Uterine Environment

From Child Health Maintenance:
Concepts in Family Centered Care
*(2nd ed., p. 109) by P. L. Chinn,
1979, St. Louis: Mosby. Copyright
1979 by C. V. Mosby Co. Reprinted
by permission.*

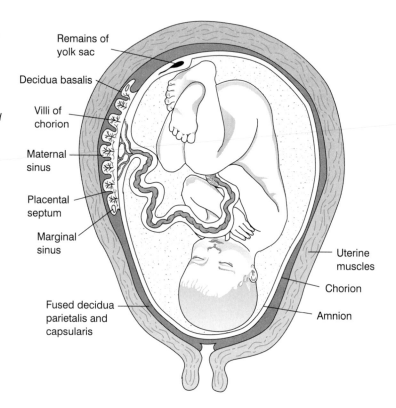

Remains of
yolk sac

Decidua basalis

Villi of
chorion

Maternal
sinus

Placental
septum

Marginal
sinus

Fused decidua
parietalis and
capsularis

Uterine
muscles

Chorion

Amnion

The loosening of the cervix, called **effacement,** is an important change in the muscle structure that must occur for the fetus to be expelled.

The exact mechanism that triggers labor remains mysterious. Many possibilities have been investigated, including both chemical (hormones) and mechanical (degree of uterine expansion) agents. The usual and desirable fetal position at the onset of labor is with the head toward the cervix, as illustrated in Figure 5–3. This position occurs in more than 80% of all childbirths. As the fetus begins to move downward into the birth canal, the pelvic girdle stretches more. The pressure of the pelvic girdle also molds the head of the fetus, so newborns often have strangely shaped heads. Later, the head returns to its natural shape.

All of this movement is generated by labor, the muscle contractions of the uterus. At the same time that the fetus moves downward, it turns counterclockwise from the effect of the uterine muscle action. Figure 5–4 shows a series of fetal positions during the birth process.

The infant's delivery usually is followed by expulsion of the placenta a few minutes later. The placenta has transmitted oxygen and nourishment to the developing child and disposed of waste during the prenatal period. Now the infant must accomplish these functions in the outside world. The respiratory tract is immediately cleared of the remaining amniotic fluid and mucus, and the infant

FIGURE 5–4
A, Engagement; B, Descent with
Flexion; C, Internal Rotation; D,
Extension; E, External Rotation;
F, Delivery; G, Lateral Flexion

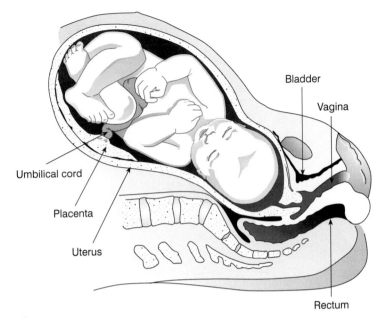

Bladder

Vagina

Umbilical cord

Placenta

Uterus

Rectum

A

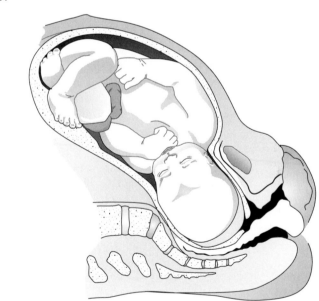

B

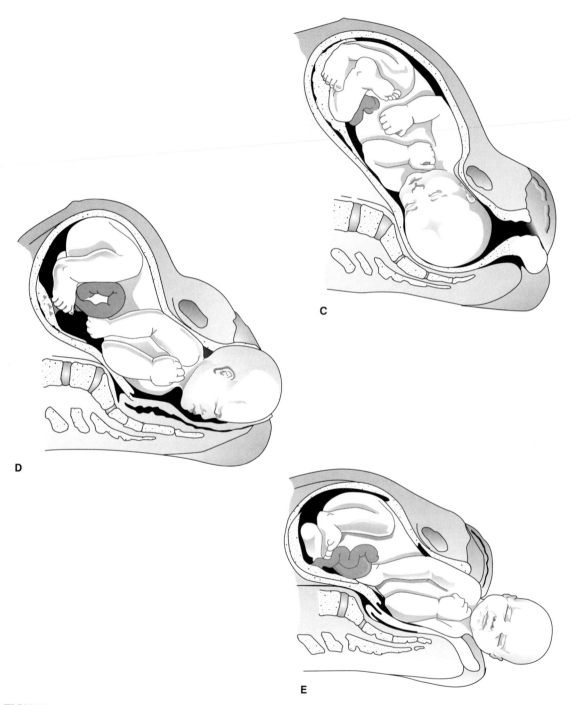

FIGURE 5–4, *continued*

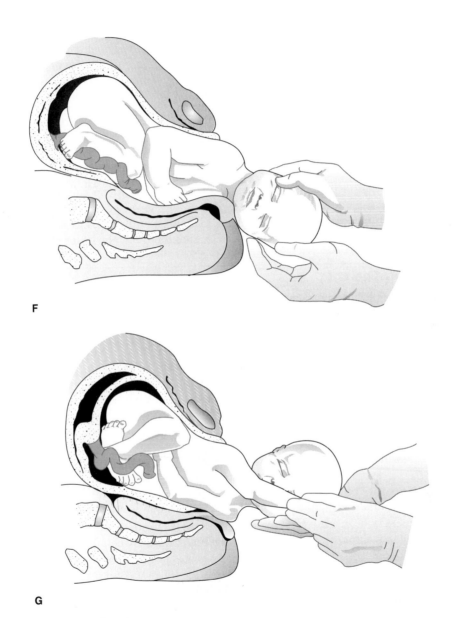

F

G

FIGURE 5–4, *continued*

From Childbirth: Family Centered Nursing *by J. Iorio, 1975, St. Louis: Mosby. Copyright 1975 by C. V. Mosby Co. Reprinted by permission.*

begins to breathe. This is the time that most new mothers and fathers remember as the first cry of their newborn. This crying serves an important function, and if the infant does not begin it spontaneously, the physician must provide stimulation. Crying expands the infant's lungs with air for the first time, causing the circulatory changes that accompany the use of the lungs and the loss of the placenta.

The birth process is very complex and, unfortunately, does not always proceed smoothly. Difficulties can arise that result in mental retardation. Some of the possible problems are discussed in Chapter 6.

NEONATAL DEVELOPMENT

The term *neonate* often is applied to the baby during the first 2 months after birth. Beyond that period, the terminology is varied and less specific. Here we examine early life, some of whose principles apply beyond the neonatal period. Later chapters treat development of the infant and the older child.

Core Concept

Many consider the time immediately following birth as the most dangerous period of human life.

The first few weeks of extrauterine life are crucial, and many authorities view the first month as being among the most dangerous in the entire life span (Berger & Thompson, 1998). Many of the developmental functions begun in utero are continuing but without the protective agents available before. In addition to physiological changes, a variety of forces initiate the neonate's rapid development in psychological and behavioral areas. As development proceeds, previous and ongoing physiological changes fuse with changes generated by environmental stimuli (e.g., learning) to form the integrated complex of responsiveness called a human being.

From a behavioral standpoint, the neonate seems to be little more than a mass of reflex actions, and at this age, assessment of reflexes is the primary method of evaluation by health-care professionals. The infant's movements seem primarily nonpurposeful and nonspecific and more often than not involve nearly the entire body. This movement pattern usually involves gross motor movements often accompanied by verbal output (crying). The frequency and intensity of movements rise between feedings and tend to diminish as the hungry neonate becomes satisfied. Cephalocaudal and proximodistal developmental trends continue after birth. These are perhaps best observable in the behavior patterns of the first 2 years of life. More mature responses tend to appear earlier in areas closest to the brain (e.g., eye movement) and progress downward and outward. The neonate's gross motor movements precede any control of more distal movements, such as those of the fingers. Infants can also usually reach for and grasp objects accurately long before they can walk.

Certain physiological changes occur very rapidly during the first period of postnatal life. The central nervous system exhibits dramatic growth during the first 4 years, with acceleration leveling off in later childhood. For example, during this growth period, brain weight increases nearly 400% over what it was at birth. In addition to quantitative changes, the brain matter is rapidly developing convolutions or folds and is developing in a number of ways that are vital to later cognitive function (Santrock, 1997; Vander-Zanden, 1997).

The progress of myelinization, which began prenatally, continues during the first 12 months after birth and declines thereafter. The progression of the myelin sheath follows the course of central nervous system development to some degree. At birth the lower or subcortical portion of the central nervous system (spinal cord, brainstem) governs the neonate, and this part of the central nervous system is first to receive the myelin covering. Later, the higher cerebral matter is involved in myelinization and likewise begins to take charge of the child's behavior. For example, functioning of the frontal lobe of the brain may be influential in developing emotional regulation (Dawson, Panagiotides, Klinger, & Hill, 1992; Yuen, 1997). The myelin sheath is essentially complete at age 2, although fragmentary myelinization apparently continues through adolescence and perhaps even middle adult life. In our consideration of mental retardation, the myelinization process becomes important when considering possible injury to the central nervous system (see Chapter 6).

The sensory organs, particularly the eyes and the ears, are nearly complete in structure at birth. Certain parts of the retina are yet to be completed, but basic sight exists at birth. For the first few weeks, the infant's eyes tend to operate independently, rather than together. By about 6 weeks, however, eye fixation is pretty well coordinated. Visual acuity appears to be imperfect during the neonatal and infant periods. Early images are blurred forms, patterns, and shapes, but visual acuity improves rather rapidly from about $20/400$ at the neonate stage (Moore & Persaud, 1998).

Hearing is apparently intact at birth. The neonate responds to a wide variety of auditory stimuli, suggesting that probably the full range of humanly detectable sound is available quite early. Additionally, the neonate seems able to identify where sounds come from. The development of auditory discrimination needs much more investigation. Part of the ability to discriminate sounds may be a learned or acquired skill.

The sense of taste is difficult to study in a very young child. However, evidence indicates that even at the neonatal stage an infant makes gross taste discriminations. Such discrimination, however, is primarily observable in different behavioral reactions to sweetness versus other tastes, such as sourness and bitterness. This sense improves with experience. The sense of smell is even more difficult to study than that of taste, so we have very little evidence about it in the neonatal period. It does seem, however, that the neonate is responsive to very dramatic or intense odors and that sensitivity increases during the infant stage.

The behavioral repertoire of the newborn is limited as noted earlier. During the first few weeks of postnatal life, verbal output is limited primarily to crying. Crying seems to be associated mostly with discomfort of some sort, although at times the source of discomfort is not evident, as parents well know. From birth, hunger is the standard stimulus for crying. Later, the young child learns to use crying as a means of communicating in a wide variety of situations that

Many environmental stimuli in this youngster's world affect development.

are unpleasurable. Other verbal output (e.g., gurgling, cooing, general noise) seems to develop considerably later, often not becoming a significant part of the behavioral repertoire until the infant is several months old.

The sucking response is an important component of neonatal behavior. In addition to its obvious value to the child in terms of feeding, it remains an important early check of well-being (Porter, 1997). A weak sucking response is a signal for concern. The neonate tends to suck in response to a variety of stimuli, both in terms of the type of stimulus and of the body part stimulated. Later, responsivity diminishes and can be elicited primarily around the mouth.

NEW ISSUES AND FUTURE DIRECTIONS

Core Concept

The knowledge gained from scientific advances both holds great promise for improving the early developmental fortunes of children and raises serious social questions. ✷

Most of this chapter has addressed matters pertaining to development from the prenatal period through birth and influential factors impinging on the young human during this time. Perhaps nowhere in the developmental life cycle have the advances of technology and research information generated so many potential treatments for health and other problems as in this time frame. This progress has created both optimism and uncertainty.

The past 30 years have seen unprecedented scientific advancement in understanding genetic function. Many of the findings have led to interventions that would have been unimaginable in the past. The level of detailed description of genetic material now possible holds enormous potential for a variety of treatments, many with implications for the field of mental retardation. Society has begun to witness early work in predicting and correcting certain genetic lesions. Such a capability provides the eventual capacity for removal of specific genes (e.g., those causing sickle cell anemia or phenylketonuria) and replacement with synthetic genes able to function normally. Although such suggestions seem like science fiction on one level, it was not long ago that in vitro fertilization was front-page news. Now thousands of children have been born as a result of in vitro fertilization, and such events hardly warrant attention.

Such advancements create marvelous possibilities, but they also cause uncertainty and controversy. One constant concern is the ethics of such interventions and, further, the possibility that the science that creates opportunities also has the potential for social and moral abuse. Many of these procedures *can* be performed, but *should* they be? Genetic engineering may hold promise for eliminating certain diseases, which might mean that more people would survive and have a better quality of life. Is such improvement of the human gene pool appropriate when the world population as a whole cannot be properly nourished? Who will decide which genetic defects should be corrected, determining who lives and who dies? Technological capability has outstripped human wisdom and the refinement of ethical thinking. This is not the first time such ethical dilemmas have had to be faced, and they continue to raise a variety of questions (e.g., Kleespies & Mori, 1998; Resnick, Cowart, & Kubrin, 1998). These questions demand serious attention and examination of how such progress affects public policy.

Core Questions

1. Compare the concepts of genotype and phenotype and discuss how they relate to the growth matrix.
2. The tabula rasa approach to explaining human growth and development differed significantly from both the preformationist and predeterministic positions. Compare and contrast these three approaches. How do you think their proponents would differ in their explanations of mental retardation, and why might the interactional view be more helpful for a major portion of those with mental retardation?
3. How are the notions of discontinuous growth and critical stages related? Discuss the views of continuous and discontinuous human growth in terms of prenatal and neonatal development.

4. In what manner does the speed of cell reproduction influence vulnerability to trauma that might cause mental retardation? How does this relate to the often noted "first trimester" of pregnancy, particularly with respect to weeks 10 through 12?

5. Why would you expect a new baby's head and arm movements to be more mature than those of its legs? What other growth gradient is also typical of early development?

6. What important physical changes in the mother prepare her for giving birth? How is the baby physically influenced during birth?

7. Why is the neonatal period a time of risk for the baby, and what important physical developments are continuing at this time?

8. How do scientific advances present technical capabilities that contribute to moral or ethical dilemmas?

Roundtable Discussion

A basic understanding of early human development is important background for the study of mental retardation. Many prenatal influences have a substantial impact on a child's status. During this time, many vital organs are being formed, and tissue growth occurs at a phenomenal rate. This is all occurring in the womb during a relatively short period of about 9 months. Biological and embryological information suggests that such processes as myelinization are taking place, central nervous system tissue is being formed, and many other matters essential to the well-being of a young child are going on.

In your study group or on your own, examine these processes as if through the eyes of a preformationist, predeterminist, tabula rasa theorist, and interactionist. Using the material presented in this chapter, as well as in other sources, explain the prenatal developments mentioned (e.g., myelinization, central nervous system development, brain development). Try to integrate the concepts of continuous/discontinuous growth and critical periods into your arguments from each theoretical perspective. Push your explanations and arguments to extremes, as early developmental theorists did. Do you find taking an extreme position the most difficult part of your tasks, or are the fundamental premises more problematic? After this examination of the basic principles of development, where do you stand theoretically as you prepare to push ahead with your study of mental retardation?

References

Albano, A. M., & Morris, T. L. (1998). Childhood anxiety, obsessive-compulsive disorder, and depression. In J. J. Plaud (Ed.), *From behavior theory to behavior therapy* (pp. 203–222). Boston: Allyn & Bacon.

Arey, L. B. (1974). *Developmental anatomy* (7th ed.). Philadelphia: W. B. Saunders Co.

Berger, K. S., & Thompson, R. A. (1998). *The developing person through the life span* (4th ed.). New York: Worth.

Burack, J. A., & Enns, J. T. (1997). *Attention, development, and psychopathology.* New York: The Guilford Press.

Chinn, P. L. (1979). *Child health maintenance: Concepts in family centered care* (2nd ed.). St. Louis: Mosby.

Dawson, G., Panagiotides, H., Klinger, L. G., & Hill, D. (1992). The role of frontal lobe functioning in the development of infant self-regulatory behavior. *Brain and Cognition, 20,* 152–175.

Didio, L. J. A. (1970). *Synopsis of anatomy.* St. Louis: Mosby.

Hall, G. S. (1904). *Adolescence: Its psychology and its relation to physiology, anthropology, sociology, sex, crime, religion, and education.* New York: Appleton-Century-Crofts.

Halpern, D. F. (1997). Sex differences in intelligence: Implications for education. *American Psychologist, 52,* 1091–1102.

Iorio, J. (1975). *Childbirth: Family centered nursing.* St. Louis: Mosby.

Kleespies, P. M. & Mori, D. L. (1998). Life and death decisions: Refusing life-sustaining treatment. In P. M. Kleespies (Ed.), *Emergencies in mental health practice: Evaluation and management* (pp. 145–173). New York: The Guilford Press.

Larsen, W. J. (1997). *Human embryology* (2nd ed.). New York: Churchill Livingstone.

Leonard, L. B. (1998). *Children with specific language impairment.* Cambridge, MA: The MIT Press.

Moore, K. L., & Persaud, T. V. N. (1998). *The developing human: Clinically oriented embryology* (6th ed.). Philadelphia: W. B. Saunders Co.

Notterman, J. M. (1997). *The evolution of psychology: Fifty years of the American psychologist.* Washington, DC: American Psychological Association.

Parisi, D. (1997). Active sampling in evolving neural networks. *Human Development, 40,* 320–324.

Piaget, J. (1926). *The language and thought of the child.* New York: Harcourt Brace.

Porter, R. H. (1997). The influence of maternal odors on the development of newborn mammals. *Enfance, 1,* 23–32.

Resnick, L., Cowart, M. E., & Kubrin, A. (1998). Perceptions of do-not-resuscitate orders. *Social Work in Health Care, 26*(4), 1–21.

Rutter, M., Simonoff, E., & Plomin, R. (1996). Genetic influences on mild mental retardation: Concepts, findings and research implications. *Journal of Biosocial Science, 28,* 509–526.

Santrock, J. W. (1997). *Life-span development* (6th ed.). Dubuque, IA: Brown and Benchmark Publishers.

Serbin, L. A. (1997). Research on international adoption: Implications for developmental theory and social policy. *International Journal of Behavioral Development, 20,* 83–92.

Sonuga-Barke, E. J. S. (1998). Categorical models of childhood disorder: A conceptual and empirical analysis. *Journal of Child Psychology and Psychiatry and Allied Disciplines, 39,* 115–133.

Thibodeau, G. A., & Patton, K. T. (1997). *Structure & function of the body.* St. Louis: Mosby.

Vander-Zanden, J. W. (1997). *Human development* (6th ed.) New York: McGraw-Hill.

Yuen, H. K. (1997). Positive talk training in an adult with traumatic brain injury. *American Journal of Occupational Therapy, 51,* 780–783.

Chapter 6

Early Influences and Causation

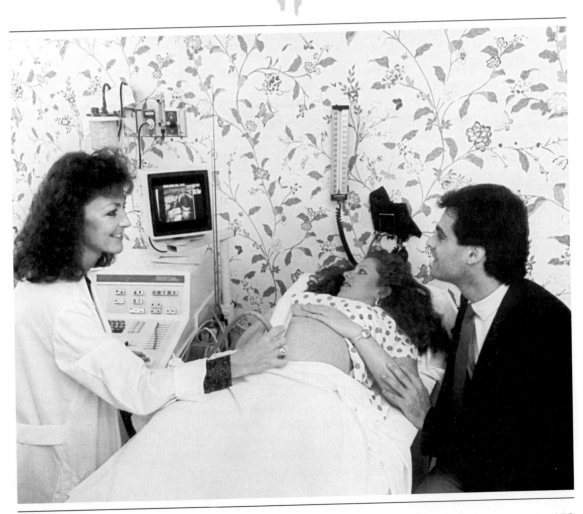

Core Concepts

- Chromosomal abnormalities and genetic errors are causative agents in a number of mental retardation syndromes.
- Inadequate birth weight and gestational age are the problems that most commonly place an infant at developmental risk. They can be caused by a number of factors.
- Various types of interactions between the mother and the unborn fetus can cause damage resulting in mental retardation.
- Fetal damage causing reduced mental functioning may occur from such factors as maternal infection and drug ingestion.
- A number of problems during the delivery of a baby may cause damage that results in mental retardation.
- Many forms of professional intervention can prevent or minimize mental retardation during the prenatal and neonatal periods.

Early life is very important in human growth and development and deserves considerable attention in the study of mental retardation. The young human is almost wholly at the mercy of the environment and is vulnerable to its impact both prenatally and after birth. Normal developmental processes during this period were examined in Chapter 5. The current chapter considers influences and causes of mental retardation in the same period (conception through early infancy).

Examination of the causes of mental retardation during prenatal and neonatal periods requires attention to certain physiological conditions and, when possible, the treatment of these conditions. Medical professionals are often the first to interact with a child at risk for mental retardation during this early period. Instead of an in-depth examination of the medical aspects of mental retardation, however, we wish to make the reader aware of influences on mental development during this period. We discuss more common types of retardation beginning at this time, as well as certain rare conditions for which intervention can prevent retardation or reduce its impact. A variety of developmental and ongoing life processes can go awry at this time and can result in reduced intellectual functioning. In fact, the beginning student occasionally wonders how any child ever manages to get through this period at all without deviation or abnormality. The vast majority of children, however, do develop to a level of functioning that is considered normal or average.

Maternal and fetal conditions both play central roles in healthy fetal development. Similarly, various maternal and fetal conditions contribute to mental retardation during early life. These influences may result in mental retardation that ranges from profound or severe to only mild deviations from normal. Such varying degrees of disability can be conceived of as a **continuum of reproductive causality**. This notion views the child with a mild disability at the less extreme end of the causality range; individuals with more severe retardation and stillborn infants are at the more extreme end. Spontaneous abortion occurring early in pregnancy may represent one extreme of the continuum; mild retardation or slight disabilities in basically normal children represent the other.

EARLY CAUSATION: THE FETUS AND INFANT AT RISK

The first portion of the life cycle is extremely important, as we have already mentioned. Many view development during the prenatal period and immediately after birth as among the most critical in the entire life span (e.g., Berger & Thompson, 1998; Reed, Claireaux, & Clockburn, 1995). Fortunately, most infants enter life outside the womb after a full, successful gestational period, with no labor and delivery complications and no factors during the first month of life that lead to serious illness or disability. When a serious problem does occur in these early months, however, the family often must adjust to having a child with a permanent mental or physical disability. Several conditions are known to place the fetus or infant at high risk for development of serious illness or permanent disability.

Genetic Causation

Core Concept

Chromosomal abnormalities and genetic errors are causative agents in a number of mental retardation syndromes.

Chromosomal and genetic errors contribute to a number of problems that occur during the prenatal period. In many cases, mental retardation resulting from such difficulties falls into well-known syndrome classes of retardation.

Chromosomal Aberrations. Chromosomal aberrations occur when some abnormality emerges in the number or configuration of the chromosomes in the body. Figure 6-1 illustrates a **karyotype,** or classification of photographed human chromosomes obtained from a blood or skin sample. The chromosomes in the sample have been stained to bring out transverse bands; chromosomes with matching bands then can be paired. The karyotype is obtained by cutting individual chromosomes out of photographs and pasting them into place. By convention, the pairs are arranged and numbered from longest to shortest and are separated into seven groups labeled A through G. In this way, determinations of the particular chromosomal anomaly causing an abnormal condition can be identified. The karyotype shown in Figure 6–1 is a normal chromosomal configuration with 44 autosomal and 2 sex chromosomes. One kind of abnormal condition involves extra chromosomes, such as 3 chromosomes in position 21 or 2 or more X or Y chromosomes. Another type of common aberration involves abnormally shaped chromosomes—for example, an excessively long "arm" on number 15.

When 45 chromosomes are present with only a single X sex chromosome, the child has the condition called **Turner syndrome,** or **gonadal aplasia.** The child is nearly always female because the Y chromosome conveys maleness to the

FIGURE 6–1
Karyotype Classification of
Human Chromosomes

From Child Health Maintenance:
Concepts in Family Centered Care
*(2nd ed.) by P. L. Chinn, 1979, St.
Louis: Mosby. Copyright 1979 by
C. V. Mosby Co. Reprinted by per-
mission.*

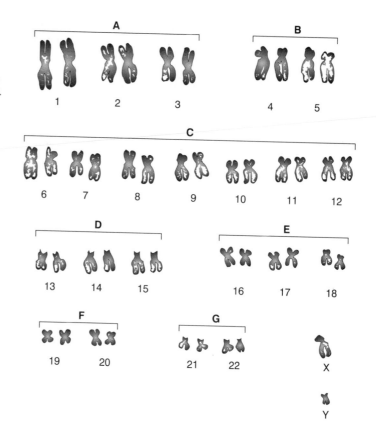

individual. Gonads are rudimentary, no secondary sex characteristics develop at puberty, and there may or may not be accompanying physical signs, such as bow-leggedness or webbed neck and abnormalities of the kidneys and heart (El-Abd, Wilson, Howlin, Patton, Wintgens, & Wilson, 1997; Reiss & Denckla, 1996). A substantial number of individuals with this problem who survive the prenatal period and reach the newborn stage have developmental difficulties and mental retardation.

A number of abnormalities occur on the chromosomes of Groups A through G. These chromosomes are referred to as **autosomal** because they contain genetic material that does not involve sexual characteristics. Down syndrome can occur from any one of three different aberrations of the autosomal chromosomes. The first type is **trisomy,** or **nondisjunction,** in which an extra chromosome occurs in Group G. This is the most common cause of Down syndrome and has a definite correlation with maternal age. The risks increase from 0.69 per 1,000 births for mothers in their early 20s to over 18 per 1,000 in mothers 40 or older. Research on fetal diagnostic procedures is ongoing, aimed at early detection of trisomy Down syndrome (e.g., Ariel, Lerer, Yagel, Cohen, Ben-Neriah, & Abeliovich, 1997; Avramopoulos et al., 1997; Kornman et al., 1997).

A second type of chromosomal difficulty resulting in Down syndrome is **translocation,** occurring in 9% of affected infants born to mothers under the age of 30 and in 2% of affected infants born to mothers over the age of 30. In translocation, some of the chromosomal material of the 21st pair in Group G detaches and becomes attached to a chromosome of the 15th pair in Group D, causing an extra long chromosome in the karyotype. A parent is sometimes the carrier of this condition, as can be detected through genetic studies of both parents and child. When the aberration is not inherited, it occurs as a result of a chance chromosomal error.

The third condition resulting in Down syndrome is **mosaicism.** In this case, the cells of the individual's body are identified as mixed. Some contain trisomies; others are normal. This error occurs during the very early cell divisions after fertilization, with some cell groups forming normally before the error occurs. Such individuals tend to exhibit milder manifestations of the condition, which may reflect the stage of development at which the chromosomal error began. As with other types of Down syndrome, research on the causal mechanism for this condition continues (e.g., Borsatto, Smith, Garcez, & Peres, 1998; Harda et al., 1998).

The physical features evident in Down syndrome vary, but are similar enough that most individuals with Down syndrome resemble one another more than they resemble their own family members. Characteristics include a lateral upward slope of the eyes; protruding tongue because of a small oral cavity; short nose with flat bondage caused by underdevelopment of the nasal bone; flattened head front and back; shortness of fingers, especially the fifth; wide space between the first and second toes; and short, stocky build. These children are more likely than the general population to have congenital heart defects and leukemia and are more susceptible to respiratory infections. Mental retardation almost always accompanies, with IQ scores in the moderate to severe retardation ranges (APA, 1994). A few individuals have IQs in the normal range, and the effect of early stimulation and education programs results in improved mental and neurological functioning for some with Down syndrome. Down syndrome occurs across all three types in about 1 to 1.5 cases per 1,000 live births. Considerable research continues on Down syndrome, including such topics as self-help skills (e.g., Spender, Stein, Dennis, Reilly, Percy, & Cave, 1996), adaptive and maladaptive behavior (Dykens & Kasari, 1997), various aspects of cognitive performance (e.g., Marcell, Busby, Mansker, & Whelan, 1998), and maternal/family matters (Helm, Miranda, & Chedd, 1998; Scott, Atkinson, Minton, & Bowman, 1997). Individuals with this condition continue to capture the attention of a significant group of researchers in mental retardation, as they have for many years.

Genetic Errors.   Genetic errors are conditions resulting from inheritance factors involving specific genes. Such disorders are rather poorly understood, and investigation of these problems is somewhat restricted because of some limitations encountered when studying human genetic material. Some areas of genetic research have achieved enormous advances while others have languished because of funding or methodological limitations (Hodapp, 1997). Although genetic disorders can be identified through study of family inheritance patterns, examination and identification of these problems can sometimes be difficult. Such conditions cannot be studied the way chromosomal disorders are.

Most genetic errors are rare, but a few that result in mental retardation happen often enough that diagnostic and treatment approaches have been developed. One example of such a condition is Prader-Willi syndrome, which occurs about once in every 15,000 births and results in mild to moderate mental retardation (Dykens & Kasari, 1997; Joseph, Overmier, & Thompson, 1997). Another example is phenylketonuria (PKU), which has become one of the most thoroughly studied genetic defects related to mental retardation (Batshaw, 1997; Griffiths, Ward, Harvie, & Cockburn, 1998). It occurs about once in every 10,000 live births and accounts for about 0.5% of patients in residential care facilities for individuals with mental retardation. It is transmitted by an autosomal recessive gene that appears with highest frequency in northern European ethnic groups; it is rare in African and Jewish groups. Affected individuals produce less of the enzyme necessary for metabolism of phenylalanine, leading to an accumulation of this product in the blood serum, cerebrospinal fluid, tissues, and urine. The effect of this metabolic malfunction on the central nervous system is grave; all untreated individuals will reach a level of severe mental retardation within the first few months of life (Diamond, Prevor, Callender, & Druin, 1997; Griffiths, Smith, & Harvie, 1997). Elevated phenylalanine in the blood or urine can be detected within a few weeks after consumption of milk, which contains the substance. Many states have established mandatory screening procedures for all infants in order to institute early treatment measures and to minimize or prevent the serious effects of the untreated condition. It is now possible to diagnose PKU prenatally, although the technique is not widely employed (Waisbren et al., 1998). In addition to mental retardation, affected children develop some degree of microcephaly and have blond hair, blue eyes, and very sensitive skin.

Specific recessive genes play a causal role in a number of other disorders. In these cases, the parents are carriers of a deficient gene but are phenotypically normal. When the recessive genetic material combines, however, the children may develop conditions that result in mental retardation. One such disorder is galactosemia, which occurs when an infant cannot properly metabolize galactose, a chemical generated during digestion of milk products. Newborns with this condition who are on milk diets rapidly develop symptoms that can become life threatening—jaundice, vomiting, and a tremendously heightened vulnerability to infection. Intellectual development also may suffer. Early detection and treatment through strict dietary means can dramatically improve the infant's potential development, although some difficulties may persist. Longitudinal research on treatment effectiveness remains inexact because of the disorder's relative rarity, a common difficulty with such genetic problems.

Prenatal Causation

A variety of problems can emerge during the prenatal period that lead to a risk condition for an infant. In some cases, circumstances result in an inadequate or incomplete development and the baby is born before he or she is ready to thrive in the outside world. Each difficulty discussed here is a condition that places the infant in one risk category or another.

Core Concept

Inadequate birth weight and gestational age are the problems that most commonly place an infant at developmental risk. They can be caused by a number of factors.

Birth Weight and Gestational Age.   The most prevalent of prenatal risk problems involve inadequate birth weight and gestational age, which result in a number of developmental difficulties (Berger & Thompson, 1998; Gazzolo, Visser, Scopesi, Santi, & Bruschettini, 1998). Although these problems occasionally do exist alone, there is more often an accompanying maternal, genetic, or traumatic condition (Hughes, 1998). Inadequate birth weight and gestational age may be the result of a number of different specific developmental difficulties, either in combination or operating singly. Although some infants who are small for gestational age exhibit a "catch-up" growth spurt after birth, there is a significant portion who do not and who experience serious difficulties including mental retardation (Newman et al., 1997). Human development at this early stage is an extremely fragile and delicate process.

Babies delivered before the 38th week of gestation generally are classified as **preterm;** those born between the 38th and 42nd weeks are referred to as **term;** and those delivered after the 42nd week are known as **postterm** infants. Great progress has been made in infant survival through improved obstetric care, even under difficult circumstances. Approximately 98% of infants born after the 32nd week of gestation now survive. Survival rates diminish substantially, however, for infants born before that time. Birth weight is a second important factor in infant mortality and neurodevelopmental deficits. Depending on the gestational age, an infant may be considered "small for gestational age," "appropriate for gestational age," or "large for gestational age." Current medical care suggests that both gestational age and birth weight should be taken into account. Because it is now possible to estimate the maturity of a newborn by physical signs of maturation, care for the infant can be more adequately geared to the particular needs that occur according to gestational age. Such improved care has led to a dramatic decrease in neonatal mortality in the United States.

Predisposing Factors.   Several factors have been identified that are related to low birth weight and inappropriate gestational age (Camp, Broman, Nichols, & Leff, 1998; Gazzolo et al., 1998). Each of the problems discussed in later sections (on infant chromosomal aberrations, maternal-infant interaction problems, and early pregnancy trauma) can be associated with early termination of pregnancy. But several other conditions also appear to lead to early pregnancy termination and inadequate birth weight.

A mother's age and pregnancy history are significant factors in risks to the fetus. Mothers under age 20 or over 35 are more likely to suffer early pregnancy termination than are women between those ages. Likewise, women who have a history of miscarriages, stillbirths, or premature deliveries tend to have as much as a 30% chance of recurrence. Socioeconomic factors also are related to the incidence of preterm and low gestational weight infants and those at risk for mental retardation (Camp et al., 1998; El DeFrawi, Hirsch, Jurkowicz, & Craig, 1996).

Premature birth rates have also been associated with ethnicity, although this factor is probably more closely aligned with extremes of socioeconomic status (wealth, poverty) than with ethnic differences per se (Camp et al., 1998; Fishbein, 1996). The percentage of infants born prematurely to White Americans is consistently about half the percentage born prematurely to non-White Americans. Viewing the extremes of socioeconomic status more specifically, 51% of all non-White (who have lower incomes as a group) births have complications, whereas only 5% of White upper-class births are so affected (Gelfand, Jenson, & Drew, 1997).

Mothers who have had multiple pregnancies account for a high percentage of infants born with low gestational age and birth weight and their concomitant problems. The reasons are complex and numerous, mainly including difficulties of placental problems that lead to ineffective transfer of nutrients across the placenta late in pregnancy and hence to fetal malnutrition. Labor and delivery often commence before term, and the infant is usually small for gestational age. Placental problems are not clearly understood and, when no other cause can be identified, often are attributed to inadequate intrauterine growth. Placental insufficiency implies an impaired exchange between mother and fetus through the placenta. Several well-defined placental lesions are associated with fetal and infant disorders (e.g., blockage of fetal vessels in the placenta, early placenta separation, a single umbilical artery).

Another factor that has long been associated with inadequate growth during fetal life is maternal smoking (Berger & Thompson, 1998; Rogers, Emmett, & Golding, 1997). Pregnant mothers who smoke more than a pack of cigarettes daily tend to have infants who are growth-retarded substantially more often than pregnant mothers who do not smoke. The precise reasons for this difference have not yet been completely delineated, although evidence suggests two probable factors: (a) smoking mothers tend to eat less, and (b) the vascular constriction caused by smoking restricts uterine blood flow. Other related factors, however, may be as important as the actual problem of maternal smoking. Recent literature raises some questions and suggests that a mother's smoking may indirectly affect fetal development (Rogers et al., 1997). It remains clear, however, that there is risk involved in maternal smoking, regardless of the specific manner in which the effect occurs.

Alcohol consumption during pregnancy can seriously injure the fetus. In its most severe form, alcohol-induced fetal injury is known as **fetal alcohol syndrome.** Some problems linked to fetal alcohol syndrome are facial abnormalities, cardiac defects, defects in joints and limbs, neurological abnormalities, autism, behavioral deficits, and mental retardation (Mattson & Riley, 1997; McCreight, 1997; Streissguth, Barr, Kogan, & Bookstein, 1997). Even moderate alcohol consumption by pregnant women can result in fetal problems, although the exact amounts and risk have not been well established (Gonzales & Jaworski, 1997; Sampson et al., 1997). It is clear, however, that alcohol consumption during pregnancy can cause decrements in measured intelligence, and fetal alcohol syndrome is associated with specific memory impairments (Kerns, Don, Mateer, & Streissguth, 1997; Mattson, Riley, Gramling, Delis, & Jones, 1998; Uecker & Nadel, 1998). Cases in which less severe damage results are now being recognized as **fetal alcohol effect,** and children who suffer from it exhibit milder but clearly evident forms of developmental problems (McCreight, 1997). The effect of maternal alcohol consumption has been recognized for nearly a century, although research on the problem was rather scarce, and fetal alcohol syndrome was first described only in the early 1970s.

Maternal nutrition is another incompletely understood factor, although evidence thus far has indicated it is very important to fetal health (Blechman & Brownell, 1998; Jacobson, Rees, Golden, & Irwin, 1997). Many families who eat poorly belong to less affluent socioeconomic groups, and the dietary practices of a subculture often influence them. Thus, it seems difficult to put a finger on the factors in this complex set of interacting variables that have contributed primarily to increased rates of low birth weight and gestational age problems. A pregnant woman has greater nutritional requirements than a nonpregnant woman. For example, caloric requirements increase by about 300 calories per day during the third trimester, which may result in about a 25-pound maternal weight gain. Additionally, both the protein and calcium requirements of a pregnant mother increase. Maternal malnutrition, which often reflects a lifelong state of inadequacy, has been implicated in damaging the fetus, particularly the fetal central nervous system. Such findings are difficult to evaluate and substantiate, however, because the direct transfer of nutrients to the fetus cannot be examined nor can the fetus's exact nutritional requirements be determined.

Associated Problems.   Newborns at risk, especially those with inadequate birth weight and gestational age, tend to be susceptible to serious stress after birth. Problems are primarily complications of respiratory and cardiac failure, infection, and nutritional disorders. They account for many of the conditions associated with birth weight and gestational age inadequacies (e.g., Beckwith & Rodning, 1996; Cosden, Peerson, & Elliott, 1997; Riniolo, Bazhenova, & Porges, 1997).

Respiratory and cardiac difficulties lead to serious interference with the delivery of oxygen to the developing fetal tissues. The central nervous system is particularly vulnerable, for even though a newborn can tolerate longer periods of anoxia (low oxygen level) than can an adult, a continuing lower level of oxygen to the tissues interferes with critical development occurring during the preterm period. Central nervous system tissue cells are still developing until about the 44th week after fertilization, and the tissue depends on oxygen for

Adequate nutrition is important to the developing fetus.

adequate development. An infant who is born at risk before term and who develops such oxygen delivery interference is particularly jeopardized with respect to developing adequate neural tissue, although the relationship between such interference and future development is not yet fully understood. With continuing improvements in neonatal care, however, including prevention of respiratory and cardiac complications and improved care for the infant with these complications, medical personnel anticipate reducing the serious neurological impact of prematurity.

Infection represents another serious complication for infants with low birth weight or gestational age problems. The fetus and the preterm infant are extremely susceptible to infection from organisms that ordinarily do not cause illness for older individuals, and infants have few physiological mechanisms with which to combat infection. An infection that begins in the skin can progress rapidly to serious illness—pneumonia, septicemia (widespread infection of the blood), or meningitis (infection of the central nervous system). And because an infant does not exhibit the usual signs of infection—for example, fever—diagnosing an infection may be difficult or impossible until it has become serious. Infection of the central nervous system in particular leads to grave and permanent consequences, affecting the child's neurological capacity in later life.

Nutrition and oxygen intake are significant problems for infants of low birth weight and inadequate gestational age. Such infants miss the optimal nutritional source of the mother through the placenta and suffer from inadequate intake of basic metabolic nutrients. Particularly important during the last few months of gestation is the supply of glucose, proteins, and oxygen through the placenta. These materials nourish all growing tissues, particularly those of the central nervous system. Central nervous system tissue depends on each of these nutrients not only for growth and development but also for survival. When an infant is born with fetal malnutrition from placental insufficiency, nutrition to help the child recuperate must be incorporated into the routine care. Oxygen administration is most complicated for infants of low birth weight or inadequate gestational age because transfer of the ambient oxygen across the lung-blood barrier cannot be measured directly. An infant may be underoxygenated while receiving large percentages of oxygen or be overoxygenated while receiving relatively low concentrations of oxygen. Excessive oxygenation causes damage to the retina of the eye and, eventually, blindness, a process known as **retrolental fibroplasia.**

Psychological and Educational Impact. Precise determination of the psychological and educational impact of inadequate birth weight and gestational age has been difficult. Part of the problem is separating these influences from the confounding variables of low socioeconomic status and racial minority groups, which consistently have more births in this category. Groups in which greater numbers of infants are born with gestational age and birth weight problems also have a higher percentage of educational and psychological problems among their young children (Gelfand et al., 1997; Hardman, Drew, & Egan, 1999). Comparison of investigations is difficult because of varying definitions of prematurity, low birth weight, and gestational age. Findings of long-term studies, which are necessary in order to determine ultimate educational impact, are often outdated by the time the data can be collected. That is, by the time a child who was born prematurely reaches 6 years of age or older, medical and nursing care for preterm infants will have progressed so much that the findings are not germane for infants born several years earlier. For example, 20 years ago, little was known about the administration of oxygen to preterm infants for the treatment of lung disorders or the prevention of anoxia. Today, great advances have been made in these and related areas, so most infants cared for in a high-risk specialty center receive optimal oxygenation of body tissues throughout the critical period of instability. It is hoped, therefore, that the seriously detrimental effects of anoxia, which may have caused many of the psychological and educational problems reported for children born in the previous two or three decades, can be offset.

Research has generally shown a number of developmental difficulty areas associated with low birth weight and prematurity (Berger & Thompson, 1998). General findings support the conclusion that premature youngsters are a high-risk group in several areas. In some cases, it appears that effects may be long term, although this is not universal; in certain circumstances, early risk appears reversible, and intervention may be rather successful. Evidence has accumulated over time that low birth weight and gestational age present substantial difficulty and are related to mental retardation.

Core Concept

Various types of interactions between the mother and the unborn fetus can cause damage resulting in mental retardation.

Influences from Maternal-Fetal Interaction.   Several abnormal maternal-fetal interactions have serious consequences for the infant. Infants of diabetic mothers, for example, are always high-risk babies because of their excessive birth weight for gestational age and their usually low gestational age. Physical anomalies are also more common among infants of diabetic mothers, and the infants are prone to several serious illnesses during the neonatal period—for example, lung disorders, seizures, hypoglycemia (low blood glucose), and hyperbilirubinemia (resulting in jaundice). The mother's diabetic condition places the child at serious risk from several standpoints. The incidence of neurological impact is largely dependent on the severity of the maternal diabetes and the neonatal course, including gestational age and complications during this period.

The problem of maternal-fetal Rh-factor incompatibility has a more direct effect on the infant's neurological capacity. In this instance, the mother has a negative Rh blood factor and the infant a positive Rh factor. The mother reacts to the infant's positive factor by developing antibodies that destroy the infant's blood cells, leading to serious consequences during fetal life and the neonatal period. The infant's condition is known as **erythroblastosis fetalis.** The higher the level of antibodies in the mother's blood, the more serious the effect on the fetus. In the most severe form, known as **fetal hydrops,** the fetus develops severe anemia, enlargement of the heart, liver, and spleen, and deterioration of the body tissues. In most cases, the fetus dies during the late second or early third trimester and is stillborn. If the child is born alive, survival is unlikely. A moderate form of erythroblastosis fetalis, known as **icterus gravis,** occurs more frequently because, in many instances, the infant's delivery is induced before term to prevent progression of the disease to the more severe form. When this preventive measure occurs, an infant is placed in the disadvantageous position of being delivered preterm, but the hazards are less than those of a more severe form of erythroblastosis fetalis. Such an infant, in addition to low gestational age, may be of low birth weight because of the condition's effect in utero. The infant is typically anemic, jaundiced, and has an enlarged spleen and liver. The high level of bilirubin, occurring from the metabolism of red blood cells, accounts for the jaundice and for any central nervous system damage. As the bilirubin level rises rapidly, adequate excretion cannot occur, and molecules enter the skin tissue, with a toxic effect known as **kernicterus.** If the infant survives the first week of life, outlook for survival is good. The possibility of impact on the neurological system, however, depends on the severity of the hyperbilirubinemia and accompanying illnesses occurring during the neonatal period. When the blood factor incompatibility effects are minimal, as is usual for the first or second infants of most Rh-negative mothers, neonatal problems are minimal and no neurological impacts are evident. Research on various aspects of the Rh factor continues, including considerable work on prevention (e.g., Robson, Lee, & Urbaniak, 1998; Thorpe et al., 1997; Urbaniak, 1998).

Core Concept

Fetal damage causing reduced mental functioning may occur from such factors as maternal infection and drug ingestion.

Trauma During Early Pregnancy.   A variety of influences can result in trauma to the fetus during the first trimester, including drug or chemical ingestion and maternal infection. The teratogenic effects of such exposures are poorly understood, but it is known that although the exact effect of most teratogens is not specified, the timing of exposure probably leads to specific kinds of anomalies. Thus, when a mother contracts rubella during the first trimester of pregnancy, resulting anomalies probably are related more to the timing of fetal exposure than to the specific effects of the virus. Teratogenic effects on the fetus include intrauterine growth retardation, central nervous system infection, microcephaly, congenital heart disease, sensorineural deafness, cataracts and/or glaucoma, and anomalies of the skin. There is a wide range of severity and variability in the occurrence of each possible condition. Again, range of severity probably is related to the timing of the infection, as well as to the possible individual susceptibility of a particular mother and fetus to the effects of the infection. The infant is likely to have a number of physical, behavioral, and intellectual handicaps.

Perinatal and Postnatal Causation

A variety of physical traumas and developmental deviations may result in mental retardation. This section focuses on influences that occur following prenatal development, during what is termed the perinatal and postnatal periods. As we address this time we begin with influences that may place a baby at risk during the birth process.

Core Concept

A number of problems during the delivery of a baby may cause damage that results in mental retardation.

The Birth Process.   The birth process has long been characterized as an extremely traumatic event in the life of the human organism. Birth trauma has been described as the basis for many psychological problems. Early proponents of the psychoanalytical school attributed a great deal of later life anxiety to the separation shock felt at birth. A variety of other phenomena, such as the content of adult dreams, have been thought, at times, to reflect birth trauma. Although there is little doubt that birth is a stressful occurrence, recent thinking places much more emphasis on its physical than its psychoanalytical aspects. From a physical trauma perspective, abnormal birth processes were a major source of later physical and mental difficulties during the early part of the 20th century. However, improvements in obstetrical procedures and practices have drastically reduced such trauma as we enter the 21st century (Hahn, 1997).

Chapter 5 outlines briefly the sequence of events that occurs during the birth of a baby. Although the birth process is a stressful time, danger is minimal if the baby is positioned head first, facing downward, and if the mother's pelvic opening is adequate for the child. This description assumes, of course, that fetal development has progressed without mishap to this point. Two general types of problems during birth can result in mental retardation: (a) physical trauma or mechanical injury and (b) anoxia or asphyxia. The first is almost self-explanatory. Physical trauma or mechanical injury refers to some occurrence during birth that injures or damages the baby so as to impair mental functioning (Meng, Ohyu, & Takashima, 1997; Yokochi & Fujimoto, 1996). In anoxia or asphyxia, the baby is deprived of an adequate oxygen supply for a period long enough to cause brain damage, thereby reducing mental functioning. Many conditions can be responsible. Although these problems are given different labels and appear to be quite dissimilar, they frequently are interrelated.

It has been mentioned that the danger of birth injury is relatively low if the fetus is positioned correctly. When labor begins, the most favorable position is head first and facing toward the mother's back. Other fetal positions are considered abnormal and can cause numerous problems, depending on the situation. Both mechanical injury and anoxia can result from abnormal fetal presentation.

The breech presentation represents one widely recognized abnormal position. Breech presentation occurs when the buttocks, rather than the head, present first. Figure 6–2 illustrates a breech presentation and can be compared with the more normal presentation illustrated earlier in Chapter 5, Figure 5–3. Physicians are becoming increasingly reluctant to deliver babies in breech position through the birth canal. Except when the delivery is conducted by extremely skilled personnel, the danger to the baby is substantial. More and more frequently, a baby lying breech within the uterus is delivered by cesarean

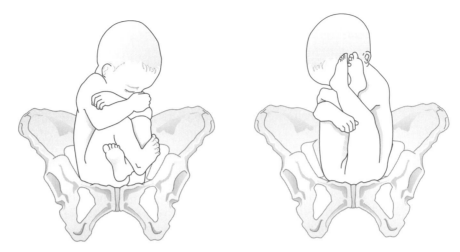

FIGURE 6–2
Examples of Breech Fetal Position

From Childbirth: Family Centered Nursing *(3rd ed.) by J. Iorio, 1975, St. Louis: Mosby. Copyright 1975 by the C. V. Mosby Co. Reprinted by permission.*

section, which involves abdominal surgery and extraction of the baby through the uterine wall.

A number of difficulties are encountered in breech birth if delivery is executed through the birth canal. Because the head presents last, it reaches the pelvic girdle (the bony hip structure of the mother) during the later, more advanced stages of labor. Contractions are occurring rapidly at this point, and the head does not have an opportunity to proceed through the slower molding process possible earlier in labor. Additionally, the molding may occur in an abnormal and damaging fashion because the skull is receiving pressure in an atypical manner (Sherer, Abulafia, & Anyaegbunam, 1998).

The abnormal pressure generated in a breech birth can result in mechanical injury to the brain matter in at least two general ways. In one way, because the skull is still quite soft, rapid compression, which crushes a portion of the brain, can cause an injury. Such damage is less likely in normal presentation because the skull is molded more gently, permitting protective fluid to absorb the pressure. In a second way, the rapid pressure and shifting of cranial bones may be severe enough to damage the circulatory system around the brain and lead to a hemorrhage in the skull, which, in turn, damages brain tissue.

Fetal anoxia may occur in a breech delivery. Because the skull is the last part of the body delivered, the baby must depend entirely on the umbilical cord as a source of oxygen until birth is complete. But the positioning can make the cord too short to remain attached while the head is expelled. In this case, the placenta can become partially or completely detached while the baby's head is still in the birth canal. This separation, of course, eliminates the oxygen supply, and oxygen deprivation can happen if delivery is not completed quickly. Severe tissue damage can result if the head is not expelled and oxygen supplied through the baby's lungs. This possibility presents an extremely serious problem if the head becomes lodged in the pelvic girdle, preventing or substantially slowing progress down the birth canal. Anoxia may occur even if the cord is long enough to remain attached throughout delivery. We already have noted that the head is the tightest fit for the baby moving through the pelvic girdle. At the beginning of delivery, a section of the umbilical cord is necessarily drawn through. Depending on how tightly the skull fits into the bony pelvic structure, the cord can become pinched and the oxygen supply shut off. If this state lasts long (as in the situation of the lodged skull noted earlier), an anoxic condition will result just as if the cord had been cut. These descriptions are only a brief look at the difficulties of breech delivery and how they can cause damaged tissue and reduced mental functioning. Such problems, as well as numerous variations, are the reason why cesarean delivery is favored in breech presentations.

Another abnormal fetal position that presents serious difficulty is the transverse position, illustrated in Figure 6–3. In this presentation, the fetus lies across the birth canal. All of the injury problems noted with the breech position are potential difficulties with this presentation, depending on how delivery proceeds, and a multitude of other problems face the attending physician (Bareggi, Sandrucci, Baldini, Grill, Zweyer, & Narducci, 1995; Hawkins, Hess, Kubicek, Joyce, & Morrow, 1995). If it is possible to rotate the fetus safely, then delivery through the birth canal may be attempted. This is particularly true if the baby

FIGURE 6–3
An Example of Transverse Fetal Position

From Childbirth: Family Centered Nursing *(3rd ed.) by J. Iorio, 1975, St. Louis: Mosby. Copyright 1975 by the C. V. Mosby Co. Reprinted by permission.*

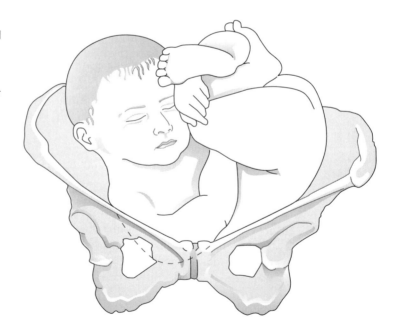

can be moved into a normal or nearly normal head-down position. If the fetus cannot be satisfactorily rotated, a cesarean section is performed.

Abnormalities of fetal presentation can cause many difficulties during birth. Such problems may result in reduced mental functioning because of mechanical injury or anoxia or both. Abnormal presentation, however, is not the only type of problem to occur during the birth process. The initial stages of labor are important for several reasons. As the fetus proceeds into the birth canal, the pelvic girdle stretches. With a normally positioned fetus, the head also is molded to permit passage through the bony pelvic structure. This process occurs during early labor, when uterine contractions are less intense and less frequent than they later become. Consequently, normal molding and stretching occur without sufficient stress to cause injury to the baby. Molding and stretching take time. Delivery of a baby after a labor of less than about 2 hours is known as **precipitous birth** and causes considerable concern about the adequacy of time for gentle skull molding. Precipitous birth increases the risk of tissue damage and increases the probability of mental retardation.

Time also may be a problem at the other end of the continuum—when labor is unusually prolonged (24 hours or more). Most deliveries do not approach 24 hours in length; 7 to 12 hours is average. A variety of conditions may accompany prolonged labor. Under certain circumstances, the uterine conditions deprive a fetus of oxygen, which after a lengthy labor results in either anoxia or a stillborn baby. This is a particular problem if the membranes have ruptured early and if labor is prolonged without delivery. Additionally, in a long period of advanced labor, the fetal skull is under an unusual amount of pressure, which can lead to intracranial hemorrhage. In either case, the probability of tissue damage and resulting mental retardation substantially increases.

This section briefly reviewed influences and causes of mental retardation occurring at birth. Our examples of conditions are the ones most prevalent, better known, and more easily understood. Even this abbreviated presentation can make readers who have just begun to study mental retardation wonder how a normal birth ever happens, but perspective must be maintained. The vast majority of babies are born normally and are ready for the challenges of the postnatal world.

Postnatal Risk and Causation.   Chapter 7 provides details regarding many facets of mental retardation risk during infancy and early childhood. The current section briefly discusses selected risk factors that may surface during the time immediately after birth. Some of these risk factors, such as abuse and neglect by caregivers, are only recently receiving significant attention in the professional literature and represent areas where research evidence is not yet mature. As mentioned earlier, clear delineation of when one developmental period ends and another begins is, in many cases, arbitrary. Likewise, the risk factors presented here cross timeline boundaries. The current section discusses selected risk factors that may surface during the time immediately after birth.

However, many of these risks are also present at other times, and statistics regarding occurrence at various specific ages are currently quite unclear.

The very young baby is quite vulnerable to various illnesses and disease states. Infections from many of the typical child sicknesses may have a more profound impact on the newborn simply because he or she is so fragile and just beginning the process of acclimating to the environment outside the womb. Of particular concern are sicknesses that may cause a high fever and damage the neurological system, which is still developing rather rapidly. Likewise, the very young baby is vulnerable to ingestion of toxic substances. For example, severe food allergies may result in an accumulation of toxins in the newborn's system and may damage the neurological system; or there may be circumstances in which the mother is being medicated and breast feeding can represent the transmission mechanism for potential toxic substances (e.g., Yoshida & Kumar, 1996). Any of these circumstances may lead to reduced mental functioning and mental retardation, brain injury resulting in other disability states, or even death to the young child.

Accidents that result in neurological injury to a newborn also present significant risks for a child to have a variety of disabilities, including mental retardation. Demographic information from the U.S. Department of Health and Human Services indicates that fatal injuries most commonly occur from severe head traumas, Shaken Baby Syndrome, trauma or injury to the abdomen and/or thorax, scalding, drowning, suffocation, and poisoning. These categories of trauma reportedly affect nearly 1 million children in the United States who are identified as substantiated victims of abuse or neglect (U.S. Advisory Board on Child Abuse and Neglect, 1995; U.S. Department of Health and Human Services, 1998, 1996). Although it is currently difficult to narrow the age ranges to our current immediately postnatal focus, it appears that perhaps as many as three fourths of these cases that result in fatalities are youngsters under the age of 4 (U.S. Department of Health and Human Services, 1998). Parents are most often identified as the perpetrators of the abuse (77%), followed by other relatives (11%), and nearly two thirds of the total group are female. Half of the triggering events or circumstances are consistent with caregiver frustration with their very young charges—specifically an infant's inconsolable crying and feeding difficulties (U.S. Advisory Board on Child Abuse and Neglect, 1995).

There are various linkages between the above-noted risk factors and causal agents of mental retardation. Abuse and neglect episodes occur in stressed family situations, with regard to parental stress as well as social and socioeconomic stressors such as poverty, substance abuse, and higher rates of domestic and community violence (Feldman, Leger, & Walton-Allen, 1997; U.S. Advisory Board on Child Abuse and Neglect, 1995). These represent many of the circumstances where higher incidence of mental retardation occurs and certainly high-risk situations for the neonate. However, research efforts and methods directly addressing these very young children remain inadequate. In many areas of the country, analyses of mortality rates for people with mental retardation are inadequate in general and may even be weaker for many at the newborn stage (Zaharia & O'Brien, 1997).

Professional Intervention

Core Concept

Many forms of professional intervention can prevent or minimize mental retardation during the prenatal and neonatal periods.

We have examined a few conditions that can result in mental retardation. Mental retardation can be prevented, or at least curtailed in many instances, through various types of professional intervention. Children born at high risk because of inappropriate birth weight or gestational age are frequently predisposed to mental retardation. As we have noted, problems often arise when prenatal care is either inadequate or nonexistent. Inadequacy or lack of prenatal care is often related to lack of financial resources, ignorance, a value system that does not include high regard for prenatal care, inefficient health-care plans, or a combination of these factors.

Financial limitations may result in inadequate prenatal dietary intake, lack of necessary drugs and vitamins, and lack of supervision by health-care specialists. Many mothers are uneducated about the necessity for prenatal care. Others who are informed do not always incorporate good prenatal care into their value systems, ignoring advice from health-care specialists. Government-supported health-care programs are frequently overburdened and inadequately staffed. Expectant mothers, frustrated by long waits and impersonal care, may become too discouraged to continue seeking prenatal care. Generally speaking, enhancing the mother's health has positive influences on the unborn child's well-being (Berger & Thompson, 1998; McGovern, Dowd, Gjerdingen, Moscovice, Kochevar, & Lohman, 1997).

Professional intervention can greatly reduce the incidence of high-risk children. Low-income families lacking the financial resources for adequate prenatal care need to be directed to the proper agencies of government-supported health care. In addition, to obtain supplemental foods, these families should be directed to various sources, such as agencies that distribute food stamps, maintain surplus food programs, and provide other types of resources to improve the diet of the entire family and especially the expectant mother. Social workers, public health staff, and other individuals working directly with the families can offer this information. It is imperative that families be advised how and where to apply for aid. Supplemental nutrition and care programs significantly improve the chances of many high-risk infants, and benefits may also extend to other family members. Many agencies require extensive documentation to verify financial need. Families should be tutored in the skills necessary to complete application forms, as well as to obtain documentation of financial need. Additionally, the heavy caseloads of physicians in government-supported programs could be much lightened by use of other health-care specialists—for example, certified nurses and midwives. The growing corps of pediatric nurse practitioners can help families achieve better postnatal care.

Professional intervention can effectively address some genetic conditions and chromosomal aberrations. Because the majority of Down syndrome cases are of the nondisjunctive or trisomy variety, a high percentage tend to be related to advanced maternal age. Health-care specialists and social workers can encourage couples to have their children at an earlier age, preferably before the prospective mother is 35. Older couples might be urged to exercise birth control methods or at least to be informed of the possible consequences of having children at more advanced ages. Young mothers who have children with Down syndrome should have a chromosomal analysis to determine whether the condition is related to translocation. If a translocation exists, then the likelihood of a genetic or inherited etiology is high. These parents can be counseled and advised of the risks involved in having other children. Under such conditions, sterilization or other forms of birth control may be considered. Amniocentesis can show the existence of a translocation in the fetus, giving the parents a chance to make an informed decision about terminating the pregnancy by means of therapeutic abortion. Issues of abortion and euthanasia remain highly controversial (e.g., Nakkula & Ravitch, 1998; Widerstrom, Mowder, Sandall, & Nickel, 1997); we discuss them at length in Chapter 13. Although abortion may or may not be acceptable to the counselor, the counselor should avoid imposing personal values on parents, who are entitled to know what their alternatives are and that the decision regarding the alternatives is rightfully theirs.

Routine screening can diagnose certain disorders, such as PKU, early. Screening for PKU can be accomplished by analyses that determines abnormal levels of phenylalanine in the urine. Other assessment also determines abnormal presence of phenylalanine through the examination of the patient's blood. Dietary restrictions often can prevent mental retardation caused by PKU (Schulpis et al., 1998). As early as possible, the child is placed on a diet that is essentially free of phenylalanine. Commercially prepared diets include Ketonil and Lofenalac. The earlier a child is placed on a restricted diet, the greater the chances of avoiding mental retardation. Although evidence suggests that a child with PKU may eventually be removed from the restricted diet, the appropriate time is specific to the individual.

Rh-factor incompatibility between mother and fetus can frequently lead to erythroblastosis fetalis and hyperbilirubinemia, which can cause brain damage and mental retardation. Bilirubin levels can be monitored effectively by periodic testing through a variety of procedures that sample the bilirubin level in the amniotic fluid. When the fetus is affected by a high bilirubin content, professional intervention may take the form of induced labor so that the child is born before the bilirubin level reaches a critical point. Some efforts also have been made toward exchange transfusion through a fetal leg extended by surgery, and exchange transfusion immediately after birth has been effective in many instances. One of the most dramatic breakthroughs in medical intervention is the development of intrauterine transfusions. Guided by X-ray films, the surgeon extends a long needle through the mother's abdomen into the peritoneal cavity in the abdomen of the fetus. Blood of the same type as the mother's then

Routine health screening may detect abnormal conditions developing in infants.

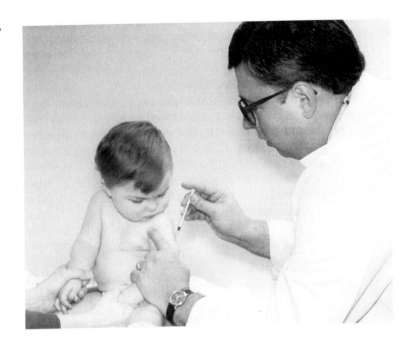

is transfused into the fetus. Thus, the incompatibility factor is eliminated, and the fetal blood is immune from the mother's antibodies.

A desensitizing medication known as **Rho immune globulin (RhoGAM)** was introduced to the general public in 1968. If RhoGAM is injected into the mother within 72 hours of her first child's birth, it desensitizes her body to the Rh-factor antibodies, and she can begin her next pregnancy without the antibodies in her bloodstream. The procedure can be performed after the birth of each child and will largely preclude the development of antibodies, provided it is done faithfully after each birth. Between intrauterine transfusions and desensitization through RhoGAM, few incidents of death or mental retardation resulting from Rh-factor incompatibility should occur in the future.

The first trimester of pregnancy is particularly vulnerable to any type of fetal insult or injury, as indicated earlier. During this period, expectant mothers must exercise extreme caution to avoid any exposure to irradiation, which may affect the fetus, or to infectious diseases. Rubella immunization is now available that can and should eliminate the possibility of widespread rubella epidemics. Parents can greatly reduce the possibility of rubella in their homes by immunizing all children in the family. This comprehensive immunization also protects future mothers from contracting the disease while pregnant.

Prevention of trauma during delivery is the major concern of adequate obstetrical management. Primary concerns include maintaining adequate fetal oxygenation during labor and delivery, ensuring appropriate delivery if a fetus-pelvis size disproportion occurs, and providing adequate observation and care of the infant during the first hour of life. Regional high-risk care centers for mothers provide an extremely high level of specialized care for both mothers and infants known to be in one of the risk categories described. These centers have significantly decreased maternal and infant mortality. One of the most important contributions that can be made in prevention of mental retardation is early identification of at-risk mothers and infants to allow their transfer to a specialized center.

NEW ISSUES AND FUTURE DIRECTIONS

As we enter the 21st century, fetal and neonatal medicine offers both promise and challenge. On the favorable side, knowledge has increased phenomenally during the past several decades. Medical, biological, and genetics research continues to present us with new and exciting knowledge and procedures, seemingly on a daily basis (Moore & Persaud, 1998). Prenatal screening and diagnosis now are available for several developmental problems relating to mental retardation (e.g., Simonoff, Bolton, & Rutter, 1996). Surgeons have progressed to the point of performing surgery to correct serious defects while the fetus is in utero and experimenting with gene therapy to correct some types of problems. However, as Bennett (1997) noted, our knowledge about many developmental errors is still incomplete and continued investigation is essential.

In many cases, advances in knowledge have been driven by progress in technology, which permits actions scarcely imaginable before; prenatal surgery is one illustration. Evidence suggests that current technology might reduce genetic caused mental retardation by 41% (Stevenson, Massey, Schroer, & McDermott, 1996). However, some significant advances such as genetic engineering and gene therapy have occurred in the boundaries of knowledge that offer potential for preventing mental retardation while sometimes treading on unstable ethical ground. Although prevention is clearly desirable, societal questions always arise when techniques have potential for abuse. Genetic mapping and its related technological capability present social and ethical issues that have yet to be fully addressed, let alone resolved.

Also challenging are the ethics of what professionals now can do to maintain life. Medical professionals are, through heroic efforts and applications of new technology, saving the lives of seriously endangered youngsters. One must ask—and many are asking—at what cost with respect to quality of life? In some cases, children are kept alive who would have died in earlier times. But in some instances, these youngsters, though alive, suffer severe mental or physical damage and may exist only in a vegetative state. This outcome raises serious ethical questions about withholding treatment. The questions are not new but remain evident in the literature and are becoming increasingly important as professionals continue to employ rapidly advancing knowledge and technology (Nakkula & Ravitch, 1998; Widersrom et al., 1997). Chapter 13 examines in more detail some of these difficult social and ethical issues.

Other challenges presented by society during the final decade of this century are also significant, and many of them affect the prenatal and neonatal development of children. In some cases, even the widely heralded advances of technology will be sorely tried if professionals intercede and prevent developmental injury. It is well known that the use of certain substances during pregnancy creates risk for the unborn fetus. As indicated earlier, concern for fetal alcohol syndrome has expanded in recent years to include fetal alcohol effect, which causes less severe fetal damage but has observable detrimental effects as the youngster matures (McCreight, 1997; Streissguth, 1997). Other substance use and abuse during pregnancy raise new questions almost daily as new drugs are developed and more is learned about diseases. Although drug and alcohol use by high school seniors peaked in the mid-1980s, it remains at a worrisome level. Effects of significant drug and alcohol use in young women during pregnancy are serious (Espy, Riese, & Francis, 1997; Laken, McComish, & Ager, 1997). Their babies are often exposed to the substance toxicity and appear to also be subjected to diminished positive parental behaviors, such as attentiveness, responsiveness, and interactions that promote cognitive development (Mayes, Feldman, Granger, Haynes, Bornstein, & Schottenfeld, 1997). On the brighter side, there are increasing reports of interventions that appear to be promising for both the young mothers and their infants (e.g., Field, Scafidi, Pickens, Prodromidis, Schanberg, & Kuhn, 1998).

Serious disease states continue to beset society and have significant implications for the health and development of young children. Perhaps the most publicized in the last part of the 20th century was human immunodeficiency virus (HIV), which is linked to AIDS. Increasing concern is evident regarding HIV and its transmission to the unborn fetus (Ahluwalia, DeVellis, & Thomas, 1998; Coreil et al., 1998; Hoover, Doherty, Vlahov, & Miotti, 1996). Certainly there is much that is not known about the effects of HIV on infants, but HIV does appear to result in diminished neuropsychological functioning as physiological aspects of the disease progress (Brouwers, Tudor-Williams, DeCarli, & Moss, 1995). Such circumstances certainly lead the youngster through progressively impaired levels of mental functioning with features that may vary greatly with the individual. Future research is essential to more completely unravel the complexities of this disease and its enormous social and health impacts in our culture.

Core Questions

1. How do different types of Down syndrome occur? Why might they relate to differing levels of intellectual functioning?
2. What factors appear to contribute to inadequate birth weight and gestational age problems? How do they place an infant at risk for mental retardation? Give examples.
3. Why is maternal-fetal interaction important? How can it contribute to the proper development of a baby and to mental retardation? Give examples.
4. Why is the first trimester of pregnancy so important to the developing fetus? How might maternal infection during this period influence the fetus?
5. Why is fetal positioning important in normal delivery of a baby? How might abnormal presentation cause mental retardation?

6. How might professional intervention with respect to maternal nutrition during the first trimester of pregnancy be important in preventing mental retardation?

Roundtable Discussion

Prenatal development is a very important phase in the life cycle of an individual, and a number of processes can malfunction during this time, to cause mental retardation. Concern has been rising about drug and alcohol use, particularly among young people. Some claim that programs aimed at curtailing abuse of such substances represent moralistic "hype" and an intrusion on the individuals' rights to privacy. Others argue that, morals aside, such programs provide important knowledge related to the health of those involved, as well as to their future children.

In your study group or on your own, examine and reflect on the information this chapter contains about early development and mental retardation. Consider this material in the light of substance abuse and discuss the pros and cons of educational and awareness programs like those you see on television.

References

Ahluwalia, I. B., DeVellis, R. F., & Thomas, J. C. (1998). Reproductive decisions of women at risk for acquiring HIV infection. *AIDS Education and Prevention, 10*(1), 90–97.

American Psychiatric Association (APA). (1994). *Diagnostic and statistical manual of mental disorders* (4th ed.). Washington, DC: Author.

Ariel, I., Lerer, I., Yagel, S., Cohen, R., Ben-Neriah, Z., & Abeliovich, D. (1997). Trisomy 2: Confined placental mosaicism in a fetus with intrauterine growth retardation. *Prenatal Diagnosis, 17*, 180–183.

Avramopoulos, D., Kennerknecht, I., Barbi, G., Eckert, D., Delabar, J. M., Maunoury, C., Hallberg, A., & Petersen, M. B. (1997). A case of apparent trisomy 21 without the Down's syndrome phenotype. *Journal of Medical Genetics, 34*, 597–600.

Bareggi, R., Sandrucci, M. A., Baldini, G., Grill, V., Zweyer, M., & Narducci, P. (1995). Mandibular growth rates in human fetal development. *Archives of Oral Biology, 40*, 119–125.

Batshaw, M. L. (1997). PKU and other inborn errors of metabolism. In M. L. Batshaw (Ed.), *Children with disabilities* (4th ed.). Baltimore: Paul H. Brookes.

Beckwith, L., & Rodning, C. (1996). Dyadic processes between mothers and preterm infants: Development at ages 2 to 5 years. *Infant Mental Health Journal, 17*, 322–333.

Bennett, F. C. (1997). Forward. In D. K. Stenson & P. Sunshine (Eds.), *Fetal and neonatal brain injury: Mechanisms, management, and the risks of practice* (v–xi). Oxford: Oxford University Press.

Berger, K. S., & Thompson, R. A. (1998). *The developing person through the life span* (4th ed.). New York: Worth.

Blechman, E. A., & Brownell, K. D. (1998). Behavioral medicine and women: A comprehensive handbook. New York: Guilford Press.

Borsatto, B., Smith, M. deA., Garcez, E. M., & Peres, C. A. (1998). Age-associated mosaicism and polyploidy in Down's syndrome. *Mechanisms of Ageing and Development, 100*, 77–83.

Brouwers, P., Tudor-Williams, G., DeCarli, C., & Moss, H. A. (1995). Relation between stage of disease and neurobehavioral measures with symptomatic HIV disease. *AIDS, 9*, 713–720.

Camp, B. W., Broman, S. H., Nichols, P. L., & Leff, M. (1998). Maternal and neonatal risk factors for mental retardation: Defining the "at-risk" child. *Early Human Development, 50*, 159–173.

Chinn, P. L. (1979). *Child health maintenance: Concepts in family centered care* (2nd ed.). St. Louis: Mosby.

Coreil, J., Losikoff, P., Pincu, R., Mayard, G., Ruff, A. J., Hausler, H. P., Desormeau, J., Davis, H., Boulos, R., & Halsey, N. A. (1998). Cultural feasibility studies in preparation for clinical trials to reduce maternal-infant HIV transmission in

Haiti. *AIDS Education and Prevention, 10*(1), 46–62.

Cosden, M., Peerson, S., & Elliott, K. (1997). Effects of prenatal drug exposure on birth outcomes and early child development. *Journal of Drug Issues, 27,* 525–539.

Diamond, A., Prevor, M. B., Callender, G., & Druin, D. P. (1997). Prefrontal cortex cognitive deficits in children treated early and continuously for PKU. *Monographs of the Society for Research in Child Development, 62*(4), 1–205.

Dykens, E. M., & Kasari, C. (1997). Maladaptive behavior in children with Prader-Willi syndrome, Down syndrome, and nonspecific mental retardation. *American Journal on Mental Retardation, 102,* 228–237.

El-Abd, S., Wilson, L., Howlin, P., Patton, M. A., Wintgens, A. M., & Wilson, R. (1997). Agenesis of the corpus callosum in Turner syndrome with ring X. *Developmental Medicine and Child Neurology, 39,* 119–124.

El DeFrawi, M. H., Hirsch, G., Jurkowicz, A., & Craig, T. J. (1996). Tardive dyskenesia and pregnancy and delivery complications. *Child Psychiatry and Human Development, 26*(3), 151–157.

Espy, K. A., Riese, M. L., & Francis, D. J. (1997). Neurobehavior in preterm neonates exposed to cocaine, alcohol, and tobacco. *Infant Behavior and Development, 20,* 297–309.

Feldman, M. A., Leger, M., & Walton-Allen, N. (1997). Stress in mothers with intellectual disabilities. *Journal of Child and Family Studies, 6,* 471–485.

Field, T. M., Scafidi, F., Pickens, J., Prodromidis, J., Schanberg, S., & Kuhn, C. (1998). Polydrug-using adolescent mothers and their infants receiving early intervention. *Adolescence, 33*(129), 117–143.

Fishbein, H. D. (1996). *Peer prejudice and discrimination: Evolutionary, cultural, and developmental dynamics.* Boulder, CO: Westview Press.

Gazzolo, D., Visser, G. H. A., Scopesi, F., Santi, F., & Bruschettini, P. L. (1998). Pregnancy-induced hypertension, antihypertensive drugs and the development of fetal behavioural states. *Early Human Development, 50*(2), 149–157.

Gelfand, D. M., Jenson, W. R., & Drew, C. J. (1997). *Understanding child behavior disorders* (3rd ed.). Fort Worth: Harcourt Brace.

Gonzales, R. A., & Jaworski, J. N. (1997). Alcohol and glutamate. *Alcohol Health and Research World, 21,* 120–127.

Griffiths, P., Smith, C., & Harvie, A. (1997). Transitory hyperphenylalaninaemia in children with continuously treated phenylketonuria. *American Journal on Mental Retardation, 102,* 27–36.

Griffiths, P., Ward, N., Harvie, A., & Cockburn, F. (1998). Neuropsychological outcome of experimental manipulation of phenylalanine intake in treated phenylketonuria. *Journal of Inherited Metabolic Diseases, 21,* 29–38.

Hahn, J. S. (1997). Correlation of clinical findings and timing of the asphyxial event. In D. K. Stenson & P. Sunshine (Eds.), *Fetal and neonatal brain injury: Mechanisms, management, and the risks of practice* (pp. 356–373). Oxford: Oxford University Press.

Harda, N., Abe, K., Nishimura, T., Sasaki, K., Ishikawa, M., Fujimoto, M., Matsumoto, T., & Niikawa, N. (1998). Origin and mechanism of formation of 45, X/47, XX, +21 mosaicism in a fetus. *American Journal of Medical Genetics, 75,* 432–437.

Hardman, M. L., Drew, C. J., & Egan, M. W. (1999). *Human exceptionality: Society, school, and family* (6th ed.). Needham Heights, MA: Allyn & Bacon.

Hawkins, J. L., Hess, K. R., Kubicek, M. A., Joyce, T. H., & Morrow, D. H. (1995). A reevaluation of the association between instrument delivery and epidural analgesia. *Regional Anaesthesia, 20,* 50–56.

Helm, D. T., Miranda, S., & Chedd, N. A. (1998). Prenatal diagnosis of Down syndrome: Mothers' reflections on supports needed from diagnosis to birth. *Mental Retardation, 36,* 55–61.

Hodapp, R. M. (1997). Direct and indirect behavioral effects of different genetic disorders of mental retardation. *American Journal on Mental Retardation, 102,* 67–79.

Hoover, D. R., Doherty, M. C., Vlahov, D., & Miotti, P. (1996). Incidence and risk factors for HIV-1 infection—a summary of what is known and the psychiatric relevance. *International Review of Psychiatry, 8,* 137–148.

Hughes, F. P. (1998). Play in special populations. In O. N. Saracho & B. Spodek (Eds.), *Multiple perspectives on play in early childhood education* (pp. 171–193). Albany, NY: State University of New York Press.

Iorio, J. (1975). *Childbirth: Family centered nursing* (3rd ed.). St. Louis: Mosby.

Jacobson, M. S., Rees, J. M., Golden, N. H., & Irwin, C. E. (1997). *Adolescent nutritional disorders: Prevention and treatment.* New York: New York Academy of Sciences.

Joseph, B., Overmier, J. B., & Thompson, T. (1997). Food- and nonfood-related differential outcomes in equivalence learning by adults with Prader-Willi syndrome. *American Journal on Mental Retardation, 101,* 374–386.

Kerns, K., Don, A., Mateer, C. A., & Streissguth, A. P. (1997). Cognitive deficits in nonretarded adults with fetal alcohol syndrome. *Journal of Learning Disabilities, 30,* 685–693.

Kornman, L. H., Morssink, L. P., Wortelboer, M. J., Beekhuis, J. R., DeWolf, B. T., Pratt, J. J., & Mantingh, A. (1997). Maternal urinary beta-core hCG in chromosomally abnormal pregnancies in the first trimester. *Prenatal Diagnosis, 17,* 135–139.

Laken, M. P., McComish, J. F., & Ager, J. (1997). Predictors of prenatal substance use and birth weight during outpatient treatment. *Journal of Substance Abuse Treatment, 14,* 359–366.

Marcell, M. M., Busby, E. A., Mansker, J. K., & Whelan, M. L. (1998). Confrontation naming of familiar sounds and pictures by individuals with Down syndrome. *American Journal on Mental Retardation, 102,* 485–499.

Mattson, S. N., & Riley, E. P. (1997). Neurobehavioral and neuroanatomical effects of heavy prenatal exposure to alcohol. In A. Streissguth & J. Kanter (Eds.), *The challenge of fetal alcohol syndrome: Overcoming secondary disabilities* (pp. 3–14). Seattle: University of Washington Press.

Mattson, S. N., Riley, E. P., Gramling, L., Delis, D. C., & Jones, K. L. (1998). Neuropsychological comparison of alcohol-exposed children with or without physical features of fetal alcohol syndrome. *Neuropsychology, 12,* 146–153.

Mayes, L. C., Feldman, R., Granger, R. H., Haynes, O. M., Bornstein, M. H., & Schottenfeld, R. (1997). The effects of polydrug use with and without cocaine on mother-infant interaction at 3 and 6 months. *Infant Behavior and Development, 20,* 489–502.

McCreight, B. (1997). *Recognizing and managing children with fetal alcohol syndrome/fetal alcohol effects: A guidebook.* Washington, DC: CWLA Press.

McGovern, P., Dowd, B., Gjerdingen, D., Moscovice, I., Kochevar, L., & Lohman, W. (1997). Time off work and the postpartum health of employed women. *Medical Care, 35,* 507–521.

Meng, S. Z., Ohyu, J., & Takashima, S. (1997). Changes in AMPA glutamate and dopamine D2 receptors in hypoxic-ischemic basal ganglia necrosis. *Pediatric Neurology, 17,* 139–143.

Moore, K. L., & Persaud, T. V. N. (1998). *The developing human: Clinically oriented embryology* (6th ed.). Philadelphia: W. B. Saunders.

Nakkula, M. J., & Ravitch, S. M. (1998). *Matters of interpretation: Reciprocal transformation in therapeutic and developmental relationships with youth.* San Francisco: Jossey-Bass.

Newman, D. G., O'Callaghan, M. J., Harvey, J. M., Tudehope, D. I., Gray, P. H., Burns, Y. R., & Mohay, H. A. (1997). Characteristics at four months follow-up of infants born small for gestational age: A controlled study. *Early Human Development, 49*(3), 169–181.

Reed, G. B., Claireaux, A. E., & Clockburn, I. (1995). *Diseases of the fetus and newborn: Pathology, imaging, genetics and management* (2nd ed.). New York: Chapman & Hall Medical Publishers.

Reiss, A. L., & Denckla, M. B. (1997). The contribution of neuroimaging to behavioral neurogenetics research: Fragile X syndrome, Turner syndrome, and neurofibromatosis-1. In G. R. Lyon & J. M. Rumsey (Eds.), *Neuroimaging: A window to the neurological foundations of learning and behavior in children* (pp. 147–167). Baltimore: Paul H. Brookes.

Riniolo, T. C., Bazhenova, O. V., & Porges, S. W. (1997). Respiratory sinus arrhythmia and ambient temperature at 5 months. *Infant Behavior and Development, 20,* 417–420.

Robson, S. C., Lee, D., Urbaniak, S. (1998). Anti-D immunoglobulin in RhD prophylaxis. *British Journal of Obstetrics and Gynaecology, 105,* 129–134.

Rogers, I. S., Emmett, P. M., & Golding, J. (1997). The incidence and duration of breast feeding. *Early Human Development, 49* (Supplement), S45–S74.

Sampson, P. D., Kerr, B., Olson, H. C., Streissguth, A. P., Hunt, E., Barr, H. M., Bookstein, F. L., & Teide, K. (1997). The effects of prenatal alcohol exposure on adolescent cognitive processing: A speed-accuracy tradeoff. *Intelligence, 24,* 329–353.

Schulpis, K. H., Papakonstantinou, E., Michelakakis, H., Theodoridis, T., Papandreau,

U., & Constantopoulos, A. (1998). Elevated serum prolactin concentrations in phenylketonuric patients on a "loose diet." *Clinical Endocrinology, 48,* 99–101.

Scott, B. S., Atkinson, L., Minton, H. L., & Bowman, T. (1997). Psychological distress of parents of infants with Down syndrome. *American Journal on Mental Retardation, 102,* 161–171.

Sherer, D. M., Abulafia, O., & Anyaegbunam, A. M. (1998). Intra- and early postpartum ultrasonography: A review. Part I. *Obstetrical and Gynecological Survey, 53*(2), 107–116.

Simonoff, E., Bolton, P., & Rutter, M. (1996). Mental retardation: Genetic findings, clinical implications and research agenda. *Journal of Child Psychology and Psychiatry and Allied Disciplines, 37,* 259–280.

Spender, Q., Stein, A., Dennis, J., Reilly, S., Percy, E., & Cave, D. (1996). An exploration of feeding difficulties in children with Down syndrome. *Developmental Medicine and Child Neurology, 38,* 681–694.

Stevenson, R. E., Massey, P. S., Schroer, R. J., & McDermott, S. (1996). Preventable fraction of mental retardation: Analysis based on individuals with severe mental retardation. *Mental Retardation, 34,* 182–188.

Streissguth, A. P. (1997). *Fetal alcohol syndrome: A guide for families and communities.* Baltimore: Paul H. Brookes.

Streissguth, A., Barr, H., Kogan, J., & Bookstein, F. (1997). Primary and secondary disabilities in fetal alcohol syndrome. In A. Streissguth & J. Kanter (Eds.), *The challenge of fetal alcohol syndrome: Overcoming secondary disabilities* (pp. 25–39). Seattle: University of Washington Press.

Thorpe, S. J., Boult, C. E., Stevenson, F. K., Scott, M. L., Sutherland, J., Spellerberg, M. B., Natvig, J. B., & Thompson, K. M. (1997). Cold agglutinin activity is common among human monoclonal IgM Rh system antibodies using the V4-34 heavy chain variable gene segment. *Transfusion, 37,* 1111–1116.

Uecker, A., & Nadel, L. (1998). Spatial but not object memory impairments in children with fetal alcohol syndrome. *American Journal on Mental Retardation, 103,* 12–18.

Urbaniak, S. J. (1998). Consensus conference on anti-D prophylaxis. *Transfusion, 38,* 97–99.

U.S. Advisory Board on Child Abuse and Neglect. (1995). *A nation's shame: Fatal child abuse and neglect in the United States.* Washington, DC: Department of Health and Human Services, Administration for Children and Families.

U.S. Department of Health and Human Services, National Center on Child Abuse and Neglect. (1996). *Third national incidence study of child abuse and neglect: Final report (NIS-3).* Washington, DC: U.S. Government Printing Office.

U.S. Department of Health and Human Services. (1998). *Child maltreatment 1996: Reports from the states to the National Child Abuse and Neglect Data System.* Washington, DC: U.S. Government Printing Office.

Waisbren, S. E., Chang, P., Levy, H. L., Shifrin, H., Allred, E., Azen, C., de la Cruz, F., Hanley, W., Koch, R., Matalon, R., & Rouse, B. (1998). Neonatal neurological assessment of offspring in maternal phenylketonuria. *Journal of Inherited Metabolic Diseases, 21,* 39–48.

Widerstrom, A. H., Mowder, B. A., Sandall, S. R., & Nickel, R. E. (1997). *Infant development and risk: An introduction* (2nd ed.). Baltimore: Paul H. Brookes.

Yokochi, K., & Fujimoto, S. (1996). Magnetic resonance imaging in children with neonatal asphyxia: Correlation with developmental sequelae. *Acta Paediatrica, 85,* 88–95.

Yoshida, K., & Kumar, R. (1996). Breast feeding and psychotropic drugs. *International Review of Psychiatry, 8,* 117–124.

Zaharia, E. S., & O'Brien, K. (1997). Mortality: An individual or aggregate variable? *American Journal on Mental Retardation, 101,* 424–429.

Part 4

Mental Retardation: Preschool and School Years

Infancy and Early Childhood

Core Concepts

- Physiological growth during infancy and early childhood plays a central role in the general development of an individual, laying the foundation for many skills and behaviors.
- Early intervention often demands partnerships between professionals and parents.
- During the early childhood years, mental retardation is likely to become evident in language development.
- Cognitive development during infancy and early childhood involves many complex processes, including some in areas where children with mental retardation have great difficulty.
- Developmental problems in social and emotional functioning can have a serious impact on a young child's ability to adapt and chances to succeed.

Growth and development during infancy and early childhood are vital to an individual's well-being. These are critical years for all children, and the importance of this period cannot be overemphasized. Experiences during infancy and early childhood can promote the attainment of optimal development potential, or they can deter the fulfillment of this potential. In the first situation, intellectual functioning may be enhanced so much that the child operates in the upper ranges of ability. In the second, experiences may detract from the developmental process so much that permanently lowered functioning results. The effects of environmental influences during infancy and early childhood are often more lasting and pervasive than during any later phase of the life cycle (Berger & Thompson, 1998; Berk, 1998). It is not surprising that this period causes stress and a variety of emotional responses in the families of youngsters with mental retardation.

This chapter addresses development during infancy and preschool years and environmental influences that promote or detract from the fulfillment of potential. We examine four broad areas of development: physical, language, cognitive, and psychosocial. Although interrelated, these also represent distinct areas of development that have been the focus of considerable research. Each of the four areas is critical in one fashion or another to a child's ability to learn. In what follows, we review pertinent research about expected traits of development, traits evident in children with mental retardation, and environmental influences.

PHYSICAL DEVELOPMENT

Core Concept

Physiological growth during infancy and early childhood plays a central role in the general development of an individual, laying the foundation for many skills and behaviors.

Several major systems are involved in a discussion of physical development. Most often considered are the gastrointestinal, renal, endocrine, skeletal, reproductive, neurological, and muscular systems. Each has an important function, although those most closely related to the learning process are the neurological, skeletal, and muscular systems. These three systems are functionally related and occasionally are thought of as one—the neuromotor system. Neurological and motor functions are influenced by important stimuli, and responses are provided by the endocrine system (Thibodeau & Patton, 1997). For the purposes of this text, we examine neuromotor development to become familiar with the physical dimensions of learning and the influences of the environment on this facet of development.

Neuromotor Development

Various parts of the neurological system are important to us here. The neurological system is composed of the brain, spinal cord, and peripheral neurons, including the autonomic system, which is functionally related to the endocrine system. Neurological pathways extend to muscle and skin tissues and provide for transmission of neurological sensations from the environment to the central nervous system. These pathways also serve as a means for neurological control and response between the central nervous system and the muscles, permitting movement and vocalization appropriate to various environmental stimuli. Neurological functioning cannot usually be studied directly, although technology developments continue to dramatically move us forward in this area. Indirect investigation often occurs by observing a variety of performance areas and comparing a given child's functioning with age-appropriate levels. Neurological maturation is critical to a child's overall development and plays an important role in cognitive, language, and psychosocial development. More complete attention is given to these areas in later portions of this chapter. For the time being, we focus directly on the development of the neuromotor system and examine certain conditions of physical development that can be detected in children with mental retardation.

Head and Brain Characteristics. A child's neurological development and capacity are related to head and brain size. The brain grows very rapidly during the prenatal period. This rapid growth continues after birth; a 2-year-old's brain is approximately 90% of adult brain size. This growth may be assessed indirectly by measuring the head circumference. Normal circumference ranges have been established for each gender at each developmental stage. For example, the mean head circumference for male infants at birth is 34.5 centimeters and reaches 49 centimeters by the age of 2. Female infants have a mean head circumference of 34 centimeters at birth and reach 48 centimeters by the age of 2. A deviation of plus or minus two standard deviations from the expected mean head circumference at any age is enough variation to warrant concern. If this anomaly occurs, the child must undergo medical testing to determine whether a pathological condition is present that threatens physical health or intellectual functioning. An example of such a condition is microcephaly, in which the head circumference is below the norm by two standard deviations or more. (Children with microcephaly are characterized by several other physical abnormalities and typically have rather severe retardation.) The child's brain size is limited, and abnormalities of brain tissue formation also may be present. Limited brain size, tissue abnormalities, or both may result from a genetic condition or from brain infections and other environmental circumstances that slows the growth of brain tissue. In either case, the neurological system is seriously impaired, and mental retardation results (Durkin, Hasan, & Hasan, 1998; Giannotti, Digilio, Mingarelli, Marino, & Dallapiccola, 1997).

A head circumference significantly larger than expected also may indicate a situation of serious concern. Hydrocephalus, for example, is a condition characterized by exceptionally large head size even though the brain may be inadequately developed or normal, depending on the precise cause of the condition. This condition is related to an increase in the amount of cerebrospinal fluid that circulates in the brain cavity and spinal column area. The excess fluid puts increased pressure on surrounding structures and leads to damage of brain tissue and ultimately to mental retardation, regardless of initial capacity.

Brain development occurs rapidly during the early years. Sulci, or convolutions, in the lobes of the brain deepen and become more prominent and numerous during this period. These continue to develop throughout life, but more gradually than during the early years (Berk, 1998). It is thought that the development of sulci reflects processes of learning, memory, and the ability to reason and form conceptualizations. A child with inadequate neuromotor control and function or showing a developmental delay may suffer from some abnormality in form or function of the brain, although the defect may not be directly detectable. Some information concerning the size and shape of the brain can be obtained by X-ray or MRI procedures. However, the primary cause of the child's lack of coordination, speaking difficulty, or limited ability to learn cannot usually be identified with certainty as defective brain tissue.

Myelinization.   As discussed in Chapter 5, myelinization is commonly accepted as an important developmental process. Myelinization involves the development of a protective insulating sheath surrounding the brain and neurological pathways. This sheath presumably operates somewhat like the insulation on an electrical wire and allows nerve impulses to travel along the nerve pathway rapidly and without diffusion. The newborn has an incomplete myelin sheath, an incompleteness that accounts for nonspecific reactions to stimuli and a lack of motor coordination. Consequently, an infant exhibits generalized body movement and crying in response to, for example, a painful stimulus to the foot, rather than specific withdrawal of the foot and attention to the source of the stimulus with specific vocalizations indicating pain. As with other growth patterns, myelinization proceeds in a cephalocaudal and proximodistal fashion, which provides for the pattern of acquisition of gross-motor control before fine-motor control. By the age of 2, a major portion of the myelin sheath is formed, and the child's motor capacity is relatively mature (Moore & Persaud, 1998; Rolland-Cachera, Deheeger, & Bellisle, 1997).

Reflexes and Voluntary Behavior.   Reflex behavior is a primitive human response compared to many that are characteristic of general human functioning. Development of reflex behavior is thought to have evolved early in human history out of necessity for protection in a harsh environment. Sophisticated cognitive skills develop later, making possible voluntary action directed toward self-protection. Much of the reflexive behavior of early infancy gradually fades as voluntary control develops through association pathways of the nervous system. Some reflexes persist throughout life, such as the knee jerk, eye blink, and reaction of the eye pupil to light.

During early childhood, voluntary movement becomes predominant for the child who is neurologically healthy, although involuntary movement on one side of the body may mirror voluntary movement on the opposite side. This involuntary mirroring action is pronounced in children who suffer damage to the central nervous system, but the phenomenon itself does not suggest damage unless it persists beyond the preschool years or is so pronounced that it interferes with the child's voluntary movements. Predominance of the one-sided voluntary function generally is established fully by the age of 4, and a child typically demonstrates a preference for right or left hand use in performing motor tasks.

Emotions and the Central Nervous System.   The limbic system of the brain is located in the central portion of the tissue and surrounds the hypothalamus. This system functions specifically to mediate emotional and temperamental dimensions of behavior. Sensations such as pleasure or discomfort and the individual meaning that such experiences develop originate and are stored in this system. Other behaviors related to these areas of functioning include excitement, anger, fear, sleep, and wakefulness. Maturity in these response areas progresses as a young child experiences a wider range of environmental stimuli and exercises more behavioral self-control, as well as control over the behavior of others. The feeling response predominates in early childhood in terms of determining behavior, indicating that the limbic system is functioning and that associations with voluntary control areas are not fully accomplished. As growth continues and these associations mature, a child becomes more effective in disguising and voluntarily controlling emotional components of behavior.

Sensory Organs and Cranial Nerves.   Development and integrity of cranial nerves and specialized sensory organs also play important roles in a young child's general functioning status. These maturational processes are essential to the child's ability to receive stimuli from the environment and integrate them into the perceptual and memory components of the central nervous system. **Cranial nerves** are distinct neural pathways that provide for the specialized sensory function and motor performance of the sensory and other essential organs and surrounding muscle structure. These nerves approach functional maturity by the age of 3 and can be tested by assessing sensory organ functions. Ears and eyes are particularly crucial for receiving stimuli related to learning. Other sensory functions, such as smell, taste, touch, and the sense of movement, however, are also important in providing essential neurological stimulation (Santrock, 1997).

Optimal functioning levels for taste and smell are reached during infancy. These senses also come under the influence of voluntary control and association with other sensory areas. A young child is able to, and often will, refuse to taste a food that looks unpleasant or that others have made negative comments about. The child is able to respond accurately to the sensation that a taste or smell arouses and learns associations between certain tastes and smells and culturally accepted values. Preferred foods in a child's culture become palatable, and foods that are not acceptable become displeasing. The role of these sensory capacities in terms of learning problems is not currently understood, but it does appear that significant learning stimuli come through these channels.

Hearing is often thought to be a very critical sense for learning. Children with hearing deficits seem to have more interference with learning than children with other types of sensory disturbances. This effect obviously varies substantially, depending on the child and the nature and severity of the deficit. The sense of hearing relies on intact tissue structures between the external ear and the brain cortex, including the important cranial nerves involved in hearing functions. Functional structures of the ear also are related to the sense of balance and movement.

An infant's hearing apparatus is mature at birth except in two areas: (a) myelinization of the cortical auditory pathways beyond the midbrain and (b) resorption of the connective tissue surrounding the ossicles of the middle ear. The infant can hear and also can respond differently to loud noises (by crying) and to soft, soothing sounds (by relaxing and becoming calm). The child's reaction to sound at this stage is characteristic of reactions to most stimuli; it is generalized and involves movements of the entire body. Typically, these movements are of a gross-motor nature and are nonspecific; they tend to be characterized by a thrashing of the arms, body, and legs or by a generalized calming. As myelinization proceeds, the child begins to exhibit an ability to localize sound direction. By the age of 2 to 3 months, the child can respond by turning the head toward the sound (Berger & Thompson, 1998).

An infant does not have fully developed hearing like an adult's, however. Adult-like hearing is not present until about age 7 and involves complex cortical functioning, including the ability to listen, to respond with discrimination, to imitate sounds accurately, and to integrate the meaning of sounds. Identification of hearing deficits during the first year of life is vital for maximally effective treatment and maintenance of optimal learning capacity (Morlet et al., 1995). If a child's hearing deficiency can be identified at this time and if some means of providing auditory stimulation is instituted, the child's ability to integrate the meaning of auditory stimuli later in life and to maintain and use these neurological pathways as an avenue for learning is substantially enhanced.

Visual acuity is rather limited at birth, although vision is fully developed by about age 6 (Berger & Thompson, 1998; Santrock, 1997). The newborn can differentiate only generally between light and dark. The development of visual acuity progresses rather rapidly during the neonatal period, however, and by the age of 6 months, an infant generally can recognize objects and people. A capacity to follow movement in the environment also begins to develop during the first months of life, and completely coordinated eye movements should be evident by the sixth month. The preschool child who is unable to see a single object when looking at it with both eyes (binocularity) has a condition known as **amblyopia.** Amblyopia creates some unusual difficulties with regard to a child's perceptual behavior. Because the child sees two separate, overlapping objects instead of a single, unified perception, he or she begins to block the perception of one eye in order to see a single object through the preferred eye. Lack of use and stimulation of the other eye leads to gradual deterioration of the neural pathways from the eye to the central nervous system. This decline can cause permanent loss of function of the eye if it continues to be unused. The effects of amblyopia illustrate the vital role of adequate stimulation in order for neurological tissue to develop and maintain adequate function.

Integration of incoming visual stimuli with existing neurological functions is very important in early learning. By about 2 to 3 years of age, the child begins to remember and recall visual images. Along with an interest in pictures, the child begins to enjoy producing geometric shapes and figures. These abilities create a readiness to recognize symbols, or to read, which typically appears by the time the child is 4 years old. A further visual discrimination that has important implications for early learning processes is color recognition. For the most part, color recognition is well established by the time the child is 5.

Summary.   A variety of complex factors contributes to neuromotor developmental advances during early childhood. Growing muscles, practicing of motor skills, continuing organization of associations between established neural pathways, and the establishing of new pathways are only a portion of the developmental process that is under way. During this period, the ability to maintain focal attention, a hallmark of early childhood, also emerges. Incredible gains are evident in cognitive and intellectual functioning, memory, consciousness, and thought. The role of each structure in the nervous system with regard to the various forms of mental retardation is not well understood. It is apparent, however, that an inadequacy in one dimension of the development of the nervous system is typically accompanied by inadequacies in the system generally. Thus, the child who evidences developmental delays in motor performance during early childhood frequently also exhibits delays in emotional development, language development, and cognitive development, because each of these dimensions of performance depends on the general adequacy of the nervous system (Berger & Thompson, 1998; Berk, 1998). Table 7–1 is a summary of selected developmental landmarks during the first 2 years of life in terms of a few motor, psychosocial, and verbal developmental features. Remember that a child who is

TABLE 7–1
Selected Developmental Landmarks

	Months							
	1	2	3	4	5	6	7	8
MOTOR								
Sitting				<		<	(Supported)	
Walking								
Sucking								
Standing								<
Crawling							<	
Creeping								
Bowel control						<		
Bladder control								
Head: prone		< Lifts head X						
sitting			< Bobs X					
PSYCHOSOCIAL								
Smiling				< Spontaneous X		Mirror image		
Reacting to others			< Follows moving people X			Discriminates		
Feeding					(Solids)		(Holds)	
Socialization	<							
VERBAL								
Crying								
Cooing			<		>			
Babbling, resembles one syllable						< Tone		
Imitation of word sounds								
Some word understanding (dada, mamma)								
Word repertoire								

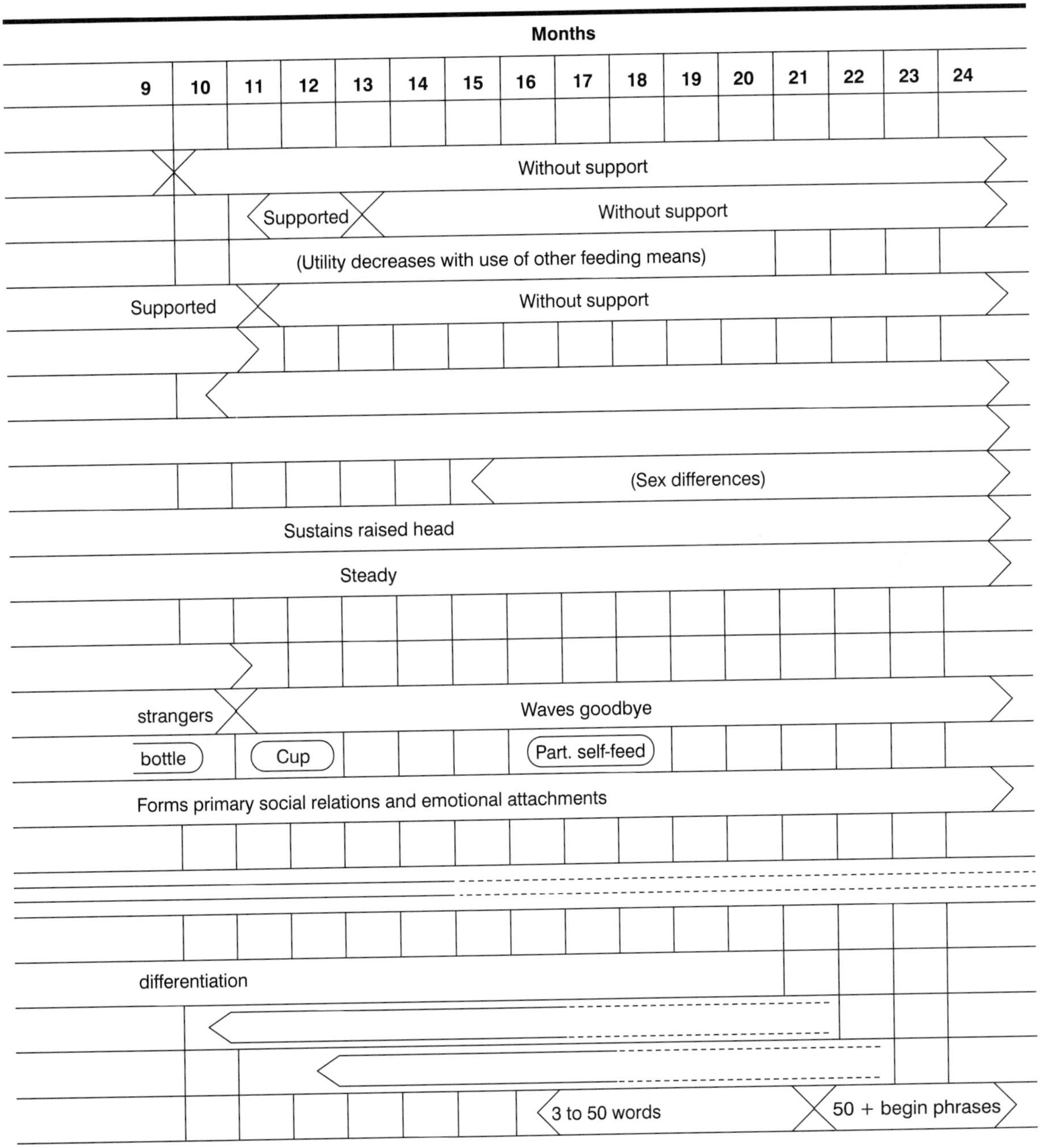

Months

9	10	11	12	13	14	15	16	17	18	19	20	21	22	23	24

Without support

Supported ✕ Without support

(Utility decreases with use of other feeding means)

Supported ✕ Without support

(Sex differences)

Sustains raised head

Steady

strangers ✕ Waves goodbye

bottle   Cup   Part. self-feed

Forms primary social relations and emotional attachments

differentiation

3 to 50 words   50 + begin phrases

delayed in one area of development is likely also to exhibit signs of delay in others. Such a child's behavior may be generally more like that of children who are chronologically younger.

Effects of the Environment

Each of the child's neuromotor capabilities has an optimal time during the developmental cycle for appearance and integration into the system as a whole. The child's development of these specific capabilities during such periods is vulnerable to disruptions that can produce either temporary or permanent problems (Guralnick, 1997). Some of these disruptions result from environmental influences. It is generally agreed that the effects of environmental conditions or stimuli on a young child are great, although the exact influences of many environmental conditions are poorly understood (Gelfand, Jenson, & Drew, 1997).

Investigations on the effects of early environmental experience represent important research in the field of mental retardation and behavioral science in general. Studies supporting the importance of early stimuli have not accumulated enough evidence to draw firm conclusions, although certain trends are emerging. For example, extreme environmental deprivation, particularly during early childhood, appears to be a potent unfavorable influence (Als, 1997). Such extreme deprivation can result in pervasive developmental delays and potential mental retardation.

Considerable evidence suggests how sensory deprivation of visual stimuli during early life affects a child. Some support comes from studies of early development in children with blindness. Significant delays appear in such infants' and toddlers' development in multiple areas, including both motor and cognitive performance (Davidson & Harrison, 1997). Such extreme cases are difficult to relate to less severe sensory deprivation that might occur in poor environments. It seems reasonable to expect that a child who does not have an opportunity to experience and practice certain sensorimotor skills will not develop such specific motor capacities. The effects of deprivation on later development of intellectual functioning, however, remain uncertain. One broadly held belief is that a wealth of sensory stimulation during the first 2 years, regardless of type, should promote favorable development of an individual's cognitive and intellectual skills. Some evidence suggests that variety in stimulation is also important in cognitive development (Berger & Thompson, 1998; Santrock, 1997). Limited environmental stimulation, a lack of systematic or ordered interpretation and mediation, or limited motivation may bring about stimulus deprivation and, with it, limitations in the development of intelligence.

A number of factors prevent a systematic accumulation of data on the effects of deprivation. The ethics of using human subjects clearly and appropriately prevents experimental manipulation of stimulus deprivation in a manner that may harm subjects (Drew, Hardman, & Hart, 1996; Gelfand et al., 1997). Occurrences of natural events that result in environmental deprivation are unsystematic and involve such situational variation that investigation of these instances provides data of only limited value. Studies like those on early visual deprivation are few and have become even more so as a result of advances in medical technology. Because of these impediments to studying deprivation, many researchers have turned to the study of stimulus enrichment in an effort to gather evidence about the influence of environmental sensory stimuli on the development of intellectual functioning. One approach to this type of investigation compares the functioning of young children who, as infants, received a natural wealth of sensory stimulation with that of children who were relatively deprived of such environmental stimulation. Although the evidence suggests some differential effect, the data are too global for inflexible conclusions. Even these investigations are not free of difficulties because, in many cases, it is unclear that presence or relative absence of environmental stimuli is the only influential variable.

Some investigators have attempted to manipulate sensory stimulation experimentally during the first few years of life (e.g., Gofin, Adler, & Palti, 1996). In large part, such studies have focused on the influences of visual stimulation during the early months of life and have demonstrated that controlled stimulation has marked effects on the rate and quality of specific aspects of development. Once again, the question whether such effects are lasting or significant with respect to the quality of future intellectual functioning remains unanswered in a clear fashion. Some results suggest that long-term effects are promising. One project generating considerable interest is the Carolina Abecedarian Project. This research involved comprehensive intervention in a variety of family environmental areas and also included direct infant stimulation (Bryant & Maxwell, 1997). As with most longitudinal research of this type, results continue to emerge. However, the findings appear quite favorable regarding improvements in intellectual and social functioning. Additional investigation clearly is needed in this area.

As additional research is conducted on nervous system stimulation it may be possible to draw more accurate conclusions regarding relationships of system development and later intellectual functioning. Such information is vital in assessing the vulnerability of the nervous system to the environment during the first 2 years of life. At this time, we can safely conclude that sensory stimulation is beneficial in affecting the rate and perhaps the quality of all traits that depend on development of the neuromotor system.

Professional and Parental Intervention

Core Concept

Early intervention often demands partnerships between professionals and parents.

Professionals working with infants and young children face multiple tasks in providing services. Minimally, these include the identification of children with developmental delays, prevention of the occurrence of delays when possible, and assistance to family and child when a developmental problem is present. Health-care workers are the professionals most often in contact with young children, particularly physicians and public-health nurses. These individuals frequently depend on the aid and cooperation of social workers, nutritionists, and dietitians to assist in providing comprehensive services to families with multiple problems and needs.

Screening is a very important process in the overall evaluation scheme (see Chapter 3) and is crucial for identifying children who may be exhibiting delays in rate and quality of development. Routine health care is essential for the child's well-being and development. During the first 6 months of life, a youngster should receive monthly checkups, with intervals increasing gradually until the child is seen annually. Health-care visits should include an assessment of the child's behavior at home since the last visit, health status, and eating patterns. Also, physical systems should be evaluated, including the neuromotor system, to determine whether development is adequate, and behavioral observations should be made to confirm the appearance of behavioral landmarks at each appropriate age. Each visit also should include discussion and guidance sessions with the child's parents on the subjects of developmental and health status. Finally, the child should receive immunizations to prevent serious contagious disease, and blood and urine tests should be made at regular intervals. The family should have developmental guidance to help prevent accidents and alleviate conditions that could lead to problems.

The routine health care just described is an important means of identifying unexpected developmental problems, but it becomes even more critical for the family of a child once a problem has been identified. Both the child with mental retardation and the family need a great deal of support and assistance to meet the challenges of daily care and health maintenance. The health-care team is well equipped to provide such assistance.

Prevention of mental retardation has always been what professionals in the field have sought to achieve. It is not, however, a subject whose principles are easy to grasp, nor is it one that is free of controversy (see Chapter 13). One of the major difficulties in conceptualizing prevention lies with the field of mental retardation. Mental retardation, as a condition, is an extremely heterogeneous phenomenon. It varies greatly in terms of causation, severity, environmental circumstances, and professional disciplines concerned. By now, the reader is well aware that mental retardation is a problem with many facets; it is sociocultural, psychological, biomedical, and much more. The complex nature of the problem makes conceptualizing prevention in any sort of global fashion most difficult. However, some notable, if limited, successes have occurred in prevention.

Screening and treatment for the enzyme-deficiency disease PKU (see Chapter 6) is a classic example of an instance in which a definite problem and subsequent treatment can result in preventing or reducing the effects of mental retardation (Waisbren et al., 1998). Continued assistance from the health-care team is critical. The child must be placed on a very restricted and expensive diet

Health-care assessment is important to the well-being of this youngsters development.

to offset the enzyme deficiency. This expense puts certain pressures on the family, and maintenance of adequate and balanced nutrition for the child and the entire family can become a serious problem. The child's health also can be in jeopardy because of increased susceptibility to infection and other factors.

Well-defined prevention programs like those implemented with PKU are scarce. But theories and research results have stimulated considerable interest among health-care workers in identifying families and children who are at risk because of inadequate environmental stimulation (Young, Davis, Schoen, & Parker, 1998). Health-care workers are often the only professional people in contact with such families on any systematic basis, so the task of identification of problems is most logically approached from a health-care standpoint. Nurses and child-development specialists have begun programs of environmental stimulation and enrichment in many communities. As the programs develop, research evidence will be forthcoming and will, it is hoped, add to our understanding of the effectiveness of this type of intervention.

The idea of enhanced stimulation is also generating increased interest in intervention beyond the prevention arena. When a child is identified as already having mental retardation and being developmentally disabled, health-care workers and child-development specialists have often begun infant stimulation programs to make the most of the child's development. As research findings suggest, such intervention in field settings has resulted in notable progress (Bryant & Maxwell, 1997; Crnic & Stormshak, 1997; Hardman, Drew, & Egan, 1999). Children normally expected to be delayed in physical neuromotor development have shown impressive acceleration in physical development. For example, a child with Down syndrome is typically delayed by several weeks or months in all aspects of neuromotor development. These delays in young Down children and other youngsters with mental retardation typically include sitting, crawling, walking, talking, eating, and a number of social behaviors (Spiker & Hopmann, 1997).

The focus of infant stimulation programs is systematic, planned stimulation of the infant in all sensory modalities. The desired result of such programming is acceleration of the child's development so that these skills appear at a time more nearly consistent with that of normal children of the same chronological age. All six perceptual systems should be stimulated, but multiple stimulation is not necessarily undertaken at any single session; one perceptual system at a time may be stimulated on a given occasion. This progression is often done to enhance clarity and specificity for parents, who frequently are involved heavily in program implementation and act as important interveners (Guralnick, 1997). At some point during the program, however, each of the senses is the focus of stimulation, including sight, hearing, touch, kinesthetic movement, smell, and taste. Thus, the parent may be instructed to strike a particular kitchen pot with a spoon near the infant, to rattle a toy, and generally to present as many hearing stimuli as possible to attract the infant's attention. As the infant responds, other perceptual systems may be stimulated, and the same stimuli are repeated but at different distances from the child. Frequently, the next step involves engaging the infant in active participation in the stimulation program. The child may be encouraged to hold the sound-producing spoon, to move the rattle, to manipulate soft cotton or a hard rock, and other such activities.

Most children born into families who are not living in poverty receive a wealth of stimulation in all sensory modalities. Such stimulation is a routine part of their environment and results from ordinary interactions and activities of the family. For the most part, these infants are wanted and loved; they are held and carried, cuddled, talked to, placed near the activities of the other children and adults in the family, and taken in the car for trips into the community. These are all a natural part of each day's activities. However, many infants are born into environments lacking some or all of the features often taken for granted by the average middle-class family. The world of such children may have substantially less stimulation than is characteristic of many middle-class environments. During their early months, they may spend a great deal of time alone, in a room with little color, and with limited interaction with other people. When they are fed or changed, they may be handled only briefly, and the bottle often may be propped beside them instead of handheld. Early experience beyond this meager environment may not exist at all for many children.

Other situations may result in reduced stimulation. For example, a relative lack of stimulation may be offered to the child born with a significant physical disability, even if the family is not of limited means. Such a child may be difficult for the family to look at or to interact with and, consequently, may be excluded from some family activities. This child is not the beautiful baby the family anticipated, and they may not wish to carry him or her into the community to participate in routine activities.

Establishing a planned sequence of stimulation for such infants is one type of effort to provide an environment that more closely resembles the rich experience that children must have for normal development. The justification for such a program does not rest on the valuation of a lifestyle found in "middle" America. Instead, it is based on the belief, reinforced by accumulating evidence, that stimulation and early intervention are of benefit to the child's intellectual development. Stimulation programs draw heavily on the child's home environment regardless of socioeconomic level. A family of limited income in a home with modest furnishings can provide interaction patterns and sensory stimulation as beneficial as those found in a family with greater means.

LANGUAGE DEVELOPMENT

Core Concept

During the early childhood years, mental retardation is likely to become evident in language development.

Mental retardation is manifested in a variety of ways and in a number of behavioral domains as evidenced by the current definition (AAMR, 1992). Perhaps the most serious and obvious deficit involves delayed language development (Berk, 1998; Owens, 1996). Expressive language even may be completely absent. Parents and teachers commonly attribute most, if not all, of the child's learning problems to language deficiencies.

Normal Language Development

Table 7–2 provides some guidelines for normal developmental landmarks, including language and prelanguage behaviors. The normal progression of language development is an important indicator of general cognitive maturation. A newborn usually is expected to cry, to make other generalized sounds, and to be cooing and babbling by 3 to 6 months. First words generally appear as babbling from 9 to 14 months, and simple sentences are formed by 18 to 24 months. Basic syntactical structures are usually in place by 3 to 4 years, and speech sounds are articulated correctly, in context, by 4 to 8 years of age. This progression suggests that for a normal child, the basic language structure is largely complete sometime between 4 and 8 years of age (Berger & Thompson, 1998). Certainly, as maturation continues beyond this point, language facility also tends to grow and expand, but such growth is largely an embellishment of existing structures.

TABLE 7–2
Normal Language and Prelanguage Development

Age	Behavior
Birth	Crying and making other physiological sounds
1 to 2 months	Cooing, as well as crying
3 to 6 months	Babbling, as well as cooing
9 to 14 months	Speaking first words, as well as babbling
18 to 24 months	Speaking first sentences, as well as words
3 to 4 years	Using all basic syntactical structures
4 to 8 years	Articulating correctly all speech sounds in context

The process involved in language development has been the source of considerable theoretical debate. A substantial portion of this debate began in 1957 with the publication of B. F. Skinner's *Verbal Behavior.* It was Skinner's contention that verbal behavior is behavior reinforced through the mediation of other people who themselves have a prolonged history that has conditioned them in ways of "precisely" reinforcing the speaker (Skinner, 1957). The mediation of others and the reinforcing consequences continue to be important to maintenance of verbal behavior after initial acquisition. This view of language development is at variance with other theories that contend that language is an innate capacity specific to the human species and dependent on the maturation of the brain and nervous system. Part of the innate capacity argument is based on the fact that the onset of language occurs in children at a similar age in all cultures of the world despite enormous cultural differences. This view often carries the assumption that teaching cannot result in language acquisition unless an individual has the innate biological propensity for language. Compromise theories

Early communication by an infant usually indicates a basic need.

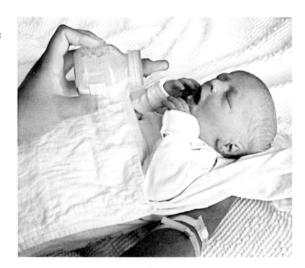

also presume a role for both learning and innate capacity (Bernstein, 1997; Hancock & Kaiser, 1996; Plumert & Nichols-Whitehead, 1996).

Theoretical debates concerning language development have enriched our considerations of how it occurs. Although it is unfortunate that so much energy has been expended in controversy and refutation, the value of different opinions should not be overlooked. Each of the theories contributes substantially, and the various hypotheses will likely blend in some fashion in the future as the process of normal language development continues to be unraveled.

Delayed Language Development

Language development is commonly delayed among children with mental retardation. Scales to measure language development of the child with mental retardation specifically have not received widespread attention, although clinical assessment of language functioning has long been a concern (Owens, 1997; Robinson & Robb, 1997; Silliman & James, 1997). Normative language development instrumentation is useful insofar as it helps identify the extent of the delay or deficiency. Numerous language development instruments have been constructed over the years (see Chapter 3). Some of these scales include the phonological (sound), semantic (meaning), morphological (word form), and syntactical (word order) skills acquired by normal children. All of these areas of assessment are important in evaluating language development both for children who appear to be progressing normally and for those who exhibit delay. For the most part, language development scales focus on the period from birth to 5 or 10 years of age. Such instrumentation provides a useful armory for those concerned with language development and particularly delayed or deficient language development.

Delayed language development presents a difficult problem, particularly for those with mental retardation in contemporary society (Owens, 1996, 1997). Exactly how delayed language relates to reduced intellectual functioning, or mental retardation, is unclear. Delayed language development is not a simple characteristic; it may be extremely obvious and debilitating, or it may be subtler (Bernstein, 1997; Leonard, 1998). For children with mental retardation, it presents some particular challenges.

For years, professionals have attempted to counteract language delay in children with mental retardation. Unfortunately, language rehabilitation efforts with this population lagged for many years because of the attitudes and perceptions of many speech and language specialists. A substantial number of such specialists have opposed working with those having mental retardation on the grounds that speech and language rehabilitation is almost impossible for these individuals. Such attitudes, although regrettable, are somewhat understandable in view of some of the theories about language development. If one believes that language development is innate to humans, many children with mental retardation are inappropriate subjects for speech and language therapy because language may not appear to be innate to them. Other theoretical schemes offer a more optimistic outlook for children with mental retardation. For example, B. F. Skinner's research provides a strong theoretical basis for working with children whose language skills fail to develop normally. Evidence is accumulating that language development during the early years is directly influenced by learning and social-experiential factors for children with mental retardation, as it is for their normal peers (Bernstein, 1997; Szagun, 1997).

Skinner's ideas have been the basis for a number of efforts at language rehabilitation for youngsters with mental retardation. Several approaches have focused on the establishment of imitative repertoires in children with retardation in order to facilitate speech and language development. These procedures have often had promising results. Although details vary from technique to technique, major characteristics include the following:

1. Imitation apparently can be learned by children who initially did not have significant imitative behavioral repertoires.
2. Imitation combined with differential reinforcement can be used to train for both simple naming or labeling and generative repertoires of plurality, simple sentences, and verb tense usage.
3. Imitation can be regarded as a particular type of learning set that exemplifies the rule "Do as the model does."
4. Language development and consequent behavior that is rule-governed can be fairly directly related to the simple training procedures of differential reinforcement and fading, which teach a child to match a series of different behaviors that are modeled.
5. A child with a widely generalized imitative repertoire can be significantly influenced by language models in the environment. Such generalization is essential to the normal acquisition of speech and language.

Some of these results have prompted programming approaches to language development stimulation that can alter the course of progress for some with mental retardation. Interestingly, it appears that effective language intervention occurs best when it is close to the natural environment, involving parents and others rather than depending only on language specialists (Tiegerman-Farber, 1997; Weiss, 1997).

COGNITIVE DEVELOPMENT

Core Concept

Cognitive development during infancy and early childhood involves many complex processes, including some in areas in which children with mental retardation have great difficulty.

An individual's developing capacity to formulate thoughts is referred to as **cognitive development.** Ordinarily, **perception** refers to sensory experiences received from the environment, whereas **cognition** is used for the meaning and thought patterns that emerge as a result of combinations of perceptions. The purposes of this book are well served by these definitions, although the explanations vary, depending on the context and the authority consulted. In this section, we discuss the work of selected theorists who have examined cognitive development and its implications for mental retardation.

Theoretical Formulations

Cognitive development theory has been substantially enriched by the work of Jean Piaget. We already have mentioned his work in previous chapters. Despite certain theoretical criticisms, Piaget's work remains worthy of discussion in the context of cognitive development. Unlike most theorists, Piaget was interested primarily in the functions and structures of intelligent activity, rather than the content of intelligence per se. He outlined stages of intelligence development that change both quantitatively and qualitatively throughout the developmental period. It was Piaget's contention that although different children progress through various stages at different rates, the sequence is always the same. Piaget's developmental stages are marked by the most recently emerging capability of the child. It is important to remember, however, that behaviors and processes preceding a given stage continue to occur and may be more intense and frequent than the newly emerging function.

Piaget provides an interesting framework from which to view cognitive development in children with mental retardation. It is speculated that these children, particularly those who are only mildly affected, do progress through Piaget's developmental stages, although somewhat more slowly than other children. The progression is demonstrable even though most individuals with retardation do not seem to develop spontaneously beyond Piaget's first two periods—sensorimotor and concrete operations. Thus, children with mental retardation often have cognitive structures more typical of chronologically younger children.

From Piaget's perspective, a child's cognitive capacities unfold naturally, although the influence of the environment is substantial. Through adaptation to the environment, a child shapes the exact nature of structures that unfold. His or her readiness to develop the next sequence of intellectual structures is governed largely by neurological capacity or readiness, whereas the stimulus for actual progression into the next stage comes from the environment. This view of cognitive development appears to have important implications for teaching children with mental retardation because education should present an environment that stimulates development of maximum potential. For Piaget, conceptualization of an idea precedes verbalization. In other words, children must experience and understand a phenomenon actively in the real world before they are able to put the event into words and demonstrate mastery of the problem. Children who have opportunities to encounter life experiences appropriate to their stage of cognitive development can be assisted in growth and development of cognitive potential through environmental stimulation. As scientists continue sorting out the interactions between system maturation and the environment, we may find that developing cognitive abilities can be a more central focus of the teaching process than it has been in the past (Bonaiuto & Fasulo, 1997; Ruffman, Perner, Naito, Parkin, & Clements, 1998).

The development of cognitive ability in individuals with mental retardation has been of great interest to behavioral scientists for many years. As discussed in Chapter 4, a number of recent theoretical developments in the area of intelligence have occurred (e.g., Gardner, Kornhaber, & Wake, 1996; Sternberg, 1997a, b). As these concepts receive additional attention from the research community, it will be interesting to see how they influence perceptions of the cognitive development in mental retardation at various levels. For example, some earlier theories held that individuals with more severe mental retardation fixate at the level of sensorimotor intelligence. From this view, such individuals simply repeat over and over the innate behaviors that are observed at birth, with very little knowledge of the objects with which they interact. Others who advance further in their development may be more closely oriented to the world around them, recognize familiar objects, and demonstrate intentionality in their behavior. They may be able to use trial-and-error experimentation with objects to produce a novel effect. Clearly, those who are less affected develop to more advanced stages, although they, too, are limited in their conceptions of such abstractions as time, space, and reality. It is anticipated that theoretical formulations of cognitive development for those with mental retardation will change as the more current conceptions of intelligence mature. The development of conceptual knowledge by children with mental retardation remains of interest to researchers and has both theoretical and practical implications (Leonard, 1998; Owens, 1997).

Implications for Professional Intervention

Early childhood specialists represent the professional group that is perhaps most concerned with the cognitive development of the preschool child, whether that child has mental retardation or is of normal intelligence. The primary goal of early childhood education is to provide an environment that stimulates maximum social and cognitive development. We already have examined the important implications of early environment for the development of optimal intellectual functioning later in life. As children progress beyond the age of 2, environmental stimulation appears to play a different role in their development. During the first 2 years, general stimulation in a wide variety of areas seems to affect individuals' ultimate level of functioning. For example, such factors as the involvement of family members are strongly related to many aspects of cognitive development (Berger & Thompson, 1998; Ruffman et al., 1998; Weiss, 1997). As the child enters the preschool period at 3, 4, and 5 years of age, general sensory stimulation does not produce the same benefits. Instead, more specific experiences with particular and focused stimulation become influential in the child's progress. Conceptualization grows out of environmental experiences, and the child develops the capacity to represent events symbolically in both thought and language.

The objective of the early childhood education specialist is to provide specific tangible experiences that are consistent with the child's cognitive capacity and that stimulate development of cognitive structures. The initial challenge for the educational specialist working with a preschooler who has mental retardation is to understand the child's level of cognitive development. If, for example, the child is functioning at the sensorimotor stage but has potential for development into the preoperational thought period, the specialist may direct efforts toward preparing the child for preoperational thinking. The child may be given experiences with a variety of spatial problems, such as physical activities that provide a contrast between objects in the environment and the child, and a recognition of how these objects can be manipulated and experienced in a consistent, predictable manner. Through such techniques, the education specialist may build a program for the young child that facilitates progression into the next cognitive stage of development. Early intervention programs are important to the developmental progression of young children with mental retardation (e.g., Guralnick, 1997).

PSYCHOSOCIAL DEVELOPMENT

Core Concept

Developmental problems in social and emotional functioning can have a serious impact on a young child's ability to adapt and chances to succeed.

A young child's growth and development involve many different components. All elements are essential to the whole with respect to development, and each is interrelated in complex ways. Psychosocial development is a vital process for all young children regardless of intellectual capacity. The development of social and emotional functioning has pervasive effects on children's intellectual functioning. When children have a serious problem in psychosocial development, it is likely to have a significant impact on their development of intellectual potential (Crick & Dodge, 1994). Thus, the development of psychosocial functioning represents a growth component of importance. In what follows, we explore some theoretical positions that are of interest in the context of the preschool period. Although broad, sweeping theories have practical limitations, they do provide general frameworks for viewing development. We examine the potential intellectual functioning of children of normal intelligence, as well as preschool-age children with mental retardation, to provide contrasting viewpoints.

Theoretical Formulations

Theories of psychosocial development are somewhat different from those in other behavioral domains. In many cases, the topics under discussion are extremely abstract, less specific with respect to behavioral definitions, and more difficult to measure (Berger & Thompson, 1998). However, they are still worth discussing, and very few readers will deny that these abstract concepts represent some behavioral reality.

Development of Trust, Autonomy, and Initiative.   Erik H. Erikson viewed child development primarily from a psychoanalytical perspective. Erikson (1968) hypothesized that infancy is the time of the child's first social achievement: basic trust. To the extent that his or her parents provide nurturance, familiarity, security, and continuity of experience, an infant can develop a basic sense of trust in both the immediate environment and the people in it. An infant's behavior reflects constant testing, experimenting, and exploring of the world to discover its predictability or the extent to which it can be trusted. Erikson believed that when an adequate mothering relationship is not present, an infant develops a sense of mistrust of the environment and the people in it. He also contended that such an experience is irreversible and influences the evolution of all subsequent stages. Clearly, all infants experience trust and mistrust to some degree; it is the predominance of one over another that is critical for successful completion of this first stage.

The maturing of autonomy and initiative also is involved in Erikson's depiction of emotional development during early childhood. Initially, children undergo a struggle to attain autonomy—a sense of self and of separateness. As part of this process, they must overcome the hazards of doubt and shame. They learn to exercise control over the processes of having and letting go. The family environment offers restraint and freedom in an appropriate balance to permit young children to experiment without becoming the victims of indiscriminate use of the abilities to hold on and to let go. As this process evolves, children develop a sense of autonomy, which is important in further development of independent functioning. Development of independence is an important step in a youngster's maturation. Failure to do so may be due to a number of complex factors (e.g., parenting, interactions with others) and can result in a personality that is overly dependent (Johnson, 1997).

Erikson also conceived of a second stage in early childhood, beginning at about the end of the 3rd year. This stage involves the struggle to gain a sense of initiative and to overcome the difficulties of guilt. The difference between this and the establishment of autonomy is likened to the difference between knowing oneself and knowing one's potential. At this point, children develop a sense of conscience, which is the regulatory or control function of the personality. If this function is overdeveloped, they may become too inhibited and even self-destructive, with a diminished capacity for creativity and initiative. As with all developmental processes, the desirable outcome is dominance of the positive task.

Development of Attachment.   Another important emotional component of personality relates to attachment. Infancy is a crucial period for the emergence of attachment behavior (Berger & Thompson, 1998; Santrock, 1997). As attachment evolves, the behaviors of the mother and other significant individuals are often caretaking behaviors. The infant's behavior reflects efforts to maintain proximity to the mother first and then to other members of the family, who, in turn, reciprocate the expressed needs for proximity. An older infant maintains proximity in many specific ways, although five basic patterns emerge: sucking, clinging, following, crying, and smiling. Some of these behaviors are evident at birth but are not manifested as self-directed attachment behavior until about the age of 4 months. As development progresses, an infant exhibits sophisticated goal-directed systems of behavior to maintain proximity to the mother. These systems of behavior usually become apparent between 9 and 18 months.

Visual and tactile contacts are crucial for the development of attachment behavior. The nature of visual and tactile interactions provides an important indication of the adequacy of attachment formation. Using the mother as a base of security from which to operate, the infant explores the larger world but maintains visual contact during the process. Tactile contact is reestablished periodically, and then exploration continues. When the child becomes frightened, distressed, or uncomfortable for any reason, he or she tries to stay close to the mother by clinging and following. When a serious threat of separation occurs, intense anxiety, anger, and violent distress result. These feelings and behaviors remain strong throughout infancy and are quite apparent during early childhood, although they lessen in intensity.

Environmental Antecedents to Self-Esteem. There has long been an interest in better understanding the influence of environmental factors on emotional and social development. Theories in this area have typically not been oriented toward child development, although their implications for infants and young children are evident (Santrock, 1997; Vander-Zanden, 1997). Early theorists have suggested that individuals need a psychological atmosphere of unconditional positive regard in order to develop to their full potential. This type of atmosphere must come from the significant others in the environment and involves total and unconditional acceptance of the feelings and values of the young child. It does not mean, however, that others must always agree with the child; they must only accept the feelings and values as real to the child. Evaluative comparison, rejecting judgments, lack of trust, and harsh punishment lead to the development of a child's underlying doubts about worthiness and competence and may block the development of self-esteem, acceptance, and assurance.

Parents and other family members play important roles in the early development of self-esteem, as they do in other areas (Berk, 1997; Ruffman et al., 1998). Children whose families give them the feeling that they mean a lot to their parents tend to develop high levels of self-esteem. Parental attention and concern, as well as restrictions on behavior, can convey such feelings. In this type of familial environment, the children are made aware of their successes, and they experience frequent success in their efforts toward development and learning. But children in these families are also made aware of situations in which they have not succeeded and are encouraged to develop the behavioral changes needed to achieve success and approval. High self-esteem seems to be related to a high level of stimulation, activity, and vigor in the family. Typically, members of the family maintain a high level of communication, including differences of opinion, dissent, and disagreement, leading to the development of mutual knowledge and respect.

Implications for Intellectual Functioning

Many of the factors of major concern in psychosocial development are also important components of intellectual functioning. For example, the role of early stimulation is immediately apparent in both psychosocial and intellectual domains (Berger & Thompson, 1998). Personality theorists focus on the crucial relationship of the infant or young child with at least one significant adult who provides the necessary care and love for the child. The child receives this adult's attention and affection primarily through the sensory channels that are so critical in the development of intellectual functioning. Thus, it appears that a significant interaction or interdependence must occur between the development of psychosocial and intellectual functions, although the precise nature of this relationship is not known. Children who are victims of potential restriction of intellectual development through environmental deprivation are also likely to exhibit signs of attenuated emotional development. Such concomitant developmental inadequacies may be evident simply because of missing elements in vital sensory stimulation. A child who is unable to develop adequate emotional security, self-esteem, or social relationships with family members and peers is also likely to be inhibited in intellectual performance. Whether the inhibiting influence becomes permanent or significant is likely the result of interaction among a number of factors. We do know, however, that supporting optimal psychological development in early life has a favorable influence on the child's ability to function intellectually (Berger & Thompson, 1998; Guralnick, 1998).

There is relatively little understanding of specific psychosocial development in the infant or preschooler with mental retardation. These children seem to show developmental lags in the psychosocial features discussed. They remain dependent and relatively immature in social interactions for a prolonged period. It is not clear, however, whether this developmental lag arises from the intimately related neurological bases for both areas of development or whether an environmentally generated psychosocial delay arises from lack of interaction with significant adults. It seems reasonable to assume that young children with mental retardation might exhibit psychosocial delays similar to their cognitive ones. All efforts possible should be made to sustain optimal psychosocial development for children with mental retardation.

Professional Intervention

Psychosocial development is no less important for the child with mental retardation than for the child of normal intelligence. Professionals working with children who have retardation must be as concerned with this area of development as they are with cognitive domains (Bihm, Sigelman, & Westbrook, 1997; Siperstein, Leffert, & Wenz-Gross, 1997). Such a child may be particularly at risk in terms of adverse environmental influences on emotional development because of unfavorable parental reactions. The family may need assistance from mental-health specialists (psychologist, psychiatrist, psychiatric social worker) to facilitate the maintenance of optimal mental health and development for all family members. Both parents and child may have glaring needs. Professionals may provide short-term assistance and intervention during periods of crisis, such as at the time of the child's birth, when the diagnosis of mental retardation is confirmed, or during periods of intense physical, social, or emotional stress in the family. Long-term assistance or intervention may be needed if the family experiences unusual or prolonged stress leading to disorganization of the family unit. It may be difficult for the family to accept such assistance because it threatens the emotional integrity of the family unit and the individual members. Accepting assistance often means recognizing a need that is most difficult to acknowledge and, for many families, represents a weakness or failure that they shun. Friends, health-care professionals, and educators should be alert to signs of need for mental-health intervention and should help the family accept such assistance. The process of adaptation and accommodation by family members to a child with mental retardation is significant, multifaceted, and ongoing (Ryff & Seltzer, 1996; Smith, 1997).

In many cases, mental retardation is not apparent at birth. Under such circumstances, a family often becomes aware of the child's disability during the first months or years of life. It is not uncommon for family members to experience particular stress and crisis as they seek to allay their fears and restore their hopes for the normal, healthy baby they thought they had. These types of reactions are relatively common for several disability areas. The longer the family has lived with the belief that the child is healthy and normal, the more difficult the adjustment. Chapters 12 and 13 discuss further the difficult emotional problems that families of retarded children experience.

NEW ISSUES AND FUTURE DIRECTIONS

Changes in programs for young children with mental retardation are sweeping, particularly with the enactment of IDEA 97 (Public Law 105-17, Individuals with Disabilities Education Act amendments of 1997). IDEA 97 Part C defines eligible infants and toddlers as those under the age of 3 needing early intervention for either 1) a developmental delay in one or more of the areas of cognitive development, physical development, communication development, social or emotional development or 2) a diagnosis of physical or mental condition that has a high probability of resulting in developmental delay (Sec. 632[1]). Early intervention services provided for by IDEA 97 go beyond the child and are to be directed at the family's needs, presumably aimed at informing and empowering the family to participate in the development of an individualized family service plan (IFSP) (Berry & Hardman, 1998).

Parents are becoming increasingly active partners in early intervention, promoting the development of children with disabilities and those who are at risk. They have moved from an ancillary role to more central involvement in collaborative planning and implementation of many aspects of intervention with their children. The IFSP considers the child's needs in the context of overall family needs and dynamics (Hardman et al., 1999). In the future, treatment and other interventions for young children with mental retardation will continue to more centrally involve parents and other family members as participants in programming.

Any discussion of infancy and early childhood requires some attention to the effectiveness of early intervention programs aimed at enhancing children's development. This is particularly true for children with mental retardation and other children at risk for handicap or developmental delay. Interpretation of early intervention outcomes, however, is not an easy task. The expectations placed on such widespread undertakings as Head Start were probably unrealistic as we look back on them. But this does not mean that such programs or other early stimulation approaches are ineffective. Overall analyses of the influence of early intervention suggests substantial gains for both at-risk children and children with disabilities. Interpretations of individual studies must be viewed cautiously, and broad, sweeping generalizations about effects in single-study investigations are always suspect (Guralnick, 1997, 1998). Still, enthusiasm about the worth of early intervention remains high among professionals in early childhood development. We anticipate that early intervention programs will flourish in the future even as more caution is exercised with respect to expectations.

Future directions and issues for the young child with mental retardation also include important contributions from the medical field. Medical technology for this group of youngsters, as for others, is developing at a dramatic pace. Medical management of these children continues to require attention to their higher incidence of chronic health problems: seizures, congenital abnormalities, and susceptibility to infectious diseases. Research and development efforts in drug and gene therapy, nutrition, and surgery (e.g., repair of birth defects, shunt implantations) will continue to have a significant impact on infants and young children with mental retardation. Some medical treatments are unconventional in the sense that they are either experimental or raise ethical questions and controversy. One such procedure involves facial surgery with Down syndrome children for cosmetic purposes and also to improve oral function (aiding speech). The appearance-normalization aspect of this procedure has raised questions by some who believe it unnecessary. Perhaps even more unconventional is the application of cell therapy with Down syndrome children. This procedure involves the injection of fresh fetal lamb brain tissue into the young child. Proponents claim dramatic alteration of developmental characteristics; others note that evidence for such change is not available and urge caution. Although such procedures may seem so unusual as to stretch the imagination, it is important to remember that altering genetic material was similarly unthinkable only a few years ago.

Core Questions

1. How does the brain develop during infancy and early childhood?
2. How can one trace the development of myelinization from a behavioral standpoint in very young children?

3. How does the early development of sensory organs influence a young child's learning?

4. How might environmental deprivation of stimuli affect the cognitive development of young children and result in mental retardation?

5. How are parents potentially important in early childhood intervention programs?

6. How is early sensory stimulation important for both emotional and intellectual development?

7. How do parents and other family members influence the development of self-esteem in a child? How can they create an environment that promotes realistic views of self-worth for a young child?

8. How would Piaget see the cognitive developmental progress of individuals with and without mental retardation as the same?

Roundtable Discussion

Human development during infancy and early childhood is extremely important. Much that occurs at this stage of life provides a foundation for many later skills and abilities. Physiological systems are developing, and they interact with aspects of cognition, language, and social development in a complex fashion that ultimately comes together to present an individual's sum potential.

In your study group or on your own, examine how physiological growth and development relate to language, cognition, and social competence. Explore the role of the environment during this time, including aspects of parental interaction and behavior. Examine how parents can be important interveners and how they might contribute to mental retardation in a child. Describe how you might discuss early childhood development with potential parents in order to facilitate their lives as parents and field-based developmental specialists.

References

Als, H. (1997). Earliest intervention for preterm infants in the newborn intensive care unit. In M. J. Guralnick (Ed.), *The effectiveness of early intervention* (pp. 47–76). Baltimore: Paul H. Brookes.

American Association on Mental Retardation (AAMR). (1992). *Mental retardation: Definition, classification, and systems of supports* (9th ed.). Washington, DC: Author.

Berger, K. S., & Thompson, R. A. (1998). *The developing person through the life span* (4th ed.). New York: Worth.

Berk, L. E. (1998). *Development through the lifespan.* Boston: Allyn & Bacon.

Bernstein, D. K. (1997). Language development: The preschool years. In D. K. Bernstein and E. Tiegerman-Farber (Eds.), *Language and communication disorders in children* (4th ed., pp. 97–126). Boston: Allyn & Bacon.

Berry, J., & Hardman, M. L. (1998). *Lifespan perspectives on family and disability.* Boston: Allyn & Bacon.

Bihm, E. M., Sigelman, C. K., & Westbrook, J. P. (1997). Social implications of behavioral interventions for persons with mental retardation. *American Journal on Mental Retardation, 101,* 567–578.

Bonaiuto, M., & Fasulo, A. (1997). Rhetorical intentionality attribution: Its ontogenesis in ordinary conversation. *British Journal of Social Psychology, 36*(4), 511–536.

Bryant, D., & Maxwell, K. (1997). The effectiveness of early intervention for disadvantaged children. In M. J. Guralnick (Ed.), *The effectiveness of early intervention* (pp. 23–46). Baltimore: Paul H. Brookes.

Crick, N. R., & Dodge, K. A. (1994). A review and reformulation of social information-processing mechanisms in children's social adjustment. *Psychological Bulletin, 115,* 74–101.

Crnic, K., & Stormshak, E. (1997). The effectiveness of providing social support for families of children at risk. In M. J. Guralnick (Ed.), *The effectiveness of early intervention* (pp. 209–225). Baltimore: Paul H. Brookes.

Davidson, P., & Harrison, G. (1997). The effectiveness of early intervention for children with visual impairments. In M. J. Guralnick (Ed.), *The effectiveness of early intervention* (pp. 483–495). Baltimore: Paul H. Brookes.

Drew, C. J., Hardman, M. L., & Hart, A. W. (1996). *Designing and conducting research in education and social science*. Needham Heights, MA: Allyn & Bacon.

Durkin, M. S., Hasan, Z. M., & Hasan, K. Z. (1998). Prevalence and correlates of mental retardation among children in Karachi, Pakistan. *American Journal of Epidemiology, 147*, 281–288.

Erikson, E. H. (1968). *Identity, youth, and crisis*. New York: Norton.

Gardner, H., Kornhaber, M. L., & Wake, W. K. (1996). *Intelligence: Multiple perspectives*. Ft. Worth, TX: Harcourt Brace.

Gelfand, D. M., Jenson, W. R., & Drew, C. J. (1997). *Understanding child behavior disorders* (3rd ed.). Fort Worth, TX: Harcourt Brace.

Giannotti, A., Digilio, M. C., Mingarelli, R., Marino, B., & Dallapiccola, B. (1997). Progeroid syndrome with characteristic facial appearance and hand anomalies in father and son. *American Journal of Medical Genetics, 73*, 227–229.

Gofin, R., Adler, B., & Palti, H. (1996). Time trends of child development in a Jerusalem community. *Paediatric and Perinatal Epidemiology, 10*, 197–206.

Guralnick, M. J. (1997). Second-generation research in the field of early intervention. In M. J. Guralnick (Ed.), *The effectiveness of early intervention* (pp. 3–20). Baltimore: Paul H. Brookes.

Guralnick, M. J. (1998). Effectiveness of early intervention for vulnerable children: A developmental perspective. *American Journal on Mental Retardation, 102*, 319–345.

Hancock, T. B., & Kaiser, A. P. (1996). Siblings' use of milieu teaching at home. *Topics in Early Childhood Special Education, 16*, 168–190.

Hardman, M. L., Drew, C. J., & Egan, M. W. (1999). *Human exceptionality: Society, school, and family* (6th ed.). Needham Heights, MA: Allyn & Bacon.

Johnson, D. W. (1997). *Reaching out: Interpersonal effectiveness and self-actualization* (6th ed.). Boston: Allyn & Bacon.

Leonard, L. B. (1998). *Children with specific language impairment*. Cambridge, MA: MIT Press.

Moore, K. L., & Persaud, T. V. N. (1998). *The developing human: Clinically oriented embryology* (6th ed.). Philadelphia: W. B. Saunders.

Morlet, T., Collet, L., Duclaux, R., Lapillonne, A., Salle, B., Putet, G., & Morgon, A. (1995). Spontaneous and evoked otoacoustic emissions in pre-term and full-term neonates: Is there a clinical application? *International Journal of Pediatric Otorhinolaryngology, 33*(3), 207–211.

Owens, R. E., Jr. (1996). *Language development: An introduction* (4th ed.). Boston: Allyn & Bacon.

Owens, R. E., Jr. (1997). Mental retardation: Difference and delay. In D. K. Bernstein and E. Tiegerman-Farber (Eds.), *Language and communication disorders in children* (4th ed., pp. 457–523). Boston: Allyn & Bacon.

Plumert, J. M., & Nichols-Whitehead, P. (1996). Parental scaffolding of young children's spatial communication. *Developmental Psychology, 32*, 523–532.

Robinson, N. B., & Robb, M. P. (1997). Early communication assessment and intervention: An interactive process. In D. K. Bernstein and E. Tiegerman-Farber (Eds.), *Language and communication disorders in children* (4th ed., pp. 155–196). Boston: Allyn & Bacon.

Rolland-Cachera, M. F., Deheeger, M., & Bellisle, F. (1997). Nutrient balance and body composition. *Reproductive Nutritional Development, 37*, 727–734.

Ruffman, T., Perner, J., Naito, M., Parkin, L., & Clements, W. A. (1998). Older (but not younger) siblings facilitate false belief understanding. *Developmental Psychology, 34*, 161–174.

Ryff, C. D., & Seltzer, M. M. (1996). *The parental experience in midlife*. Chicago: University of Chicago Press.

Santrock, J. W. (1997). *Life-span development* (6th ed.). Dubuque, IA: Brown and Benchmark Publishers.

Silliman, E. R., & James, S. (1997). Assessing children with language disorders. In D. K. Bernstein and E. Tiegerman-Farber (Eds.), *Language and communication disorders in children* (4th ed., pp. 197–271). Boston: Allyn & Bacon.

Siperstein, G. N., Leffert, J. S., & Wenz-Gross, M. (1997). The quality of friendships between children with and without learning problems. *American Journal on Mental Retardation, 102,* 111–125.

Skinner, B. F. (1957). *Verbal behavior.* New York: Appleton-Century-Crofts.

Smith, G. C. (1997). Aging families of adults with mental retardation: Patterns and correlates of service use, need, and knowledge. *American Journal on Mental Retardation, 102,* 13–26.

Spiker, D., & Hopmann, M. R. (1997). The effectiveness of early intervention for children with Down Syndrome. In M. J. Guralnick (Ed.), *The effectiveness of early intervention* (pp. 271–305). Baltimore: Paul H. Brookes.

Sternberg, R. J. (1997a). The triarchic theory of intelligence. In D. P. Flanagan & J. L. Genshaft (Eds.), *Contemporary intellectual Assessment: Theories, tests, and issues* (pp. 92–104). New York: Guilford Press.

Sternberg, R. J. (1997b). Educating intelligence: Infusing the triarchic theory into school instruction. In R. J. Sternberg & E. L. Grigorenko (Eds.), *Intelligence, heredity, and environment* (pp. 343–362). New York: Cambridge University Press.

Szagun, G. (1997). A longitudinal study of the acquisition of language by two German-speaking children with cochlear implants and of their mothers' speech. *International Journal of Pediatric Otorhinolaryngology, 42,* 55–71.

Thibodeau, G. A., & Patton, K. T. (1997). *Structure & function of the body* (10th ed.). St. Louis: Mosby.

Tiegerman-Farber, E. (1997). Social cognition: The communication imperative. In D. K. Bernstein and E. Tiegerman-Farber (Eds.), *Language and communication disorders in children* (4th ed., pp. 26–59). Boston: Allyn & Bacon.

Vander-Zanden, J. W. (1997). *Human development* (6th ed.) New York: McGraw-Hill.

Waisbren, S. E., Chang, P., Levy, H. L., Shifrin, H., Allred, E., Azen, C., de la Cruz, F., Hanley, W., Koch, R., Matalon, R., & Rouse, B. (1998). Neonatal neurological assessment of offspring in maternal phenylketonuria. *Journal of Inherited Metabolic Diseases, 21,* 39–48.

Weiss, A. L. (1997). Planning language intervention for young children. In D. K. Bernstein and E. Tiegerman-Farber (Eds.), *Language and communication disorders in children* (4th ed., pp. 272–323). Boston: Allyn & Bacon.

Young, K. T., Davis, K., Schoen, C., & Parker, S. (1998). Listening to parents. A national survey of parents with young children. *Archives of Pediatric and Adolescent Medicine, 152,* 255–262.

Chapter 8

The Elementary School-Age Child with Mental Retardation

Core Concepts

- Challenges associated with mental retardation often become a reality for children during the school years.
- For children with moderate to profound mental retardation, deficits in intellectual and social functioning are evident before the school years.
- The intellectual development of the child with mental retardation can be described in terms of stages or periods of growth.
- The memory capabilities of children with mental retardation are deficient in comparison with those of their nondisabled peers.
- Distributed practice in a learning situation enhances the learning performance of children with mental retardation.
- Children with mental retardation are able to grasp concrete concepts in a learning situation much better than abstract concepts.
- Children with mental retardation develop learning sets at a slower rate than their nondisabled peers.
- Children with mental retardation may benefit from instruction in basic or functional academic programs.
- School-age children with mental retardation will need to develop and apply adaptive skills in such areas as communication, self-care, home living, social skills, community use, self-direction, health and safety, functional academics, leisure, and work.
- Children with mental retardation may become failure avoiders, rather than success strivers.
- The more severe the mental retardation, the greater the probability that the child will exhibit physical differences.
- Several genetic and environmental factors can contribute to health problems for children with mental retardation.
- The major provisions of IDEA focus on multidisciplinary and nonbiased assessment, a free and appropriate public education, an IEP, parental rights, and education in the least restrictive environment.
- Successful inclusion of students with mental retardation in regular education settings is dependent on the availability of both formal and natural supports.
- Regular class placement with support services includes both the consulting teacher and resource room models.
- Students with mental retardation may be educated in a part-time special education classroom in the regular school building.
- Full-time special education classes and special day schools are considered more restrictive educational settings for students with mental retardation.
- For students with mental retardation, learning in the school setting is a continual process of adaptation.
- Instruction in academic areas may include a foundation and/or a functional approach to learning.

- Adaptive skills are necessary to decrease an individual's dependence on others and to increase opportunities for school and community participation.
- Students with mental retardation often benefit from instruction that incorporates assistive technology devices or activities.
- Culturally different children with mental retardation need an educational experience that focuses on learning how to learn.
- Educational reform efforts that focus on individualization in the schools and the effectiveness of social integration will benefit students with mental retardation.

Core Concept

Challenges associated with mental retardation often become a reality for children during the school years.

The beginning of elementary school is generally an exciting time for both children and their parents. It is a time to make new friends and begin associations. Even for the "typical" child, the beginning of school is filled with uncertainty, as well as anticipation. For children with mental retardation and their families, school may be the beginning of or further enhance the challenges associated with disability. For many parents, the challenges of mental retardation first become a reality when their child enters school. A 6-year-old child with mild mental retardation may have a developmental delay of only about 1 year. This maturational lag may have been so slight during early childhood that it was viewed as insignificant or not even noticed by the parents and family physician. This often happens in the absence of physical or health problems. The child's differences surface when he or she is confronted with the academic and social demands of elementary school and may become compounded if proper educational services and supports are not provided. A teacher may attribute difficulties to immaturity and not refer the child for special education during early primary grades.

Core Concept

For children with moderate to profound mental retardation, deficits in intellectual and social functioning are evident before the school years.

Whereas deficits associated with mild mental retardation may not be apparent by the time the child enters school, conditions characterizing moderate, severe, and profound retardation are clearly evident. The term *education* takes on an entirely different meaning for these children. Before the passage of federal and state legislation in the 1970s, many children with moderate to profound retardation were excluded from public schools because they were unable to meet academic or social requirements. A different set of values has emerged over the past 25 years, establishing two goals for public education: (1) to raise the functioning level of the child to the next highest developmental level regardless of the severity of the disability and (2) to create through instruction an adaptive fit between the student and the learning environment (Hardman, Drew, & Egan, 1999). For children with severe mental retardation, the emphasis is not on academic learning but on the development and application of skills that increase independence within the school, home, and community (e.g., self-help skills, mobility, communication).

Intellectual development, learning, personality, emotional development, motivation, and physical health characteristics of children with mental retardation and related theories are discussed in this chapter. In most instances, these characteristics and theories are not limited to school-age children with mental retardation but may follow the individual throughout life. We elected to present these characteristics in this chapter because it is often at the beginning of formal schooling that many of them initially manifest themselves to professionals working with the individual with mental retardation.

COGNITIVE DEVELOPMENT

Core Concept

The intellectual development of the child with mental retardation can be described in terms of stages or periods of growth.

To gain some understanding of the cognitive development of the school-age child, we briefly return to the theory of Jean Piaget (1969). Piaget referred to the span from 2 to 7 years as the period of **preoperational thought** and the span from 7 to 11 years as the period of **concrete operation.** During the preoperations subperiod, perceptions are the child's dominant mental activity. At about the age of 7, the child begins to move into a period in which perceptions are dominated by intellectual operations, the dominant mental activity of the concrete operations period. The ability to order and relate experiences to an organized whole begins to develop. Rather than being bound to irreversibility, as before, the child begins to develop mobility in thought processes and can reverse some mental operations and return to the starting point.

By 4 years old, the child is less self-centered and more able to take into account another person's point of view. Instead of centering on a one-dimensional property of a situation, the child is able to focus on several properties in sequence and to move quickly from one to another. This phase is termed "concrete" because the child's mental operations still depend on the ability to perceive concretely what has happened. No mental experimentation can take place without prior perception. The basic ability from which concrete operations develop is the ability mentally to form ordering structures, which Piaget called **groupings** and **lattices.** Lattices are a special form of groupings in which the focus is on the connection between two or more objects and the objects that are connected. Using lattices, the child can develop a classification hierarchy system in which he or she can understand that all humans are animals but that not all animals are human.

Children begin to conserve numbers around the age of 7 years, to conserve quantity (substance, amount of space occupied by an object) around ages 7 or 8 years, and to conserve weight around 9 years of age.

During the preoperational period, the child's egocentrism is evident in conversations with other children. During this developmental period, conversations with other children of the same age consist of collective monologues. Each child pursues a private, personal conversation regardless of what the other child says. During the concrete operational period, however, these children begin to take into account the other child's point of view and to incorporate these views into their own conversations. Thus, more meaningful communication emerges, and the children carry on dialogue, each responding to what the other has just said.

Children with mental retardation move through the same states of development as their nondisabled peers but at a slower rate (Agran, Salzberg, & Stowitchek, 1987). School-age children with mild mental retardation are slower in progressing from the preoperational stage into concrete operations, with delays as long as 3 to 4 years. Children with moderate retardation may fixate at the preoperational level and not reach even the most basic stages of concrete operations until later adolescence. Children with severe and profound levels of mental retardation may fixate at the sensorimotor and preoperational stages and never reach the more advanced periods.

LEARNING CHARACTERISTICS

When children with mental retardation are compared with their nondisabled age-mates, they perform more poorly on tasks of learning and retention. Research on learning and mental retardation has increased dramatically since the early 1950s, but the understanding of how these individuals learn still needs considerable expansion. In this section, we discuss the learning characteristics of children with mental retardation. In addition, our attention is directed not only to the pertinent research in this area but also to some of its implications for classroom practice.

Memory

Core Concept

The memory capabilities of children with mental retardation are deficient in comparison with those of their nondisabled peers.

The greater the severity of intellectual deficit, the greater the deficits in memory. Memory problems in children with mental retardation have been attributed to several factors, including the inability to focus on relevant stimuli in a learning situation (Benson, Aberdanto, Short, Nuccio, & Mans, 1993; Westling & Fox, 1995).

Literature on the memory of learned material strongly indicates that ability is related to the type of retention task. Short-term memory, the ability to recall material over a period of seconds or minutes, has long been a topic of interest as it relates to children with mental retardation. Early work in the area drew a somewhat confusing picture. Some research suggested the performance of children with mental retardation was no different from that of nondisabled individuals; other work indicated quite the opposite. Many methodological limitations with this early memory research made interpretation very difficult (Drew, Hardman, & Hart, 1996). There is little question, however, that the child with mental retardation may take longer to understand the nature of a task than nondisabled peers. Procedures can be used in the classroom to compensate for these deficiencies (Stokes & Osnes, 1988; Westling & Fox, 1995). The following are some possible ways to enhance short-term memory skills in children with mental retardation:

1. Teach as often as possible in the setting where you want the behavior(s) to occur.
2. Reduce extraneous environmental stimuli, which tend to distract students, and increase stimulus value of the task.
3. Present each component of stimuli clearly and with equivalent stimulus value initially.
4. Begin with simpler tasks, moving to the more complex.
5. Avoid irrelevant materials within the learning task.
6. Label stimuli.
7. Minimize reinforcement to avoid interference from anticipation of reward.
8. Provide practice in short-term memory activities.
9. Integrate practice material with new subject fields, making use of the child's successful experiences.
10. Dramatize skills involving short-term memory, making them methodologically central to the program.

Studies on long-term memory in persons with mental retardation are even less conclusive than those on short-term memory. As before, although some researchers obtained results indicating long-term memory deficits, others found very different results. The research on long-term memory has been plagued by methodological problems similar to those on short-term memory.

More current research has moved away from the long- and short-term memory model. Much of the thinking in cognitive psychology has turned to information-processing theories for exploration of these capabilities. Information-processing theorists study how a person processes information from sensory stimuli to motor output (Sternberg, 1985, 1997). Sternberg and Spear (1985) described the memory deficits of people with mental retardation as the underdevelopment of metacognitive processes. Metacognitive processes are "used to plan how to solve a problem, to monitor one's solution strategy as it is being executed, and to evaluate the results of this strategy once it has been implemented" (p. 303). Even though children with mental retardation may be unable to use the best strategy when confronted with new learning situations, other researchers have suggested that they can be taught ways to do so (Agran, Fodor-Davis, Moore, & Deer, 1989; Borkowski, Peck, & Damberg, 1983; Glidden, 1985).

Self-Regulation

Self-regulation is the ability to regulate one's own behavior (Whitman, 1990). In order to regulate behavior, a person must be able to develop efficient learning strategies, such as the ability to rehearse a task (practice a new concept either out loud or to oneself over and over). While most people will rehearse to try to remember, it does not appear that individuals with retardation are able to apply this skill. Children with mental retardation appear to be unable to find, monitor, or evaluate the best strategy to use when confronted with a new learning situation. However, research suggests that they can be taught to change their control processes (Borkowski et al., 1983; Glidden, 1985).

Distribution of Practice

Core Concept

Distributed practice in a learning situation enhances the learning performance of children with mental retardation.

Many individuals appear to be able to function well by using massed practice, such as cramming for examinations. However, distributed practice, compared with massed practice, enhances the learning performance of children with mental retardation more than it does for individuals without cognitive disabilities (Mulligan, Guess, Holvoet, & Brown, 1980). The teacher should provide the child with mental retardation short but frequent practice sessions on day-to-day tasks. The teacher also should allow for practice in a variety of situations and contexts and for the meaningful introduction of overlearning. This should not only result in an increased rate of acquisition but also ensure a greater degree of retention.

Cipani and Spooner (1994) discussed the use of **naturally distributed trials**—that is, "trials that may occur as the skill would normally be performed in a natural school or home routine" (p. 89). Several authors have suggested that the use of naturally distributed trials may improve both acquisition of a skill and its generalization to another setting (Bambara, Warren, & Komisar, 1988; Neel & Billingsley, 1989; Westling & Fox, 1995).

Learning Concrete and Abstract Concepts

Core Concept

Children with mental retardation are able to grasp concrete concepts in a learning situation much better than abstract concepts.

The more concrete the material, the more apt the child with mental retardation is to learn. The teacher or parent may be advised to teach nothing with inanimate objects if the *natural*, real, living object is available. The child with mental retardation will grasp concepts more readily if the natural object, rather than a picture of the object, is present. Instead of reading and looking at pictures of buses, the child with mental retardation will learn more and faster if given the opportunity to ride a bus in his or her local community.

Learning Sets and Generalization

Core Concept

Children with mental retardation develop learning sets at a slower rate than their nondisabled peers.

Learning sets and generalization appear to be interrelated in a person's ability to solve problems. Whereas **learning set** refers to an individual's ability to learn how to learn, **generalization** happens "when a learned response is seen to occur in the presence of 'untaught' stimuli" (Cipani & Spooner, 1994, p. 157). *Generalization*, then, is the ability to apply learning from previous experiences to new situations with similar components.

Children with mental retardation develop learning sets at a slower rate than nondisabled children of comparable chronological age (Hughes, 1992; Turner, Dofny & Dutka, 1994; Stokes & Osnes, 1988). The formation of learning sets, however, can be facilitated in the classroom. Payne, Polloway, Smith, & Payne (1981) offered the following suggestions:

1. Prevent the development of failure sets that interfere with learning by providing for success experiences.
2. Present content to be learned in easy-to-hard progressions.
3. Present factual and conceptual information in sequence.
4. Assist the child in developing rules and generalizations (mediation strategies) to transfer learned information to new experiences.
5. Reinforce correct responses to stress successful experiences. (p. 29)

Generalization is described as the third stage of learning, following **acquisition** (learning to perform accurately) and **fluency building** (going beyond accuracy to efficiency) (Cipani & Spooner, 1994). Research suggests that for the child with mild mental retardation, the ability to transfer is not significantly impaired (Evans & Bilsky, 1979) but that children with moderate to severe levels of mental retardation exhibit deficiencies in this area (Fox, 1989; Haring, 1988). The following are some suggestions for working with the child with mental retardation who is deficient in the development of generalization skills:

1. Age seems to make a difference in the ability to generalize learning for all children, those with mental retardation and nondisabled. Younger children generalize learning with greater ease than older children.
2. The individual with mental retardation can generalize learning best when both the initial task and the new task are very similar. Generalization is most effective if a considerable number of the operations involved in the first task can be performed as a unit in the new task.

3. Meaningfulness is extremely important to the person's ability to generalize. A more meaningful task is both easier to learn initially and easier to generalize to a second setting.

Educational Achievement

Core Concept

Children with mental retardation may benefit from instruction in basic or functional academic programs.

Children with mild mental retardation require a systematic instructional program that accounts for differences in the rate of learning, but they may achieve as high as fourth- or fifth-grade level in reading and arithmetic. In a review of the literature on reading and mental retardation, Westling (1986) reported that "reading is generally considered the weakest area of learning, especially reading comprehension. Comparatively, students with mild mental retardation tend to do better on reading words than on understanding what they have read" (p. 127).

A significant relationship appears to exist between measured IQ and reading achievement. This relationship seems to suggest that reading instruction should be limited to higher functioning children with mental retardation. A growing body of research, however, indicates that children with mental retardation can be taught to read at least a protective, or survival, vocabulary-sometimes referred to as **functional reading**. Browder and Snell (1993) describe functional academics as the "skills to enhance independence in daily living" (p. 443). A functional reading program uses materials that are a part of a person's normal routines in work, everyday living, and leisure activities.

Children with mental retardation are also deficient in arithmetic skills, but the majority of those with mild retardation can learn basic addition and subtraction. However, these children will have significant difficulty in the areas of mathematical reasoning and problem-solving tasks (Beirne-Smith, Ittenbach, & Patton, 1998). Arithmetic skills are taught most efficiently through the use of money concepts. The immediate practical application motivates the student. Regardless of the approach used, arithmetic instruction must be concrete and practical to compensate for the child's deficiencies in reasoning ability.

ADAPTIVE SKILLS

Core Concept

School-age children with mental retardation will need to develop and apply adaptive skills in such areas as communication, self-care, home living, social skills, community use, self-direction, health and safety, functional academics, leisure, and work.

The AAMR (1992) identifies limits in adaptive skills as important criteria for defining mental retardation. For an individual to meet the criterion for mental retardation, limitations must occur in two or more applicable adaptive skill areas—communication, self-care, home living, social skills, community use, self-direction, health and safety, functional academics, leisure, and work. For educational purposes, **adaptive skill development** for the school-age child may be defined as the ability (or lack thereof) to apply basic information learned in school to naturally occurring daily activities. Depending on the age of the child with mental retardation, the need is to develop appropriate skills for coping in school, for developing interpersonal relationships, for developing language skills, for developing emotionally, and for taking care of personal needs (see Table 8–1).

The child with mild mental retardation may have difficulty in both learning and applying adaptive skills, due to distractibility, inattentiveness, failure to read social cues, and problem behaviors (Benavidez & Matson, 1993; Bergen & Mosley, 1994; Gresham & MacMillan, 1997; McAlpine, Kendall, & Singh, 1991; Merrill & Peacock, 1994). As such, these children will need to be taught appropriate reasoning, judgment, and social skills that lead to more positive social relationships and personal competence.

Siperstein and Leffert (1997) studied the social acceptance of children with mental retardation among nondisabled peers in regular education classrooms. The researchers identified the characteristics of 20 socially accepted and 20

Interacting with peers is important for children with mental retardation.

TABLE 8–1
Adaptive Skills of Children with Mental Retardation

Adaptive skill	Examples of skills needing possible training and support
Coping with the demands of school	Attending to learning tasks
	Organizing work tasks
	Following directions
	Managing time
	Asking questions
Developing interpersonal relationships	Learning to work cooperatively with others
	Responding to social cues in the environment
	Using socially acceptable language
	Responding appropriately to teacher directions and cues
	Enhancing social perception (drawing appropriate conclusions from experiences with others)
Developing language skills	Understanding direction
	Communicating needs and wants
	Expressing ideas
	Listening attentively
	Using proper voice modulation and inflection
Developing emotionally	Seeking out social participation and interaction
	Decreasing avoidance of work and social experiences (e.g., tardiness, idleness, social withdrawal)
Taking care of personal needs	Practicing appropriate personal hygiene
	Dressing independently
	Taking care of personal belongings
	Getting around from one place to another

socially rejected students with mental retardation. Characteristics of socially accepted children included a higher level of social skills. These children were not perceived by their nondisabled peers as aggressive in their behavior. The authors suggest there is value in recognizing and teaching the skills that distinguish between those children who are accepted and those who are not.

Adaptive skill deficits for children with more severe mental retardation may include head rolling, body rocking, twirling, teeth grinding, and inappropriate vocalizations. Children with severe retardation may also engage in self-injurious acts, including self-biting, head banging, and face slapping.

MOTIVATION

Core Concept

Children with mental retardation may become failure avoiders, rather than success strivers.

Children with mental retardation are often described as lacking motivation—an unwillingness or inability to initiate new tasks or complete existing ones, to take responsibility, and to be self-directed. In fact, this apparent lack of motivation may be more attributable to the way these children learn to avoid situations because of a fear of failure. The child, with a history of failure in school, may be afraid to take risks or participate in new situations. The result of failure is often learned helplessness, or the feeling that "no matter what I do or how hard I try, I will not succeed." To overcome learned helplessness, the child with mental retardation needs to have experiences that have high probabilities for success. The opportunity to seek success, rather than avoid failure, is a very important learning experience for these children.

Prestige, success, and self-respect, which fulfill the need for esteem, may be formidable goals for children with mental retardation. Although the child may never be able to match the accomplishments of their nondisabled peers, children with mental retardation can find considerable satisfaction and contentment in being the best at whatever they can do, in being well liked by both disabled and nondisabled peers, and in contributing to a better life for themselves and their families.

PHYSICAL AND HEALTH CHARACTERISTICS

Physical Differences

Core Concept

The more severe the mental retardation, the greater the probability that the child will exhibit physical differences.

The vast majority of children with mental retardation do not differ from nondisabled children in their physical appearance. A positive correlation does exist, however, between severity of intellectual deficit and degree of physical anomaly (APA, 1994). With more severe mental retardation comes a greater probability that the child will exhibit physical problems. Among children with mild mental retardation, no differences may be noticeable because the retardation is not usually associated with physiological factors. For more severely disabled children, physical differences are more evident and sometimes can be traced to biomedical conditions (e.g., Down syndrome, hydrocephaly).

Motor development of children with mental retardation may be significantly below the norms for children who are not disabled. Children with mental retardation are generally less developed in areas such as equilibrium, locomotion, and manual dexterity. Research has also suggested a higher prevalence of vision and hearing impairments among children with mental retardation (Hardman et al., 1999).

Speech problems as well are more prevalent among children with mental retardation (Bernstein & Tiegerman, 1993). In a study by Epstein, Polloway, Patton, & Foley (1989) of more than 100 students' individualized education programs (IEPs), speech and language problems were identified as the most frequent secondary disability to mental retardation. The most common speech problems are articulation, voice, and stuttering problems (Hardman et al., 1999). Fink (1981), in a survey of Oregon service providers, reported severe speech delays in nearly 90% of 1,700 children with mental retardation. Most children with severe and profound retardation have multiple disabilities, exhibiting difficulties in nearly every aspect of cognitive and physical development.

Health Differences

Core Concept

Several genetic and environmental factors can contribute to health problems for children with mental retardation.

Health problems for children with mental retardation may be associated with either genetic or environmental factors. For example, there is a higher probability that people with Down syndrome will have a higher incidence of congenital heart defects and respiratory problems directly linked to their genetic condition (Marino & Pueschel, 1996). On the other hand, some children with mental retardation experience health problems due to their living conditions. A significantly higher percentage of children with mental retardation come from low socioeconomic backgrounds in comparison to nondisabled peers. Children who do not receive proper nutrition and are exposed to inadequate sanitation have a greater susceptibility to infections. Health services for families in these situations may be minimal or nonexistent, depending on whether they are able to access government medical support. As such, children with mental retardation may become ill and end up being absent from school more often than their nondisabled peers.

EDUCATIONAL PROGRAMS AND PLACEMENT

The Individuals with Disabilities Education Act (IDEA)

Core Concept

The major provisions of IDEA focus on multidisciplinary and nonbiased assessment, a free and appropriate public education, an IEP, parental rights, and education in the least restrictive environment.

The education of students with mental retardation historically has meant segregated programs and services. Before the 1960s, most special education services were available only in self-contained classrooms that segregated the children with retardation from their nondisabled peers. Additionally, special education services were available primarily to the child with mild retardation who was defined as "educable," a term implying that although the child had mental retardation, he or she still could benefit from some of the traditional academic curriculum taught in the public schools. Children functioning at lower levels (as determined solely by IQ tests) generally were excluded from public schools because they required "training" in such areas as self-help, language development, gross-motor skills, and academic readiness. The needs of children labeled "trainable" were not within the purview of the public education curriculum. For children with more severe mental retardation, exclusion from the public schools was nearly universal. The pervading view was that these children needed habilitation, not education. Children with severe and profound retardation often were labeled "custodial," implying that care and management were the intended outcomes for these individuals.

The passage of the Education for All Handicapped Children Act (Public Law 94-142) in 1975 was the culmination of years of litigation dealing with discrimination against students with disabilities, including those with mental retardation, in this nation's schools. Public Law 94-142 (renamed the Individuals with Disabilities Education Act in 1990) mandated that all eligible children with disabilities in the nation's schools must be provided a *free and appropriate* public education. IDEA requires that these students, regardless of the extent or type of disability, receive at public expense the special education services necessary to meet their individual needs. Special education means specially designed instruction, at no cost to parents, provided in all settings (such as the classroom, in physical education, at home, and in hospitals or institutions). IDEA 97 stipulates that students with disabilities are to receive any related services necessary to ensure that they benefit from their educational experience. **Related services** include

> transportation, and such developmental, corrective, and other supportive services (including speech-language pathology and audiology services, psychological services, physical and occupational therapy, recreation, including therapeutic recreation, social work services, counseling services, including rehabilitation counseling, orientation and mobility services, and medical services, except that such medical services shall be for diagnostic and evaluation purposes only) as may be required to assist a child with a disability to benefit from special education, and includes the early identification and assessment of disabling conditions in children. (Sec. 602[22])

IDEA requires that in order to be eligible for special education services, a child must meet two criteria. First, the child must be identified as having one of the 13 disability conditions identified in federal law or their counterparts in a state's special education law. One of these conditions may be mental retardation. However, the 1997 amendments gave states and local education agencies (LEA) the option of eliminating categories of disability (such as mental retardation or specific learning disabilities) for children up to the age of 9. For this age group, a state or LEA may define a child with a disability as

> (i) experiencing developmental delays, as defined by the State and as measured by appropriate diagnostic instruments and procedures, in one or more of the following areas: physical development, cognitive development, communication development, social or emotional development, or adaptive development; and (ii) who, by reason thereof, needs special education
> and related services. (Sec. 602[3][B])

The second criteria for eligibility is the student's demonstrated need for specialized instruction and related services in order to receive an appropriate education. This need is determined by a multidisciplinary team of professionals and parents (discussed below). Both criteria for eligibility must be met. If this is not the case, it is possible for a student to be identified as being disabled but not eligible to receive special education services under federal law. These students may still be entitled to accommodations or modifications in their educational program under Section 504 of the Americans with Disabilities Act.

Originally, IDEA allowed states to exclude from the mandate all children under 5 years of age. In 1986, however, the provisions of the law were extended under Public Law 99-457, Education of the Handicapped Act Amendments, to children ages 3 to 5. Additionally, a new early intervention program for infants and toddlers was initiated.

In the 1994-95 school year, over 5.2 million students with disabilities, living in the United States, and between the ages of 3 and 21 years were served under IDEA. Of these 5.2 million students, about 12% (570,855) are defined as having mental retardation (U.S. Department of Education, 1997).

Specifically, the requirements of IDEA provide for the following:

- Nondiscriminatory and multidisciplinary assessment of educational needs
- A free and appropriate public education
- Development and implementation of an IEP for each student
- Parental involvement in the development of each student's educational program
- Education in the least restrictive environment

Nondiscriminatory and Multidisciplinary Assessment. The assessment provisions of IDEA required that students be tested in their native or primary language and that all evaluation procedures be free of cultural or racial discrimination. Assessment is to be conducted by a **multidisciplinary team** that works together in determining the needs of each child relative to a free and appropriate public education.

A Free and Appropriate Public Education (FAPE).   Every student with a disability is entitled to a free and appropriate public education (FAPE) based upon individual ability and need. The IDEA provisions related to FAPE are based on the Fourteenth Amendment to the U.S. Constitution, guaranteeing equal protection of the law. No student with a disability can be excluded from a public education based on a disability. In 1982, a major interpretation of FAPE was handed down by the U.S. Supreme Court in *Hendrick Hudson District Board of Education v. Rowley* (1982). The Supreme Court declared that an appropriate education consist of a "specially designed instruction and related services" that are "individually designed to provide educational benefit." Often referred to as the "some educational benefit" standard, the ruling mandates that a state need not provide an ideal education but must provide a beneficial one for students with disabilities.

The Individualized Education Program (IEP).   The individualized education program (IEP) is developed by professionals from the multidisciplinary team, parents, and the student, where appropriate. As per IDEA 1997, the team should consist of the student's parents, at least one special education teacher, at least one regular (general) education teacher if the child is, or may be, participating in the regular (general) education environment, and a representative of the LEA. The LEA representative must be qualified to provide or supervise the provision of specially designed instruction to meet the unique needs of children with disabilities. This individual must also be knowledgeable about the general curriculum and the availability of resources within the LEA.

At the discretion of the parents or the LEA, the IEP team may also include an individual who can interpret the instructional implications of evaluation results; other individuals who have knowledge or special expertise regarding the child may also participate in the IEP process, including related services personnel as appropriate and, whenever appropriate, the student with disability.

IDEA 97 requires that each child's IEP must include the following:

- Each child's IEP must include a statement of the child's present levels of educational performance, including how the child's disability affects involvement and progress in the general curriculum. For preschool children the statement must describe how the disability affects the child's participation in appropriate activities.
- It must include a statement of measurable annual goals, including benchmarks or short-term objectives related to meeting the child's needs that result from the disability. The annual goals should enable the child to be involved and make progress in the general curriculum and meet each of the child's other educational needs that result from the disability.
- It must include a statement of the special education and related services and supplementary aids or services to be provided to or on behalf of the child. The statement must include (1) any program modifications or supports for school personnel that will be provided for the child to advance

appropriately toward attaining the annual goals, (2) how the child will be involved and progress in the general curriculum and participate in extracurricular and other nonacademic activities, (3) how the child will be educated and participate with other children with disabilities and nondisabled children, and (4) an explanation of the extent, if any, to which the child will not participate with nondisabled children in the regular [general education] class and in the activities described above.

- The IEP must include a statement of any individual modifications in the administration of state or district-wide assessments of student achievement that are needed in order for the child to participate in such assessment. If the IEP team determines that the child will not participate in a particular state or district-wide assessment of student achievement (or part of such an assessment), there must be a statement of why that assessment is not appropriate for the child and how the child will be assessed.

- It must include the projected date for the beginning of the services and modifications, and the anticipated frequency, location, and duration of those services and modifications.

- Lastly, it must include a statement of how the child's progress toward the annual goals will be measured and how the child's parents will be regularly informed (by such means as periodic report cards), at least as often as parents are informed of their nondisabled children's progress, of their child's progress toward the annual goals. The statement should include the extent to which that progress is sufficient to enable the child to achieve the goals by the end of the year (Sec. 614[d]).

Parental Involvement. IDEA requires parent involvement in the IEP process for two reasons. First, the requirement creates an opportunity for parents to be more involved in decisions regarding their child's education program. Second, the student and the family are protected from decisions that could adversely affect their lives. Families would be more secure in the knowledge that every reasonable attempt was being made to educate their child appropriately.

Provisions under IDEA for parents granted them rights to the following:

- Consent in writing before the child is initially evaluated
- Consent in writing before the child is initially placed in a special education program
- A request for an independent education evaluation if they think the school's evaluation is inappropriate
- A request for an evaluation at public expense if a due-process hearing decision is that the public agency's evaluation was inappropriate
- Participation on the committee that considers the evaluation, placement, and programming of the child
- Inspection and review of educational records and to challenge information believed to be inaccurate, misleading, or in violation of the privacy or other rights of the child

- A request for a copy of information from their child's educational record
- A request for a hearing concerning the school's proposal or refusal to initiate or change the identification, evaluation, or placement of the child, or the provision of a free appropriate public education.

IDEA 97 added a new mandate to the requirements for parent involvement, requiring that schools regularly inform parents about their son or daughter's progress in meeting IEP goals and objectives. "Regularly inform" means as often as parents of students without disabilities are informed. Figure 8–1 lists 10 reasons why it is so important for schools to establish a collaborative partnership with parents.

Education in the Least Restrictive Environment (LRE).   Students with disabilities, including those with mental retardation, must be educated in the least restrictive environment (LRE). The LRE concept requires that all students with disabilities receive their education with nondisabled peers to the maximum extent appropriate. To meet this mandate, IDEA regulations describe a continuum of placements to be made available, ranging from placement in regular classrooms with support services to homebound and hospital programs. Figure 8–2 presents educational service options for students with disabilities. Levels I through IV of the continuum involve inclusion of students with mental retardation in a regular education classroom with their nondisabled age-mates for at least some part of the school day. Some advocates and professionals have emphasized the full inclusion of all students with mental retardation into regular education classrooms.

FIGURE 8–1
Ten Reasons Why Schools Should Have a Collaborative Partnership with Families of School-Age Children

From Lifespan Perspectives on the Family and Disability *(p. 199) by J. Berry and M. L. Hardman, 1998, Boston: Allyn & Bacon.*

1. Recognizes that the child is a member of a home and a school community. Each influences the other.
2. Enables family and school to work together toward a common outcome.
3. Increases opportunities for students to succeed.
4. Includes the parents, who play a primary role in the child's development throughout the school years and have an important influence on the child's learning.
5. Creates a positive relationship between home and school.
6. Helps teachers learn more about the family, which increases effectiveness with the student.
7. Addresses concerns about the student as they arise.
8. Allows for mutual problem solving.
9. Encourages collaborative decision making.
10. Fosters shared responsibility for implementation of school program and home activities.

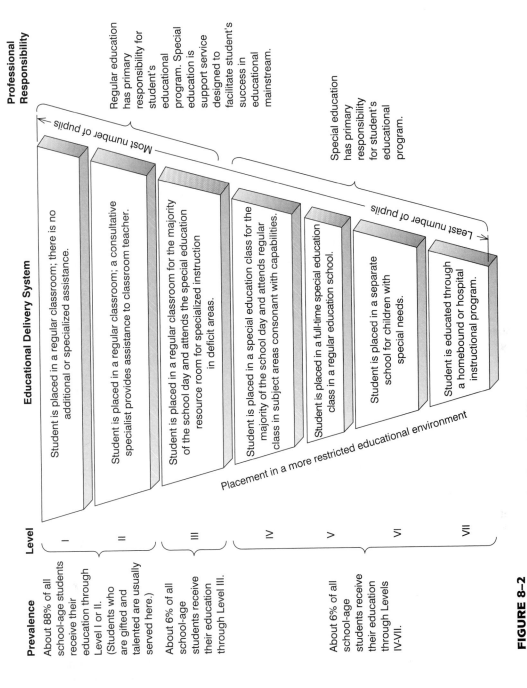

Professional Responsibility

Regular education has primary responsibility for student's educational program. Special education is support service designed to facilitate student's success in educational mainstream.

Special education has primary responsibility for student's educational program.

Educational Delivery System

Most number of pupils

I — Student is placed in a regular classroom; there is no additional or specialized assistance.

II — Student is placed in a regular classroom; a consultative specialist provides assistance to classroom teacher.

III — Student is placed in a regular classroom for the majority of the school day and attends the special education resource room for specialized instruction in deficit areas.

IV — Student is placed in a special education class for the majority of the school day and attends regular class in subject areas consonant with capabilities.

V — Student is placed in a full-time special education class in a regular education school.

VI — Student is placed in a separate school for children with special needs.

VII — Student is educated through a homebound or hospital instructional program.

Least number of pupils

Placement in a more restricted educational environment

Level

I

II

III

IV

V

VI

VII

Prevalence

About 88% of all school-age students receive their education through Level I or II. (Students who are gifted and talented are usually served here.)

About 6% of all school-age students receive their education through Level III.

About 6% of all school-age students receive their education through Levels IV-VII.

FIGURE 8–2
Educational Service Options for Exceptional Students

From Human Exceptionality: Society, School, and Family (6th ed., p. 28) by M. L. Hardman, C. J. Drew, and M. W. Egan, 1999, Boston: Allyn & Bacon. Copyright 1999 by Allyn & Bacon, Inc. Reprinted by permission.

Inclusion of Students with Mental Retardation in Regular Education Settings

Core Concept

Successful inclusion of students with mental retardation in regular education settings is dependent on the availability of both formal and natural supports.

Although the concept of the least restrictive environment is imbedded in federal law (IDEA) for students with disabilities, a growing number of educators are calling for a more *inclusive* educational approach for these students. Hardman et al. (1999) suggested that the term **inclusion** may be defined by "the level of participation and support the individual receives in the [regular] educational setting" (p. 5). Inclusion is most often described as full or partial participation in a regular education class. **Full inclusion** of students with mental retardation in a regular education classroom is an approach in which all instruction and support services come to the student; the student is not pulled out of the regular class into a special education program. Under the full inclusion approach, a special education teacher and other support personnel collaborate with the regular education teacher to meet the needs of the student with mental retardation in the context of a class that is made up of primarily nondisabled students. In the **partial inclusion** approach, students may receive most of their education in the regular classroom but are "pulled out" into a special education program when the multidisciplinary team considers it appropriate to their individual needs.

The proponents of the full inclusion approach argue that any "pull-out" of students with mental retardation into a separate special educational setting is not in the individual's best interest. It results in a fragmented approach to instruction in which regular and special educators do not work together and individual student needs go unmet (Lipsky & Gartner, 1996; Sailor, Gee, & Karasoff, 1993; Stainback & Stainback, 1991; Stainback, Stainback, & Ayres, 1996).

Those opposing full inclusion suggest that the regular education teacher does not have the training or expertise to meet the diverse needs of students with mental retardation. These teachers are already significantly overburdened with large class sizes and little support to meet the needs of their nondisabled students (Fuchs & Fuchs, 1991; Hocutt, 1996; Kauffman, 1991; Lieberman, 1996). Opponents also argue that specialized academic and social instruction can best be provided in a specialized (pull-out) setting for which special educators have been specifically trained and have access to the specialized resources necessary to meet the needs of students with mental retardation (see Figure 8–3).

Whether a full or partial inclusion approach, it is clear that the success of any inclusive educational program for students with mental retardation will be dependent on the availability of supports to both the student with mental retardation and the regular classroom teacher. These supports can be described as both formal and natural. **Formal supports** may include the availability of quali-

FIGURE 8–3
Should students with mental retardation spend all of their time in regular classrooms?

From The Education of Students with Mental Retardation: Preparation for Life in the Community, *position statement, ARC-A National Organization on Mental Retardation, 1998, www.the arc.org/welcome. html.*

Education programs for students with mental retardation must be individualized to meet the unique characteristics and needs of each individual. Some students with mental retardation will benefit from instruction outside school environments, such as the community-based settings. As such, an appropriate learning environment will not be exclusively in the regular classroom. Other students with mental retardation may require related services that necessitate time out of the regular classroom. The IEP process should identify the appropriate program for each student and determine what arrangement best meets the student's needs.

Nonetheless, all students should be integrated in some way into regular education buildings, classrooms, and activities with same age peers who are not disabled. This does not mean that every student in the regular classroom must learn the same material nor does it mean that students with disabilities enter regular classrooms only for social benefits. It means that with adequate support, adaptation, and respect for individual differences, all students with mental retardation can benefit educationally and socially from integration.

fied regular and special education teachers, access to paraprofessionals and peer tutors, appropriate multilevel instructional materials, and technology aids (e.g., talking computers, language boards). **Natural supports** are most often described as the student's family, friends, and classmates (Hardman et al., 1999). Jorgensen (1992) suggested that "natural supports bring children closer together as friends and learning partners rather than isolating them" (p. 183).

Core Concept

Regular class placement with support services includes both the consulting teacher and resource room models.

Regular Class Placement with Support Services.   As depicted in Figure 8–2, placement at Level II means that the student remains in the regular classroom with support services. The regular classroom teacher is responsible for any adaptation that may be necessary for the student's success in this environment. Consequently, this teacher must have the skills to develop and adapt curricula to meet individual needs. Approximately 9% of students with mental retardation are in a regular education classroom for the full day (U.S. Department of Education, 1997).

Because regular teachers are an integral part of a successful educational experience for the child with mental retardation, it is important that they receive expanded university preparation in the education of children with disabilities. The

This youngster is progressing academically, although more slowly than peers without mental retardation.

National Council for the Accreditation of Teacher Education (NCATE) and the National Advisory Council on Education Professions Development support this position. Necessary skills for the regular classroom teacher include an understanding of how a disabling condition can affect the ability to learn academic skills or to adapt in social situations. The teacher must also be able to recognize a learning or behavior problem and to seek out appropriate school resources that will facilitate the implementation of an appropriate individualized program. School districts also have a responsibility to the teacher and the child. Appropriate resources and consultative personnel must be available to assist the regular classroom teacher, and time must be set aside for planning and coordinating activities for the child. Figure 8–4 highlights strategies for regular and special educators to locate and use the supports necessary to meet the needs of students in an inclusive class setting.

The **consulting teacher,** sometimes referred to as a curriculum specialist, itinerant teacher, or master teacher, provides assistance to the regular classroom teacher or the child while the child remains in the regular classroom. This specialist may help a teacher identify the child's specific problem areas and recommend appropriate assessment techniques and educational strategies. Schulz, Carpenter and Turnbull (1991) suggest that effective consultants have several important characteristics. They are often professionals with advanced training beyond the basic teacher certification program and are "knowledgeable about a variety of instructional strategies." They are able to build mutually trusting relationships through positive interactions with other professionals, are responsive

---

FOR REGULAR CLASS TEACHERS

- Seek out assistance in your classroom from other professionals, emphasizing a cooperative or team approach to all children.

- Explore/observe a variety of teaching methods to learn different ways to tailor instruction to the multiple needs and learning styles of your students.

- Accept that not all students will cover the same material at the same time and that a variety of curricula (e.g., functional literacy, community mobility, and college preparation) are equally valid for different students.

- Above all, **be flexible.** This type of change takes time, and every teacher makes mistakes along the way as he or she learns to work with increasingly diverse students.

FOR SPECIAL EDUCATORS (Teachers and Administrators)

- Recognize that the best service a special educator can provide his or her student is to enable the student to function independently in the real world. Each school should model that environment rather than create asylums for children. Special educators should define their role as enriching or supplementing the general education program, through consultation and in-class support, rather than providing an alternative program.

- Creating an inclusive system will not mean that there will be fewer special educators but that special educators will do a substantially different job. Discretionary monies should be focused on *joint* special education/general education teacher training efforts that build on the strengths of both fields.

- The school restructuring movement provides a window of opportunity for truly including students with special needs into the general student population. Special educators should be a part of every school governing council that has teacher representatives.

FIGURE 8–4
Strategies for Regular and Special Educators in Inclusive Class Settings

From Winners All: A Call for Inclusive Schools *(pp. 38–39) by the National Association of State Boards of Education, October 1992, Alexandria, VA: Author.*

to others, and have a good understanding of the dynamics of social interaction. They view consultation as a learning experience for themselves as well as the professionals and students they serve. Effective consultants are also very concrete and specific in making suggestions to improve students' educational experiences but are capable of looking at issues from broad theoretical perspectives. Finally, Lipsky and Gartner (1996) suggest that effective consultants are good researchers who know how to locate and use resources effectively.

Working with a consultant, regular classroom teachers are supported in their own backyard, so to speak, with emphasis on adapting the classroom environment to the needs of the child with mental retardation. If the child requires more support than a consultant can give, however, a more restricted setting, such as a resource room, may be necessary.

The consultant can also assist the regular class teacher in the implementation of a cooperative learning program between students with mental retardation and their nondisabled peers. Peers can be a powerful support system within the classroom in both academic and behavioral areas. They often have more influence on their classmates' behavior than the teacher does. Peer support programs may range from simply creating opportunities in the class for students with disabilities to socially interact with their nondisabled peers on a general education basis to highly structured programs of peer-mediated instruction. Peer-mediated instruction involves a structured interaction between two or more students under the direct supervision of a classroom teacher.

A student with mental retardation placed at Level III in the cascade of services remains in the regular classroom most of the school day and goes to a **resource room** for a portion of his or her instructional programming. The U.S. Department of Education (1997) estimates that about one out of every four students with mental retardation are served in resource room programs.

This resource room still requires collaboration between regular classroom teachers and other consulting professionals. Services may range from assisting a teacher in the use of tests or modification of curriculum to direct instruction with students in the regular classroom. The regular education teacher must participate as a member of a multidisciplinary team involved in the planning of appropriate educational services for the child. This team may include special educators, communication specialists, occupational or physical therapists, school psychologists, social workers, physical education specialists, and the child's parents.

The resource room also reflects a philosophy of sharing of responsibility between regular education and special education for children with retardation. The resource room represents another effort to integrate children as much as possible into regular education and still offer them special education support services when needed. This approach allows the child to remain with nondisabled age-mates for the majority of the school day while removing a great deal of the stigma associated with separate full-day special education classrooms.

In the resource room program, children with mental retardation are assigned to a regular education teacher in the elementary grades and to a regular education homeroom teacher in the upper grades. These children are primarily in regular education and will participate in as many regularly scheduled activities as possible. Assignments, possibly with modifications, approximate those of the other children. The two teachers arrange times for the children in resource programs to meet with the special education resource teacher.

The resource room teacher maintains a room within the school building and is a regular member of the school faculty. The special education teacher's function is essentially twofold. The first responsibility is to provide instructional support services to the child with a disability. These services can include orientation to the school for new students, tutorial services, counseling, and training of instructional aides if needed. A second major function for the resource room teacher is to serve as a liaison between the regular classroom teacher and the child. The resource room teacher is responsible for facilitating understanding between regular class teachers and the child, aiding regular class teachers in understanding the needs and nature of children with mental retardation, and supporting the child academically and in areas of personal and social adjustment.

Core Concept

Students with mental retardation may be educated in a part-time special education classroom in the regular school building.

The Part-Time Special Education Classroom in the Regular School.   The part-time special class (Level IV) involves the sharing of responsibility for the child by both regular and special education teachers. The major difference between a part-time special class and a resource room rests in the area of primary responsibility. In the resource room, the child with mental retardation is primarily a student in the regular classroom with support services from special education. In the part-time special class, the students are assigned to a special education teacher and class and remain in the same room with the same teacher for a large portion of the day. During the remainder of the day, these students are included in as many regular education activities as possible. In most instances, the child remains in the special classroom for academic subjects. Inclusive classes are typically less academically oriented and include music, shop, home economics, physical education, and art. Proponents of the part-time special class suggest that a student has the advantage of a nonthreatening academic setting, along with inclusion into the social mainstream.

Full-Time Special Education Classes and Schools

Core Concept

Full-time special education classes and special day schools are considered more restrictive educational settings for students with mental retardation.

The Full-Time Special Class.   A traditional approach to providing educational services to children with mild mental retardation is the full-time special class (Level V) in the regular education school. This approach also has been used more recently for children with both moderate and severe retardation. The U.S. Department of Education (1997) estimates that about 58% of students with mental retardation are educated in full-time special education classrooms. The special class has been criticized because it segregates students from their nondisabled peers (Jenkins, Pious, & Jewell, 1990). This approach, however, has had its share of supporters over the years. Some research in the 1950s indicated that social adjustment for children with mental retardation in full-time special education classrooms may exceed that of children with mental retardation in regular education classes, although academic performance between the two groups does not differ (Cassidy & Stanton, 1959). Indications are that children with mental retardation in special classes have less fear of failure than peers in regular classrooms (Jordan & deCharms, 1959). It also has been suggested that a child in a special class has a greater opportunity to excel and become a "star" (Baldwin, 1958). Proponents also argue that the self-contained class has a teacher who is thoroughly prepared and fully understands the needs and nature of children with mental retardation.

The Special School.   Some classes for children with moderate and severe levels of mental retardation are located in special schools exclusively for students with mental retardation. Approximately 7% of students with mental retardation are educated in public or private special schools (U.S. Department of Education, 1997).

Proponents of special schools argue that they provide services for large numbers of children with mental retardation and therefore offer greater homogeneity in grouping and programming for children. They also support this type of arrangement because it allows teachers to specialize in their teaching areas. For example, one teacher might specialize in art for children with mental retardation, another in physical education, and a third in music. In smaller programs with only one or two teachers, these individuals may have to teach subjects as diverse as art and home economics and academics.

Special schools also allow for centralization of supplies, equipment, and special facilities for children with mental retardation. Smaller, isolated programs may not be able to justify the purchase of expensive equipment used only occasionally, but the special school can justify expenditures based on more frequent use by a larger number of classes.

Results of research studies on the efficacy of special schools do not support the arguments of the proponents. Several authors (Gee, 1996; Halvorsen & Sailor, 1990; McDonnell, Hardman, McDonnell, & Kiefer-O'Donnell, 1995; Stainback et al., 1996) contend that regardless of the severity of their disability, children with mental retardation do benefit from placement in a regular education facility where opportunities for inclusion with nondisabled peers are systematically planned and implemented. As discussed above, several studies have indicated that educational outcomes for students are significantly improved in an inclusive setting. Additionally, in appropriately implemented inclusive settings, no substantiated detrimental outcomes have been found for students with severe disabilities. Systematically planned interactions between students with severe mental retardation and nondisabled peers yield improved attitudes and interaction patterns (Gee, 1996; Halvorsen & Sailor, 1990; McDonnell et al., 1995; Stainback et al., 1996).

The courts, too, have affirmed the application of the least restrictive environment clause of IDEA to students with severe disabilities (*Armstrong v. Kline*, 1980; *Campbell v. Talladega Board of Education*, 1981; *Fialkowski v. Shapp*, 1975;

Roncker v. Walters, 1983). Specifically, students with severe mental retardation are to be educated to the maximum extent appropriate with their nondisabled peers, which includes attending regular schools, unless extenuating individual circumstances preclude this as an appropriate placement decision.

Critics argue that although administratively convenient to operate, special schools deprive children with mental retardation of many of their basic rights. First, these schools are quickly identified as being different and exclusively for children with mental retardation. With a stigma attached to such schools, both the children and their parents may suffer. Critics also argue that the real world of society is not naturally segregated and that special schools remove children from the mainstream of society and education, thus depriving them of valuable experiences with nondisabled peers.

INSTRUCTIONAL APPROACHES

Core Concept

For students with mental retardation, learning in the school setting is a continual process of adaptation.

Students with mental retardation can and will learn if provided an appropriate instructional program and a teaching process oriented to their individual needs. The specific instructional program, based on annual goals and short-term objectives, is a critical factor in the implementation of an appropriate educational program. The selection of curricula for learners with mental retardation, however, has been a problem for educators because of the students' heterogeneous needs. Because they do not learn as quickly or as effectively as their nondisabled peers, the traditional approach to teaching basic academic skills is often not appropriate for these students. For students with moderate and severe mental retardation, academic skills such as reading, writing, and arithmetic may not be a priority. Given the limited instructional time available in the schools, instruction for these children may necessarily be oriented more toward adaptive living skills. In the following section, we discuss some instructional approaches for children with mental retardation that emphasize the acquisition of both functional academic and adaptive skills.

Teaching Functional Academic Skills

Core Concept

Instruction in academic areas may include a foundation and/or a functional approach to learning.

The primary instructional approach in the public schools emphasizes learning of foundation skills in the basic academic areas. For example, reading is learned as a set of sequenced skills that can be divided into three phases: (a) the development of readiness skills (left-to-right sequencing, visual and auditory discrimination skills, and memory skills); (b) word recognition or decoding skills (breaking the code and correctly identifying the abstract symbols in sequence); and (c) reading comprehension (giving symbols meaning). Each step in the process is a prerequisite for the next, and the whole forms a framework for higher levels of functioning. The learner with mental retardation, however, may not efficiently acquire the necessary prerequisites within the time frame the schools prescribe. Many children with mental retardation just need more time to learn the skills for an instructional approach to be effective. Others may better invest their time and energy in such areas as personal management, mobility, or communication.

Another approach to learning academic skills is often termed **functional** and is consistent with an adaptive learning curriculum. In this approach, the basic academic tools are taught in the context of daily living activities and in the natural setting as much as possible (home, community). A functional life program in the area of reading focuses primarily on those words that facilitate adaptation in the child's environment (see Figure 8–5). Functional mathematics skill development may relate more to environmental needs like telling time or spending money. Whatever the academic area, a functional approach pairs the skill being taught with an environmental cue. Browder and Snell (1993) stressed that when attempting to functionalize learned skills, the teacher must use instructional materials that are realistic. Traditional materials—workbooks, basal readers, flash cards, and so on—are not practical because the student is unable to relate the materials to his or her world.

The curricular approaches discussed above are not necessarily mutually exclusive. A foundation approach can incorporate many functional elements to reduce the abstract nature of the academic subjects and facilitate efficient learning for the student with mental retardation.

Go	Up	Dynamite	School
Slow down	Down	Explosives	School bus
Stop	Men	Fire	No trespassing
Off	Women	Fire escape	Private property
On	Exit	Poison	Men working
Cold	Entrance	Wet paint	Yield
Hot	Danger	Police	Railroad crossing
In	Be careful	Keep off	Boys
Out	Caution	Watch for children	Girls

FIGURE 8–5
A Functional Reading Vocabulary

Teaching Adaptive Skills

Core Concept

Adaptive skills are necessary to decrease an individual's dependence on others and to increase opportunities for school and community participation.

The public schools, which excluded many children with mental retardation for the better part of this century, now face the challenge of providing an educational experience consistent with the individual needs of these children. Educational programming has been expanded to include the learning of adaptive skills necessary to decrease an individual's dependence on others and to increase opportunities for school and community participation. The teaching of adaptive skills to children with mental retardation is based on the premise that if these skills are not taught through formal instruction, they will not be learned. For children without mental retardation, teaching these skills is often unnecessary because they are acquired through daily experiences.

Adaptive skill content areas for school-age children with mental retardation include motor, personal management (self-care), social, communication, and functional academic skills. The development of gross- and fine-motor skills is a prerequisite to successful learning in other adaptive areas. Gross-motor skills development relates to general mobility-balance and locomotor patterns. This includes neck and head control, rolling, body righting, sitting, creeping, crawling, standing, walking, running, jumping, and skipping. Fine-motor training includes learning to reach, grasp, and manipulate objects. For the child to develop motor skills, he or she must be able to fix on an object visually and track a moving target. The coordination of fine-motor skills and visual tracking (eye-hand coordination) is both a prerequisite to object-control skills that are required in vocational situations and a basis for learning leisure activities.

Personal management skills are essential to the child's independence at home and at school. The primary personal management areas are safety, dressing, hygiene, and eating. Westling and Fox (1995, p. 388) describe a five-step task analysis for teaching a student to eat finger foods:

1. Reaching to locate the food
2. Grasping the food
3. Lifting the food from the table to the mouth
4. Putting the food into the mouth
5. Chewing and swallowing the food

Dressing skills involve learning to button, zip, buckle, lace, and tie. Personal hygiene skills include toileting, face and hand washing, bathing, brushing teeth, and shampooing and combing hair. Eating skills include learning to finger feed, use proper utensils, drink from a cup, and serve food.

Instruction in social skills applies many of the self-care areas to the development of positive interpersonal relationships. Social-skill training stresses appropriate physical appearance, etiquette, use of leisure time, and sexual behavior. Communication is closely related to social-skill development because without communication there is no social interaction. The communication may be verbal or manual (e.g., sign language, language boards), but most important is that some form of communication be present.

Using Assistive Technology

Core Concept

Students with mental retardation often benefit from instruction that incorporates assistive technology devices or activities.

Assistive technology includes any item, piece of equipment, or product system that can be used to increase, maintain, or improve the functional capabilities of students with disabilities (Public Law 100-407, Technology-Related Assistance for Individuals with Disabilities Act). There are several categories of assistive technology:

- Mobility (wheelchairs, lifts, adaptive driving controls, scooters, laser canes)
- Seating and positioning (assistance in choosing and using a wheelchair)
- Computers (environmental control units, word processors, software, keyboards)
- Toys and games (software, switch-operated toys)
- Activities of daily living (feeders, lifts, watch alarms, memory books)
- Communication (touch talkers, reading systems, talking keyboards (Wehman, 1997, p. 475).

Students with mental retardation who have communication deficits or delays will benefit from assistive technology devices or activities that promote the use of augmentative communication strategies (see Strategies for Augmenting Communication). Mirenda, Iacono, and Williams (1990) suggest that augmentative communication may include (a) adapting existing vocal or gestural abilities into meaningful communication; (b) teaching manual signing (such as American Sign Language), static symbols, or icons (such as **Blissymbols**); and (c) using manual or electronic communication devices (such as electric communication boards, picture cues, or synthetic speech).

EDUCATING THE CULTURALLY DIFFERENT CHILD WITH MENTAL RETARDATION

Core Concept

Culturally different children with mental retardation need an educational experience that focuses on learning how to learn.

Strategies for Augmenting Communication

There are many ways to augment communication including the use of communication boards. A communication board is a collection of images, including icons and photographs. When an image is pointed to or chosen, it sends a message to the person an individual is trying to communicate with. In turn, that choice evokes a response. For example, an icon of a stop sign can be used to represent the command, "Stop." When pointed to, the "offender" knows to *stop* to honor the command.

When planning a communication strategy, it is important to start simply. Here are some everyday examples of ways to use a communication board or picture system to provide the opportunities to make choices.

Creating a Snack or Meal Time Menu

- Cut out labels from food packaging typically found in the refrigerator or pantry.
- Glue the labels on unlined index cards or poster board. Laminate the cards for extended use.
- Single hole punch them and place them on a metal ring, which can be purchased from a hobby or office supply store.
- Place the ring on the refrigerator or pantry door handle for easy access.
- Encourage the individual to thumb through the cards and select choices for drinks, snacks, etc.

- Consider grouping food groups together by using different colored poster board. For instance, put drinks on blue poster board, fruits on yellow, vegetables on green, desserts on red, and so on.

After a while, it can become tiring to make communication boards by cutting with scissors, copying, and pasting pieces of paper. A solution is to consider using Mayer-Johnson's Boardmaker™ software. Available for both Mac and Windows, Boardmaker™ is designed for finding, copying, and pasting icons quickly to design communication boards. Icons are provided for many trademark symbols for such things as Coca-Cola™ and McDonald's™, as well as numerous icons for various daily activities. Icons can be resized by the computer and placed in premade guides, or placed in customized ones. Communication boards can be printed in either color or black and white. And additional "libraries" can be created for personally drawn images, as well as digital or scanned photos. This provides easy accessibility, as well as the opportunity to use the images over and over again.

Source: From "Augmenting Communication" by K. Voss, July/August 1997, *Disability Solutions 2*(2), pp. 7, 9.

Because disproportionately large numbers of ethnic minority children are in some classes for children with mental retardation (Baca & deValenzuela, 1998; Shapiro, Loeb, & Bowermaster, 1993; Willig & Greenberg, 1986), there is a critical demand for teachers who are sensitive to the needs of these students. Teaching about different cultures and their value may be important in reducing racial and ethnic conflict and promoting respect and tolerance for human differences. As suggested by Hallahan and Kauffman (1997), "multiculturalism aims to change educational institutions and curricula so that they will provide equal educational opportunities to students regardless of their gender, social class, ethnicity, race, disability or other cultural identity" (p. 86).

To meet the educational needs of culturally diverse children with retardation, the teacher needs to focus on learning how to learn, in addition to memorizing facts and acquiring basic skills. These children may have linguistic limitations both in their native dialect or language and in Standard English. Thus, reading material should be primarily experience oriented so that the child can draw from his or her own perceptions and experiences.

Chinn and McCormick (1986) suggested four topics that should be considered in curriculum development for culturally diverse students: "(1) teaching values that support cultural diversity and individual uniqueness; (2) encouraging and accepting the qualitative expansion of existing ethnic values; (3) supporting exploration in alternative and emerging life styles; and (4) encouraging multiculturalism, multilingualism, and multidialectism" (p. 99). Because more than 1 million minority children and youths drop out of school every year, the curriculum must convince these students that school is a positive social institution in which they are valued by teachers and age-mates. Ethnic studies should focus on the use and meaning of societal labels and the image of culturally diverse people portrayed through the media. The curriculum for the culturally different child with mental retardation who is also living in poverty should include instruction on available resources for food assistance and medical care. In light of the limited financial resources of the child's family, effective money management and consumer skills must be emphasized. Finally, classroom teachers must believe in and communicate the basic tenet that people in this society exist in a pluralistic culture that values the intrinsic worth of every individual.

NEW ISSUES AND FUTURE DIRECTIONS

Core Concept

Educational reform efforts that focus on individualization in the schools and the effectiveness of social inclusion will benefit students with mental retardation.

School Reform and Students with Mental Retardation

As professionals move through an era of reform and restructuring in this nation's schools, several emerging issues will directly affect the lives of students with mental retardation. For example, will future school reform movements focus exclusively on improving academic achievement for college-bound students, or will these efforts be directed more to improvements at the school building level, with an orientation to individualized instruction and fostering of full participation for all students in a community setting (National Research

Council, 1997)? Obviously, reform efforts that focus only on improving academic achievement fail to acknowledge diversity and inevitably will result in the wholesale exclusion of students with mental retardation from the process. School-based reform initiatives, however, will be more responsive to the needs of students with mental retardation because the change process accommodates individual student need while recognizing that there must be a common vision of excellence for all students in this nation's schools. Reform that deals with individual variability should take into account the needs of each student and match these needs against the demands of life in a community setting. For students with mental retardation, the curriculum needs to be broadened beyond academic performance to participation and access within their family setting, neighborhood, and community at large. This curriculum may include skills for independent living, adaptive behavior, recreation, and employment preparation.

A new requirement in IDEA 97 mandates that students with disabilities must have access to the general education curriculum when appropriate, as well as participate in state or local performance assessments. The requirement raises some important curriculum issues for students with mental retardation. Will the general education curriculum be broadened to include the "life skills" appropriate to the needs of these students? On what basis will the decision be made to include or exclude students with mental retardation from the general education curriculum? If these students are to participate in state or local performance assessments, will appropriate accommodations (such as more time to take the test or oral testing) be made available? If a student with mental retardation is excluded from the state testing, how will the schools be accountable for ensuring satisfactory educational progress?

Teacher Education Reform and the Education of Students with Mental Retardation

University teacher education is critical to the success of effective educational programs for students with mental retardation. During the past two decades, these programs have begun to expand their curricula to include more functional, community-based, and social inclusion instruction. University teacher education programs in special education are beginning to concentrate efforts on ways to facilitate collaboration with regular education colleagues and school administrators to address the needs of all students, including those with mental retardation (Joseph P. Kennedy, Jr., Foundation, 1997). These programs also will need to assist potential teachers in special education to organize and use schools' resources more effectively (e.g., peer tutors, paraprofessionals) to meet the needs of students with mental retardation. Additionally, teacher education candidates from both elementary and secondary teacher programs, as well as potential school administrators, will require strategies that facilitate the success of students with mental retardation in an inclusive public school setting. These strategies could include (a) functioning as a member of a multidisciplinary team, (b) supporting students with mental retardation to function in the social network of the school, and (c) developing effective pedagogy for students in a regular education setting (Hardman, McDonnell, & Welch, 1997).

The Social Inclusion of Students with Mental Retardation

As discussed earlier in this chapter, the issue of social inclusion in the public schools for all students with mental retardation continues to be hotly debated. Although the principle of normalization and the least restrictive environment clause of IDEA indicate a strong preference for having every student with mental retardation participate in settings that are as close as possible to those available to nondisabled students, some professionals and parents still openly advocate socially segregated programs. As a report by the National Council on Disability (1989) stated, "A highly emotional discussion is taking place about the role of separate schools and the unique instructional needs of students with specific disabilities" (p. 31). To understand and meet the needs of students with mental retardation better in the least restrictive setting, in the future this debate must move from the realm of emotions to that of realities. Comparative studies across environments and functioning levels are needed before one can draw conclusions about what role, if any, segregated educational environments for students with mental retardation should play.

Core Questions

1. Discuss the various stages of development and periods of growth as they relate to children with mental retardation.
2. How do the memory capabilities of children with mental retardation compare with those of their nondisabled peers?
3. Compare massed and distributed practice in relationship to the learning performance of children with mental retardation.
4. Discuss several suggestions for working with children who have difficulty transferring learning from one situation to another.
5. Identify examples of adaptive skills that children with mental retardation may need to learn during the school years.
6. What are the major provisions of the Individuals with Disabilities Education Act?
7. Identify examples of both formal and natural supports that will facilitate the success of the child with mental retardation in an inclusive school setting.
8. Describe adaptive skill content areas that children with mental retardation may need to learn.
9. Why is it important for students with mental retardation that school reform efforts concentrate more on school-based issues than on a top-down approach to declining academic achievement?

Roundtable Discussion

This chapter discussed several aspects of the education of children with mental retardation in both inclusive and more segregated educational environments. It also emphasized the need to provide for both formal and natural supports in the regular education setting if inclusion is to be successful.

In your study group or on your own, discuss the rationale for including children with mental retardation in both regular school and regular classroom environments. Given support for the inclusion of children with mental retardation in the regular school, discuss ideas for planning appropriate interactions between children with mental retardation and nondisabled peers both in and out of school.

References

Agran, M., Fodor-Davis, J., Moore, S., & Deer, M. (1989). The application of a self-management program on instruction following skills. *Journal of the Association for Persons with Severe Handicaps, 14,* 147–154.

Agran, M., Salzberg, C. L., & Stowitchek, J. (1987). An analysis of the effects of a social skills training program using self-instructions on the acquisition and generalization of two social behaviors in a work setting. *Journal of the Association for Persons with Severe Handicaps, 12*(2), 131–139.

American Association on Mental Retardation (AAMR). (1992). *Mental retardation: Definition, classification, and systems of supports* (9th ed.). Washington, DC: Author.

American Psychiatric Association (APA). (1997). *Diagnostic and statistical manual of mental disorders* (4th ed.). Washington, DC: Author.

The ARC-A National Organization on Mental Retardation (1998). *The Education of Students with Mental Retardation: Preparation for Life in the Community.* www.the arc.org/welcome.html.

Armstrong v. Kline, 476 F. Supp. 583 (E.D. Pa. 1979), aff'd 78-0172 (3rd cir. July 15, 1980).

Baca, L., & deValenzuela, J. S. (1998). Development of the bilingual special education interface. In L. M. Baca & H. T. Cervantes (Eds.), *The bilingual special education interface* (3rd ed., pp. 98–118). Upper Saddle River, NJ: Merrill/Prentice Hall.

Baldwin, W. D. (1958). The social position of the educable mentally retarded in the regular grades in the public schools. *Exceptional Children, 25,* 106–108.

Bambara, L. M., Warren, S. F., & Komisar, S. (1988). The individualized curriculum sequencing model: Effects on skill acquisition and generalization. *Journal of Persons with Severe Handicaps, 13,* 8–19.

Beirne-Smith, M., Ittenbach, R. F., & Patton, J. R. (1998). *Mental retardation.* Upper Saddle River, NJ: Merrill/Prentice Hall.

Benavidez, D., & Matson, J. L., (1993). Assessment of depression in mentally retarded adolescents. *Research in Developmental Disabilities, 14,* 179–188.

Benson, G., Aberdanto, L., Short, K., Nuccio, J. B., & Mans, F. (1993). Development of a theory of mind in individuals with mental retardation. *American Journal on Mental Retardation, 98*(6), 427–433.

Bergen, A. E., & Mosley, J. L. (1994). Attention and attention shift efficiency in individuals with and without mental retardation. *American Journal on Mental Retardation, 98*(6), 732–743.

Bernstein, D. K., & Tiegerman, E. (1993). *Language and communication disorders in children.* Upper Saddle River, NJ: Merrill/Prentice Hall.

Berry, J., & Hardman, M. L. (1998) *Lifespan perspectives on the family and disability.* Boston: Allyn & Bacon, p. 199.

Borkowski, J. G., Peck, V. A., & Damberg, P. R. (1983). Attention, memory, and cognition. In J. L. Matson & J. A. Mulich (Eds.), *Handbook of mental retardation* (pp. 479–497). New York: Pergamon.

Browder, D. M., & Snell, M. E. (1993). Functional academics. In M. E. Snell (Ed.), *Systematic instruction of persons with severe handicaps* (pp. 442–479). Upper Saddle River, NJ: Merrill/Prentice Hall.

Campbell v. Talladega Board of Education, U.S. District Court (1981).

Cassidy, V. M., & Stanton, J. E. (1959). *An investigation of factors involved in educational placement of mentally retarded children: A study of differences between children in special and regular classes in Ohio* (Project No. 043, U.S. Office of Education Cooperative Research Program). Columbus: Ohio State University.

Chinn, P. C., & McCormick, L. (1986). Cultural diversity and exceptionality. In N. G. Haring & L. McCormick (Eds.), *Exceptional children and youth* (pp. 95–117). Upper Saddle River, NJ: Merrill/Prentice Hall.

Cipani, E., & Spooner, F. (1994). *Curricular and instructional approaches for persons with severe disabilities.* Needham Heights, MA: Allyn & Bacon.

Drew, C. J., Hardman, M. L., & Hart, A. W. (1996). *Designing and conducting research in education and social science.* Needham Heights, MA: Allyn & Bacon.

Epstein, M. H., Polloway, E. A., Patton, J. R., & Foley, R. (1989). Mild mental retardation: Student characteristics and services. *Education and Training in Mental Retardation, 24*(1), 7–16.

Evans, R. A., & Bilsky, L. H. (1979). Clustering and categorical list retention in the mentally retarded. In N. R. Ellis (Ed.), *Handbook of mental deficiency: Psychological theory and research* (2nd ed.). Hillsdale, NJ: Erlbaum.

Fialkowski v. Shapp, 405 F. Supp. 946 (E.D. Pa. 1975).

Fink, W. (1981). *The distribution of clients and their behavioral characteristics in programs for the mentally retarded and other developmentally disabled throughout Oregon.* Eugene: Oregon Mental Health Division.

Fox, L. (1989). Stimulus generalization skills and persons with profound mental handicaps. *Education and Training in Mental Retardation, 24,* 219–229.

Fuchs, D., & Fuchs, L. (1991). Framing the REI debate: Abolitionists versus conservationists. In J. W. Lloyd, N. N. Singh, & A. C. Repp (Eds.), *The regular education initiative: Alternative perspectives on concepts, issues, and models* (pp. 241–255). Sycamore, IL: Sycamore.

Gee, K. (1996). Least restrictive environment: Elementary and middle school. In The National Council on Disability, *Improving the implementation of the Individuals with Disabilities Education Act: Making schools work for all children* (Supplement), (395–425). Washington, DC: The National Council on Disability.

Glidden, I. M. (1985). Semantic processing, semantic memory, and recall. In N. R. Ellis (Ed.), *International review of research in mental retardation* (Vol. 13, pp. 247–278). New York: Academic Press.

Gresham, F. P., & MacMillan, D. L. (1997). Social competence and affective characteristics of students with mild disabilities. *Review of Educational Research, 67*(4), 377–415.

Hallahan, D. P., & Kauffman, J. P. (1997). *Exceptional children* (7th ed.). Needham Heights, MA: Allyn & Bacon.

Halvorsen, A. T., & Sailor, W. (1990). Integration of students with severe and profound disabilities: A review of research. In R. Gaylord-Ross (Ed.), *Issues and research in special education* (pp. 110–172). New York: Teachers College Press.

Hardman, M. L., Drew, C. J., Egan, M. W. (1999). *Human exceptionality: Society, school, and family* (6th ed.). Boston: Allyn & Bacon.

Hardman, M. L., McDonnell, J., & Welch, M. (1997). *Preparing special education teachers in an era of school reform.* Washington, DC: Federal Resource Center, Academy for Educational Development.

Haring, N. G. (Ed.). (1988). *Generalization for students with severe handicaps: Strategies and solutions.* Seattle: University of Washington Press.

Hendrick Hudson District Board of Education v. Rowley, 485 U.S. 176 (1982).

Hocutt, A. M. (1996) Effectiveness of special education: Is placement the critical factor? In The Center for the Future of Children, *Special education for students with disabilities, 6*(1) 77–102. Los Angeles, CA: The Center for the Future of Children.

Hughes, C. (1992). Teaching self-instruction utilizing multiple exemplars to produce generalized problem solving among individuals with severe mental retardation. *American Journal on Mental Retardation, 97*(3), 302–314.

Jenkins, J. R., Pious, C. G., & Jewell, M. (1990). Special education and the regular education initiative: Basic assumptions. *Exceptional Children, 56*(6), 479–491.

Jordan, T. E., & deCharms, R. (1959). The achievement motive in normal and mentally retarded children. *American Journal of Mental Deficiency, 64,* 80–84.

Jorgensen, C. M. (1992). Natural supports in inclusive schools: Curricular and teaching strategies. In J. Nisbet (Ed.), *Natural supports in school, at work, and in the community for people with disabilities* (pp. 179–215). Baltimore: Paul H. Brookes.

Joseph P. Kennedy, Jr., Foundation (1997). *Preparing special education teachers for the 21st century.* Washington, DC: Author.

Kauffman, J. M. (1991). Restructuring in sociopolitical context: Reservations about the effects of current reform proposals on students with disabilities. In J. W. Lloyd, N. N. Singh, & A. C. Repp (Eds.), *The regular education initiative: Alternative perspectives on concepts, issues, and models* (pp. 57–66). Sycamore, IL: Sycamore.

Lieberman, L. M. (1996). Preserving special education for those who need it. In W. Stainback & S. Stainback (Eds.), *Controversial issues confronting special education: Divergent perspectives* (2nd ed., pp. 16–27). Boston: Allyn & Bacon.

Lipsky, D. K., & Gartner, A. (1996). Inclusive education and school restructuring. In W. Stainback & S. Stainback (Eds.), *Controversial issues confronting special education: Divergent perspectives* (2nd ed., pp. 3–15). Boston: Allyn & Bacon.

Marino, B. R., & Pueschel, S. M. (1996). Heart disease in persons with Down syndrome. Baltimore: Paul H. Brookes.

McAlpine, C., Kendall, K. A., & Singh, N. N. (1991). Recognition of facial expressions of emotion by persons with mental retardation. *American Journal on Mental Retardation, 96,* 29–36.

McDonnell, J., Hardman, M., McDonnell, A. P., & Kiefer-O'Donnell, R. (1995). *Introduction to persons with severe disabilities.* Boston: Allyn & Bacon.

Merrill, E. C., & Peacock, M. (1994). Allocation of attention and task difficulty. *American Journal on Mental Retardation, 98*(5), 588–593.

Mirenda, P., Iacono, T. & Williams, R. (1990). Communication options for persons with severe and profound disabilities: State of the art and future directions. *Journal of the Association for Persons with Severe Disabilities, 15,* 3–21.

Mulligan, M., Guess, D., Holvoet, J., & Brown, F. (1980). The individualized curriculum sequencing model (I): Implications from research on massed, distributed or spaced trial learning. *Journal of the Association for the Severely Handicapped, 7,* 48–61.

National Association of State Boards of Education. (1992, October). *Winners all: A call for inclusive schools.* Alexandria, VA: Author.

National Council on Disability. (1989). *The education of students with disabilities: Where do we stand?* Washington, DC: Author.

National Research Council (1997). Educating one and all: Students with disabilities and standards-based reform. Washington, DC: National Academy Press.

Neel, R. S., & Billingsley, F. F. (1989). *IMPACT: A functional curriculum handbook for students with moderate to severe disabilities.* Baltimore: Paul H. Brookes.

Payne, J. S., Polloway, E. A., Smith, J. E., & Payne, R. A. (1981). *Strategies for teaching the mentally retarded* (2nd ed.). Upper Saddle River, NJ: Merrill/Prentice Hall.

Piaget, J. (1969). *The theory of stages in cognitive development.* New York: McGraw-Hill.

Roncker v. Walters, 700 F.2d 1058 (6th cir. 1983).

Sailor, W., Gee, K., & Karasoff, P. (1993). School restructuring and full inclusion. In M. Snell (Ed.), *Systematic instruction of persons with severe handicaps* (4th ed., pp. 1–30). Upper Saddle River, NJ: Merrill/Prentice Hall.

Schulz, J. B., Carpenter, C. D., & Turnbull, A. P. (1991). Mainstreaming exceptional students: A guide for classroom teachers. Boston: Allyn & Bacon.

Shapiro, J. P., Loeb, P., & Bowermaster, D. (1993, December 13). Separate and unequal. *U.S. News and World Report,* pp. 46–60.

Siperstein, G. N., & Leffert, J. S. (1997). Comparison of socially accepted and rejected children with mental retardation. *American Journal on Mental Retardation, 101*(4), 339–351.

Stainback, S., Stainback, W., & Ayres, B. (1996). Schools as inclusive communities. In W. Stainback & S. Stainback (Eds.), *Controversial issues confronting special education: Divergent perspectives* (pp. 31–43). Boston: Allyn & Bacon.

Stainback, W., & Stainback, S. (1991). Rationale for integration and restructuring: A synopsis. In J. W. Lloyd, N. N. Singh, & A. C. Repp (Eds.), *The regular education initiative: Alternative perspectives on concepts, issues, and models* (pp. 225–240). Sycamore, IL: Sycamore.

Sternberg, R. J. (1985). Beyond IQ: *A triarchic theory of intelligence.* New York: Cambridge University Press.

Sternberg, R. J. (1997). The triarchic theory of intelligence. In D. P. Flanagan, J. Genshaft, & P. L. Harrison (Eds.), *Contemporary intellectual assessment:: Theories, tests, and issues* (pp. 92–104). New York: Guilford.

Sternberg, R. J., & Spear, L. C. (1985). A triarchic theory of mental retardation. In N. R. Ellis (Ed.),

International review of research in mental retardation (Vol. 13, pp. 301–326). New York: Academic Press.

Stokes, T. F., & Osnes, P. G. (1988). The developing applied technology of generalization and maintenance. In R. H. Horner, G. Dunlap, & R. L. Koegel (Eds.), *Generalization and maintenance* (pp. 5–19). Baltimore: Paul H. Brookes.

Turner, L., Dofny, E., & Dutka, S. (1994). Effective strategy and attribution training on strategy maintenance and transfer. *American Journal on Mental Retardation, 98*(4), 445–454.

U.S. Department of Education, Office of Special Education Programs. (1997). *Nineteenth Annual Report to Congress on the Implementation of the Individuals with Disabilities Education Act.* Washington, DC: Author.

Voss, K. (1997, July/August). Augmenting communication. *Disability Solutions 2*(2), 5–10.

Wehman, P. (1997). Traumatic brain injury. In P. Wehman (Ed.), *Exceptional individuals in school, community, and work* (pp. 451–485). Austin, TX: Pro-Ed.

Westling, D. (1986). *Introduction to mental retardation.* Upper Saddle River, NJ: Merrill/Prentice Hall.

Westling, D. & Fox, L. (1995). *Teaching students with severe disabilities.* Upper Saddle River, NJ: Merrill/Prentice Hall.

Whitman, T. L. (1990). Self-regulation and mental retardation. *American Journal on Mental Retardation, 94*(4), 347–362.

Willig, A. C., & Greenberg, H. F. (1986). *Bilingualism and learning disabilities: Policy and practice for teachers and administrators.* New York: American Library.

Chapter **9**

The Adolescent with Mental Retardation and the Transitional Years

Core Concepts

- Components of an effective high school program for adolescents with mental retardation include a comprehensive curriculum that focuses on employment preparation, the teaching of adaptive skills, and instruction in functional academics when appropriate.
- Work is important not only for monetary rewards but also for personal identity and status.
- Two important pieces of legislation that have had significant impact on employment training for adolescents with mental retardation are the Vocational Rehabilitation Act and IDEA.
- Career education focuses on preparation for life and personal social skills, in addition to instruction in occupational skills.
- Work experience is a method of training in which the student may participate in occupational activities in the community under actual working conditions.
- In a community-referenced training approach, the demands of the work setting and the functioning level of the individual determine goals and objectives.
- Socialization training includes the development of positive interpersonal relationships with family and peers, as well as the acquisition of behaviors appropriate in a variety of community settings.
- Adolescents with mental retardation may need to learn the critical skills necessary to speak up for themselves and manage their personal needs as they move into adult life.
- Recreation and leisure activities may contribute to the adolescent's emotional, psychological, and affective development.
- The purpose of teaching academic tool subjects to adolescents with mental retardation is to enhance opportunities for their independence in the classroom, family, and community.
- Although effective educational and adult service models can provide greater opportunities for individuals with mental retardation in community settings, significant long-term changes may not result without transition planning.
- Effective transition planning is ongoing and begins with goals and objectives established from the time the student enters school.
- The needs of adults with mental retardation are diverse and vary with the severity of the condition and the demands of the environment.
- The purposes of transition planning are to establish a working relationship between students/parents and adult service agencies, to identify resources for employment and community participation, to access services before graduation, and to locate systems that will help maintain needed services.
- Parents must have the opportunity to learn as much as possible about adult service systems before their son or daughter leaves school.

- The successful transition of the adult with mental retardation to life in an inclusive community setting begins with integration during the school years.

Core Concept

Components of an effective high school program for adolescents with mental retardation include a comprehensive curriculum that focuses on employment preparation, the teaching of adaptive skills, and instruction in functional academics when appropriate.

Adolescence is a period of transition that encompasses the personal, social, and educational life of the individual. Adolescents are suspended between childhood and adulthood for several years, attempting to free themselves from the child's role but not yet ready to assume an adult's responsibilities. They work toward emancipation from the family unit while developing social and educational characteristics that help them gain greater acceptance in society. For adolescents with mental retardation, educational goals during this period are directed toward employment opportunities and preparation for life as an adult.

The challenges of adolescence are intensified for the individual with mental retardation. Many adolescents with retardation have the same physical attributes as their nondisabled peers but lack the capacity to cope with the demands of their environment or their own desires for emancipation from childhood. Adolescents with moderate or severe retardation, whose physical and cognitive differences may be readily apparent, focus on achieving as much social and employment independence as possible.

In this chapter, we consider the educational and employment training programs that schools may offer adolescents with retardation. Our discussion concentrates on expected outcomes of secondary education programs for students with mental retardation, as well as on the elements of an effective high school experience. During the adolescent years, educational programs for students with mental retardation primarily focus on the skills necessary to make the successful transition from school to adult life. For individuals with mild retardation, greater emphasis on applying such academic tools as reading and arithmetic to employment and personal/social needs begins during the junior high years. For children with moderate or severe mental retardation, many of these skill areas are a central focus of the curriculum, from the time they enter school.

EXPECTED OUTCOMES OF SECONDARY EDUCATION PROGRAMS

A critical measure of the effectiveness of any educational program is the success of its graduates. Although 1995 marked the 20th anniversary of the passage of Public Law 94-142 (renamed IDEA in 1990), the educational opportunities afforded by this landmark legislation have not yet led to full participation of special education graduates in the social and economic mainstream of their local communities (Bursuck & Rose, 1992; Gartin, Rumrill, Serebreni, 1996).

Results of several follow-up studies of special education graduates suggested that these adults were unable to participate fully in community activities, had little or no social life outside the family or primary care givers, and were isolated from both disabled and nondisabled peers (Peraino, 1992; Rusch, 1996; Valdes, Williamson, & Wagner, 1990; Wagner & Blackorby, 1996). The vast majority of these adults were not employed (Hasazi, Johnson, Hasazi, Gordon, & Hull, 1989; Rusch, 1996; Wagner & Blackorby, 1996). In fact, a 1994 Lou Harris poll found that (1) only three of ten adults with disabilities were working full- or part-time, (2) 79% of those not working and of working age indicated that they would like to have jobs, and (3) a comparison of working and non-working individuals with disabilities revealed that those who were working were more satisfied with life, had more money, and were less likely to blame their disability for preventing them from reaching their individual potential (Harris & Associates, 1994).

The National Longitudinal Transition Study of the U.S. Department of Education (Valdes et al., 1990; Wagner & Blackorby, 1996) reported that paid employment during high school had become more common, with 42% of students with disabilities being placed in community vocational or employment programs. However, one out of four of these students worked less than 10 hours per week and was paid below minimum wage. Most students, including those with mental retardation were in service and manual labor positions. Five years out of high school, 57% of students with disabilities were in competitive employment, with 43% of this group working full-time. The employment rate of individuals with disabilities lagged far behind those of nondisabled adults. Table 9–1 provides a summary of the study's results for students categorized as mentally retarded.

Because special education graduates are not fully accessing community services and programs, the need is to identify what should be expected of high school programs. Goals for these individuals are described most often as establishing social relationships with family and friends, access to services and activities within the local community, and involvement in the economic life of the community (McDonnell, Hardman, McDonnell, & Kiefer-O'Donnell, 1995; McDonnell, Wilcox, & Hardman, 1991; Nisbet, 1992). To be effective, a high school program for students with mental retardation must be directed toward meeting each of these goals. Components of an effective high school program include a comprehensive curriculum that focuses on employment preparation, the teaching of adaptive skills for adult life, and instruction in functional academics where appropriate (McDonnell, Mathot-Bucker, & Ferguson, 1996; Udvari-Solner, Jorgensen, & Courchane, 1992). Secondary education programs also should incorporate inclusion with nondisabled peers, consistent parental involvement, and the implementation of systematic transition planning (McDonnell et al., 1996; McDonnell et al., 1995).

TABLE 9–1
Employment Characteristics of Adolescents with Mental Retardation

From The National Longitudinal Transition Study of Special Education Students, Statistical Almanac Volume 5: Youth Categorized as Mentally Retarded *by K. A. Valdes C. L. Williamson, and M. M. Wagner, 1990, Menlo Park, CA: SRI.*

| | Age | | |
Characteristics	15–16	17–18	19 and older
Percentage of adolescents with mental retardation[1] who are:			
• unemployed	72%	50%	50%
• in sheltered work only	0%	1%	9%
• competitively employed			
part-time	15%	14%	11%
full-time	2%	7%	11%
• in work study only	6%	20%	13%
• earning less than $3.00 per hour	47%	28%	27%
Average hourly wage for employed adolescents with mental retardation[2]	$3.10	$3.30	$3.30

[1]N = 187 (15–16 year olds), 283 (17–18 year olds), 436 (19 years and older)
[2]N = 26 (15–16 year olds), 61 (17–18 year olds), 143 (19 years and older)

EMPLOYMENT PREPARATION

Core Concept

Work is important not only for monetary rewards but also for personal identity and status.

The person with mental retardation is often characterized as one who consumes services, rather than as one who contributes to the community. A consumer of services is dependent on the charity of others. Employment assists in removing this image and in placing the individual in the role of contributor. Work is important as a means to earn wages and, through wages, to obtain material goods that contribute to quality of life. Work also confers personal identity and status.

From Colonial days to the 20th century, the pervasive belief in the United States has been that individuals should have the opportunity to seek their own livelihoods. This belief, however, has not applied equally to all. For persons with mental retardation, access to employment training and placement has been negligible throughout most of U.S. history. Even today, many people with mental retardation are unemployed or underemployed, despite the dramatic increases in employment research and development of the 1980s and 1990s (Harris & Associates, 1989, 1994; Valdes et al., 1990; Wagner & Blackorby, 1996). Many explanations for this problem are proffered, some of which are recounted by the National Council on Disability (1989):

> Traditionally, many high schools have focused their employment preparation programs on a general assessment of student interests and strengths, and the teaching of vocational readiness skills in a classroom setting. This approach places high schools in a passive role in preparing students for employment. The instruction focuses more on general preparation for employment rather than training for a specific job(s). (p. 42)

In this section, we examine the issues surrounding employment preparation for persons with mental retardation, reviewing various approaches to training including career education, work experience, and community-referenced training. Our discussion begins with the legislative mandates that have played such a vital role in the development of vocational services for citizens with retardation.

Legislative Mandates for Employment Training

Core Concept

Two important pieces of legislation that have had significant impact on employment training for adolescents with mental retardation are the Vocational Rehabilitation Act and IDEA.

Federal legislation has given broad support to comprehensive employment preparation that is accessible to all persons with mental retardation. Two pieces of legislation are particularly important: the Vocational Rehabilitation Act and IDEA. These two laws have had a significant impact on the development and quality of employment training services to individuals with mental retardation.

Persons with mental retardation have been eligible for vocational services under the Barden-LaFollet Act ever since 1943, but few received any services until the 1960s. The Vocational Rehabilitation Act of 1973 (Public Law 93-112) greatly enhanced access to vocational rehabilitation services. The act established vocational training as a mandatory service for all qualified persons with disabilities. Section 504 of this act contains basic civil rights legislation for persons with disabilities, which makes it illegal to discriminate against these individuals in access to vocational training and employment. Subsection 84.11 of the Federal Regulations for Section 504 states, "No qualified handicapped person shall, on the basis of handicap, be subjected to discrimination in employment under any program or activity to which this part applies" (*Federal Register,* 1977). Discrimination is prohibited in the following areas:

1. Recruitment, advertising, and processing of applications
2. Hiring, alterations in job status, rehiring
3. Rates of pay and other forms of compensation

4. Job assignments and classifications, lines of progression, and seniority
5. Leaves of absence and sick leave
6. Fringe benefits
7. Selection and financial support for training, conferences, and other job-related activities
8. Employer-approved activities, including social and recreational programs.

The passage of this law did not mean that long-established negative attitudes toward persons with disabilities suddenly disappeared. It was, however, a first step toward opening new doors for people with disabilities in general and for persons with retardation in particular. Career and vocational education for individuals with retardation became more important than ever. Section 503 of the same act emphasizes the regulations for affirmative action to employ people with disabilities. If individuals with retardation are properly educated and can perform competitively for jobs, the federal government stands behind these individuals both in promoting affirmative action in their employment and in prohibiting any discrimination in their hiring. It is critical to reemphasize here that persons with retardation need to be educated and trained as competent employees. (See Chapter 11 for more information on nondiscriminatory practices in the employment of persons with mental retardation under the Americans with Disabilities Act [ADA].)

In addition to reaffirming the civil rights of persons with disabilities, the Vocational Rehabilitation Act has several other objectives:

- To promote expanded employment opportunities for persons with disabilities in all areas of business and industry
- To establish state plans for the purpose of providing vocational rehabilitation services to meet the needs of persons with disabilities
- To conduct evaluations of the potential rehabilitation of persons with disabilities and to expand services to them, as well as to those who have not received any or received inadequate rehabilitation services
- To increase the number and competence of rehabilitation personnel through retraining and upgrading experiences

Current provisions of the Vocational Rehabilitation Act mandate services on a priority basis, with the most severely disabled as the highest priority. Research studies published in the 1970s, however, indicated that many of these people continued to be excluded from vocational rehabilitation services (Halpern, 1973; Sowers, Thompson, & Connis, 1979). In 1986, Congress passed new amendments to the Vocational Rehabilitation Act (Rehabilitation Act Amendments of 1986, Public Law 99-506) that strengthened the mandate to serve the most severely handicapped individuals. The amendments include provisions for supported employment (see Chapter 10 for a more detailed explanation of supported employment). This new dimension in employment models for persons with mental retardation is described in Section 103 of Public Law 99-506 as follows:

Competitive work in integrated work settings for individuals with severe handicaps for whom competitive employment has not traditionally occurred, or for individuals for whom competitive employment has been interrupted or intermittent as a result of a severe disability, and who because of their handicap, need on-going support services to perform such work.

In 1992, Congress once again amended the Vocational Rehabilitation Act, encouraging stronger collaboration and outreach between the schools and rehabilitation counselors in transition planning. Greater linkages between education and vocational rehabilitation are expected to benefit the student with mental retardation in moving on to postsecondary education or in obtaining employment.

Additional federal legislation, under the Carl Perkins Vocational and Applied Technology Education Act of 1990, has enhanced employment training opportunities for adolescents with mental retardation. This act provides increased access for all students, including those with disabilities, to vocational education training during the high school years.

IDEA requires that all students with disabilities who are between the ages of 3 and 22 years receive a free and appropriate education. The provisions of this act are the basis for current employment training for youths with mental retardation. Several researchers have substantiated the need for appropriate employment preparation programs for adolescents with more severe retardation (Brolin, Durand, Kromer, & Muller, 1989; Hasazi, Gordon, & Roe, 1985a; Hasazi, Gordon, Roe, Finck, Holl, & Salembier, 1985b; Inge & Wehman; 1993; Wehman & Kregel, 1994).

In 1990 and 1997, Congress passed amendments to IDEA that strengthened employment training through planning for the transition from school to adult life. These amendments are discussed later in this chapter under the heading "Transition Planning."

Career Education

Core Concept

Career education focuses on preparation for life and personal social skills, in addition to instruction in occupational skills.

Career education begins in the early elementary years and continues throughout high school. Its purpose is to make work, either paid, or unpaid, a meaningful component of the student's life (Hoyt, 1993). Patton, Beirne-Smith, and Payne (1990) describe career education as going beyond job training to preparing students for the diverse roles of adult life.

Career education models have been developed by Brolin (1993, 1995) and Clark and Kolstoe (1995). Brolin's model consists of several competencies, experiences, and stages clustered into three curriculum areas: daily living skills, personal-social skills, and occupational guidance and preparation. Brolin (1995, p. 3) conceptualizes career education into four progressive and interrelated stages:

1. *Career awareness* begins at the elementary level and is intended to make students aware of the existence of work . . . and workers and how students will fit into the work-oriented society in the future.
2. *Career exploration* . . . emphasized at the middle school/junior high level, is intended to help students explore their interests and abilities in relation to life-style and occupations.
3. *Career preparation*, emphasized at the high school level, is a period for career decision making and skills acquisition.
4. *Career assimilation* is the transition of the student into post-secondary training and community-adjustment situations.

As a means to infuse career education into the regular education program, Brolin (1993) developed the Life-Centered Career Education (LCCE) Curriculum model. The LCCE teaches 22 major life skill competencies across the four stages of career development (see Table 9–2).

In 1979, Clark developed a school-based career education model for students with disabilities that begins at the elementary school level. Clark and Kolstoe (1995) applied the model to adolescents with disabilities as they transition from school to adult life. The model consists of four elements: (a) values, attitudes, and habits, (b) human relationships, (c) occupational information, and (d) acquisition of job and daily living skills. Career education is a total educational concept that systematically coordinates all school, family, and community components, thus facilitating the individual's potential for economic, social, and personal fulfillment.

Work Experience

Core Concept

Work experience is a method of training in which the student may participate in occupational activities in the community under actual working conditions.

Work experiences vary according to the philosophy of each particular program. Some programs begin work experiences in the school setting and eventually ease the student into community settings; others may have the student work in the community immediately. The difficulty and the type of assignment are usually dependent on the needs and nature of each student. Before placements are made, each student's ability and interests are evaluated carefully. During the years spent in a vocational class, the student may have an opportunity to work in a variety of settings to maximize exposure to different types of job-related experiences and possibly allow the student to find the permanent placement he or she would like at the completion of school. The primary purpose of the work experience, however, is not to develop specific vocational skills but rather to enable the student to develop the work habits and interpersonal skills necessary to get and keep any job. If, in the course of training, specific skills are acquired, these naturally could be helpful in obtaining specific jobs at the end of school.

TABLE 9–2
Possible LCCE Competency Instructional Subject Areas

Competency	Elementary	Middle School/ Junior High	Senior High
Daily Living Skills			
1. Managing personal finances	Math, language, reading	Business, math	Home economics, math
2. Selecting and managing a household	Language, social studies	Home economics, vocational education	Home economics
3. Caring for personal needs	Science, health	Home economics, health	Home economics
4. Raising children and meeting marriage responsibilities	Health	Home economics	Home economics
5. Buying, preparing, and consuming food	Reading, language	Home economics	Home economics
6. Buying and caring for clothing	Reading, language	Home economics	Home economics
7. Exhibiting responsible citizenship	Social studies	Social studies, music	Social studies, music
8. Utilizing recreational facilities and engaging in leisure	Health, physical education	Physical education, art, music, counselors	Physical education, art, music, counselors
9. Getting around the community	Health, science	Home economics	Driver's education
Personal-Social Skills			
10. Achieving self-awareness	Language, social studies	Music, physical education, counselors	Art, music, counselors
11. Acquiring self-confidence	Health, science	Art, music, physical education, home economics, counselors	Physical education, counselors, social studies, art, vocational education, music

But specific competencies must not be emphasized at the expense of the affective dimensions of vocational behavior.

Community-Referenced Training

Core Concept

In a community-referenced training approach, the demands of the work setting and the functioning level of the individual determine goals and objectives.

Competency	Elementary	Middle School/ Junior High	Senior High
12. Achieving socially responsible behavior— community	Social studies, language	Physical education, counselors	Social studies, music
13. Maintaining good interpersonal skills	Language, social studies	Counselors	Music, counselors
14. Achieving independence	Social studies, language	Counselors	Counselors
15. Making adequate decisions	Language, social studies	math, counselors	Science, counselors
16. Communicating with others	Language, reading	Language arts, music, speech, physical education	Language arts, speech, music, art
Occupational Skills			
17. Knowing and exploring occupational possibilities	Reading, social studies	Vocational education, home economics, counselors	Counselors
18. Selecting and planning occupational choices	Language, social studies	Business, vocational education, home economics	Counselors
19. Exhibiting appropriate work habits and behaviors	Science, art	Vocational education, math, home economics, art	Home economics, vocational education, music
20. Seeking, securing, and maintaining employment	Language, social studies	Counselors	Counselors
21. Exhibiting sufficient physical-manual skills	Art, physical education	Vocational education, home economics	Vocational education, home economics
22. Obtaining specific occupational skills	Social studies, art, music	Vocational education, home economics	Vocational education, home economics

From Career Education: A Functional Life Skills Approach *(3rd ed., p. 72) by D. E. Brolin, 1995, Upper Saddle River, NJ: Merrill/Prentice Hall.*

The community-referenced approach to employment training, though similar to work-experience programs in some ways, has some very notable differences. The idea that people with mental retardation must have acquired a certain level of skills prior to going into community work settings is not acceptable in this approach. Training focuses directly on the activities to be accomplished in the community work setting, rather than on the development of skills in the class-room. Consequently, goals and objectives develop from the demands of the

Instruction and transition planning during adolescence may still include one-to-one work with the teacher.

work setting considered in conjunction with the functioning level of the individual. Research has clearly indicated that individuals with retardation, including those with moderate and severe disabilities, can work in community employment settings with adequate training and support (Wehman & Revell, 1996).

Effectively preparing adolescents with mental retardation for community work settings requires a comprehensive employment training program in the high school. The critical characteristics of an employment training program based on a community-referenced approach to instruction include the following:

- A curriculum that reflects the job opportunities available in the local community
- An employment training program that takes place at actual job sites
- Training designed to sample the individual's performance across a variety of economically viable alternatives
- Ongoing opportunities for students to interact with nondisabled peers in the work setting
- Training that culminates in specific job training and placement
- Job placement linked to comprehensive transition planning, which focuses on establishing interagency agreements that support the individual's full participation in the community.

TEACHING ADAPTIVE SKILLS

Socialization

Core Concept

Socialization training includes the development of positive interpersonal relationships with family and peers, as well as the acquisition of behaviors appropriate in a variety of community settings.

Adaptive skills teaching for students with mental retardation generally falls into three categories: socialization, personal management, and recreational/leisure time. **Socialization** training includes developing positive interpersonal relationships with family and peers, as well as acquiring behaviors appropriate in a variety of community settings. It is important for adolescents with mental retardation to become aware of their strengths and limitations as they interact with adults and peers in a social context.

One of the greatest needs in the area of socialization for adolescents with retardation is access to social activities. Adolescents with mental retardation may lack the sophistication that most nondisabled individuals learn through observation. The challenges for these adolescents include locating transportation, as well as planning and financing social activities.

Transportation is a problem for many teenagers with mental retardation. Some are unable to drive because they lack access to an automobile or because they can't pass driver's education. If the adolescent is unable to pass driver's training, the school must offer instruction in the use of public transportation. The ability to use public transportation may be important not only for social reasons but also for employment. If public transportation is not available, then parents, school staff, or volunteers must provide it. For those able to profit from it, driver's education is usually available in the high school. Driver's education may be perceived as controversial for the adolescent with mental retardation. It has been argued that only the most capable students with mental retardation should be encouraged to drive. These would include students who possess the coordination and ability to think critically in difficult situations and emergencies.

The adolescent with mental retardation is often unable to take the initiative in planning social activities. As such, the responsibility to provide social activities rests with volunteer groups, local associations for people with retardation, and parents. Many social functions can be planned at school with the assistance of teachers and staff. If a university or college is nearby, special education and recreational therapy majors might be available to assist in planning and supervising functions (see "Best Buddies").

The learning of appropriate social interaction skills should begin early in the home and continue throughout the school years. Most adolescents with mental retardation are eager to learn because they would like to be as much like their nondisabled peers as possible.

Best Buddies:

The Only Way to Have a Friend Is to Be One

American poet and philosopher Ralph Waldo Emerson wrote: "The only way to have a friend is to be one." However, for people with mental retardation, few avenues exist by which these individuals can find and keep friendships over time. The reality for most people with mental retardation is that opportunities to establish relationships are often limited to immediate family members and paid service workers. What people with mental retardation want to have is friends outside the immediate family who are not paid to be there.

Best Buddies was founded by Anthony Shriver (son of Eunice Kennedy Shriver and nephew of President John F. Kennedy) in 1989. It is a national service program that provides an opportunity for people who are not disabled to get to know persons with mental retardation and possibly become friends. People without disabilities are recruited to share their lives by participating in various activities with a person with mental retardation. Activities are selected based on mutual interests, needs, and abilities and can range from going to a movie or sharing a meal to hanging out with friends.

Best Buddies High Schools, an exciting new program, began in October 1994. In today's schools, students with mental retardation often enter the same building and walk the same hallways as their peers, but they are left out of social activities. By introducing Best Buddies as a service program in local high schools, the invisible line is crossed that too often separates those with disabilities from those without.

Best Buddies Colleges is a highly successful program on college and university campuses throughout the United States, England, Canada, and Greece. Best Buddies Colleges has grown from only two campuses in 1989 to over 200 in 1997, thanks to the participation of thousands of college students.

Best Buddies Citizens takes friendship from the campus to the community by pairing corporate employees, church members, and others in one-to-one friendships with people with mental retardation. The Citizens program is creating friendships in Florida, Utah, Connecticut, Pennsylvania, and Maryland.

Historically, the United States has a strong tradition of community participation. Americans vote, pay taxes, join the PTA, serve on the school board, and so on. Unfortunately, people with mental retardation tend to be left out of community activities because of the general public's misunderstanding of and inexperience with people with differences.

In becoming friends with a person with mental retardation, High School Buddies, College Buddies, and Citizen Buddies learn to appreciate the person first. Such an awareness opens doors for people with mental retardation to more fully enter community workplaces and neighborhoods. Kathy Koski, a former Best Buddies student leader, expressed the importance of Best Buddies this way:

> You will never know the impact you are making on your Buddy's [person with mental retardation] life, or, for that matter, the impact you are making on the community. Every time you and your Buddy go out, someone realizes that your Buddy is a capable and contributing member of society.

The community impacted includes parents, siblings, and other family members (of persons with mental retardation) who are frustrated at the lack of social opportunities available for a family member with special needs. Beverly Clark, mother of a person with mental retardation matched in a Texas Chapter, said it this way:

> A few weeks ago, when I arrived home from work, [my daughter] Pamela greeted me at the

door. Pamela told me that her Best Buddy, Erica, had called and asked if she could go to a football game, that they would also eat dinner out, and could she go. I held back my tears of joy until she left for the evening, acting as though it was a normal occurrence. I felt the joy most parents take for granted! (I know, because

with my daughter Laura, I take this sort of everyday activity for granted.)

For more information about Best Buddies, call 1-800-89-BUDDY or write Best Buddies, 100 S.E. 2nd Street, Suite 1990, Miami, FL 33131.

Source: Best Buddies, 100 S.E. 2nd Street, Suite 1990, Miami, FL 33131

Self-Determination and Personal Management

Core Concept

Adolescents with mental retardation may need to learn the critical skills necessary to speak up for themselves and manage their personal needs as they move into adult life.

While still in school, many adolescents with mental retardation will need to learn the critical skills necessary to succeed or, at the very least, become more independent, during the adult years. Personal management skills include the ability to problem-solve and make decisions, develop an understanding of sex-role expectations, and take care of personal appearance and hygiene.

The ability to problem-solve and make life decisions is referred to as "self-determination." Hughes and Agran (1998) describe self-determination as "people speaking up for themselves and making and acting on their own lifestyle choices (i.e., living their lives pretty much like everybody else hopes to and, to some extent, probably does" [p. 1]).

Learning self-determination helps adolescents with mental retardation to play a major role in choosing and achieving their goals as they make the transition into adult life; it also helps them to understand the barriers they may face. Ultimately, the student comes away from school with a more well-developed sense of personal worth and social responsibility (Deci, Vallerand, Pelletier, & Ryan, 1991).

One area requiring considerable decision-making skills during adolescence is sexual behavior. Sexual interest is a defining characteristic of adolescence, and for high schools, it represents the difficult challenge of identifying what role, if any, the school will have in providing instruction in this area.

The onset of puberty brings about many changes in the adolescent. These changes include physiological and behavioral differences, the most noticeable being the attainment of sexual function. As these physical changes occur, estrogen, progesterone, and testosterone production levels also increase. These hormones are essential for secondary sex characteristics (e.g., broadening of the shoulders and increased muscle mass in boys; widening of the hips in girls). Changes occur in reproductive systems and in distribution of body hair and adipose tissue. When and how fast these changes happen varies. Puberty changes in girls generally begin between the ages of 10 and 14 years, and in boys, between 12 and 16 years.

The beginning of reproductive capabilities is evident with the beginning of menstruation for girls and seminal emission for boys. Menstruation is usually irregular and not accompanied by ovulation for several months. Likewise, for boys, mature sexual capabilities may not occur for several months after the first indications of development. Unless adolescents with mental retardation are prepared for the dramatic physiological changes brought about by puberty, they may come as traumatic experiences. The adolescent female with mental retardation who has not been prepared for menstruation may find her initial experience frightening and may be too embarrassed to seek help.

Who is responsible for providing sex education? That is a hotly debated issue. Whereas some individuals believe that sex education belongs in the school, others consider sex education primarily, if not exclusively, the responsibility of the parents. Sex education is one of the most controversial subjects confronting American public schools today.

Teachers are hesitant to offer sex education without authorization. Peers are the only constant source of information about sex, but the ideas of adolescents are often distorted or highly inaccurate. This problem is certainly not unique to those with mental retardation, but it may be more acute because they are often less able to locate accurate information. The adolescent with mental retardation may not be able to read or comprehend the written information even if it is made available.

Parents may have difficulty discussing their child's sexual maturation with the family pediatrician. Even though they may recognize the need for information to deal effectively with their son or daughter's needs, they may be reluctant to ask questions. Many parents will not seek help until the natural course of physical development forces the issue of sex education into the open.

Success in dealing with sex-related issues depends on the willingness of adults to give adolescents permission to ask questions or to wonder about sexual matters. Although our Puritan heritage has imposed inhibitions that influence society's official attitude, there are opposing views with regard to sexual permissiveness. There is little doubt that sexual activity among adolescents is on the increase.

Related to the increase of sexual activity among adolescents is an increasing incidence of sexually transmitted diseases, including AIDS. Some adolescents, including those with mental retardation, will continue to engage in sexual activity with or without the approval of society. Unless they receive adequate sex education, unwanted pregnancies and sexually transmitted diseases are inevitable. Although school board members, parents, and the public argue over

Personal appearance becomes increasingly important for the youngster with mental retardation during adolescence.

who should take responsibility for sex education, many adolescents with mental retardation remain in ignorance, victims of indecision.

In addition to changes in sexual function, puberty may also bring about changes in personal appearance. Acne frequently causes emotional scarring far more significant and permanent than any physical scarring. Adolescents who are not disabled have the advantage of being able to read and ask questions. Some go to a dermatologist to help protect their appearance. Adolescents with mental retardation may have difficulty in locating necessary help. Some lack the financial resources to receive treatment from a dermatologist. Unable to care for themselves adequately and to maintain an acceptable appearance, adolescents with mental retardation may find social acceptance very difficult.

Unfortunately, some parents of children with mental retardation make the assumption that their son's or daughter's intellectual limitations render physical appearance of little consequence. Yet most adolescents with retardation strive constantly to be as much like their nondisabled peers as possible. They do not want to draw attention to the fact that they are different. Being less well groomed first draws attention and then hinders or even precludes social acceptance. Parents and teachers must be aware that looks usually have a bearing on self-concept and that programs and curricula must include attention to appearance in the education of adolescents.

Parents may lack ability or desire to teach hygiene skills to adolescents with mental retardation. In such situations, responsibility also falls on the schools. Instruction in this area may take several forms. Class discussion is one way to address this need. Guest speakers from clothing and cosmetic stores can be brought into the schools, or the teacher can take students into these stores for a demonstration. Students with mental retardation may also be able to learn to sew their own clothing through participation in home economics courses.

For students with skin problems who are unable to access a dermatologist, the school nurse should be able to provide the necessary information about skin care and treatment of acne. Beauty colleges that train cosmetologists are frequently willing to provide their services to teach students with mental retardation how to shampoo and take care of their hair.

Recreation and Leisure

Core Concept

Recreation and leisure activities may contribute to the adolescent's emotional, psychological, and affective development.

The opportunity to participate in community recreation and leisure activities may vary considerably depending upon the age and severity of the individual's mental retardation. For many adults with mental retardation, television is the only consistent leisure experience (Hardman, Drew, & Egan, 1999). However, this picture is changing for the better. Some agencies and communities are initiating new programs specifically for persons with mental retardation. Many colleges and universities have developed special or adaptive physical education, recreation, and therapeutic recreation programs that prepare professionals to work with people who are disabled. Other programs, such as Special Olympics, are expanding throughout the United States and worldwide. Special Olympics provides children and adults with mental retardation the opportunity to participate in sports competition. Recently, Special Olympics expanded into the Unified Sports Program, a program that involves both nondisabled individuals and people with mental retardation in integrated team sports.

Although the development of structured leisure programs for adolescents with mental retardation is encouraging, much remains to be done. It is disconcerting to realize that most free-time activities for adolescents with mental retardation revolve around watching television. Yet, training programs in the development of leisure skills, like those used in therapeutic recreation, can be effective. The goal of therapeutic recreation is to help people with mental retardation take advantage of leisure opportunities as a means to enhance their independence in the community (Hardman et al., 1999).

TEACHING ACADEMIC SKILLS

Core Concept

The purpose of teaching academic tool subjects to adolescents with mental retardation is to enhance opportunities for their independence in the classroom, family, and community.

The objectives of an academic skills program for adolescents with mental retardation are primarily functional. Such programs are oriented to daily living activities, leisure time, and employment preparation. For the adolescent with mild mental retardation, basic academics may be a higher priority than for the student with more severe mental retardation. This is because adolescents with mild retardation may be better able to assimilate academic skills into their daily living and employment preparation activities. Because adolescents with moderate and severe retardation have a diminished ability to apply academic tools to daily living, it is necessary to emphasize adaptive skill training for these students.

A functional academics program includes instruction in reading, language, and mathematics. A functional reading program focuses on protection and information. A protective (sometimes referred to as survival) vocabulary teaches the student to read building signs (e.g., push/pull, men/women, entrance/exit), street signs (e.g., walk/don't walk, stop, caution, railroad crossing), and common environmental safety words (e.g., *keep out, danger, poison, hazard, do not enter*). An informational reading program teaches functional skills related to employment (e.g., components of a job application form, reading classified ads), daily living

Teaching academic skills to students with mental retardation is one of many areas where computer technology may be effectively used.

(e.g., use of maps, telephone directories, catalogs), and leisure activities (e.g., movie listings, newspapers).

Functional language programs focus on the use of expressive and receptive skills. Instruction in expressive language includes effective oral skills in carrying on a conversation, talking on the telephone, and responding to questions. Some degree of writing proficiency also may be necessary to enhance independence in community and employment activities. These skills range from the basic ability to write one's name to the more complex task of filling out a job application form. Receptive skills also are needed for daily conversations and job interviews. Good oral skills are not helpful if the individual is unable to understand what others say.

The intended outcomes for a functional mathematics program are generally basic management of personal finances, consumer skills, and telling time. A personal finance program instructs the adolescent in several areas, including budgeting money, establishing and using credit, taxes, insurance, and wages. Consumer skills include identifying coins and bills of all denominations, making change, and reading bus or train schedules and timetables.

The decision of whether to include functional academics as a component of a student's instructional program must be looked at in the context of each student's prioritized needs. As such, Browder and Snell (1993) recommended that five factors be addressed in deciding whether to include functional academics as a program focus:

1. Current and future academic skill needs
2. Other skill needs
3. Chronological age
4. The prior rate of learning in academics
5. The student's and parents' preferences (p. 443)

TRANSITION PLANNING

Core Concept

Although effective educational and adult service models can provide greater opportunities for individuals with mental retardation in community settings, significant long-term changes may not result without transition planning.

Each year, approximately 50,000 adolescents with mental retardation leave school and face life as adults in their local communities. The transition from school to adult life is not easy. Many adults with retardation find that they cannot get services critical for success in the community (Harris & Associates, 1994; Hasazi et al., 1989; Rusch, 1996; Wagner & Blackorby, 1996). These individuals may face long waiting lists for employment and housing services.

Transition planning must facilitate the coordination and expansion of services within the community for each adult with retardation (McDonnell et al., 1995; McDonnell et al., 1996). Professionals and parents have come to the realization that a systematic transition planning process must begin during the school years and carry over into adulthood.

Federal and state initiatives for transition planning were begun in 1983; they focused on the development of new programs to facilitate transition from school to adult life. The federal requirement that every student with a disability is to receive transition services was mandated into law in 1990 and expanded by Congress in IDEA 97. Under IDEA 97, transition services for students with disabilities

- are designed within an outcome-oriented process, which promotes movement from school to post-school activities, including post-secondary education, vocational training, integrated employment (including supported employment), continuing and adult education, adult services, independent living, or community participation
- are based upon the individual student's needs, taking into account the student's preferences and interests
- include instruction, related services, community experiences, the development of employment and other post-school adult living objectives, and, when appropriate, acquisition of daily living skills and functional vocational evaluation. (Sec. 602[30])

IDEA 97 requires that beginning at age 14 and updated annually, a student's IEP include a statement of the transition services that relate to various courses of study (such as participation in advanced-placement courses or a vocational education program). Beginning at age 16 (or younger, if determined appropriate by the IEP team), an IEP must include a statement of the needed transition services, including, when appropriate, a statement of the interagency responsibilities (such as vocational rehabilitation) or any other needed linkages.

The critical components of transition planning include (a) effective high school programs that prepare students to work and live in the community, (b) a broad range of adult service programs that can meet the various support needs of individuals with handicaps, in employment and community settings, and (c) comprehensive and cooperative transition planning between educational and community service agencies in order to develop needed services for graduation (McDonnell et al., 1991; McDonnell et al., 1995; McDonnell et al., 1996; Will, 1984).

The remainder of this section focuses on a process designed to address the critical components of transition planning and to facilitate coordination and expansion of services within the community for each individual with retardation.

Coordinating Transition Planning

Core Concept

Effective transition planning is ongoing and begins with goals and objectives established from the time the student enters school.

The foundation for a formal transition planning process begins in elementary school and comes to fruition during the high school years. High schools must organize their programs and activities to produce outcomes that facilitate success for the individual during the adult years. Outcomes for the adult with mental retardation include the ability to function as independently as possible in daily life. The individual should be involved in the economic life of the community, both in paid and/or unpaid work. He or she should also be able to participate in social and leisure activities that are part of community living. The role of school personnel includes assessing individual needs, developing an individualized transition plan (ITP) for each student, coordinating transition planning with adult service agencies, and participating with parents in the planning process (Hardman et al., 1999; Hardman & McDonnell, 1987; McDonnell et al., 1996).

Determining Individual Need

Core Concept

The needs of adults with mental retardation are diverse and vary with the severity of the condition and the demands of the environment.

For some adults with mild mental retardation, support may be unnecessary following school. Others may need a short-term support system. For adults with moderate to severe retardation, the support necessary to ensure appropriate access to community services may have to be long-term and intense. An effective transition planning system must take into account both the short- and long-term service needs of the individual. McDonnell et al. (1995) stated that to identify the level of support an individual will require, parents and school staff must look at the individual's performance during high school in a variety of areas (i.e., personal management, work, residential living, recreational and leisure time). Assessment in personal management includes such activities as shopping for groceries, using public transportation, crossing streets, and maintaining a schedule.

Developing an ITP

Core Concept

The purposes of transition planning are to establish a working relationship between students/parents and adult service agencies, to identify resources for employment and community participation, to access services before graduation, and to locate systems that will help maintain needed services.

Approximately two years before the student leaves school, work should begin on a formal ITP (see Table 9–3 for the basic steps involved in the formulation of such a plan). As stated previously, IDEA 97 mandates that transition services must include a statement of the needed transition services, including, when appropriate, a statement of the interagency responsibilities or linkages (or both), before the student leaves the school setting.

TABLE 9-3
Basic Steps in the Formulation of an ITP

Step One: Organize ITP teams for all transition-age students.
- Identify all students who are transition age.
- Identify appropriate school service personnel.
- Identify adult services and agencies.

Step Two: Organize a circle of support.
- Meet with transition-age student and small circle of friends, family members, coworkers, neighbors, church members, and staff to establish individual's needs and preferences for adult life.

Step Three: Identify key activities.
- Identify those items that are most important to the individual in the transition from school to adult years.

Step Four: Hold initial ITP meetings as part of annual IEP meetings.
- Schedule the ITP meeting.
- Conduct the ITP meeting.
- Develop the ITP.

Step Five: Implement the ITP.
- Operate according to guidelines defined in local interagency agreements.
- Use a transdisciplinary and cross-agency approach.

Step Six: Update the ITP annually during the IEP meetings and implement follow-up procedures.
- Phase out involvement of school personnel while increasing involvement of adult service personnel.
- Contact persons responsible for completion of ITP goals to monitor progress.

Step Seven: Hold an exit meeting.
- Ensure most appropriate employment outcome.
- Ensure most appropriate recreation outcome.
- Ensure most appropriate community living outcome.
- Ensure referrals to all appropriate adult agencies and support services.

Adapted from Life Beyond the Classroom: Transition Strategies for Young People with Disabilities *(2nd ed., pp. 78–98) by P. Wehman, 1996, Baltimore: Paul H. Brookes.*

A transition plan serves several purposes: (a) establishment of a formal working relationship between parents and postschool case managers and adult service providers, (b) identification of the services and resources that will ensure meaningful employment and community participation, (c) access to services before graduation, and (d) identification of systems that will facilitate the maintenance of needed services (McDonnell et al., 1995). To address each purpose, parents and professionals must work together to review potential services that are now or should be made available as the student leaves school. They identify activities that will facilitate access to these services and establish timelines and responsibilities for completion.

Following are the components of an ITP:

1. *Employment training and placement.* Specify the type of training and placement most appropriate for the student. Determine how the resources between school and postschool service programs will be coordinated to ensure that appropriate jobs are identified and that the student is trained for them.

2. *Residential placement.* Determine which residential alternative is the most appropriate for the student. If the family believes it is in the best interest of their son or daughter with retardation to remain home for some time after leaving school, then appropriate family support services need to be in place. If the individual is to move into a residential placement immediately following school, then alternative living arrangements must be made.

3. *Leisure alternatives.* Identify the leisure activities most important to the student. Activities should be planned to ensure that the student has the necessary resources or skills to participate in the activities regardless of where he or she chooses to live after leaving school. Resources or skills include financing the activity, finding transportation, and locating a peer to accompany the student.

4. *Income and medical support.* Balance the potential array of service alternatives with the individual's supplemental security income program. Ensure that needed cash awards or medical benefits are not jeopardized by other services.

5. *Transportation.* Determine specific transportation needs for employment, residential, and leisure alternatives. Identify alternatives for each activity, the method of financing transportation, and strategies to coordinate transportation between school and adult service providers.

6. *Long-term support and care.* Identify the need for guardianship and/or specific trusts or wills. Parents will need legal assistance in drawing up these documents.

Involving Parents in Transition Planning

Core Concept

Parents must have the opportunity to learn as much as possible about adult service systems before their son or daughter leaves school.

Parent education during the high school years should include information regarding the characteristics of adult services agencies, criteria for evaluating adult service programs, and potential as well as current service alternatives for the adult with mental retardation. It is very helpful for school personnel to offer ongoing educational programs for parents to acquaint them with the issues involved in the transition from school to adult life. School personnel should develop and use a transition planning guide to help parents complete critical planning activities (Berry & Hardman, 1998).

INCLUSION WITH NONDISABLED PEERS

Core Concept

The successful transition of the adult with mental retardation to life in an inclusive community setting begins with integration during the school years.

Inclusion may be described as one of the most important factors in promoting successful community living for adults with mental retardation (O'Brien & O'Brien, 1992). Interaction between adolescents with mental retardation and nondisabled peers is important. Such interaction provides opportunities for nondisabled peers to develop (a) positive attitudes about persons with disabilities, (b) the skills to support persons with disabilities during school, at work, and in neighborhood settings, and (c) meaningful friendships with persons with disabilities (Giangreco & Putnam, 1991).

During the transition years, the inclusion of students with mental retardation with their nondisabled peers may take place in several contexts. First, it may occur in the regular education classroom. The student with mental retardation may participate in a variety of academic content or nonacademic classes (e.g., physical education, shop, art, music). Second, the student, although receiving some formal instruction within a self-contained special education classroom, may participate in general school activities (e.g., school assemblies, lunch, hall interaction). The student also may have the chance to interact with nondisabled peers in the special education classroom through such programs as peer tutoring.

Peer tutors volunteer to assist students with mental retardation as part of their high school educational experience. Peer tutors may assist the student in any context within the classroom, such as employment training, adaptive learning, or recreational and leisure activities. In a review of best practice indicators for educating learners with severe disabilities (see Figure 9–1), several authors have suggested that the student with a disability *must* have access to the same environments as nondisabled peers (Falvey, 1989; Fox et al., 1986; Gee, 1996; Halvorsen & Sailor, 1990; Stainback, Stainback, & Ayres, 1996). As suggested by Fox et al., "A primary goal of social integration should be to increase the *number* of integrated community and school environments in which learners . . . can participate" (p. 4).

NEW ISSUES AND FUTURE DIRECTIONS

For adolescents with mental retardation, the effective high school experience of the future will be comprehensive in its approach and involve a transition planning process oriented to individual needs, preferences, and environments.

FIGURE 9–1
Best Practice Indicators for Successful Inclusion

Adapted from Human Exceptionality *(6th ed., p. 343) by M. L. Hardman, C. J. Drew, and M. W. Egan, 1999, Boston: Allyn & Bacon.*

- Are students with mental retardation physically placed in general education classrooms and/or high schools with nondisabled peers?
- Does the high school actively create and support opportunities for interaction between students with mental retardation and their nondisabled peers?
- Does the high school provide specific instruction intended to increase the competence of students with mental retardation in interacting with students who are not disabled?
- Are there highly trained teachers in the school who are competent in the necessary instructional and assistive technology that facilitates social interaction between students with and without disabilities?

Hardman et al. (1999) reported that many students with disabilities have not been involved in transition planning as a component of their high school program. The Harris Poll (1989, 1994) also found that fewer than half of students with disabilities received any job counseling during high school and that of those who did, their parents did not consider it to be effective.

Now, at the beginning of the 21st century, schools need to develop transition planning that is outcome driven, focusing directly on providing access to natural environments to teach and apply different skills. Depending on individual student needs and abilities, transition planning must focus on further access to postsecondary education and/or preparation for life, including employment. In the area of employment preparation, many high schools have focused more on getting the student ready by teaching vocational skills in the classroom, rather than in an actual job setting. This emphasis places schools in a passive role, rather than an active one in which professionals prepare students and place them in jobs. A study on the employment status of students with mental retardation after they leave high school emphasized the need for active involvement of school personnel in job preparation. Hasazi et al. (1989) found that graduates with disabilities who had secured a job placement before leaving school were more likely to stay employed.

To facilitate employment preparation at the high school level in future years, it will be necessary for family and adult service providers to be integrally involved in transition planning. School staff cannot do this task alone. Coordination of family, schools, and adult service agencies should concentrate on identifying specific roles and responsibilities for all participants in the student's transition plan.

Core Questions

1. What are the three components of an effective high school program for adolescents with mental retardation?

2. What basic civil rights were established under Section 504 of the Vocational Rehabilitation Act?
3. Distinguish between career education and work-experience programs.
4. Identify the components of a community-referenced employment preparation program.
5. What challenges face the adolescent with mental retardation in attempting to manage personal needs?
6. What is the value of recreational and leisure activities?
7. Discuss the objectives of a functional academics program for an adolescent with mental retardation.
8. Discuss the school's role in the transition planning process.
9. Why is inclusion with nondisabled peers an important aspect of a quality educational experience for adolescents with mental retardation?

Roundtable Discussion

Adolescence is accurately described as a period of transition from childhood to adult life. In recent years, some professionals have advocated that educational programs for adolescents with more moderate to severe mental retardation focus more on performance required for successful adjustment to community life as adults and less on basic academics. This chapter has discussed a process for transition planning that focuses on matching the individual's functional capabilities with the demands that will be placed on him or her as an adult.

In your study group or on your own, design a transition plan for a student with mental retardation. Take into account the individual's capabilities in relation to preparation for employment, residential living, and access to recreational and leisure experiences. You may choose to use the components of the transition planning process as discussed in this chapter as a guideline for the development of your plan.

References

Berry, J., & Hardman, M. L. (1998). Lifespan perspectives on family and disability. Boston: Allyn & Bacon.

Brolin, D. E. (1993). *Life-centered career education: A competency-based approach* (rev. ed.). Reston, VA: Council for Exceptional Children.

Brolin, D. E. (1995). *Career education: A functional life skills approach* (3rd ed.). Upper Saddle River, NJ: Merrill/Prentice Hall.

Brolin, D., Durand, R., Kromer, K., & Muller, P. (1989). Post-school adjustment of educable retarded students. *Education and Training for the Mentally Retarded, 24,* 144–148.

Browder, D. M., & Snell, M. E. (1993). Functional academics. In M. E. Snell (Ed.), *Instruction of students with severe disabilities* (4th ed., pp. 442–479). Upper Saddle River, NJ: Merrill/Prentice Hall.

Bursuck, W. D., & Rose, E. (1992). Community college options for students with mild disabilities. In F. R. Rusch, L. Destefano, J. Chadsey-Rusch, L. A. Phelps, & E. Syzmanski (Eds.), *Transition from school to adult life* (pp. 71–91). Sycamore, IL: Sycamore.

Clark, G. M. Kolstoe, O. P. (1995). *Career development and transition education for adolescents with disabilities* (2nd ed.). Boston: Allyn & Bacon.

Deci, E. L., Vallerand, R. J., Pelletier, L. G., Ryan, R. M. (1991). Motivation and education: The self-determination perspective. *Educational Psychologist, 26,* 325–346.

Falvey, M. A. (1989). *Community-based curriculum: Instructional strategies for students with severe handicaps.* Baltimore: Paul H. Brookes.

Federal Register. (1977, May 4). Federal Code of Regulations, Public Law 94-142, p. 42, 495.

Fox, W., Thousand, J., Williams, W., Fox, T., Towne, P., Reid, R., Conn-Powers, C., & Calcagni, L. (1986). *Best educational practices '86: Educating learners with severe handicaps* (Monograph series). Burlington: University of Vermont, Center for Developmental Disabilities.

Gartin, B. C., Rumrill, P., & Serebreni, R. (1996). The higher education transition model: Guidelines for facilitating college transition among college-bound students with disabilities. *Teaching Exceptional Children, 29*(1), 30–33.

Gee, K. (1996). Least restrictive environment: Elementary and middle school. In *The National Council on Disability, Improving the implementation of the Individuals with Disabilities Education Act: Making schools work for all children* (Supplement) (pp. 395–425). Washington, DC: The National Council on Disability.

Giangreco, M. F., & Putnam, J. W. (1991). Supporting the education of students with severe disabilities in regular education environments. In L. H. Meyer, C. A. Peck, & L. Brown (Eds.), *Critical issues in the lives of people with severe disabilities* (pp. 245–270). Baltimore: Paul H. Brookes.

Halpern, A. S. (1973). General unemployment and vocational opportunities for EMR individuals. *American Journal of Mental Deficiency, 78,* 123–127.

Halvorsen, A. T., & Sailor, W. (1990). Integration of students with severe and profound disabilities: A review of research. In R. Gaylord-Ross (Ed.), *Issues and research in special education* (pp. 110–172). New York: Teachers College Press.

Hardman, M. L., Drew, C. J., Egan, M. W. (1999). *Human exceptionality: Society, school, and family* (6th ed.). Boston, MA: Allyn & Bacon.

Hardman, M. L., & McDonnell, J. (1987). Implementing federal transition initiatives for youths with severe handicaps: The Utah Community-Based Transition Project. *Exceptional Children, 53*(6), 493–498.

Harris, L., & Associates. (1989). *International Center for the Disabled survey III: Employing disabled Americans.* New York: Author.

Harris, L., & Associates. (1994). National Organization on Disability/Harris Survey of Americans with Disabilities. New York: Author.

Hasazi, S. B., Gordon, L. R., Roe, C. A. (1985a) Factors associated with the employment status of handicapped youth exiting high school from 1975 to 1983. *Exceptional Children, 51,* 455–469.

Hasazi, S. B., Gordon, L. R., Roe, C. A., Finck, K., Holl, M., & Salembier, G. (1985b). A statewide follow-up on post high school employment and residential status of students labeled "mentally retarded." *Education and Training of the Mentally Retarded, 20,* 222–234.

Hasazi, S. B., Johnson, R. E., Hasazi, J., Gordon, L. R., & Hull, M. (1989). Employment of youth with and without handicaps following school: Outcomes and correlates. *Journal of Special Education, 23,* 243–255.

Hoyt, K. B. (1993). Reaction to the three solutions for transition from school to employment. *Youth Policy, 15*(6&7), 36.

Hughes, C., & Agran, M. (1998). Introduction to the special section: Self-determination: Signaling a systems change? *Journal of the Association for Persons with Severe Handicaps, 23*(1), 1–4.

Inge, K., & Wehman, P. (Eds.). (1993). *Designing community-based vocational programs for students with severe disabilities.* Richmond, VA: Virginia Commonwealth University Rehabilitation Research and Training Center.

McDonnell, J., Hardman, M. L., McDonnell, A., & Kiefer-O'Donnell, R. (1995). *Introduction to people with severe disabilities.* Needham Heights, MA: Allyn & Bacon.

McDonnell, J., Mathot-Bucker, C., & Ferguson, B. (1996). *Transition programs for students with moderate/severe disabilities.* Pacific Grove, CA: Brooks/Cole.

McDonnell, J., Wilcox, B., & Hardman, M. L. (1991). *Secondary programs for students with developmental disabilities.* Needham Heights, MA: Allyn & Bacon.

National Council on Disability. (1989). *The education of students with disabilities: Where do we stand?* Washington, DC: Author.

Nisbet, J. (1992). *Natural supports in school, at work, and in the community for people with severe disabilities.* Baltimore: Paul H. Brookes.

O'Brien, J., & O'Brien, C. L. (1992). Members of each other: Perspectives on social support for people with severe disabilities. In J. Nisbet (Ed.), *Natural supports in school, at work, and in the community for people with severe disabilities* (pp. 11–16). Baltimore: Paul H. Brookes.

Patton, J. R., Beirne-Smith, M., & Payne, J. (1990). *Mental retardation* (3rd ed.). Upper Saddle River, NJ: Merrill/Prentice Hall.

Peraino, J. M. (1992). Post-21 follow-up studies: How do special education graduates fare? In P. Wehman (Ed.), *Life beyond the classroom: Transition strategies for young people with disabilities* (pp. 21–70). Baltimore: Paul H. Brookes.

Rusch, F. (1996). Transition. In *Improving the implementation of the Individuals with Disabilities Education Act: Making schools work for all of America's children* (Supplement) (pp. 477–492), Washington, DC: National Council on Disability.

Sowers, J., Thompson, L., & Connis, R. (1979). The food service vocational training program: A model for training and placement of the mentally retarded. In G. T. Bellamy, G. O'Conner, & O. Karan (Eds.), *Vocational rehabilitation of severely handicapped persons.* Baltimore: University Park Press.

Stainback, S. Stainback, W., & Ayres, B. (1996). Schools as inclusive communities. In W. Stainback & S. Stainback (Eds.), *Controversial issues confronting special education: Divergent perspectives* (pp. 31–43). Boston: Allyn & Bacon.

Udvari-Solner, A., Jorgensen, J., & Courchane, G. (1992). Longitudinal vocational curriculum: The foundation for effective transition. In F. R. Rusch, L. Destefano, J. Chadsey-Rusch, L. A. Phelps, & E. Szymanski (Eds.), *Transition from school to adult life: Models, linkages, and policy* (pp. 285–320). Sycamore, IL: Sycamore.

Valdes, K. A., Williamson, C. L., & Wagner, M. M. (1990). *The National Longitudinal Transition Study of Special Education Students, statistical almanac volume 5: Youth categorized as mentally retarded.* Menlo Park, CA: SRI.

Wagner, M., & Blackorby, J. (1996). Transition from high school to work or college: How special education students fare. In The Center for the Future of Children, *Special education for students with disabilities,* 6(1) 103–120. Los Angeles, CA: The Center for the Future of children.

Wehman, P. (1996). *Life beyond the classroom: Transition strategies for young people with disabilities* (2nd ed.). Baltimore: Paul H. Brookes.

Wehman, P., & Kregel, J. (1994). At the crossroads: Supported employment ten years later. In P. Wehman & J. Kregel (Eds.), *New Directions in supported employment.* Richmond: Virginia Commonwealth University, Rehabilitation Research and Training Center.

Wehman, P., & Revell, W. G. (1996). Supported employment. In *Improving the implementation of the Individuals with Disabilities Education Act: Making schools work for all of America's children* (Supplement) (pp. 501–525). Washington, DC: National Council on Disability.

Will, M. (1984). *OSERS program for the transition of youth with disabilities: Bridges from school to working life.* Washington, DC: Office of Special Education and Rehabilitative Services.

Part 5

Adulthood and Mental Retardation

Chapter 10

The Adult with Mental Retardation

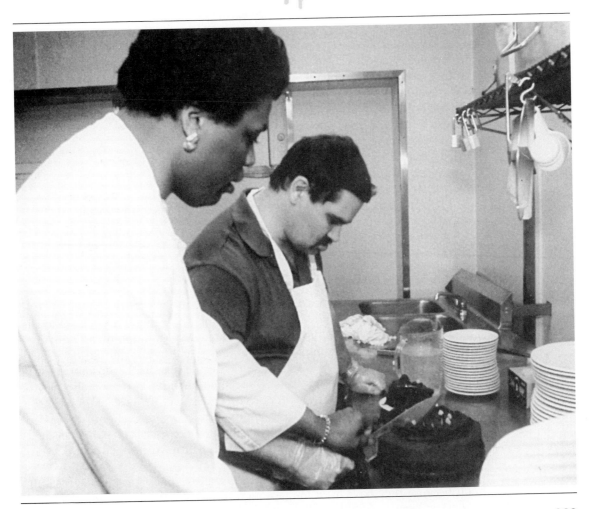

Core Concepts

- Self-determination, an outgrowth of the principle of normalization, involves people with mental retardation speaking up for themselves, making their own lifestyle choices, and being able to act on them.
- The purpose of the Americans with Disabilities Act (ADA) is to end discrimination against persons with disabilities in private-sector employment, public services, public accommodations, transportation, and telecommunications.
- Small community residential models for adults with mental retardation include group homes, semi-independent homes and apartments, and foster care.
- While supported living opportunities facilitate adults with mental retardation living on their own, some people never move away from their primary family. Parents or siblings may be the individual's primary support for a lifetime.
- Recreational and leisure activities are an important source of pleasure and relaxation for the adult with mental retardation.
- Many individuals with mental retardation desire and value marriage and sexual intimacy.
- Adults with mental retardation are capable of self-sufficiency and social adaptation within the community.
- For individuals with mental retardation, institutional living is widely viewed as detrimental to intellectual, psychological, and physical development.
- There are three alternatives for competitive employment for persons with mental retardation: employment with no support services, employment with time-limited support services, and employment with ongoing support services.
- The purpose of a sheltered workshop is to prepare the person with mental retardation for competitive employment or to provide a terminal sheltered job.

Adulthood generally marks a time of transition from relative dependence to increasing independence and responsibility for one's life. There is some disagreement about when adulthood begins. From a legal standpoint, an individual becomes an adult on reaching a specific age. Legal age for adulthood varies from 18 years in some states to 21 years in others. Thus, the law instantaneously transforms adolescents into adults on a specified birthday. A person also may be transformed from adolescent to adult or vice versa by crossing state lines.

Public schools have viewed the completion of a high school program or reaching a certain age (often 21 years) as the point at which their responsibility ends. Presumably, by this time, the individual will have reached some understanding of what it means to be an adult.

Adults with mental retardation are a paradox. They have achieved adulthood because they have lived long enough to deserve the distinction. However, many of these individuals may be unable to be completely independent. They often lack the ability to meet typical high school graduation requirements and do not have the necessary adaptive skills for successful adult functioning.

Although the pressure associated with school may end, other demands find their way into the life of an adult with mental retardation. What does society expect of an adult? An adult works, earns money, and buys the necessities of life and as many of the pleasures as he or she wants or can afford. An adult socializes, often marries, has children, and tries to live as productively and happily as possible. The adult with mental retardation may be unable to find or hold a job, particularly without a formal support system in place. If jobs are available, wages may be so low that even the basics of life may be out of reach. What if the adult with mental retardation has no one to socialize with, no one to love or be loved by? What if he or she must become dependent on parents for mere existence and the parents die or become too old to help? There are many such "what ifs" for the adult with mental retardation, who just may exchange the academic and social pressures of adolescence for new and sometimes more difficult ones.

There is little extant research on the lives of adults with mental retardation. (Hardman, Drew, & Egan, 1999). Most studies have focused on children with mental retardation and the schools. It was not until 1973 that the Association for Retarded Children changed its name to the Association for Retarded Citizens (now the ARC-A National Organization on Mental Retardation). Although this association has long campaigned for the rights of all people with mental retardation, the name change was indicative of a growing recognition of the need to emphasize support at all stages of life. Interestingly, one thing we do know from the limited research available on adults with mental retardation is that they require ongoing support from family, friends, neighbors, and co-workers throughout life in order to live and work successfully in a community setting (O'Brien & O'Brien, 1992). The individual will probably be an adult three times as long as he or she is a child or an adolescent. Therefore, it seems only appropriate for us to devote more time to the needs and nature of adults with mental retardation.

COMMUNITY LIVING

In its most basic form, successful adult living may be defined as (a) earning a living, (b) having access to further education when desired and appropriate, (c) personal autonomy and independence, (d) social interaction and community participation, and (e) ongoing involvement within the life of the family. As one reaches the age of majority, there are decisions that have to made relative to each of these five areas. What kind of career or job do I desire? Should I further my education to increase my career choices? Where shall I live and whom shall I live with? How shall I spend my money? Whom do I choose to spend time with? Who will be my friends? While most people face these choices as a natural part of growing into adult life, the issues facing adults with mental retardation and their families may be very different.

Making Adult Choices: Issues of Competence and Self-Determination

Core Concept

Self-determination, an outgrowth of the principle of normalization, involves people with mental retardation speaking up for themselves, making their own lifestyle choices, and being able to act on them.

Everyone is considered mentally competent—that is, able to make rational and reasoned choices about their lives—at the age of majority, unless legally determined to be otherwise. The legal presumption of mental competence removes from parents the obligation and power to make decisions for their adult child—a power that until this point in life could not be usurped unless it was abused. For professionals, this means no longer seeking parental advice or consent on issues related to the person who has reached the age of majority but respecting the rights of the individual as an adult. Respecting these rights involves the obligation to maintain confidentiality from parents and others if the person so desires.

While the legal presumption is that everyone is competent at the age of majority, this supposition can be overturned or set aside by the courts in certain circumstances. An adult can be deemed incompetent through a process known as adjudication. In adjudication, those seeking to have the individual declared incompetent must provide a preponderance of evidence that the person does not have the capacity to make rational choices.

- Does the person have the capacity to consistently make rational and reasoned decisions that are in his or her best interests and those of others that the individual has direct contact with?
- Is the individual *partially* competent and thus able to make some rational decisions at varying levels of complexity?
- Is the individual *totally* incompetent and thus unable to make any reasoned decisions on his or her behalf?

Determining incompetence is a very sensitive and complex process. It is further complicated by a somewhat unclear judicial criteria as to what differentiates complete or partial competence from total incompetence. It is important to remember that competence is not "an all-or-nothing" proposition. Certainly, few people are completely competent in everything; correspondingly, few people are totally incompetent as well. Any decision to remove or reduce an individual's right to make choices must be weighed very heavily, since such rights are fundamental to adult status, from a legal, moral, and practical standpoint.

One of the first challenges facing families when their son or daughter with mental retardation reaches the age of majority is weighing that son or daughter's right to self-determination against the mental competence to make reasoned choices. As mentioned in Chapter 9 of this text, Hughes and Agran (1998, p. 1) describe self-determination as "people speaking up for themselves and making and acting on their own lifestyle choices (i.e., living their lives pretty much like everybody else hopes to and, to some extent, probably does)."

Self-determination is an extension of a concept first introduced in the 1960s that became widely known as "the principle of normalization." First articulated in Scandinavia (Bank-Mikkelsen, 1969; Nirje, 1969) and later expanded on in the United States (Wolfensberger, 1972), **normalization** means "making available to the mentally retarded patterns and conditions of everyday life which are as close as possible to the norms and patterns of mainstream society" (Nirje, p. 181). Normalization does not mean just providing a normative situation, like a home in the community. Without supports, the individual with mental retardation may not be able to meet the demands of the community.

In 1983, Wolfensberger suggested a rethinking of the term *normalization* and introduced the concept of social role valorization-giving value to the individual with mental retardation. He stated, "The most explicit and highest goal of normalization must be the creation, support, and defense of valued social roles for people who are at risk of social devaluation" (p. 234). It is important to attain socially valued roles and life conditions for people whom society now devalues. Strategies to accomplish this goal would enhance the individual's social image or perceived value in the eyes of others and enhance individual competence within society.

As we reach the 21st century, the term *self-determination* embodies the view that persons with mental retardation should act as the primary causal agent in their lives and be able to make choices and decisions about their quality of life without interference (Schloss, Alper, & Jayne, 1993; Wehmeyer, 1996). Turnbull, Turnbull, Bronicki, Summers, and Roeder-Gordon (1989) indicate that there should be more focus on teaching and promoting personal choice and self-advancement and less on decision making by family members and service providers. Making self-determination a reality is not always easy. In "Standing Together," Christian's mother, while advocating strongly for his independence, often faced situations where he made decisions that she did not agree with or that she saw as clearly dangerous. It took a great deal of inner strength for Christian's mother to come to a realization that while "not all his choices were safe, physically or emotionally," they were his choices.

Self-determination may be characterized by several factors, including (a) optimal challenge and empowerment, (b) autonomy, (c) competence, (d) involvement, (e) acknowledging individual feelings, and (f) self-regulation (Deci & Chandler, 1986; Wehmeyer, 1996). Activities that optimally challenge students are those that are neither too easy nor too difficult (Deci & Chandler, 1986). Excessive repetition, overlearned tasks, or activities far beyond a person's achievement level decreases motivation. The issue of optimal challenge is particularly salient to people with mental retardation. These individuals often require repeated exposure to a task to learn a skill.

Development of opportunities to express preference, make choices, and experience the outcomes of these choices are characteristics of environments that support autonomy and empowerment. Unfortunately, many professionals

Standing Together:

One Family's Lessons in Self-Determination

Self-determination is not synonymous with independence. Rather, it is best facilitated by interdependence: connections and support from those around us. Our brain, our spirit, our emotions, our psyche, and our sexuality all function better in social interaction than in isolation. For my son, Christian, it has been this positive interaction that has allowed him to experience more choices and opportunities, leading to his determined spirit. These are some examples that he would like shared with everyone:

- Christian stood up and lowered his eyes. He spoke clearly and was firm. "I will not take Speech and Language anymore. It's always the same thing and it's for babies. I will take a language class, but no more therapy!"

- It was the second week on a new job and Christian noticed that all the employees went to a meeting, but that he was not included. He said nothing, but brought home his anger. The next day he went to his supervisor and said, "I work here too. Why can't I go to the meetings?"

- He woke at 5:30 every morning and caught the bus for school at 6:15, arriving home at 4:30. Of those 10 hours, half were spent on the bus. In addition to the frustrations of this demanding schedule, he had a new job "experience" across town starting at 1:00. The criteria for success established by his school was that his work had to approach 95% of the quantity and quality of a person without mental retardation. He failed . . . week after week. On the fifth week he announced, "I keep telling you, this is the best that I can do. If it isn't good enough I'm not coming anymore."

I am always in awe of Christian's tenacity. I remember all the days and nights in hospitals, feeling helpless to free him from painful, restrictive treatments and procedures. I remember being unable to speak up when he was treated as if he were invisible by doctors and teachers, simply because he was a child . . . and "retarded." I remember the past 18 years of special education and IEPs and feeling incompetent and alone at the table at which professionals typically used acronyms and language I didn't understand or agree with. The words "severe," "profound," "can't," "flat scale," and "inappropriate" will always send shivers up my spine. I remember when the neighbor kids started the name calling: "fag," "retard," and "cripple."

It was difficult for me to move past the pity and protection. However, my basic values dictated that I raise all of my four children in a home that valued their voices and encouraged discussions about their thoughts and feelings. Also, before I ever had children, I knew that the first priority to teach them was compassion. I didn't know anything about self-determination, but Christian was able to risk saying the wrong thing or making a mistake because he knew no matter what happened, home was a place where he was valued, accepted, and loved.

By the time Christian was seven, he was frustrated and angry about his disability. My first reaction was to protect him from experiences that would cause pain or frustration. I felt that was part of my job description as a parent. By the time he was 10, I knew I was not doing him a favor. I began to question if I was responding out of pity or love. I quit feeling sorry for Christian. We regularly discussed how he had to live with himself and learn to understand what seizures were and what mental retardation meant for him. At the same time the family, including his brother and sisters, supported

continues on next page

continues from previous page

and went to bat for him when attitudes and programs he experienced demeaned and devalued him.

Self-advocacy and self-determination begin with advocacy. Christian observed his dad, myself, and his siblings all standing up for his rights. Not only did that allow him to learn behaviors, but he knew he was worth the fight. For example, it was wrong for a teacher to set up a classroom reward system with criteria that never allowed success for Christian. When he displayed anger, he was called psychotic; we went through due process. It was also wrong for hospital staff to continue to insist on further sedation when they had already administered a high enough does to put a 200-pound man out cold; we left AMA (Against Medical Advice).

As an advocate I could be in charge and direct the course of action and be the decision maker. The real challenge for me was when adolescence arrived. All the skills I'd hoped Christian would have, appeared. I was disjointed, fearful, confused, and struggled with his "noncompliant, inappropriate, and aggressive" behaviors. Oops! The change meant I had to look at my values again in order to step back and support Christian in decisions I didn't always agree with and often thought were dangerous. I needed to believe that he would make decisions that would keep him safe physically and emotionally. In the beginning I also needed to believe that "the world" would view his contributions as important. I struggled with my perceptions of mental retardation beginning at the bottom of the disability list and the possibility that he would have no caring person in his adult life. Not all the choices that Christian has made have been safe, physically or emotionally, but they have been his choices.

For instance, Christian's first major purchase with his SSI money was a chain saw. In another instance, Christian, who cannot drive a car, bused around the city, found a 19 foot boat to purchase, and now is looking for a "friend" (paid or unpaid) to get the boat to water. Two days ago he was at the corner waving cars down and offering to pay $100 for a drive to a lake. He recently announced that there must not be any available women who could possibly like him so he was going to pay for that service also. I have learned to spend a great deal of time taking hot baths or putting invisible masking tape over my mouth.

Self-determination requires that a person have rich and abundant experiences. In order for growth in confidence and the ability to make choices, a person must have successful and unsuccessful experiences. Christian has used that chain saw and other power tools to help clear a wooded area and build a deck. He is currently enrolled in a technical college in the chef program, using meat cleavers and very sharp knives; a few supportive people in the decision-making role decided not to be afraid that he would have a seizure and get hurt. When he goes to the lake with the family, Christian drives that 19 foot boat and skillfully docks it because his dad and I decided that to risk paying for a dent in another boat was worth building Christian's confidence. Christian can say no to drugs, alcohol, and abuse because his siblings have included him in their typical teen parties and he's had the opportunity to say no.

Christian may still be vulnerable, and may still get frustrated by his mistakes and angry about attitudes that isolate him. But, he has a strong determination to know, understand, and like himself . . . And he knows that he is worth it.

Source: From "Standing Together: One Family's Lessons in Self-Determination" by K. Schoeller, Winter 1993–94, *IMPACT,* (6)4, 1, 19.

have not focused on developing these opportunities (Bambara, Cole, Koger, 1998; Wehmeyer, 1992). As stated by Brown, Gothelf, Guess, & Lehr, 1998: "For years, professionals decided what was best for people with disabilities and their families. Now . . . the field is moving away from an emphasis on care taking and fitting people to pre-existing services toward an emphasis on personal control, flexible support, and a rich, varied lifestyle" (p. 27).

Competence and involvement are considered basic human needs (Deci & Ryan, 1991). Competence involves understanding how to attain various outcomes and being efficacious in performing the required actions to achieve these outcomes. This notion is also referred to as self-efficacy—that is, having confidence in being able to perform a particular task (Gillespie & Hillman, 1993). Involvement is dependent upon an individual developing secure and satisfying connections with others in his or her social environment (Deci, Vallerand, Pelletier, & Ryan, 1991). The most desirable outcomes for individuals are achieved when involvement or "caring" occurs in conjunction with support for autonomy and competence (Bambara et al., 1998; Deci & Chandler, 1986).

Self-determination may be also enhanced by acknowledging the individual's feelings. While everyone has to engage in tasks they feel are uninteresting, self-determination is strengthened when a reason for participation is provided and the individual's questions or concerns are acknowledged (Bambara et al., 1998; Deci & Chandler, 1986).

While providing opportunities for students to make choices and decisions is paramount in developing self-determination, *it is also important for parents and professionals to assist youths* in (1) identifying options from a range of alternatives, (2) identifying the associated consequences, (3) selecting and implementing options, (4) evaluating results, and (5) adjusting future directions. Self-regulation techniques are skills supportive of autonomy. The development of these skills is a complex and long-term process. Instructional programs that promote self-determination must begin laying the groundwork early in the child's life. Abery (1994) has suggested that "striving to attain self-determination doesn't begin (or end) during adolescence or early adulthood. Rather it is initiated shortly after birth and continues until we have breathed our least breath" (p. 2).

One strategy to create opportunities for people with mental retardation to learn and apply self-determination skills in work and community life, and thus to enhance their perceived value, is through legislative reform. One such major reform effort came to fruition in 1990 with the passage of ADA.

The Americans with Disabilities Act (ADA)

Core Concept

The purpose of the Americans with Disabilities Act (ADA) is to end discrimination against persons with disabilities in private-sector employment, public services, public accommodations, transportation, and telecommunications.

ADA (Public Law 101-336) mandates that barriers of discrimination against people with disabilities in private-sector employment, all public services, and public accommodations, transportation, and telecommunications are to be broken down. ADA requires businesses that serve the public to remove architectural barriers, such as curbs on sidewalks, narrow doorways, or shelving and desks, that prevent access by a person with a disability. The business community must provide "reasonable accommodations" to people with disabilities in hiring or promotion practices, in restructuring jobs, and in modifying equipment. Under ADA, all new public transit facilities (e.g., buses or train stations) must be accessible, and transportation services must be available to people with disabilities who cannot use fixed bus routes. ADA also requires that public accommodations (e.g., restaurants, hotels, retail stores) and state and local government agencies be accessible to people with disabilities. By the year 2010, all Amtrak train stations must be accessible. Telecommunication devices for people who are deaf must be made available by all companies that offer telephone service to the general public.

The ADA's purpose is to provide people with disabilities an "equal playing field" as they seek access to the same opportunities afforded those who are not disabled (Hardman et al., 1999). As important as this law is to people with disabilities, including those with mental retardation, it is only social policy. The law must be translated from policy into everyday practice as an accepted way of life for communities across the United States if it is to be truly successful in breaking down discrimination.

Most individuals take many areas of everyday living for granted, such as shopping, crossing streets, making daily purchases, and getting transportation. Yet unless people with mental retardation receive the necessary support in these areas, their opportunities certainly will be curtailed. In the following sections, we address various aspects of life in the community. These include supported living, parents or siblings as primary caregivers, community participation, marriage and sexuality, and adjustment to community life.

Supported Residential Living

Core Concept

Small community residential models for adults with mental retardation include group homes, semi-independent homes and apartments, and foster care.

As the 21st century begins, the vast majority of people with mental retardation, along with their families and professionals, are advocating nationwide expansion of small community-based residences located in residential neighborhoods with support from trained personnel. Adults with mental retardation who are living in these settings would use existing services in the community for education, work, health care, and recreation.

As is true for people without disabilities, community supports for people with mental retardation should promote personal autonomy, social inclusion, and choice of lifestyle. For the vast majority of individuals with mental retardation, **supported living** is the most appropriate residential arrangement. Braddock, Hemp, Bachelder, and Fujiura (1994, p. 26) define supported living as

> housing in which individuals with developmental disabilities choose where and with whom they live, housing which is owned by someone other than the support provider (i.e., by the individual, the family, a landlord, or a housing cooperative), and housing in which the individual has a personalized support plan which changes as her or his needs and abilities change.

Several types of community residential programs have been developed over the years (Baker, Seltzer, & Seltzer, 1977; Campbell & Bailey, 1984; McDonnell, Hardman, McDonnell, & Kiefer-O'Donnell, 1995; Nisbet, Clark, & Covert, 1991; Schalock, 1986). In this chapter, we discuss three widely used residential models for adults with mental retardation living in the community: group homes, semi-independent homes and apartments, and foster care.

Group Homes.   Considerable variation is found in organization and alternatives within the group home model. A small group home is usually a community residence with two to four persons living in a single dwelling. A large group home may have as many as 8 to 15 or more residents.

Living arrangements for adults with mental retardation may involve a number of options.

Trained professionals usually provide support to persons with mental retardation living in these homes, regardless of the size, and they often have an assistant to serve as a relief person when they are off duty. In some instances, a house director works on a full- or half-time basis to handle administrative matters. Many group homes now are employing shift workers who are on duty for 4 to 7 days at a time as a team. Small group homes are usually more integrated into residential neighborhoods. The homes emphasize programs that provide daily living experiences as similar as possible to those of nondisabled individuals. Government funding supplemented by fees paid by the residents usually finance these homes.

Semi-Independent Homes and Apartments.   The semi-independent home or apartment represents the least supervised and least restrictive of all supervised residential models (see "One Man's Walk Through Modern History of Residential Services"). Several variations on the semi-independent home or apartment have been developed over the years:

1. *Apartment clusters.* Comprised of several apartments fairly close together, they function to some extent as a unit and are supervised by a resident staff member who lives in one of the apartment units.
2. *Single co-residence home or apartment.* This consists of a single home or apartment in which an adult staff member shares the dwelling with one or more roommates who have mental retardation.
3. *Single home or apartment.* This consists of a home or apartment owned and/or occupied by an adult with mental retardation whom a nonresident staff member assists. This is the most independent kind of living arrangement in the model.

These three variations provide different degrees of independence, and individuals living in this type of residential model require fewer supports than those living in other residential models. Most residents are responsible for or contribute to apartment maintenance, meal preparation, and transportation to place of employment.

Foster Family Care.   The purpose of foster family care is to provide a surrogate family for the individual with mental retardation. One goal of foster family care is to integrate the individual into the family setting, with the assumption that within the normal family environment and with the foster family's understanding, he or she will learn adaptive skills and work in a community setting. One problem with this model is that a person with mental retardation living in a surrogate family may assume a dependent, childlike role and become overprotected. In general, these placements offer residents adequate productive daytime activities and opportunities to manage their physical environment, both fundamental components of normalization. Those who operate the foster homes generally receive a per capita fee from the state. These settings accommodate from one to six adults. Activities and quality of care are, to some extent, at the

One Man's Walk Through Modern History of Residential Services

When I lived at Lake Owasso State institution in Minnesota, you had to ask for everything: "Can you let me out?," "Can I have a can of pop?," "Can I stay up a little bit longer?"

When I moved into a group home, I had to follow all of the rules. I had to go to bed at a certain time, and when I was in bed, I had to be asleep; that was that. I lived with two other guys. We were being watched all the time, 24 hours a day, seven days a week.

Two years ago I got married. My wife and I moved into our own apartment. Now that I have my own place, I make the decisions. I have my own keys. I can let myself out, and let myself back in.

Now I can come and go when I want. I can make my own food, and I decide whether I want to have breakfast or lunch, when I'm ready for a snack. We can invite friends to stay over. My wife and I decide when the staff come over. They help us with some things, but we make our own decisions.

Source: From *Guidebook on Consumer Controlled Housing* by T. Fields K. C. Lakin, 1995, Minneapolis, MN: ARC-Minnesota and the Institute on Community Integration.

discretion of the operator. If the operator's goal is to make a profit, he or she may spend very little on the foster residents to increase profits.

Another setting that some consider a community residential alternative is the sheltered village. Sheltered villages for adults with mental retardation usually are located in rural areas; they are secluded and spread over several buildings. Although rules, activities, and relative freedom within each sheltered village vary, they do have one common characteristic: In this setting, the individual with mental retardation is isolated from the outside community. The rationale is that residents are better off in isolation than exposed to the potential failures, frustrations, and demands of the outside world. Many of these facilities are private, and a number are church supported. Of the community models we have discussed, the sheltered village conflicts most with the principle of normalization.

Living with Parents and Siblings

Core Concept

While supported living opportunities facilitate adults with mental retardation living on their own, some people never move away from their primary family. Parents or siblings may be the individual's primary support for a lifetime.

In a study of adults with disabilities, Heller and Factor (1993) found that 63% of those interviewed indicated that they wanted to remain in the family home. In fact, 85% of adults with mental retardation live under the supervision of their parents for most of their lives (Seltzer & Krauss, 1994). Living with parents or siblings during the adult years may result from a lack of formal resources for the family or from the family's decision to keep the individual at home. This is not to say that parents who choose to keep their adult offspring at home aren't in need of government funded supports and services. They may need respite care, in-home assistance, and counseling/training services.

Respite Care and In-Home Assistance.   Respite care and in-home assistance provides relief and help for parents attempting to cope with the challenges of an adult with mental retardation living in the home. In-home respite care may involve a paid companion spending some time with the adult who is disabled. Out-of-home respite care may be provided by parent cooperatives, day-care centers, community recreational services, and families who are licensed to take adults with disabilities into their home for a limited period of time (Levy & Levy, 1986). Nisbet et al. (1991) suggest that respite care services may "enable family members to become more socially active and in turn reduce their feelings of social isolation" (p. 135). In-home assistance could come from, for example, a professional homemaker, who might reduce the family's time in dealing with household management tasks, or a personal attendant, who might help with daily routines.

Extended family members are also sources of respite care and in-home assistance. These family members may periodically help with meals, clean the house, provide transportation, or just listen when everyone is overwhelmed. Hardman et al. (1999) suggest that grandparents and other extended family members are a critical resource for helping parents who choose to keep an adult family member at home.

Counseling and Training.   In addition to respite care and in-home assistance, families may also receive counseling services and training to help them cope with the daily stress of caring for an adult with mental retardation. Counseling services and family training programs often focus on the relationships and interactions between and among the members, not just on the adult with mental retardation. Such an approach, referred to as a "family systems perspective," is based on the premise that "all parts of the family are interrelated; furthermore, each family has unique properties, understood only through careful observation of the relationships and interactions among all members" (Turnbull & Morningstar, 1993, p. 22).

A relatively new approach to counseling and training is psychoeducational support groups that are intended to assist parents whose adult child remains fully or partially dependent on the family for a lifetime (Smith, 1995). The purpose of these groups is to provide an opportunity for older and aging parents to share their needs and concerns with others in similar circumstances regarding such issues as "making plans for when they can no longer care for their offspring due to their own disability or death" (Smith, Majeski, & McClenny, 1996, p. 173). These support groups, facilitated by professionals knowledgeable in the areas of disability and the family, generally have five major goals:

to (a) inform parents about the residential, financial, and legal aspects of [futures] planning; (b) promote acceptance of the relinquishment of care to others; (c) foster coping skills to deal with the impact of age-related changes on care giving; (d) encourage knowledge and use of both formal and informal supports; and (e) instill solidarity among participants. (Smith et al., p. 173)

While some attention has been paid to the role of parents during the adult years, little has been written about sibling responsibilities. During adulthood, sibling concerns center on the following questions:

"Who is going to take care of my brother or sister?"
"When my parents die, who will be responsible?"
"Am I going to have to take care of my brother or sister all of my life?"

Griffiths and Unger (1994) found that a majority of siblings believe that families should be responsible for the care of their disabled members. Most indicated that they were "willing to assume future care giving responsibilities for their brothers/sisters" (p. 225). In a longitudinal study of families who had adults with mental retardation still living at home, Krauss, Seltzer, Gordon, and Friedman (1996) found that many siblings remained very actively involved with their brother or sister well into the adult years. These siblings had frequent contact with their brothers or sisters and were knowledgeable about their lives. In addition, they played a major role in their parents' support network. Approximately one in three of these siblings indicated that they planned to reside with their brother or sister at some point during adult life.

The reality is that sibling roles with a brother or sister who has mental retardation may vary considerably depending on the attitudes and values of their parents, their own attitudes about responsibility, and the proximity to their brother or sister (Hardman et al., 1999; McHale, Sloan, & Simeonsson, 1986). There are siblings who develop negative feelings very early in childhood and carry these feelings through to adult life. These siblings grew up resenting the time and attention parents gave to their disabled brother or sister, eventually becoming bitter and emotionally neglected adults. Such negative feelings often result in guilt that further isolates the individual from the primary family. Adult siblings, resentful of their brother or sister, may actively disengage themselves from parents and the disabled family member for long periods of time (Seligman, 1991; Forbes, 1987). However, some siblings play a crucial role during adult life, providing ongoing support to parents and spending time with their mentally retarded brother or sister.

Recreation and Leisure in a Community Setting

Core Concept

Recreational and leisure activities are an important source of pleasure and relaxation for the adult with mental retardation.

Many adults with mental retardation have busy and active work schedules. For these individuals, recreational and leisure activities provide a much-needed change from daily work schedules. Other adults with mental retardation have little, if any, work or regular daily activity. These individuals need recreational activities as a means to achieve more satisfaction and independence in their lives.

Fain (1986) suggested that adults with retardation are too often lonely and inactive, when meaningful leisure activities could be an integral part of their lives. Shannon (1985) found that adults with retardation spend significant amounts of time alone at home. Typical activities include watching television, listening to music, and looking at books and magazines. A more recent study by Valdes, Williamson, and Wagner (1990) found that the time spent alone by adults with mental retardation may be decreasing. In a follow-up investigation of young adults with mental retardation between the ages of 19 and 22, these authors found that about 75% of these individuals got together with friends at least once per week. Approximately 21% of the respondents were with friends more than five times per week.

Peck, Apolloni, and Cooke (1981) found that successful training in leisure time could come about through the incorporation of systematic assessment, highly structured training procedures, and rigorous evaluation components. The adult with retardation is fully entitled to the pleasures of well-planned recreational activities. Efforts in this direction by recreational therapists, churches, schools, and family can help make life more meaningful for these adults.

Marriage and Sexuality

Core Concept

Many individuals with mental retardation desire and value marriage and sexual intimacy.

Heshusius (1982) reviewed the literature on marriage and sexuality of persons with mental retardation, sorting the statements according to common elements. These generalized statements reflected a desire for and enjoyment of sexual contact, as well as a fear of sexual intimacy. Many of those with retardation believed that sexual intimacy belonged with marriage. Also evident was a lack of knowledge about basic facts regarding sexual relations. Heshusius stressed the need for more sensitivity on the part of society to the need for sexual intimacy by a person with mental retardation.

Persons with mental retardation desire and value marriage and sexual intimacy. As a group, however, they are apparently not as successful as nondisabled peers in finding mates; this may result partly from their desire to marry nondisabled individuals or at least individuals who have had no previous association with an institution (Edgerton & Bercovici, 1976). This particular need dovetails with the overall preference to live as normal a life as possible.

Sex education is a major concern, but it is often deliberately ignored despite the fact that individuals with mental retardation can learn new social/sexual skills (Abramson, Parker, & Weisberg, 1988; Foxx, McMorrow, Storey, & Rogers, 1984). As adults in the community, these persons are free, in many instances, to conduct their personal lives as they choose, and the results of their interpersonal relationships may depend on the instruction and training they receive in sex education. The sexual behavior of people with mental retardation is learned and directly affected by environmental factors. Abramson et al. (1988) suggested that people with mental retardation be guaranteed sex education and training: "This training must be designed to facilitate informed consent, sexual hygiene, and when desired, conscientious contraception" (p. 332).

Another issue concerning sexuality and people with mental retardation is the practice of sterilization. In past years, sterilization was viewed as a means of eliminating or curtailing mental retardation, preventing individuals with retardation from having unwanted children, or preventing them from having children because of their alleged incompetence. In 1927 Justice Oliver Wendell Holmes issued his famous opinion for the Supreme Court, which upheld a state compulsory sterilization law. He stated that "three generations of imbeciles are enough" (*Buck v. Bell*, 1927). Following the Holmes opinion came a marked increase in the practice of sterilization. As many as 8,000 people were legally sterilized without their permission in the state of Virginia between the 1920s and the 1970s (Smith, 1989).

The prime targets for compulsory sterilization appear to have been individuals with mental retardation who are in the process of being released from institutions. In a 1967 study, Edgerton found that 44 of the 48 former patients studied at Pacific State Hospital, a California residential institution, had undergone "eugenic" sterilization. During the period of their institutionalization, sterilization was considered a prerequisite to release. Form letters were sent to parents or guardians to gain consent for the procedure. These letters strongly implied that sterilization could permit parole and would be in the best interest of the individual. Unless there was strong objection, the surgery was routinely performed. By 1935 people with mental retardation constituted 44% of those sterilized in this country; by 1946 the percentage had increased to 69%. The rate of sterilization had increased through 1937 but leveled off by 1942 because of the shortage of medical personnel during the war years (Goldstein, 1964). Gamble (1951) reported that by 1951, 26,000 individuals with mental retardation had been sterilized and, thus, rendered fit for parole from institutions.

The concern of discriminatory sterilization laws should not be limited exclusively to the institutional group. The question of whether society has the right to impose sterilization on any individual with retardation has great relevance for parents, professionals, and the individuals themselves.

Who decides who must be sterilized and what criterion is used to determine the decision? Should all individuals with retardation, those in institutions and those in the community, be sterilized? What are the criteria for determining sufficient mental retardation to warrant compulsory sterilization? These are the primary issues being debated.

Research on Adjustment to Community Living

Core Concept

Adults with mental retardation are capable of self-sufficiency and social adaptation within the community.

The 1980s and 1990s were an era of expansion in supported community living alternatives for persons with mental retardation. Significant advances have been made in understanding the factors that promote successful inclusion into community living (McDonnell et al., 1995; Nisbet et al., 1991; President's Committee on Mental Retardation, 1995). Much remains to be done, however, to use the information available effectively and to identify more specifically those variables associated with success in community programs.

Follow-up studies of individuals with retardation date back to 1919. Fernald (1919) studied individuals discharged from an institution over a 25-year period and found considerable variability in their adjustment to community life. In the 1930s and 1940s, several studies compared the community adjustment of individuals with retardation with control groups of individuals without mental retardation. These include studies by Fairbanks (1931), Baller (1936), and Kennedy (1948). Fairbanks and Kennedy conducted their studies during periods when economic and general employment conditions were generally favorable. Baller's study was conducted in the middle of the Great Depression.

When economic conditions are poor, individuals with retardation are among those most severely affected. Employers may consider them the most dispensable of their employees, so they are often the first to be laid off. This is particularly evident in Baller's study: Only 20% of the subjects with retardation were gainfully employed, as opposed to 50% of the control group (normal subjects). In Fairbanks's and Kennedy's studies, however, those with mental retardation compared very favorably with the controls with respect to gainful employment. In all three studies, the marital status of the person with mental retardation appeared to be somewhat comparable with the control subject. Home ownership, as reported by Fairbanks and Kennedy, also appeared comparable. These studies suggest that the majority of persons with retardation were able to make acceptable adjustments to community life. They were employed in semiskilled and unskilled jobs. Economic conditions and the type of community may have had some effect on their ability to adjust. Follow-up studies of the subjects suggest that even in later years, community adjustment of these individuals can be considered successful (Baller, Charles, & Miller, 1966; Kennedy, 1966).

A study in the 1960s (Edgerton, 1967) examined the posthospital lives of a number of individuals released from Pacific State Hospital. The subjects of Edgerton's study were individuals with mild retardation who had received the benefit of vocational rehabilitation training programs both in the hospital and in the community. These individuals were considered among the more intellectually, socially, and emotionally capable in the institution. As a group, Edgerton found the subjects generally living comfortably, with most of them married and enjoying various leisure activities. Largely, their existence was rather inconspicuous. Edgerton suggested that one of the greatest problems faced by this group was the stigma of the label of mental retardation. These individuals could not and would not accept the "fact" that they had (or ever had) mental retardation. To do so would have humiliated them and devalued their feelings of self-worth. Thus, much of their effort went to convince others, as well as themselves, that they were normal individuals. Many attributed their relative incompetence to the years spent in the institution, locked up and deprived of the knowledge and experience that society requires for competent living and functioning.

In a follow-up to the 1967 study, Edgerton and Bercovici (1976) examined the lives of many of the same individuals several years later to determine what effect the passage of time had on their community adaptation. They managed to locate 30 of the original 48 subjects. In this follow-up, the subjects expressed far less concern for passing as "normal," and stigma was less evident. Additionally, Edgerton and Bercovici found that "normal" benefactors played a smaller role. Overall, dependence on benefactors lessened over time. This may have been the result of less need for benefactors or a lessening availability of them. Edgerton and Bercovici concluded that the reduction in stigma may have helped decrease the need for benefactors and that the additional years of experience in community living may have reduced the need for assistance. Although Edgerton and Bercovici rated the life circumstances for the total group as slightly worse, compared with their status in the earlier study (1967), in general the subjects considered their circumstances happier. Their happiness was not necessarily a function of vocational success; rather, happiness may have been more a function of being normal, and in periods of high unemployment, many normal people may not be working.

A second follow-up to Edgerton's 1967 study was conducted in 1982 (Edgerton, Bollinger, & Herr, 1984). This follow-up study focused on the personal and social resources of 15 persons with mild retardation originally studied in 1960 and 1961. These authors found still less dependence on others than reported in the previous investigations. These subjects, now ranging between 47 and 68 years of age, were described by the investigators as more hopeful, confident, and independent.

In the 1970s, several studies (Bellamy, O'Conner, & Karan, 1979; Close, 1975; Gold, 1973) demonstrated that under carefully controlled conditions, even people with severe and profound mental retardation are capable of self-sufficiency and social adaptation within a community setting. In the 1980s, investigations (Conroy & Bradley, 1985; Haney, 1988; O'Neill, Brown, Gordon, & Schonhorn, 1985) focused on the feasibility of small community living situations for people with moderate and severe mental retardation.

In 1993, Edgerton conducted a third follow-up to his seminal 1967 study on former patients of the Pacific State Hospital. While continuing to deal with challenges of living in the community, the lives of these people had remained relatively stable over the past 25 years. They were generally happy and had a

Community participation for adults with mental retardation may include many activities undertaken by individuals without mental retardation.

continuing optimism about life. Edgerton suggested that the majority of people with mental retardation find varying levels of success in the community. Adjustment to community living stabilizes over time.

In their summary of the research on community living over the past three decades, Nisbet et al. indicated the following:

> Persons with disabilities who move out of large residential environments do better in smaller ones when there is sufficient attention paid to their individual characteristics. . . . When individuals with disabilities or their families are provided with individualized support, there are greater chances of programmatic success and satisfaction. (1991, p. 115)

INSTITUTIONAL LIVING

Core Concept

For individuals with mental retardation, institutional living is widely viewed as detrimental to intellectual, psychological, and physical development. ✷

Institutions for persons with mental retardation go under many different labels—for example, school, hospital, colony. Characteristics of an institution include the following: (a) all aspects of life go on in the same place and under the same single authority; (b) activities are carried on in the immediate company of others, all of whom are treated alike and required to do the same things together; (c) a system of explicit formal rulings and a body of officials govern tightly scheduled activities; (d) social mobility is grossly restricted; (e) work is defined as treatment, punishment, or rehabilitation; and (f) a system of rewards and punishments takes in the individual's total life situation (Goffman, 1975).

The deinstitutionalization movement in the United States came about because many institutions for those with mental retardation had become dehumanizing warehouses with no adequate treatment programs (Balla, 1976; Blatt, Ozolins, & McNally, 1979; *Homeward Bound v. Hissom Memorial Center,* 1988; *Staff Report,* 1985; *Wyatt v. Stickney,* 1972; Zigler, 1973). For persons with mental retardation, institutional living is widely viewed as a detriment to intellectual, psychological, and physical development.

Menolascino, McGee, and Casey (1982) suggested that an abundance of information and research data is available, indicating the following:

> (1) Prolonged institutionalization has destructive developmental consequences. . . . (2) appropriate community-based residential settings are generally more beneficial than institutional placements. . . . and (3) mentally retarded individuals with a wide spectrum of disabilities including the severely and profoundly retarded can be successfully served in community-based settings. (p. 65)

The most harmful aspect of institutional living is the emphasis on a restrictive regimen, with no attempt to personalize programs or living conditions to the needs of the residents (Hardman et al., 1999).

The legal and moral debate continues regarding what is a good or bad institution or whether there is a need for any large residential facility for persons with mental retardation. Some institutions for those having mental retardation have attempted, in recent years, to provide a more family-like environment for the resident, instead of restricted dormitory living conditions. Changes include efforts to provide private or semiprivate bedrooms, family dining facilities, individual clothing and hairstyles, and private possessions. Neither parents nor professionals have agreed on criteria for determining whether any institution is an appropriate living and learning environment for any person with mental retardation. We can say, however, that the accomplishments of institutions in the past 90 years add up to very little.

The institution of the 20th century has been more concerned with social management than with the physical and psychological growth of the person with mental retardation. Across the United States, these large public facilities continue to serve fewer and fewer residents each year, and a number of states have closed or are moving toward closure of large institutions. Braddock et al. (1994) reported that since 1977, the number of people living in state-operated institutions has been reduced by half, falling from 149,681 to 77,712. These authors further reported that 94 institutions are scheduled for or have completed closure in 20 states.

COMPETITIVE EMPLOYMENT

Core Concept

There are three alternatives for competitive employment for persons with mental retardation: employment with no support services, employment with time-limited support services, and employment with ongoing support services.

From childhood on, everyone fantasizes about job and occupation choices. Fantasy may follow a person through life; aspirations, however, tend to fit actual abilities better as the individual grows. Because an individual's lifestyle and ultimate personal satisfaction are often related to employment satisfaction, counselors attempt to direct and aid students in finding acceptable job choices. People with mental retardation are no different from others with respect to employment aspirations, but because of their intellectual limitations and misinformation or a lack of knowledge on the part of employers, they may find it more difficult to obtain jobs that fulfill their aspirations.

Sustained, competitive employment for persons with mental retardation is a laudable societal goal. Employment is important for many reasons beyond monetary rewards, including adult identity, social contacts, integration with peers, and the perception of contributing to society. Yet research on adults with mental retardation clearly indicates that these people are underemployed or unemployed (Harris & Associates, 1994; Valdes et al., 1990).

The high unemployment rates of people with mental retardation seem to be attributable to several factors. First, traditional employment models have been oriented to either no training for the individual after leaving school or to short-term training programs with the expectation that the individual will not need ongoing support while on the job. Second, the emphasis has been on sheltered or protected work settings, where the individual is placed for training but does not earn significant wages. The individual with mental retardation may remain in such settings for most, if not all, of his or her adult years.

There are, however, some good reasons to be optimistic about competitive employment for people with mental retardation (see "Can a Person with Mental Retardation Really Perform on the Job?"). Greater emphasis now is put on improvement of employment services. Research knowledge is expanding, and more emphasis is placed on employment with both state and national policymakers (McDonnell et al., 1995; McDonnell, Mathot-Buckner, & Ferguson, 1996; Rusch, Chadsey-Rusch, & Johnson, 1991; Tines, Rusch, McCaughrin, & Conley, 1990).

The concept of competitive employment for persons with mental retardation has changed dramatically in recent years (West, Revell, & Wehman, 1992). As

Can a Person with Mental Retardation Really Perform on the Job?

People with mental retardation can be effective and successful on the job. Employers describe them as dependable employees who genuinely want to work. Boeing Corporation in Seattle, Washington, reports a strong work ethic and above average safety records among its workers with disabilities. The company also finds improved co-worker morale.

Roger Beach, of Beach Brothers Printing in Rockville, Maryland, has employed two men with developmental disabilities in the bindery for more than 10 years. "They are extremely valuable employees who are good at what they do. In fact, they have a talent for the job! Typically their hourly rate is higher than that of other workers in the same job, and they have brought a stability to the job that didn't exist before."

Marriott Hotels' "Bridges . . . from School to Work" project has placed 75 students with mental retardation in paid internships during the past 2 years. Seventy percent of the interns were later hired for permanent positions to their host employers.

Thermo King in Hastings, Nebraska, has six employees with mental retardation. Although all were initially supported by job coaches in specially created jobs, some of these employees have moved into competitive-wage jobs.

Source: From *The Untapped Resource: The Employee with Mental Retardation* by the Joseph P. Kennedy, Jr., Foundation, 1993, Washington, DC: Author.

stated previously, competitive employment now can be described in terms of three service alternatives: employment with no support services, employment with time-limited support services, and employment with ongoing support services.

Employment with No Support Services

The adult with mental retardation may be able to locate and maintain a community job with no additional supports from public or private agencies. The individual finds a job independently either through contacts made during school vocational preparation programs or through such sources as a job service, want ads, family, and friends. For the person with mild retardation, competitive employment without support is most often possible if adequate employment training and experience are available during the school years. A major concern of professionals preparing individuals with mental retardation for competitive employment is identification of characteristics related to employment success. If these characteristics can be identified, employment training programs can be developed during the school years to emphasize the positive characteristics that tend to enhance job success.

Employment with Time-Limited Training and Support Services

After the individual with mental retardation finishes school, he or she may have access to several services on a short-term basis, including vocational rehabilitation, vocational education, and on-the-job training. As Will (1985) wrote, "Access to such time-limited services is generally restricted to individuals thought capable of making it on their own after services are completed." Vocational rehabilitation services are the best known of time-limited employment services.

Vocational rehabilitation is a federally funded program intended to help persons with disabilities obtain employment. Under the Vocational Rehabilitation Act of 1973 (amended under Public Law 102-569 in 1992), federal funds are passed to the states to provide services in counseling and job placement. To qualify for vocational rehabilitation, the individual must have an employment-related disability. The expectation is that the individual will be employed independently, following rehabilitation training. After the individual completes the training, rehabilitation services terminate unless the individual fails on the job and has to be retrained.

Over the years, vocational rehabilitation has been viewed by policymakers as a good investment, backed up by cost-benefit studies that indicate a positive ratio between government investment and the wages of former clients. More recently, however, the efficacy of rehabilitation services has been called into question (Government Accounting Office, 1993). The issues raised regarding services provided under the Vocational Rehabilitation Act of 1973 are focused on whether vocational rehabilitation "is able to serve all those who are eligible and desire services, whether the services provided are sufficient in scope and suitably targeted to meet the needs of a diverse client, and whether the program's effects persist over the long term" (Government Accounting Office, 1993, p. 11). A program that responds directly to the issues of client diversification and long-term employment outcomes is the supported employment model.

Employment with Ongoing Support Services: The Supported Employment Model

Supported employment is defined as work in an integrated setting for individuals with severe disabilities (including those with mental retardation) who probably will need some type of ongoing support and for whom competitive employment traditionally has not been possible (Wehman & Revell, 1996). As defined in the legislation (1986 amendments to the Vocational Rehabilitation Act and the Developmental Disabilities Act of 1984), supported employment placements must meet the following criteria:

1. The job must provide between 20 and 40 hours of work weekly and be consistent with the individual's stamina.
2. The individual must earn a wage either at or above minimum wage or a wage commensurate with production level and based on the prevailing wage rate for the job.
3. Fringe benefits should be similar to those provided for nondisabled workers performing the same type of work.
4. Employment must be community based and provide the individual with regular opportunities for integration with nondisabled workers or with the public as a regular part of working.

5. Work should take place in settings where no more than eight persons with disabilities work together.

On the basis of these criteria, the federal government established programs to fund states to initiate supported employment services through cooperative inter-agency services (education, vocational rehabilitation, developmental disabilities). State dollars to match federal funds or to stand alone are being allocated for supported employment services in nearly every state in the United States.

In a relatively short time, supported employment has become a viable alter-native for rehabilitation training and employment of individuals with severe disabil-ities. Research on the effectiveness of supported employment services has docu-mented the success of this delivery system (Baer, Simmons, Flexer, & Smith, 1995; Braddock et al., 1994; McCaughrin, Ellis, Rusch, & Heal, 1993; Revell, Wehman, Kregel, West, & Rayfield, 1994; Rusch et al., 1991; Wehman & Revell, 1996).

Although the efficacy of supported employment services has been well docu-mented by research and demonstration, the growing fear is that the rapid expan-sion of this employment service delivery system in the United States will result in failure to safeguard the essential elements of the concept. As expansion continues, the need for trained personnel in administrative positions is more acute.

Bellamy and Horner (1987) highlighted four critical features of supported employment. The first critical feature is that remuneration for the individual is a program goal. Wages are a primary index of employment success. Noble and Conley (1986) compared the wages earned in supported employment with those of more conventional day programs. They reported that individuals in sup-ported work placements earned significantly higher wages. Clients in integrated employment also worked more hours than persons in sheltered employment and work activity centers. In addition, client earnings were not correlated with severity of disability.

Although earnings are primary to the success of supported employment, they are not the sole indicator of quality. Bellamy and Horner's second critical feature is that work should take place in socially integrated settings, rather than in segregated facilities. Job placement in an integrated setting allows the individ-ual to learn appropriate social and vocational skills side by side with nondisabled peers and to apply the skills in the environment. The nondisabled employer and co-workers also learn about the potential of the disabled individual as a reliable employee and friend.

The third critical feature is that support on the job is continuous, based on individual need, and not time limited. Time-limited services such as traditional vocational rehabilitation or vocational education have been restricted to individ-uals with disabilities who are supposed to need no support after reception of ser-vices. These time-limited services, then, terminate after the individual enters the workforce. Unlike time-limited services, continuous services are made available as needed. Support does not end with placement in an employment setting or after a specified time for follow-up. Services are provided on the job and consist of whatever support is necessary to maintain employment. Continuous supports

Employment options for adults with mental retardation may include working with others and performing a variety of tasks.

include job development, job placement, ongoing postemployment training, skill maintenance and generalization, and follow-up services. The amount and type of continuous support are related to individual need, job demand, and the organizational structure of the supported employment program.

The fourth critical feature is that supported employment is for people with mental retardation who have not usually been served in vocational programs. According to Bellamy and Horner, "There is . . . the clear possibility that supported employment may become the nation's first zero-reject employment program" (1987, p. 498).

Supported Employment Within the Framework of Community Living. It is important for supported employment to be viewed in the larger context of supported living. Supported living is an opportunity for people with mental retardation to live in a home wherever they want and with whomever they choose while receiving all the support needed. Supported employment fits within the framework of a supported life network for people with mental retardation. Services are defined by individual preference and need, rather than by availability of facilities.

The goals for the individual within a supported life network include increased independence, community integration, and productivity. Services must reflect these individualized goals, which will result in an improvement in the quality of life for the person with a disability. Services that focus directly on increasing independence promote higher adaptive behavior levels and greater opportunities for choice in residence, recreation, and employment. Services that support community integration will result in greater access to and participation in the community, including generic community services and programs such as restaurants, swimming pools, theaters, and parks. Services that focus on increasing the individual's productivity move the individual from consumer to contributor through identity in the workforce, wages to spend in the community, and taxpayer status. Supported employment is a service that increases productivity. Supported employment is defined as wage-generating work with an emphasis on continuous support determined as much as possible by the individual and congruent with other aspects of the person's supported living network. People with mental retardation can live and work successfully in as many different situations as nondisabled individuals. Work and living options are constrained only by inadequate support.

Structural Features of Supported Employment.   The development of supported employment services as the basic structure of a vocational service system for individuals with mental retardation has several implications: (a) the evaluation of the employment program based on client outcomes, (b) the elimination of the continuum of employment alternatives based on the "getting people ready" philosophy of vocational services, and (c) the development of training and advocacy services that are directly linked to employment success.

The success of an employment service may be evaluated in several ways. For example, in the vocational rehabilitation system, success is determined by closure of an individual's file, based on completion of training and job placement and maintenance for a specified length of time. Other means of evaluation relate more to the process of establishing a vocational service than to client outcomes. Process questions may include the following: Is the client eligible for the vocational service? Is an individualized work plan in place? Is the work plan consistent with a standardized vocational assessment of the individual? and Does the plan contain goals and objectives? These questions are concerned with ensuring that a standardized process is in place that is consistent across all programs.

Although supported employment does not ignore process questions, its primary focus is on results for the individual. Does the vocational service provide good employment outcomes for the individual served? Measures for success are meaningful wages and benefits, access to generic services and resources, contact with nondisabled peers, and job security. Where more conventional vocational services emphasize a broader rehabilitation function, supported employment focuses on work and wages. Because employment outcomes are the key variables in the evaluation process, programs must become more effective in identifying, developing, and maintaining work opportunities.

The traditional philosophy of "getting people ready" (the flow-through model) for jobs is not consistent with the supported employment concept. The basis for supported employment is that individual support needs determine program placement. Individual functioning level and performance demands in a given work environment are matched. And supported employment takes into account the job's compatibility with the individual's life needs, as well as consideration for family values and constraints. The underlying principle of supported employment is not to move people to less restricted job placements as a result of training but to provide the necessary resources to support individuals in their current work site.

The purpose of supported employment is to achieve community-integrated employment success for the individual with a severe disability. Therefore, all training programs and advocacy efforts must be directed toward this goal. Developing skills for various job tasks is only one component of a supported employment training program. Program training objectives might include riding the mass transit systems, grooming, self-monitoring, and evaluation of work performance. These objectives facilitate the individual's participation in the social network of the business.

Supported Employment Models.   Three basic models of supported employment currently are recognized: individual placement, the community work crew, and the enclave. Each model differs in terms of intensity of long-term support, training, support structure, organizational strategy and business base, number of workers per site, and levels of integration (see Table 10–1).

In the individual placement model, a job coach gives each person intensive one-on-one training aimed at successful performance of specific job tasks and nonwork behaviors around the job setting. Initial training is usually continuous throughout the workday but may be reduced eventually to no more than an hour or less per day. The job coach may be responsible for as many as eight employees at sites throughout a community. Training and assistance also may be available through co-workers willing to support the individual in completion of job tasks or to act as friends in the workplace. The type of work available in individual placements varies from entry-level custodial or food service jobs to jobs in high-technology industries.

A community work crew usually consists of five or six individuals (maximum of eight) with disabilities, who are supervised by a crew supervisor. Work crews generally perform service jobs (e.g., custodial, food service) that are contracted with two or more businesses, industries, or private individuals. Training and support from the crew supervisor may be continuous and long term, focusing on completion of the service task and fostering community-integration activities. Work crews are usually mobile, moving from site to site in the performance of their contract. Under such circumstances, integration with nondisabled individuals may be difficult to achieve. Systematic efforts must be made to create opportunities for social interaction between work crew members and nondisabled people.

In the enclave model, two to eight individuals with disabilities work in an industrial or business setting alongside nondisabled people. The enclave usually

TABLE 10–1

Comparison of Three Supported Employment Models

	Supported Jobs	Enclave	Mobile Crew
Organizational strategy and business base	• Nonprofit support to individuals and employers • Varied types of jobs	• Nonprofit support to host company • Target manufacturing companies	• Nonprofit • Crews operate from a van • Rural • Service contracts
Number of workers per job site	One per job	Six to eight	Five per crew
Cost	Not yet known, expected to be similar to day programs	Less than half the cost of other day programs	Same as traditional day programs
Intensity of support	Low. Continuous initially, scaling to no more than 1 hour a day after several months	Medium. Continuous and long term	Medium. Continuous and long term
Training	Individual training for up to 4 months on: • job tasks • nonwork behaviors in and around job setting	Individual training on: • production tasks • nonwork behaviors in job setting	Individual training on: • service tasks • community integration activities
Supervisor	Two or three supervisors for 12 employees in separate businesses	• One supervisor for six to eight employees in host company • Host company assigns model employee as backup to supervisor	• One supervisor for five employees • Continuous presence of one supervisor on service jobs for all five employees
Integration	High. Daily and continuous integration in individual job sites	High. Daily and nearly continuous with nonhandicapped peers, in work area, breaks, and lunchtimes	Medium. Breaks and lunch occur in community settings; work performed in community settings, but interaction with nonhandicapped persons is low

Adapted from Pathways to Employment for Adults with Developmental Disabilities *(p. 149) by W. E. Kiernan and J. A. Stark (Eds.), 1986, Baltimore: Paul H. Brookes. Copyright 1986 by Paul H. Brookes Publishing Co. Adapted by permission.*

is supervised by a single nondisabled person trained in the requirements of a single host company or industry. Job support is usually continuous and long term; training focuses on production tasks, appropriate nonwork behaviors in the job environment, and community integration. Jobs include manufacturing and small-item assembly. Kiernan and Stark (1986) indicated that the level of social integration is high in enclaves, with opportunities for integration in the work area, during breaks, and at lunch. It is possible, however, for enclaves to be physically isolated within a business operating on different work, break, and lunch times. Conscious efforts are sometimes necessary to integrate enclaves with the nondisabled workforce.

All three supported employment models give training in specific job skills at the work site. On-the-job training involves job analysis, development of systematic training programs, and the use of effective training strategies. The primary difference between the models in relationship to on-the-job training is the number of individuals being trained at a time. For example, in the individual placement model, training is always one on one. In a work crew, any number of individuals may be trained together.

In summary, the three supported employment models provide the opportunity for individuals with mental retardation to work successfully in community employment settings with adequate training and long-term support. At the same or less public expense, these individuals can be competitively employed, instead of attending segregated day-care centers.

Since the passage of IDEA, research and demonstration programs clearly have made improvements in employment training and placement of persons with mental retardation. Supported employment is being used successfully to place and maintain individuals with mental retardation in jobs in the community. Research findings clearly indicate that ongoing training and assistance in the job setting are more effective than vocational services in segregated settings (Rusch et al., 1991).

The components of an effective community employment program include (a) placement in a job that is consistent with the abilities and interests of the individual, (b) on-the-job training that includes direct instruction by a trained professional and that enables the individual to perform all skills the job calls for, (c) continuous assessment and monitoring of the individual's job performance, and (d) availability of systematic follow-up services to ensure skill retention years after the initial placement.

SHELTERED EMPLOYMENT

Core Concept

The purpose of a sheltered workshop is to prepare the person with mental retardation for competitive employment or to provide a terminal sheltered job.

Sheltered employment provides both occupational training and remuneration for persons with mental retardation. There are several common characteristics of sheltered workshops:

1. Clients/employees usually work on contractual jobs.
2. These contract jobs are usually of short duration; therefore, a staff person is needed to bring in new jobs.
3. Most tasks are broken into small steps.
4. Jobs usually proceed in an assembly line fashion; one part is added at each step of the process until a final product is completed.
5. The facility may or may not provide vocational assessment and training for persons outside the center. (Payne & Patton, 1981, p. 278)

Some sheltered workshops operate exclusively for clients with mental retardation; others serve a wider variety of individuals with disabilities, such as those with visual impairments, cerebral palsy, or emotional disturbance. Some are operated by national programs, such as Goodwill Industries of America, Inc., which has more than 100 centers, and Jewish Vocational Service agencies, with more than 20 locations. Other workshops are community based and may be supported by the United Fund, religious groups, private endowments, or, more recently, public schools.

Typically, sheltered workshops restore or repair clothing or household articles and then sell them. Items come from collections or strategically located depositories. Other workshop revenue comes from contracts with various businesses or industries.

Workshop clients usually are compensated on a piecework basis at a rate comparable to that of other workers in that industry. Thus, if the typical industry worker is paid $4 for 10 units of work per hour, the workshop client should be paid $2 for 5 units. Some workers are relatively productive and may earn more than $10 per day. Others are less capable and may earn less than $1 per day.

Over the years, the sheltered workshop model has been criticized as a segregated approach that provides low wages and fails to move people with mental retardation into less restricted employment settings (Schuster, 1990). Questions have been raised about the value of sheltered work for individuals who earn little. From a purely economic standpoint, the justification for maintaining services for these individuals is questionable. Their wages are so low as to be of next to no value even to themselves, and their productivity is so low that their contribution to the employment field also may be considered nearly negligible. Workshops have been criticized also for not having systematic procedures to evaluate the production capabilities of clients and for failure to provide vocational tasks consistent with their clients' range of capabilities.

In many respects, the sheltered workshop contradicts any focus on community living and gainful employment. Industry employs workers to turn out a product. In the sheltered workshop, the product is often the means to produce workers. And for many workers, the sheltered setting becomes the permanent work setting.

Day habilitation and work activity centers are intended to provide programming that will prepare the person for more advanced work, preferably in a competitive employment situation. The results, at least for people with mental retardation, have not reflected the stated philosophy. Current rates of progress in day activity and work activity programs suggest that people with mental retardation will spend the better part of their adult lives being "prepared" for competitive employment.

NEW ISSUES AND FUTURE DIRECTIONS

Historically, human-services programs for adults with mental retardation have focused primarily on protection and care. The objective of such programs was to protect the individual from society and society from the individual. This philosophy resulted in services that isolated the individual in large institutions and that offered physical care in place of preparation for life in a heterogeneous world. With the international movement of the past two decades to educate students with disabilities in the public school system, new goals have become clear: (a) employment, useful work, and valued activity; (b) personal autonomy, independence, and adult status; (c) social interaction, community participation, leisure, and recreation; and (d) roles within the family.

Society must recognize that expectations for adults with mental retardation are no different from those for people without disabilities. Although the characteristics of a "quality life" are certainly individual and personal, several indicators seem to be widely accepted in Western society. These are as follows:

All people are empowered to make their own choices about adult living, including selecting friends, where they will live, and what jobs they will hold. Empowerment has three aspects: control of the environment, involvement in community life, and social relationships. Quality of life can be assessed by the answers to such questions as "Do you have a key to the house in which you live?" (controlling the environment); "Do you earn enough money to pay for your basic needs, including housing and food?" (involvement in the community); and "Do you have the opportunity of interacting with friends and neighbors?" (social relationships).

Each person is valued as an individual capable of personal growth and development. As such, everyone is treated with dignity and has the opportunity to participate in all aspects of community life. Participation in community life includes access to adequate housing, opportunities to exercise citizenship (e.g., voting), access to medical and social services as needed, and access to recreational and personal services (e.g., parks, theaters, grocery stores, restaurants, public transportation).

Each person has the opportunity to participate in the economic life of the community. Work is important for reasons beyond its monetary rewards—for example, social interaction, personal identity, and contribution to the community. Work removes the individual from being viewed solely as a consumer of service. Important personal needs include adequate and fair compensation, safe and healthy environments, development of human capacities, growth and security, social integration, constitutionalism (the rights of the worker and how these rights can be protected), the total life space (the balanced role of work in one's life), and social relevance (when organizations act in socially irresponsible ways, employees see their work and careers as less valuable).

Several indicators of a "quality of work life" for nondisabled adults have been identified by assessing the degree of employer satisfaction with the work process. These indicators include (a) adequate and fair compensation, (b) safe and healthy environments, (c) development of human capacities, (d) growth and security, (e) social integration, (f) affirmation and protection of worker rights, and (g) a balance between work and personal life. In the light of the such indicators, the question is whether there should be separate standards of quality for persons with mental retardation. In fact, quality indicators do differ for the more conventional models of employment preparation for people with mental retardation (day habilitation, sheltered workshops, work activity centers).

Sheltered workshops are designed as protected places for long-term employment, and people with mental retardation may be placed in these settings with little or no reassessment of their competitive employment potential. Supported employment differs significantly from conventional work programs. The goals for people with mental retardation in a supported employment program are the same as those for nondisabled people: What income does the job provide? What kind of lifestyle does the income allow? How attractive is the work life (co-workers, challenge, safety, status)? and How good is job security?

Core Questions

1. Define and discuss the principle of normalization. Why is self-determination described as an extension of the normalization principle?
2. Describe three widely used community residential models for adults with mental retardation.
3. Identify supports needed by parents or siblings who choose to live with an adult family member with mental retardation?
4. Why is knowledge regarding sexuality especially important for persons with mental retardation?
5. Summarize the research on the adjustment of persons with mental retardation to community living.
6. Why is institutionalization considered detrimental to the intellectual, psychological, and physical growth of the individual?
7. Discuss some of the reasons for high unemployment among persons with mental retardation.
8. Define and discuss the concept of supported employment.
9. What are some of the criticisms of sheltered employment?

Roundtable Discussion

The principle of normalization emphasizes that the person with mental retardation should have the same opportunities and access to services as nondisabled individuals. It is much more than just the opportunity to live or work in the community because it means providing the support services necessary to assist the individual in successfully meeting the demands of adult life.

In your study group or on your own, discuss the range of activities and services that must be available for an adult with mental retardation to live and work successfully in the community. How would you ensure that these supports are available?

References

Abery, B. (1994). Self-determination: It's not just for adults. *IMPACT, 6*(4), 2. (ERIC Document Reproduction Service No. ED 368 109)

Abramson, P. R., Parker, T., & Weisberg, S. R. (1988). Sexual expression of mentally retarded people: Educational and legal implications. *American Journal of Mental Retardation, 93*(3), 328–334.

Baer, R., Simmons, T., Flexer, R., & Smith, C. (1995). A study of the cost and benefits of supported employees with severe physical and multiple disabilities. *Journal of Rehabilitation Administration, 18*(1), 46–57.

Baker, B. L., Seltzer, G. B., & Seltzer, M. M. (1977). *As close as possible: Community residences for retarded adults.* Boston: Little, Brown.

Balla, D. (1976). Relationship of institution size to quality of care: A review of the literature. *American Journal of Mental Deficiency, 81,* 117–124.

Baller, W. R. (1936). A study of the present social status of a group of adults who, when they were in elementary schools, were classified as mentally deficient. *Genetic Psychology Monographs, 18,* 165–244.

Baller, W. R., Charles, C., & Miller, E. (1966). *Midlife attainment of the mentally retarded: A longitudinal study.* Lincoln: University of Nebraska Press.

Bambara, L. M., Cole, C. L., & Koger, F. (1998). Translating self-determination concepts into support for adults with severe disabilities. *Journal of the Association of Persons with Severe Handicaps, 23*(1), 27–37.

Bank-Mikkelsen, N. E. (1969). A metropolitan area in Denmark: Copenhagen. In R. B. Kugel & W. Wolfensberger (Eds.), *Changing patterns in residential services for the mentally retarded* (pp. 227–254). Washington, DC: President's Committee on Mental Retardation.

Bellamy, G. T., & Horner, R. H. (1987). Beyond high school: Residential and employment options after graduation. In M. E. Snell (Ed.), *Systematic instruction of persons with severe handicaps* (3rd ed., pp. 491–510). Upper Saddle River, NJ: Merrill/Prentice Hall.

Bellamy, G. T., O'Conner, G., & Karan, O. (1979). *Vocational rehabilitation of severely handicapped persons: Contemporary service strategies.* Baltimore: University Park Press.

Blatt, B., Ozolins, A., & McNally, J. (1979). *The family papers: A return to purgatory.* New York: Longman.

Braddock, D., Hemp, R., Bachelder, L., & Fujiura, G. (1994). *The state of the states in developmental disabilities: Fourth national study of public spending for mental retardation and developmental disabilities in the United States.* Chicago: University of Illinois at Chicago, Institute on Disability and Human Development.

Brown, F., Gothelf, C. R., Guess, D., & Lehr, D. (1998). Self-determination for people with the most severe disabilities: Moving beyond chimera. *Journal of the Association of Persons with Severe Handicaps, 23*(1), 17–26.

Buck v. Bell, 274 U.S. 200 (1927).

Campbell, V. A., & Bailey, C. J. (1984). Comparison of methods for classifying community residential settings for mentally retarded individuals. *American Journal of Mental Deficiency, 89,* 44–49.

Close, D. W. (1975, May). *Normalization through skill training: A group study.* Paper presented at the Annual Convention of the American Association on Mental Deficiency, Portland, OR.

Conroy, J. W., & Bradley, V. J. (1985). *The Pennhurst Longitudinal Study: A report of five years of research and analysis.* Philadelphia: Temple University Developmental Disabilities Center.

Deci, E. L., & Chandler, C. L. (1986). The importance of motivation for the future of the LD field. *Journal of Learning Disabilities, 19,* 587–594.

Deci, E. L., & Ryan, R. M. (1991). A motivational approach to self: Integration in personality. In R.

Dienstbier (Ed.), *Nebraska Symposium on Motivation Vol. 38. Perspectives on motivation*, (pp. 237–288). Lincoln: University of Nebraska Press.

Deci, E. L., Vallerand, R. J., Pelletier, L. G., Ryan, R. M. (1991). Motivation and education: The self-determination perspective. *Educational Psychologist, 26*, 325–346.

Edgerton, R. B. (1967). *The cloak of competence*. Berkeley: University of California Press.

Edgerton, R. B. (1993). *The cloak of competence* (revised and updated). Berkeley: University of California Press.

Edgerton, R. B., & Bercovici, S. M. (1976). The cloak of competence years later. *American Journal of Mental Deficiency, 80*, 485–497.

Edgerton, R. B., Bollinger, M., & Herr, B. (1984). The cloak of competence: After two decades. *American Journal of Mental Deficiency, 88*(4), 345–351.

Fain, G. S. (1986). Leisure: A moral imperative. *Mental Retardation, 24*(5), 261–283.

Fairbanks, R. F. (1931). The subnormal child: Seventeen years later. *Mental Hygiene, 17, 177–208.*

Fernald, W. E. (1919). After-care study of the patients discharged from Waverly for a period of twenty-five years. *Ungraded, 5, 25–31.*

Forbes, E. (1987). My brother, Warren. *Exceptional Parent, 17*(5), 50–52.

Foxx, R. M., McMorrow, M. J., Storey, K., & Rogers, B. M. (1984). Teaching social/sexual skills to mentally retarded adults. *American Journal of Mental Deficiency, 89*(1), 9–15.

Gamble, C. J. (1951). The prevention of mental deficiency by sterilization. *American Journal of Mental Deficiency, 56*, 192–197.

Gillespie, D. & Hillman, S. B. (1993, August). *Impact of self-efficacy expectations on adolescent career choice.* Paper presented at the meeting of the American psychological Association, Toronto, Ontario, Canada.

Goffman, E. (1975). Characteristics of total institutions. In S. Dinitz, R. R. Dynes, & A. C. Clarke (Eds.), *Deviance: Studies in definition, management, and treatment* (p. 410). New York: Oxford University Press.

Gold, M. W. (1973). Research on the vocational rehabilitation of the retarded: The present, the future. In N. R. Ellis (Ed.), *International review of research in mental retardation* (Vol. 6, pp. 97–147). New York: Academic Press.

Goldstein, H. (1964). Social and occupational adjustment. In R. Heber & H. Stevens (Eds.), *Mental retardation.* Chicago: University of Chicago Press.

Government Accounting Office. (1993). *Vocational rehabilitation: Evidence of federal program's effectiveness is mixed.* Washington, DC: Author.

Griffiths, D. L., & Unger, D. G. (1994, April). Views about planning for the future among parents and siblings of adults with mental retardation. *Family relations, 43*, 221–227.

Haney, J. I. (1988). Toward successful community residential placements for individuals with mental retardation. In I. W. Heal, J. I. Haney, & A. R. Novak Amado (Eds.), *Integration of developmentally disabled individuals into the community* (2nd ed., pp. 125–168). Baltimore: Paul H. Brookes.

Hardman, M. L., Drew, C. J., & Egan, M. W. (1999). *Human exceptionality: Society, school, and family* (6th ed.). Needham Heights, MA: Allyn & Bacon.

Harris, L., & Associates. (1994). National Organization on Disability/Harris Survey of Americans with Disability. New York: Author.

Heller, T., & Factor, A. R. (1993). Support systems, well-being, and placement decision-making among older parents and their adult children with developmental disabilities. In E. Sutton, A. R. Factor, B. A. Hawkins, T. Heller, & G. B. Seltzer (Eds.), *Older adults with developmental disabilities* (pp. 107–122). Baltimore: Paul H. Brookes

Heshusius, L. (1982). Sexuality, intimacy, and persons we label mentally retarded: What they think, what we think. *Mental Retardation, 20*(4), 164–168.

Homeward Bound v. Hissom Memorial Center, U.S. District Court (1988).

Hughes, C., & Agran, M. (1998). Introduction to the special issue on self-determination: Signaling systems change. *Journal of the Association of Persons with Severe Handicaps, 23*(1), 1–4.

Joseph P. Kennedy, Jr., Foundation (1993). *The untapped resource: The employee with mental retardation.* Washington, DC: Author.

Kennedy, R. A. (1966). *A Connecticut community revised: A study of the social adjustment of a group of mentally deficient adults in 1948 and 1960.* Hartford: Connecticut State Department of Health, Office of Mental Retardation.

Kennedy, R. J. R. (1948). *The social adjustment of morons in a Connecticut city.* Willport, CT: Commission to Survey Resources in Connecticut.

Kiernan, W. E., & Stark, J. A. (1986). *Pathways to employment for adults with developmental disabilities.* Baltimore: Paul H. Brookes.

Krauss, M. W., Seltzer, M. M., Gordon, R., & Friedman, D. H. (1996, April). Binding ties: The roles of adult siblings of persons with mental retardation. *Mental Retardation, 34*(2), 83–93.

Levy, J. M., & Levy, P. H. (1986). Issues and models in the delivery of respite services. In C. L. Salisbury & J. Intagliata (Eds.), *Respite care: Support for persons with developmental disabilities and their families* (pp. 99–116). Baltimore: Paul H. Brookes.

McCaughrin, W. B., Ellis, W. K., Rusch, F. R., & Heal, L. W. (1993). Cost-effectiveness of supported employment. *Mental Retardation, 31*, 41–48.

McDonnell, J., Hardman, M., McDonnell, A., & Kiefer-O'Donnell, R. (1995). *Introduction to persons with severe disabilities.* Needham Heights, MA: Allyn & Bacon.

McDonnell, J., Mathot-Buckner, C., & Ferguson, B. (1996). Transition programs for students with moderate/severe disabilities. Pacific Grove, CA: Brooks/Cole.

McHale, S. M., Sloan, J., & Simeonsson, R. J. (1986). Sibling relationships and adjustment of children with disabled brothers and sisters. *Journal of Children in Contemporary Society, 16,* 131–158.

Menolascino, F. J., McGee, J. J., & Casey, K. (1982). Affirmation of the rights of institutionalized retarded citizens (Implications of *Youngberg v. Romeo*). *TASH Journal, 8,* 63–71.

Nirje, B. (1969). The normalization principle and its human management implications. In R. B. Kugel & W. Wolfensberger (Eds.), *Changing patterns in residential services for the mentally retarded* (pp. 179–195). Washington, DC: President's Committee on Mental Retardation.

Nisbet, J., Clark, M., & Covert, S. (1991). Living it up! An analysis of research on community living. In L. H. Meyer, C. A. Peck, & L. Brown (Eds.), *Critical issues in the lives of people with severe disabilities* (pp. 115–144). Baltimore: Paul H. Brookes.

Noble, J., & Conley, R. (1986, November). *Accumulating evidence on the benefits and costs of supported and transitional work for persons with severe disabili-*

ties. Paper presented at the Annual Meeting of the Association for Persons with Severe Handicaps, San Francisco.

O'Brien, J., & O'Brien, C. L. (1992). Members of each other: Perspectives on social support for people with severe disabilities. In J. Nisbet (Ed.), *Natural supports in school, at work, and in the community for people with severe disabilities* (pp. 17–64). Baltimore: Paul H. Brookes.

O'Neill, J., Brown, M., Gordon, W., & Schonhorn, R. (1985). The impact of deinstitutionalization on activities and skills of severely/profoundly retarded multiply handicapped adults. *Applied Research in Mental Retardation, 6,* 361–371.

Payne, J. S., & Patton, J. R. (1981). *Mental retardation.* Upper Saddle River, NJ: Merrill/Prentice Hall.

Peck, C. A., Apolloni, T., & Cooke, T. P. (1981). Rehabilitation services for Americans with mental retardation: A summary of accomplishments in research and development. In E. L. Pan, T. E. Backer, & C. L. Vash (Eds.), *Annual review of rehabilitation* (Vol. 2). New York: Springer.

President's Committee on Mental Retardation. (1995). *The journey to inclusion.* Washington, DC: Author.

Revell, W. G., Wehman, P., Kregel, J., West, M., & Rayfield, R. (1994). Supported employment for persons with severe disabilities: Positive trends in wages, models, and funding. *Education and Training in Mental Retardation and Developmental Disabilities, 29*(4), 256–264.

Rusch, F. R., Chadsey-Rusch, J., & Johnson, J. R. (1991). Supported employment: Emerging opportunities for employment integration. In L. H. Meyer, C. A. Peck, & L. Brown (Eds.), *Critical issues in the lives of people with severe disabilities* (pp. 145–170). Baltimore: Paul H. Brookes.

Schalock, R. (1986). *Transitions from school to work.* Washington, DC: National Association of Rehabilitation Facilities.

Schloss, P. J., Alper, S., & Jayne, D. (1993). Self-determination for persons with disabilities: Choice, risk, and dignity. *Exceptional Children, 60,* 215–225.

Schuster, J. W. (1990). Financial and philosophical liabilities. *Mental Retardation, 28,* 233–239.

Seligman, M. (1991). Siblings of disabled brothers and sisters. In M. Seligman (Ed.), *The family with a handicapped child* (2nd ed.). Boston: Allyn & Bacon.

Seltzer, M. M., & Krauss, M. W. (1994). Aging parents with resident adult children: The impact of lifelong care giving. In M. M. Seltzer, M. W. Krauss, & M. P. Janicki (Eds.), *Life course perspectives on adulthood and old age* (pp. 3–18). Washington, DC: The American Association on Mental Retardation.

Shannon, G. (1985). *Characteristics influencing current recreational patterns of persons with mental retardation.* Unpublished doctoral dissertation, Brandeis University, Waltham, MA.

Smith, G. C. (1995). Preventive approaches to building competencies. In G. C. Smith, S. S. Tobin, E. A. Robertson-Tchabo, & P. W. Power (Eds.), *Strengthening aging families: Diversity in practice and policy* (pp. 221–234). Newbury Park, CA: Sage.

Smith, G. C., Majeski, R. A., & McClenny, B. (1996). Psychoeducational support groups for aging parents: Development and preliminary outcomes. *Mental Retardation, 34*(3), 172–181.

Smith, J. D. (1989). *The sterilization of Carrie Buck.* New York: New Horizons.

Staff Report on the Institutionalized Mentally Disabled. (1985). Washington, DC: U.S. Senate Subcommittee on the Handicapped, Committee on Labor and Human Resources.

Tines, J., Rusch, F. R., McCaughrin, W., & Conley, R. W. (1990). Benefit-cost analysis of supported employment in Illinois: A statewide evaluation. *American Journal on Mental Retardation, 96,* 55–67.

Turnbull, A. P., & Morningstar, M. E. (1993) Family and professional interaction. In M. E. Snell (Ed.), *Systematic instruction of persons with severe handicaps* (pp. 31–60). Upper Saddle River, NJ: Merrill/Prentice Hall.

Turnbull, A. P., Turnbull, H. R., Bronicki, G. J., Summers, J. A., & Roeder-Gordon, C. (1989). *Disability and the family: A guide to decisions for adulthood.* Baltimore: Paul H. Brookes.

Valdes, K. A., Williamson, C. L., & Wagner, M. M. (1990). *The National Longitudinal Transition Study of Special Education Students, statistics almanac volume 5: Youth categorized as mentally retarded.* Menlo Park, CA: SRI.

Wehman, P., & Revell, W. G. (1996). Supported employment. In *Improving the implementation of the Individuals with Disabilities Education Act: Making schools work for all America's children* (Supplement) (pp. 501–525). Washington, DC: Author.

Wehmeyer, M. (1992). Self-determination: Critical skills for outcome-oriented transition services steps in transition that lead to self-determination. *Journal for Vocational Special Needs Education, 16*(1), 3–7.

Wehmeyer, M. L. (1996). Self-determination as an educational outcome: Why is it important to children, youths, and adults with disabilities? In D. J. Sands & M. L. Wehmeyer (Eds.), *Self-determination across the life span: Independence and choice for people with* disabilities (pp. 17–36). Baltimore: Paul H. Brookes.

West, M., Revell, W. G., & Wehman, P. (1992). Achievement and challenges I: A five-year report on consumer and system outcomes from the supported employment initiative. *Journal of the Association for Persons with Severe Handicaps, 17,* 227–235.

Will, M. (1985). OSERS programming for the transition of youth with disabilities: Bridges from school to working life. In S. Moon, P. Goodall, & P. Wehman (Eds.), *Critical issues related to supported competitive employment* (pp. 12–29). Richmond: Virginia Commonwealth University, Rehabilitation Research and Training Center.

Wolfensberger, W. (1972). *Normalization: The principle of normalization in human services.* Toronto: National Institute on Mental Retardation.

Wolfensberger, W. (1983). Social role valorization: Proposed new term for the principle of normalization. *Mental Retardation, 21*(6), 234–239.

Wyatt v. Stickney, 344 F. Supp. 387; 344 F. Supp. 373 (M.D. Ala. 1972).

Zigler, E. (1973). The retarded child as a whole person. In D. K. Routh (Ed.), *The experimental psychology of mental retardation.* Chicago: Aldine.

Chapter 11

The Older Person with Mental Retardation

Core Concepts

- Problems in research methodology have contributed to the relative lack of information on elderly individuals with mental retardation. Some problems relate to aging research generally; others arise specifically from mental retardation.
- Identifying the elderly with mental retardation has been difficult because of disagreement on who is old and problems in actually finding such individuals.
- Age-related changes in mental functioning of older people with mental retardation are of great interest and often are compared with changes in peers without mental retardation.
- The social and personal functioning of elderly people with mental retardation provides some extremely interesting areas of study. Evidence currently is confusing and, in some ways, may challenge the normalization principle.
- Service programs and living arrangements for elderly people with mental retardation also raise interesting questions about normalization.

The study of elderly people with mental retardation continues the progression through the developmental cycle. In some ways, the content of this chapter extends the material in Chapter 10, although the focus is altered to suit the group. Distinguishing between the aged and adults is not as simple as it may appear. There is, however, legitimate reason to give special attention to the latter part of adulthood—the final phase of the life cycle. Interest in aging and geriatrics has grown dramatically in the past decade. This growth may be partially because society can afford to be increasingly humanitarian. Another reason, however, is the highly visible presence of an increasing number of older persons. As medical sophistication has progressed and survival needs have been satisfied, the longevity of the general population has increased (Lemme, 1995).

Aging: What does it mean? Who is an old person? Certainly, these are questions most people can answer. An old person is perhaps one's grandmother or grandfather. An old person may be one who is retired. But a child's definition of an old person is very different from that of a 45-year-old. For the most part, people's perceptions of age involve specific examples from personal experience or individual conceptualizations. One does not have to probe very far to see that answers vary a great deal. It follows that the conceptual basis from which a behavioral scientist operates also must vary. If aging is considered from a physiological viewpoint, it looks very different from its appearance from a cultural standpoint. Different individuals and characteristics emerge from the different definitions, and the problem is compounded further by different attitudes, philosophies, social views, and public policy perspectives (Dietz, 1996; Lemme, 1995; Pushkar, Bukowski, Schwartzman, Stack, & White, 1998). What appears on the surface to be a rather uncomplicated question is not so simple on further consideration.

This chapter focuses on the aging of the population of people with mental retardation. We have emphasized throughout this volume that people with mental retardation represent one part of the complete spectrum of humanity. Although they are different from those without mental retardation in some respects, they are similar in many others. To ignore this fact is to be blinded by either attitude or lack of information. The process of aging must be given attention for the elderly with mental retardation, as well as for the population in general. The major emphasis of both research and service for those having mental retardation has largely fixed on childhood and more recently has included more focus on adolescence. One only need scan the literature that has accumulated over the years to note that attention and research on many conditions, including mental retardation, declines dramatically as one progresses up the age scale (e.g., Pushkar et al., 1998; Shore, 1998). Children with mental retardation do, however, grow up, and they grow old and die.

RESEARCH ON AGING AND RETARDATION

In comparison with many areas of behavioral science, relatively little study of aging in populations with mental retardation has been conducted. In fact, the information available has been so limited that it was characterized in earlier editions of this book as nearly nonexistent. With rare exceptions (e.g., Kaplan, 1943), little interest in this area has been evident until recently. Although the need is still urgent for additional study, aging is gaining priority (LeBlanc & Matson, 1997; Shultz, Aman, & Rojahn, 1998).

We mentioned the lack of clarity about identifying the elderly with mental retardation. Some of the reasons for this lack of clarity receive additional attention in this section. We review research in an attempt to explore how the elderly with mental retardation are both like and unlike their peers without retardation. Because we have limited research data on older people with mental retardation, we sometimes use those without retardation as a reference group.

Methodological Problems

Core Concept

Problems in research methodology have contributed to the relative lack of information on elderly individuals with mental retardation. Some problems relate to aging research generally; others arise specifically from mental retardation.

A number of factors contribute to the paucity of research in the area of aging and mental retardation. Some involve lack of interest and an uncaring attitude toward the population, although such perspectives appear to be changing. Others involve the methodological problems of conducting research on aging in general and with the population having mental retardation specifically (e.g., Nelson, Lott, Touchette, Satz, & D'Elia, 1995; Shultz et al., 1998).

Some of the methodological problems encountered in investigations on aging involve fundamental difficulties in research design (Bass & Caro, 1995; Belsky, 1997; Drew, Hardman, & Hart, 1996). These difficulties represent serious impediments to increasing knowledge on aging. Consequently, we need to examine these design problems before we can interpret existing data on the elderly and on the process of growing old.

Two of the most common approaches to studying aging are the cross-sectional design and the longitudinal design. **Cross-sectional studies** sample subjects from several age levels (say, ages 40 to 49, 50 to 59, 60 to 69, and 70 to 79) and compare certain measures among groups. **Longitudinal studies** select a single group of subjects and follow it through the years to compare behaviors at different ages. Each approach compares attributes at different ages to determine how the aging process affects them. Although on the surface these approaches appear suited to their purpose, problems have arisen that make reliable interpretation of data difficult.

The cross-sectional design is by far the more convenient procedure because all subjects are assessed at approximately the same time. A sample of subjects at each level is selected, and the investigator records the desired data. Data then are compared among age levels to find any differences among groups (e.g., Berg, Strough, Calderone, Sansone, & Weir, 1998; Lifshitz, 1998). The problem is that the investigator may incorrectly attribute differences to aging. Although observed differences may be caused by age differences, other explanations also are possible. Differences between the group that is 40 and the group that is 70 years old, for example, could be the result of sociocultural change over the 30 years that have passed since the older group was 40. It is quite likely (and observations of the past 25 years would confirm) that many social and cultural changes have occurred in such a period of time, creating cohort differences among groups that are not due to aging. People with mental retardation also may be affected by the enormous changes in treatment over the years. Differences among groups may be from aging, different sociocultural influences, different treatments, or combinations of all three. Researchers on aging must be cautious in their interpretations in order to determine age-related and other contextual information in cross-sectional research (Berg et al., 1998; Drew et al., 1996).

Longitudinal investigations are not plagued by the problem of sociocultural change in the same fashion as cross-sectional studies. Because the same sample is followed through a period of years (even a life span), generation gap differences are not as potent. It cannot be denied, however, that a given person changes behaviors in response to altered sociocultural influences. A more serious difficulty is the problem of sample attrition during the period of the study. Because subjects inevitably are lost during the investigation, the sample available at age 70 years is likely to be quite different from the initial sample at 40 years. Thus, differences might result because the composition of the sample has changed, rather than from the effects of age. This difficulty has been called "experimental mortality" and is an inherent design problem of longitudinal studies (Drew et al., 1996; Gelfand, Jenson, & Drew, 1997). An additional difficulty of longitudinal studies is that the researcher may die before the investigation is over. This misfortune sometimes leads to the use of retrospective studies that do not directly assess status at earlier ages but rely on reports based on the subjects' memory or that of others close to them. Such studies are rife with problems of reliability and accuracy.

These methodological problems are serious threats to the soundness of research on the effects of aging. They do not, however, imply that the study of aging is impossible or should not be undertaken. It is merely important that one keep them in mind when reading and interpreting research on the elderly. Obviously, at times, research results need to be interpreted cautiously in order not to generalize beyond the data or to make unsound inferences based on preliminary findings.

Identifying the Older Person with Mental Retardation

Core Concept

Identifying the elderly with mental retardation has been difficult because of disagreement on who is old and problems in actually finding such individuals.

Investigators studying the aging process in mental retardation face even more difficulties than those who study aging in general. Because little research has focused specifically on this population, little information is available for use as a point of departure. Although progress has been made recently in research on the elderly in general, and those with mental retardation, difficulties are still inherent in identifying, detecting, and analyzing data on such individuals (Belsky, 1997; McNellis, 1997).

Researchers are forced to address some fundamental questions as they consider investigating aging in mental retardation. One of the basic questions immediately raised was mentioned earlier: Who is an old person with mental retardation? Among people with mental retardation, age ranges for the elderly have varied considerably and have been rather arbitrary. Ages as young as 40 and 55 years have appeared in the literature—hardly what some would consider old. Some current research on people with mental retardation still employs age ranges in the 40s and 50s as elderly (e.g., Lifshitz, 1998; Shultz et al., 1998). Early literature in the area speculated that a person with mental retardation who lives to 45 or 50 years of age may be considered old. This speculation was based on the view that persons with mental retardation may be subject to double or triple jeopardy with regard to the normal loss pattern associated with advancing age. This does not mean that the aging process (physiologically) is necessarily more rapid in the population with mental retardation. In part this speculation was based on such factors as where the person resides and what minimal services are available for the elderly with disabilities. Factors such as poverty, marital status, gender, services available, and housing or living status are important considerations in the study of aging (Enright, 1994; Pushkar et al., 1998). Agreement about who is old among people with mental retardation remains a problem, as it does for many researchers in gerontology.

Noting that identifying the elderly with mental retardation is not simple, we find that a related task is thereby complicated—determining the size of the population. Determining demographic information and various associated characteristics for older people with mental retardation remains as research to be undertaken (McNellis, 1997; Shultz et al., 1998). Estimates vary widely with the nature of the population studied, the age used as a lower limit, and the procedures employed for calculating prevalence. If age 65 is used as the cutoff, a prevalence rate of 1% generates 347,000 individuals who might be considered elderly with mental retardation (U.S. Census Bureau, 1997). Estimates based on a younger age, like the mid-50s, would clearly result in a much larger number. Thus our beginning question of what is considered old among people with mental retardation is an important one. Without a clear point of demarcation, policy matters related to service will lag.

Because of the absence of a firm knowledge base regarding this group, variability in the data raises some extremely interesting questions about aging and mental retardation. Where are the elderly with mental retardation? Perhaps the use of population percentage projections is inappropriate for this group, although no particular logic explains why. Are they hidden or invisible because of a lack of services and, therefore, not on anyone's records? Do they have a shorter life span? Have they adapted to the point that they are no longer evident as having mental retardation? These types of questions are central to the study of aging in those with mental retardation, and definitive answers remain among the forthcoming.

CHARACTERISTICS OF THE OLDER PERSON WITH MENTAL RETARDATION

The absence of a complete picture of elderly people with mental retardation is not surprising. Problems encountered in the study of aging generally are compounded by additional complications specific to the population with mental retardation. Interest in this area is growing, however, and some evidence is accumulating about the characteristics of this population. We examine two broad areas: mental functioning and social and personal functioning.

Mental Functioning

Core Concept

Age-related changes in mental functioning of older people with mental retardation are of great interest and often are compared with changes in peers without mental retardation.

Mental functioning includes a number of specific cognitive skills. At this time, we are unable to discuss all of these skill areas separately because the accumulated body of research pertaining to older people with mental retardation is relatively immature. Although we know more about the older population without mental retardation, some comparisons are only broadly inferred because of limited data.

Mental functioning is a performance domain that often is assumed to decline with advancing age, and some research supports this assumption (e.g., Raz, Gunning-Dixon, Head, Dupuis, & Acker, 1998). Most people would agree that older people they know are frequently less mentally alert and generally not as mentally capable as younger individuals. Additionally, people often compare the present functioning of a particular older person with recollections of his or her functioning when younger—a comparison fraught with error for many reasons. Although many questions about this perception are unanswered, it is a widely held view in our culture.

Elderly persons with mental retardation may engage in a variety of activities to enrich their lives.

This perspective appears to have substantially influenced research on aging, which often seems to presume that aging erodes cognitive ability. Although it may be true that a decline in mental functioning occurs as age increases, when such a perspective unduly influences scientific investigation, the resulting knowledge base may be biased. Consequently, we must be cautious in interpreting results as they now exist. Although evidence does suggest that some areas of mental functioning decline with aging, this is not a universal pattern of performance, and the type of decline varies greatly among individuals (Shapiro & Tate, 1997; Snowdon, 1997; Stuart-Hamilton & Rabbitt, 1997). For example, the type of memory that stores information as abstract symbols and relations between them is known as **secondary memory.** This type of memory performance does seem to decline in older people. In other mental performance areas, however, such a trend does not appear. Thus memory performance includes several different dimensions and some of these, but not all, seem to show a decline that is related to aging (Belsky, 1997; Kim & Muller, 1997). Table 11–1 presents a summary of certain typical myths regarding aging and mental functioning, along with abstracted research evidence pertaining to that area of performance.

One question related to our particular focus concerns the influence of aging on older people with retardation. Do such people experience a further or marked decline in mental functioning as they age? Does the rate of mental decline occur in a fashion similar to that for peers without mental retardation? Precise answers to these questions remain elusive even with more attention being paid to populations of elders with mental retardation. Table 11–1 presents some of the myths often held that pertain to the association of aging and mental functioning generally. Some common beliefs about decline in mental functioning also have influenced the field of mental retardation. These views generally presume not only a general decline of intelligence with age but also a more rapid decline in the mental retardation population. However, solid research evidence on the general nature of intellectual change as a function of age is unclear.

Research literature in mental retardation suggests that the elderly in this population appear to mirror many of the same cognitive trends of their counterparts who do not have mental retardation (LeBlanc & Matson, 1997; McNellis, 1997). In some cases, impairments do seem to appear at a higher rate in older people with mental retardation, although they are a heterogeneous population with many different influences causing their reduced intellectual functioning (Cherry, Matson, & Paclawskyj, 1997). Some subgroups appear to show a decline in cognitive capacity with age; the performance of other subgroups seems related to specific detrimental influences other than aging, such as depression (Nelson et al., 1995; Sung et al., 1997). For example, evidence is accumulating that older adults with Down syndrome are affected by Alzheimer's disease or Alzheimer's-type dementia more frequently and at an earlier age than their peers without retardation (Prasher, Chowdhury, Rowe, & Bain, 1997; Visser, Aldenkamp, van Huffelen, Kuilman, Overweg, & van Wijk, 1997). It is worth noting, however, that despite this susceptibility, not all elders with Down syndrome show evidence of Alzheimer's disease (Chicoine & McGuire, 1997).

TABLE 11–1
Myths About Aging and Mental Functioning

Myth	Best available evidence
Most old persons suffer from severe memory impairments and cannot remember such basic information as the names of their loved ones and where they live.	Secondary memory does decline significantly with increasing age, but not to this extent. Memory impairments of this magnitude typically result from severe illnesses, such as Alzheimer's disease or other dementias. Memory declines in healthy middle-aged and elderly adults are likely to take the form of absentmindedness, such as forgetting what one said an hour ago and repeating it to the same listener or deciding to do something 10 minutes from now and then forgetting to do so.
Most middle-aged and elderly adults conform to the maxim, "You can't teach an old dog new tricks."	This is true only for certain kinds of tasks. Older adults perform more poorly on tasks that involve learning new motor skills, the cognitive reorganization of material between the stimulus and the response, dividing attention among several tasks simultaneously, and highly speeded tasks. On many other kinds of tasks, middle-aged and elderly adults are capable of significant amounts of learning.
Because of age-related declines in memory and learning, most older people should not be given complicated and challenging jobs.	Although older adults do perform more poorly on difficult memory tests, most jobs are not as demanding. So older adults usually can do well by relying on their experiences.
If you have not made any creative contributions by about age 40, you probably never will.	Creativity does tend to peak prior to middle age, but numerous important creative works have been produced during the latter part of the creator's life.
There is a universal decline in intelligence with increasing age. Thus, you are very likely to suffer serious and widespread deterioration in intellectual ability during your old age.	Some intellectual abilities do show significant decrements as we grow older, especially after middle age. But the declines in other abilities are small and do not appear to have much effect on one's daily functioning. Age-related changes in intelligence test scores may not accurately reflect true changes in intelligence because of cohort effects, extraneous variables, selective attrition, and/or other methodological problems. The majority of elderly adults do not suffer extreme deterioration in intelligence, although some losses may be expected in such areas as perceptual integration, response speed, and certain aspects of memory.

From Adult Development and Aging: Myths and Emerging Realities *(2nd ed., pp. 148, 182) by R. Schulz and R. B. Ewen, 1993, Upper Saddle River, NJ: Merrill/Prentice Hall. Adapted by permission.*

Thus older individuals with mental retardation appear to have mental functioning *trends* similar to those of people without mental retardation, although rates may be higher and some subgroups more vulnerable than others. Like most groups, specific health problems may influence cognitive performance and other functioning, and the specific effects of aging alone are difficult to identify (Cooper, 1998; Prasher, Chung, & Haque, 1998). It should be emphasized that focused research on some of the more specific cognitive skills noted for general populations (e.g., secondary memory) have yet to be investigated. It is also important to underscore the need for longitudinal research to isolate more clearly the effects of age from the cohort effects found in cross-sectional studies. With rare exceptions, research to date on aging in older people with mental retardation has predominantly employed cross-sectional methodology (Prasher et al., 1998).

Interpreting these research results warrants caution for a variety of reasons. Situational factors, such as the testing itself, can substantially alter an individual's performance. The immediate circumstances or environment may cause enhanced or diminished performance, depending on the individual and the situation. Such influences have long been recognized by psychologists and those in the field of gerontology (e.g., Gelfand et al., 1997; Ross & Lichtenberg, 1997). One factor that may well result in declining test scores is an apparent increase in cautiousness observed in older people in general. Behavior occasionally interpreted as increased cautiousness, however, might also be viewed as test anxiety in the elderly. Such a characteristic often stands out most prominently in tasks with a time limit. It may also come into play in situations that have the potential to produce additional anxiety by their very nature, such as the presence of a nonroutine authority figure (the psychometrician). Both of these conditions often exist in a testing situation. If older people with retardation exhibit the same situational anxiety as older people in general (and there is no reason to expect that they would not), the timed responses required by testing may have a substantial negative influence on their scores (Elias, Robbins, & Elias, 1996). They simply may fail to respond within the allotted time. In fact, the presence of a psychometrician may create some special concern for the elderly person with retardation. A mental test is an important occurrence in the life of such a person—an event that is likely to have a significant personal history. The possibility is also good that much of that history has not been particularly pleasant. A number of disagreeable or troubling associations may be made with the presence of a psychometrician and the process of a psychological test. All of these matters may contribute to anxiety and serve to suppress test performance.

A number of factors may contribute to the apparent decline in mental functioning by older people with retardation. It should be noted once again that these points are largely speculative because research on these topics comes mainly from the general field of gerontology, rather than from the field of mental retardation. For example, age deficits tend to be evident on tasks that are paced, tasks that require a constant switching of attention, and tasks that involve free recall, rather than recognition. Such research remains to be systematically conducted with subjects having mental retardation. However, there is little reason to believe that similar studies done with this population would not produce similar results. The tasks noted are also reminiscent of the activities included in an intelligence test.

Cognitive performance in elderly people also seems to be negatively influenced by self-perceptions of poor health and by symptoms of depression (Carmelli, Swan, LaRue, & Eslinger, 1997). In these areas the individuals' actual health status also seems to influence cognitive functioning, although here too the evidence suggests individual differences and variability regarding the type of health problems. For example, some cardiovascular problems do not seem related to mental functioning, while chronic bronchitis does have a negative impact (van Boxtel, Buntinx, Houx, Metsemakers, Kottnerus, & Jolles, 1998). There are some data suggesting that stress-related circumstances may relate to poor health, although separating out other risk factors is difficult (Barak, Achiron, Kimh, & Lampi, 1996; Yadava, Yadava, & Vajpeyi, 1997). The concept of cumulative effects of multiple risk factors on a person's functioning is emerging as health-care workers, psychologists, and gerontologists view some trends of declining performance with age. General trends appear to support enhanced life qualities, including cognitive functioning, in later years, trends associated with higher exercise and activity patterns and healthy lifestyle practices (van Boxtel et al., 1998; Vita, Terry, Hubert, & Fries, 1998).

Another area of cognitive or mental functioning that has generated some interest in aging research is rigidity—a reduced ability to change as situations or tasks are altered. This, too, is among the characteristics that are commonly associate with aging (Kahana & Morgan, 1998; McDaniel, Hepworth, & Doherty, 1997). It may be related also to the performance of tasks that require one to switch attention, as noted previously. Mental retardation has also played a role in theories about cognitive and behavioral rigidity in addition to the perception that there is an increasing tendency to exhibit rigid behavior (e.g., Berkson, Gutermuth, & Baranek, 1995; Switzky, 1997). Dulaney and Ellis (1997) note that much of the empirical evidence suggests both cognitive and motivational elements play roles in rigid behavior. Increasing chronological age generally seems related to increased rigid behavior, and increased mental age relates to decreased rigidity (Dulaney & Ellis, 1997). Clearly further research is needed to delineate this aspect of mental functioning. Additionally, research specifically on older people with mental retardation needs to be undertaken. Early research suggested that those with mental retardation are particularly susceptible to the formation of learning sets, diminishing their ability to transfer training well. Although this susceptibility seems related to rigidity, further study is needed.

Social and Personal Functioning

Core Concept

The social and personal functioning of elderly people with mental retardation provides some extremely interesting areas of study. Evidence currently is confusing and, in some ways, may challenge the normalization principle. ⚙

Social and personal functioning is a very broad theme and potentially covers an enormous range of topics. This type of section heading is useful in the current discussion for two reasons. First, we still are examining performance areas for which the body of research evidence still is accumulating and information regarding subtopics is relatively scarce. Second, social and personal functioning, though a broad subject, relates to normalization, an important concept for those working in mental retardation.

We presented the principle of normalization in earlier chapters of this volume. Essentially, it reflects the general concern for educating, placing, and treating individuals with mental retardation as nearly normally as possible. Normalization emerged in the literature during the late 1960s and early 1970s and is related to the least restrictive alternative concept. It has continued to be of interest in a variety of conceptual formats and under some divergent terminology (e.g., social valorization, inclusion) (Hardman, Drew, & Egan, 1999). Normalization ideas have a number of applications as we consider the quality of life for older people with mental retardation.

Many aspects of one's quality of life relate to personal health and an ability to function in the environment. Personal health and health care have become topics of vital concern as the general population has become older (Kavanagh & Broom, 1998; Klein & Bloom, 1997). Some general indicators are that the health status of those with mental retardation does not compare favorably with their counterparts without retardation, although these indicators are not necessarily age related (Cooper, 1998; Kapell, Nightingale, Rodriguez, Lee, Zigman, & Schupf, 1998; Newcomer & Benjamin, 1997). For example, general mortality rates appear higher for those with mental retardation and seem to be related to severity of retardation. In some cases, underlying causation of the mental retardation appears associated with death, which would be expected in circumstances in which the etiology is physiologically based. However, much of the research addressing these topics is plagued with methodological limitations like those outlined in the beginning of this chapter. Sound longitudinal investigation is needed to delineate more adequately the age-related variables affecting this group as they grow older. Such information is vital as policymakers plan for the future of cost-effective health-care delivery to those with mental retardation (Kastner, Walsh, & Criscione, 1997; Pulcini & Howard, 1997).

Mental health problems, such as depression, seem to emerge more frequently in older populations and have been the focus of increased study in such groups (Hernandez, Hinrichsen, & Lapidus, 1998; Meltzer et al., 1998; Deeg, Kriegsman, & Beekman, 1996). As usual it is difficult to separate the various influences in such research. Does depression really appear more frequently with increased age or are the various other maladies associated with becoming older more linked to such mental health states (e.g., reduced independence, physical limitations, fewer social relationships)? Interest in depression and other psychopathologies and their relationships to mental retardation also appears in the literature with increasing frequency, although direct analysis of the relationship needs attention (Cherry et al., 1997; Mitchell, 1998; Raitasuo, Virtanen, & Raitasuo, 1998). It is unlikely that the factors of aging, mental retardation, and the emergence of depression or other mental health difficulties represent relationships that are linear or easily investigated.

Additional questions of interest remain regarding the quality of life of the elderly with mental retardation (Hatton, 1998). What are their social and personal lives like? Where do their support systems lie? These are difficult questions for older people generally, and the picture for those with mental retardation is not an appealing one. The variety of supports tend to be different and of variable effectiveness for those with mental retardation (Jameson, 1998; Mank, Cioffi, & Yovanoff, 1997). For many people without mental retardation, growing older means an increased dependence on informal support systems, as well as on governmental agencies. Family members often shoulder a significant burden of support and caregiving (Smith, 1997). However, for those older individuals with mental retardation, the family may not be available for a variety of reasons. In many cases, no spouse is available to provide care and support because the person was not married, and siblings may not be a reliable source of care and support. Although it is promising to see social agency networks increasingly serving elderly people with mental retardation, such assistance may be a low-quality substitute for family support (Braddock & Hemp, 1997; Smith, 1997). Further, family support networks for older people with mental retardation may be limited. There is a serious need for additional systematic research on the family structures of older citizens having mental retardation.

Adaptive behavior skills become increasingly important as a greater numbers of adults, including older adults with mental retardation, are moved from institutions to community living arrangements. This is an area of escalating interest and concern among professionals working in mental retardation, since therapeutic services may be less available or require more individual initiative outside of an institutional setting (Stancliffe & Hayden, 1998). Problem solving in the interpersonal domain is a skill that is likely to be of heightened importance as one lives in a community setting and represents a set of skills where age differences are clearly evident. Older adults appear to employ different strategies for interpersonal problem definition (Berg et al., 1998). Some features of the social circumstances of elderly adults suggest less desirable situations (e.g., diminished interpersonal contact and support) and behavioral profiles that do not promote interpersonal contact as a group (Newsom & Schulz, 1996; Smith & Baltes, 1997). As we have found in other areas, individual differences clearly have nearly preemptive influences, and declines in adaptive behavior are not evident in all investigations (Prasher et al., 1998). These topics must, however, be the focus for future research as we observe the juncture of increased life spans and community living for our citizens with mental retardation, a circumstance that increases the importance of interpersonal competence and life decision making (Stancliffe & Abery, 1997).

Research has demonstrated a decline in adaptive behavior functioning in Down syndrome subjects as a function of aging (Prasher et al., 1998). Such evidence, however, may include some significant other influences beyond aging effects. For example, this particular population has also been shown repeatedly to be affected by a relatively early onset of Alzheimer's disease or Alzheimer's-type dementia (e.g., Prasher et al., 1997; Visser et al., 1997). The presence of such a condition may certainly contribute to behavior that most would consider to be nonadaptive. Not surprisingly, adults with mental retardation seem significantly influenced by their environmental circumstances. For example, a general increase in socially related activities seem characteristic of individuals in supported living arrangements compared with those in institutional circumstances (Howe, Horner, & Newton, 1998). Current evidence is as complicated as the settings in which the research must necessarily be undertaken. However, solid rigorous research methods now in use allow and promote such investigation (Drew et al., 1996; Gelfand et al., 1997). Further research on the personal and adaptive functioning of elderly people with mental retardation is extremely important, particularly in community settings.

A comprehensive picture of the social and personal functioning of the elderly person with mental retardation is still not available. Many dimensions of this topic remain relatively unexplored. The emergence of community living as a preferred alternative for many with mental retardation opens new areas needing investigation. Although some elements of the family circumstances for older people with mental retardation may seem rather depressing, other pieces of data provide much more hope (Howe et al., 1998).

PROGRAMMING AND FUTURE RESEARCH

Core Concept

Service programs and living arrangements for elderly people with mental retardation also raise interesting questions about normalization.

The development of programs for older people with mental retardation varies greatly throughout the nation. Reports of state service plans range from programs that are already implemented to circumstances in which policies have yet to be articulated (Braddock & Hemp, 1997; Howe et al., 1998). As noted earlier, however, the nearly standard and strong impetus is for educating, placing, and treating individuals with retardation as nearly normally as possible. Some of the positive outcomes of such placements (Howe et al., 1998) prompt further interest in these types of arrangements. Future programming plans increasingly must anticipate changes in this population as health care of all types continues to improve. Additionally, there may well be some additional risks generated by the normalization of living arrangements for adults and older citizens with mental retardation. To some degree, normalization brings with it some of the self-inflicted hazards that we all live with on a daily basis (Rimmer, Braddock, & Fujiura, 1994).

Community living arrangements for adults with mental retardation have raised considerable controversy periodically. Objections often come from neighborhood residents who are fearful for the physical well-being of their families or who believe that the value of their property will be reduced by the proximity of facilities for people with retardation. These arguments have been the most prominent in objections to community living placements. However, we must also consider an issue that surfaces only occasionally in the heat of such controversy—the well-being of the individual.

Evidence is accumulating that demonstrates advantages of community living for those with mental retardation. In some cases, such living arrangements require alterations in the way service is conceived and provided. Modification of staffing arrangements in group homes, for example, allows for the additional health-care services that may be required by older residents experiencing some added physical needs with age. New relationships are being suggested between service providers and clients in order to promote some citizens with disabilities being able to live most productively in the community. We are learning more regarding what is needed and are beginning to see even larger areas where additional research is required. The base of research information regarding living arrangements for the elderly with mental retardation, though growing, remains limited when compared with that regarding the general population.

Considerable research is necessary for a better understanding of the elderly with mental retardation in general. The empirical knowledge based on this population remains rather thin. We do not have a firm grasp on how many aged people with retardation there are or where they are in general. Such information, plus a clear definition of what old means in this group, is fundamental to further research. It is difficult to describe characteristics and to prescribe programming coherently unless these basic questions are answered. Investigation of the aged population with mental retardation is obviously a rich area of study for beginning researchers. It represents an area of specialization that promises an exciting career. Future researchers in this area will have to study both mental retardation and gerontology and then synthesize the two for use with the elderly with retardation. The research needed is unlikely to come from either mental retardation or gerontology singly.

Who are the elderly with mental retardation, and what are their characteristics? These were general questions with which we began this chapter, and they have been answered only partially. The final part of the life cycle of the individual with mental retardation has had little examination in comparison with earlier phases. We still do not know whether people with retardation tend to age more rapidly than their peers without retardation. In individual cases (e.g., some Down syndrome individuals), they do seem to become prematurely old, but what of the population as a whole? Certainly people of the ages under discussion in this chapter (i.e., the 50s) are not considered old in the general population. If, in fact, this population does age more quickly, it is not at all clear whether it results from factors related to mental retardation or to environmental factors that may be associated with mental retardation, such as poor health care. More likely, we are seeing a phenomenon that is a social construct; we see these people in a particular way and with certain expectations.

It is interesting to note that people with mental retardation seem not to experience middle age to any marked degree. They often are thought of as being in an extended childhood and adolescent phase for a large part of their lives. This also is likely the result of how people have viewed them. It is a view that may well change as the literature on adults with mental retardation grows, as it has begun to do.

When older people with mental retardation are placed in nursing homes, they tend to be grouped with patients who are senile. This classification may be one factor that contributes to the invisibility of elderly people with retardation. No one distinguishes their behaviors from those of elderly patients in general, so they lose their diagnosis of mental retardation. Obviously, one must question whether such programming practices are appropriate for and in the best interests of these individuals. If the practices are appropriate and in the best interests of these individuals (a matter not yet determined), is it advisable to relabel these people with a term that carries such negative connotations? Mental retardation is a complex problem that involves interaction of many forces and influences. It is a problem that society has at least partially created, and society must address it. The life of the aged individual with retardation continues to reflect these interacting variables.

NEW ISSUES AND FUTURE DIRECTIONS

A number of questions have been examined in this chapter, several of which began the chapter and remain only partially answered. The literature available on the latter part of the life span has expanded in recent years. The future of services to the elderly with mental retardation, however, depends heavily on consolidating knowledge about this population. Policymakers have a difficult time enacting legislative support for a problem that has an undetermined size, and there remains a great deal to be learned about the size and age distribution of this group. Although the literature has grown, the results also remain mixed in terms of identifying their special problems. Issues like these are vital to our knowledge base on older people with mental retardation and our ability to serve them.

We are also somewhat confused about what we should do with older people in general, let alone those with mental retardation. The aging of our population presents a variety of problems, and some of those matters become very personal when they involve an individual in our own family. As individuals we may have made some decisions that are effective to some degree. But as a population there is much that needs attention about our older citizens, and policies and services for them will also impact that segment that has mental retardation.

There are also ethical concerns that may be particularly relevant to this age-group. Some of the dilemmas that recur with older individuals having mental retardation illustrate certain similarities and differences between this group and the general population of elderly people. One dilemma of particular note is competence to refuse recommended treatment—an issue that recently has received more widespread attention (Cetron & Davies, 1998; O'Donnell & Safford, 1997; Safford, 1997). However, one important difference in older people with mental retardation is that they may be considered incompetent by reason of mental ability irrespective of age. Does this factor really make such individuals less competent to refuse treatment? This question remains unanswered but is one that faces care providers in a very real, perhaps personal way when considering an individual with whom they have formed a service relationship. These are no longer hypothetical issues when real people are involved.

The future of services for elderly people with mental retardation is still relatively uncharted territory. Balancing real life with the hypothetical ideal presents many challenges for people working with this population. It is important to think carefully as we enter these unknown areas, to draw on the desirable as professionals develop service plans that will work within the constraints of society's ability to provide. Nearly 15 years ago Cotten and Spirrison (1986) articulated many elements of a desirable quality of life for the elderly with mental retardation. These are presented in Figure 11–1 as a bill of rights that might be desirable for all elderly people.

Core Questions

1. How have the general methodological problems encountered in conducting gerontological research contributed to problems in the investigation of the elderly with mental retardation?
2. Why might elderly people with retardation be characterized as an "invisible" group?
3. What effect does invisibility have on social services for the elderly with retardation?
4. How does disagreement about who is old contribute to research difficulties on elderly people with mental retardation?
5. The general perception of older people is that they have a reduced level of mental functioning. Does this perception hold for older individuals with mental retardation?
6. Do people with mental retardation decline in mental functioning more rapidly than people in the general population?
7. What factors, other than reduced mental functioning, may enter the picture in terms of mental performance for older populations?
8. Why do some people object to community-based living arrangements for older individuals with mental retardation?

Roundtable Discussion

Throughout this volume, the notions of mainstreaming and normalization have been much in evidence at many stages of the life cycle. In some ways, these principles represent an imposition of what one group (mental retardation professionals) believes is best for another group (people with mental retardation). When people reach the level of old age, these considerations take on other meanings and may require additional planning.

FIGURE 11–1

The Bill of Rights for the Elderly
Person with Mental Retardation

*From "The Elderly Mentally
Retarded Developmentally Disabled
Population: A Challenge for the
Service Delivery System" by P. D.
Cotten and C. L. Spirrison, in S. J.
Brody and G. E. Ruff (Eds.),* Aging
and Rehabilitation *(pp. 159–187),
1986, New York: Springer. Copy-
right 1986 by Springer-Verlag New
York, Inc. Reprinted by permission.*

1. The right to an adequate standard of living, economic security, and protective work.

2. The right to humane services designed to help them reach their fullest potential.

3. The right to live as independently as they are able in the community of their choice, in as normal a manner as possible.

4. The right to an array of services that is generally available to other elderly groups.

5. The right to choose to retire. In addition, the opportunity to retire "to something," rather than just "from something."

6. The right to participate as a member of the community, having reciprocal interdependency.

7. The right to be considered a person and not merely "elderly" or "retarded."

8. The right to protected, personal well-being and to a qualified guardian, when required.

9. The right to be involved in setting one's goals and in making one's decisions. The right to fail, if necessary.

10. The right to a positive future, and having enough involvement with life to prevent a preoccupation with death.

11. The right to be romantic, not asexual.

12. The right to sufficient activity and attention to permit continued integrity of self, individual identity, and purpose.

13. The right to an interesting environment and lifestyle, with availability of sufficient mobility to provide a variety of surroundings.

14. The right to live and die with dignity.

In your study group or on your own, examine the principles of mainstreaming and normalization with regard to the elderly with mental retardation. Consider that the notions seem more complicated by the fact that some older people with mental retardation have been institutionalized for many years. How might this influence their perceptions of satisfaction? How do these matters influence the way you might plan services for elderly people with mental retardation during the next decade?

References

Barak, Y., Achiron, A., Kimh, R., & Lampi, Y. (1996). Health risks among shift workers: A survey of female nurses. *Health Care for Women International, 17,* 527–534.

Bass, S. A., & Caro, F. G. (1995). Older people as researchers: Benefits to research and the community. *Educational Gerontology, 21,* 467–478.

Belsky, J. (1997). *The adult experience*. St. Paul, MN: West Publishing.

Berg, C. A., Strough, J., Calderone, K. S., Sansone, C., & Weir, C. (1998). The role of problem definitions in understanding age and context effects on strategies for solving everyday problems. *Psychology and Aging, 13,* 29–44.

Berkson, G., Gutermuth, L., & Baranek, G. (1995). Relative prevalence and relations among stereotyped and similar behaviors. *American Journal on Mental Retardation, 100,* 137–145.

Braddock, D., & Hemp, R. (1997). Toward family and community mental retardation services in Massachusetts, New England, and the United States. *Mental Retardation, 35,* 241–256.

Carmelli, D., Swan, G. E., LaRue, A., & Eslinger, P. J. (1997). Correlates of change in cognitive function in survivors from the Western Collaborative Group Study. *Neuroepidemiology, 16,* 285–295.

Cetron, M., & Davies, O. (1998). *Cheating death: The promise and the future impact of trying to live forever.* New York: St. Martin's Press.

Cherry, K. E., Matson, J. L., & Paclawskyj, T. R. (1997). Psychopathology in older adults with severe and profound mental retardation. *American Journal on Mental Retardation, 101,* 445–458.

Chicoine, B., & McGuire, D. (1997). Longevity of a woman with Down syndrome: A case study. *Mental Retardation, 35,* 477–479.

Cooper, S. A. (1998). Clinical study of the effects of age on the physical health of adults with mental retardation. *American Journal on Mental Retardation, 102,* 582–589.

Cotten, P. D., & Spirrison, C. L. (1986). The elderly mentally retarded developmentally disabled population: A challenge for the service delivery system. In S. J. Brody & G. E. Ruff (Eds.), *Aging and rehabilitation* (pp. 159–187). New York: Springer.

Deeg, D. J., Kriegsman, D. M., & Beekman, A. T. (1996). Association of chronic physical and mental conditions with physical test performance and mortality. *Gedrag and Gezondheid: Tijdschrift voor Psychologie and Gezondheid, 24,* 323–333.

Dietz, B. E. (1996). The relationship of aging to self-esteem: The relative effects of maturation and role accumulation. *International Journal of Aging and Human Development, 43,* 249–266.

Drew, C. J., Hardman, M. L., & Hart, A. W. (1996). *Designing and conducting research in education and social science.* Needham Heights, MA: Allyn & Bacon.

Dulaney, C. L., & Ellis, N. R. (1997). Rigidity in the behavior of mentally retarded persons. In W. E. MacLean, Jr. (Ed.), *Ellis' handbook of mental deficiency, psychological theory and research* (3rd ed., pp. 175–195). Mahwah, NJ: Erlbaum.

Elias, M. F., Robbins, M. A., & Elias, P. K. (1996). A 15-year longitudinal study of Halstead-Reitan neuropsychological test performance. *Journals of Gerontology: Series B: Psychological Sciences and Social Sciences, 51B,* 331–334.

Enright, R. B., Jr. (Ed.). (1994). *Perspectives in social gerontology.* Needham Heights, MA: Allyn & Bacon.

Gelfand, D. M., Jenson, W. R., & Drew, C. J. (1997). *Understanding child behavior disorders* (3rd ed.). Fort Worth: Harcourt Brace.

Hardman, M. L., Drew, C. J., & Egan, M. W. (1999). *Human exceptionality: Society, school, and family* (6th ed.). Needham Heights, MA: Allyn & Bacon.

Hatton, C. (1998). Whose quality of life is it anyway? Some problems with the emerging quality of life consensus. *Mental Retardation, 36,* 104–115.

Hernandez, N. A., Hinrichsen, G. A., & Lapidus, L. B. (1998). An empirical study of object relations in adult children of depressed elderly mothers. *International Journal of Aging and Human Development, 46,* 143–156.

Howe, J., Horner, R. H., & Newton, J. S. (1998). Comparison of supported living and traditional residential services in the State of Oregon. *Mental Retardation, 36,* 1–11.

Jameson, C. (1998). Promoting long-term relationships between individuals with mental retardation and people in their community: An agency self-evaluation. *Mental Retardation, 36,* 116–127.

Kahana, R. J., & Morgan, A. C. (1998). Psychoanalytic contributions to geriatric psychiatry: Psychotherapy, clinical psychoanalysis, and the theory of aging. In G. H. Pollock and S. I. Greenspan (Eds.), *The course of life* (Vol. 7, pp. 161–196). Madison, CT: International Universities Press.

Kapell, D., Nightingale, B., Rodriguez, A., Lee, J. H., Zigman, W. B., & Schupf, N. (1998). Prevalence of chronic medical conditions in adults with mental retardation: Comparisons with the general population. *Mental Retardation, 36,* 269–279.

Kaplan, O. (1943). Mental decline in older morons. *American Journal of Mental Deficiency, 47,* 277–285.

Kastner, T. A., Walsh, K. K., & Criscione, T. (1997). Technical elements, demonstration projects, and fiscal models in Medicaid managed care for people with developmental disabilities. *Mental Retardation, 35,* 270–285.

Kavanagh, A. M., & Broom, D. H. (1998). Embodied risk: My body, myself? *Social Science and Medicine, 46,* 437–444.

Kim, K. A., & Muller, D. J. (1997). Memory, self-efficacy, and adaptability in Korean American older adults: A collective study of four cases. *Educational Gerontology, 23,* 407–423.

Klein, W. C., & Bloom, M. (1997). *Successful aging: Strategies for healthy living.* New York: Plenum Press.

LeBlanc, L. A., & Matson, J. L. (1997). Aging in the developmentally disabled: Assessment and treatment. *Journal of Clinical Geropsychology, 3,* 37–55.

Lemme, B. H. (1995). *Adult development and aging.* Boston: Allyn & Bacon.

Lifshitz, H. (1998) Instrumental enrichment: A tool for enhancement of cognitive ability in adult and elderly people with mental retardation. *Education and Training in Mental Retardation and Developmental Disabilities, 33,* 34–41.

Mank, D., Cioffi, A., & Yovanoff, P. (1997). Analysis of the typicalness of supported employment jobs, natural supports, and wage and integration outcomes. *Mental Retardation, 35,* 185–197.

McDaniel, S. H., Hepworth, J., & Doherty, W. J. (1997). *The shared experience of illness: Stories of patients, families and their therapists.* New York: BasicBooks.

McNellis, C. A. (1997). Mental retardation and aging: Mental health issues. *Gerontology and Geriatrics Education, 17*(3), 75–86.

Meltzer, C. C., Smith, G., DeKosky, S. T., Pollock, B. G., Mathis, C. A., Moore, R. Y., Kupfer, D. J., & Reynolds, C. F. (1998). Serotonin in aging, late-life depression, and Alzheimer's disease: The emerging role of functional imaging. *Neuropsychopharmacology, 18,* 407–430.

Mitchell, K. (1998). Assessing dementia and depression in adults with mental retardation. In A. F.

Rotatori and J. O. Schwenn (Eds.), *Advances in special education, Vol. 11: Issues, practices and concerns in special education* (pp. 255–264). Greenwich, CT: Jai Press.

Nelson, L., Lott, I., Touchette, P., Satz, P., & D'Elia, L. (1995). Detection of Alzheimer disease in individuals with Down syndrome. *American Journal on Mental Retardation, 99,* 616–622.

Newcomer, R. J., & Benjamin, A. E. (1997). *Indicators of chronic health conditions: Monitoring community-level delivery systems.* Baltimore: Johns Hopkins University Press.

Newsom, J. T., & Schulz, R. (1996). Social support as a mediator in the relation between functional status and quality of life in older adults. *Psychology and Aging, 11,* 34–44.

O'Donnell, M., & Safford, F. (1997). Death, bereavement, loss, and growth: Two perspectives. In F. Safford and G. I. Krell (Eds.), *Gerontology for health professionals: A practice guide* (2nd ed., pp. 179–204). Washington, DC: NASW Press.

Prasher, V. P., Chowdhury, T. A., Rowe, B. R., & Bain, S. C. (1997). ApoE genotype and Alzheimer's disease in adults with Down syndrome: Meta-analysis. *American Journal on Mental Retardation, 102,* 103–110.

Prasher, V. P., Chung, M. C., Haque, M. S. (1998). Longitudinal changes in adaptive behavior in adults with Down syndrome: Interim findings from a longitudinal study. *American Journal on Mental Retardation, 103,* 40–46.

Pulcini, J., & Howard, A. M. (1997). Framework for analyzing health care models serving adults with mental retardation and other developmental disabilities. *Mental Retardation, 35,* 209–217.

Pushkar, D., Bukowski, W. M., Schwartzman, A. E., Stack, D. M. & White, D. R. (1998). *Improving competence across the lifespan: Building interventions based on theory and research.* New York: Plenum Press.

Raitasuo, S., Virtanen, H., & Raitasuo, J. (1998). Anorexia nervosa, major depression, and obsessive-compulsive disorder in a Down's syndrome patient. *International Journal of Eating Disorders, 23,* 107–109.

Raz, N., Gunning-Dixon, F. M., Head, D., Dupuis, J. H., & Acker, J. D. (1998). Neuroanatomical correlates of cognitive aging: Evidence from structural magnetic resonance imaging. *Neuropsychology, 12,* 95–114.

Rimmer, J. H., Braddock, D., & Fujiura, G. (1994). Cardiovascular risk factor levels in adults with mental retardation. *American Journal on Mental Retardation, 98,* 510–518.

Ross, T. P., & Lichtenberg, P. A. (1997). Effects of age and education on neuropsychological test performance: A comparison of normal versus cognitively impaired geriatric medical patients. *Aging, Neuropsychology, and Cognition, 4*(1), 74–79.

Safford, F. (1997). Advance directives: Choices and challenges. In F. Safford and G. I. Krell (Eds.), *Gerontology for health professionals: A practice guide* (2nd ed., pp. 205–235). Washington, DC: NASW Press.

Schultz, R., & Ewen, R. B. (1993). *Adult development and aging: Myths and emerging realities* (2nd ed.). Upper Saddle River, NJ: Merrill/Prentice Hall.

Shapiro, E., & Tate, R. B. (1997). The use and cost of community care services by elders with unimpaired cognitive function, with cognitive impairment/no dementia and with dementia. *Canadian Journal on Aging, 16,* 665–681.

Shore, M. F. (1998). Beyond self-interest: Professional advocacy and the integration of theory, research, and practice. *American Psychologist, 53,* 474–479.

Shultz, J. M., Aman, M. G., & Rojahn, J. (1998). Psychometric evaluation of a measure of cognitive decline in elderly people with mental retardation. *Research in Developmental Disabilities, 19,* 63–71.

Smith, G. C. (1997). Aging families of adults with mental retardation: Patterns and correlates of service use, need, and knowledge. *American Journal on Mental Retardation, 102,* 13–26.

Smith, J., & Baltes, P. B. (1997). Profiles of psychological functioning in the old and oldest old. *Psychology and Aging, 12,* 458–472.

Snowdon, D. A. (1997). Aging and Alzheimer's disease: Lessons from the nun study. *Gerontologist, 37,* 150–156.

Stancliffe, R. J., & Abery, B. H. (1997). Longitudinal study of deinstitutionalization and the exercise of choice. *Mental Retardation, 35,* 159–169.

Stancliffe, R. J., & Hayden, M. F. (1998). Longitudinal study of institutional downsizing: Effects on individuals who remain in the institution. *American Journal on Mental Retardation, 102,* 500–510.

Stuart-Hamilton, I., & Rabbitt, P. (1997). Age-related decline in spelling ability: A link with fluid intelligence? *Educational Gerontology, 23,* 437–441.

Sung, H., Hawkins, B. A., Eklund, S. J., Kim, K. A., Foose, A., May, M. E., & Rogers, N. B. (1997). Depression and dementia in aging adults with Down syndrome: A case study approach. *Mental Retardation, 35,* 27–38.

Switzky, H. N. (1997). Individual differences in personality and motivational systems in persons with mental retardation. In W. E. MacLean, Jr. (Ed.), *Ellis' handbook of mental deficiency, psychological theory and research* (3rd ed., pp. 343–377). Mahwah, NJ: Erlbaum.

U.S. Census Bureau (1997). *Data base news in aging: Federal interagency forum on aging-related statistics.* Aging Studies Branch, Population Division, U.S. Bureau of the Census, Washington, DC.

Van Boxtel, M. P. J., Buntinx, F., Houx, P. J., Metsemakers, J. F. M., Kottnerus, A., & Jolles, J. (1998). *Journals of Gerontology: Series A: Biological Sciences and Medical Sciences, 53A,* 147–154.

Visser, F. E., Aldenkamp, A. P., van Huffelen, A. C., Kuilman, M. Overweg, J., & van Wijk, J. (1997). Prospective study of the prevalence of Alzheimer-type dementia in institutionalized individuals with Down syndrome. *American Journal on Mental Retardation, 101,* 400–412.

Vita, A. J., Terry, R. B., Hubert, H. B., & Fries, J. F. (1998). Aging, health risks, and cumulative disability. *New England Journal of Medicine, 338,* 1035–1041.

Yadava, K. N. S., Yadava, S. S., & Vajpeyi, D. K. (1997). A study of aged population and associated health risks in rural India. *International Journal of Aging and Human Development, 44,* 293–315.

Part 6

Family and Social Issues

Chapter 12 : Mental Retardation and the Family

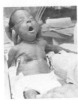

Chapter 13 : Social and Ethical Issues

Mental Retardation and the Family

Core Concepts

- Parents of children with mental retardation may progress through stages ranging from awareness to acceptance.
- Denial is a common parental reaction, especially during the initial stage of adjustment.
- Parents may project blame for the child with mental retardation on others.
- Common fears of parents are associated with having other children, loss of friends, a lifetime of care, and impact on the family unit.
- When parents of children with mental retardation are unable to blame someone else, they may blame themselves.
- When parents realize that their child has mental retardation, they may react with grief or mourning.
- Parents may choose to isolate themselves because of their feelings of shame and guilt.
- Parents may show rejection of the child through strong underexpectations of achievement, unrealistic goals, escape, and reaction formation.
- The final step in adjustment is acceptance of the child's disability, the child, and oneself.
- Families need government-sponsored services, as well as the assistance of an informal support network of family and friends.
- Parents of children with mental retardation must have their needs and feelings recognized and understood by each other, friends, family, and professionals.
- Parents' search for a cause is generally aimed in one of two directions: theological or medical.
- When parents have accepted their child's condition, they usually seek out a "cure."
- Parent and professional organizations can provide valuable information and support to parents.
- A family with a child with mental retardation must be able to maintain typical functioning as nearly as possible.
- One of parents' greatest concerns is what the future will hold for their child when they are no longer able or available to provide care.
- Children with mental retardation are more similar to their nondisabled peers than they are different from them.
- Every child with mental retardation can grow and develop.
- The effect a child with mental retardation has on siblings is receiving increasing attention from professionals.
- Siblings who are not disabled often become neglected members of the family.
- The parent/professional partnership needs to be reinforced and expanded into the 21st century.

The family is the oldest and most enduring of all human institutions. It has survived empires, wars, famines, plagues, depressions, recessions, and the constant changes of social values (Goldenberg & Goldenberg, 1996). Today, the family is characterized as a diverse and evolving social system. Forty years ago, approximately 60% of all U.S. households consisted of a working father, a mother who stayed at home, and about two school-age children. Today, approximately 25% of all children are living in single-parent families, with the mother as the head of the household in 90% of the cases. Approximately 50% of American children will experience living in a single-parent household at some time before the age of 18. About 60% of mothers whose youngest child is over 2 years of age are in the workforce (Berry & Hardman, 1998). As expressed by McDonnell, Hardman, McDonnell, and Kiefer-O'Donnell (1995), "the reality of the 1990s is that the traditional family consisting of a mother, father, and children all under one roof is now only one of many different family constellations that may range from single-parent households to formal family support systems (such as foster care)" (p. 49).

Regardless of the structure of the unit, the family is centered around an emotional bond between parents and children. Family systems exist for various reasons, including the need for security, belonging, and love. The family provides a socially acceptable vehicle for bringing children into the world. Many individuals see children as an extension of themselves; others perceive their children as a means to attain some degree of immortality. Unfortunately, the conception of some children is unplanned, and the children are unwanted.

A child may have a positive or negative effect on the relationship between husband and wife. The child may draw the parents closer together with a commitment toward a common goal. However, the child's presence also may result in discord and conflict. Either way, the arrival of a child usually represents a dramatic change in lifestyle for a couple. Financial problems may plague new parents. Recreational and social activities have to be curtailed or modified. Travel over long distances may become difficult because of expense, inconvenience, and sometimes the uncooperative behavior of the child. Entertainment may become a problem because of the expense or difficulty of obtaining baby-sitters.

Couples with children may find that their childless friends do not understand the needs and nature of children and parenthood. This dissimilarity may result in a change in friendship patterns, marking an end to a relatively independent and carefree lifestyle. Housing needs may change significantly. The small apartment that once seemed most adequate suddenly becomes confining. The comfortable and socially convenient "adults only" apartment complex must be vacated for one that is less to their tastes. A two-seater sports car may no longer be practical because the space needed for the child and his or her belongings dictates a larger, more practical but less enjoyable mode of transportation.

The list of complications, inconveniences, expenses, and changes in lifestyles brought on by a new child is endless. Many of these negative aspects of parenthood are most often overshadowed by the sheer joy and pleasure that the child brings to the new parents. The displeasures of diaper changing and the sleepless nights caused by the infant's crying tend to fade away with the first smile, the first step, and the first spoken word. With these first accomplishments, parents begin to envision the fruition of their dreams and hopes of parenthood: healthy, bright, capable, beautiful children doing all of the things the parents did or wished they could have done.

The parents of children with disabilities, including those with mental retardation, may need a great deal of additional support from society, professionals, friends, and other family members to find the happiness that compensates for the frustrations and inconveniences of having a child (Knoll, 1992; Turnbull & Turnbull, 1990). The children's developmental delays may impede their ability to smile at their parents, mimic voices, or take their first steps at the same times as nondisabled infants. Dreams and hopes for the children's future are often shattered, or at least readjusted. The children may threaten the parents' self-esteem, feelings of self-worth, and dignity. Some individuals view the parenting of healthy children as one of the main purposes of existence. The birth of a child with mental retardation may cause parents to view themselves as failures in what they consider one of their fundamental purposes in life. For some parents, these feelings of failure and loss of self-worth are temporary. For others, these emotions may last a lifetime. What can be said with certainty is that the process of adjustment for parents is continuous and distinctly individual (Hardman, Drew, & Egan, 1999).

No response, reaction, or feeling can be considered typical, mature, good, or bad. Parental reaction to the growth and development of a child with mental retardation is unpredictable. Reactions are based on emotions, and for the parents, the magnitude of their feelings and reactions is as great as they perceive the problem to be.

In this chapter, we address the impact of the child with mental retardation on the family. The needs of the child, the parents, and the siblings are discussed in the context of the needs of the family unit and of its relationship with professionals.

THE IMPACT OF THE CHILD WITH MENTAL RETARDATION ON THE FAMILY

Core Concept

Parents of children with mental retardation may progress through stages ranging from awareness to acceptance.

A child with mental retardation has a profound impact on the family. The condition may be apparent at birth or may become evident only with the passage of time. As parents recognize differences in the development of their child, their reactions can be highly variable. Some move through distinct stages and phases; others exhibit no emotional pattern (Kroth & Edge, 1997; Simpson, 1996).

Stages from Awareness to Acceptance

One of the first authors to suggest that parents of children with mental retardation move through a series of stages was Rosen (1955). He addressed five stages through which parents of children with mental retardation may progress from the time they first become aware of a problem until they accept the child. Rosen's five stages are referred to throughout this chapter: (a) awareness of a general problem in the child's growth and development, (b) recognition that the basic problem is mental retardation, (c) search for a cause for the retardation, (d) search for a cure, and (e) acceptance of the child.

It is important to emphasize that although some parents go through distinct periods of adjustment, others cope without passing through any set sequence of stages. As Blacher (1984) pointed out, "The question of whether sequential stages of parental adjustment to a handicapped child are clinically and scientifically derived fact, or an artifact of researchers' attempts to perpetuate ideas from the literature, remains to be determined" (p. 67).

The severity of the retardation is always an important variable in this adjustment process. A child with mild mental retardation may not have any physically distinguishing characteristics that suggest mental retardation, and thus the parents may be unaware that the child has mental retardation until the school suggests that the child is not keeping up academically. The degree of impact, frustration, or disappointment, however, does not necessarily correlate directly with the degree of mental retardation. Nonetheless, parents of children with severe mental retardation may find it easier to acknowledge differences because the child's disability is obvious to these parents; thus, acknowledgment (not necessarily acceptance) generally comes quickly.

The religious background of the parents may affect their attitude toward mental retardation. Etiology and age of onset are also important factors. Physical traumas that may permanently disable a child who has developed normally may be more debilitating to the parents than congenital retardation.

The family's socioeconomic and intellectual status also has an impact on its members' reception of a child with mental retardation. Some families at lower socioeconomic levels place less emphasis on cognitive development and skills and, at times, more emphasis on the development of physical attributes. This is particularly true when members of the family work primarily in occupations that are physically, rather than cognitively, demanding. However, in a family that places great emphasis on cognitive development and whose members work primarily in professional settings requiring a higher level of education, reactions may, at least initially, be quite different. A child with mental retardation born into a family in which education and white-collar careers are held in high regard may be a greater threat and disappointment to the family.

For the parents of children with severe mental retardation, awareness and recognition of the basic problem may come simultaneously. Parents of children with mild mental retardation become aware of the problem only gradually as the child fails to develop or progress as anticipated. Learning difficulties may be more obvious to parents with other children who have developed normally.

For many parents, although inconsistent growth and developmental patterns may be indicated, the actual problem does not manifest itself until the child is in school, fails academically, and is evaluated and declared by the school psychologist to have "mental retardation." When the parents are informed that their child has mental retardation, they may acknowledge the condition and recognize it for what it is, or they may resort to a variety of defense mechanisms to aid in coping. The initial impact may take on several forms. It may result in some sort of a transient stress problem for the parents, or it may have a permanently debilitating effect on the family unit (Dyson, 1993). It may attack the foundations of a marriage by inciting powerful emotions in both parents, including feelings of shared failure. Seligman and Darling (1989), however, suggested that following the diagnosis of disabilities, some families with a child who is disabled have no more frequent problems than those who do not. In fact, parents may report an improvement in their marriage (Hardman et al., 1999).

Other authors (Cleveland, 1980; Lamb, 1983) indicated that fathers and mothers may react very differently to the child. The mother may take on the role of physical protector and guardian of the child's needs, while the father may take a more reserved role. He may cope by withdrawing and internalizing his feelings. However, Willoughby and Glidden (1995) reported that fathers who routinely care and nurture their children with disabilities strengthen the marital bond with their wives.

The presence of a child with mental retardation need not create a family crisis. How the event is defined by the family determines whether a real crisis exists. There are few families, however, in which the stigma of mental retardation that society imposes will not cause the event to be interpreted as a crisis. The professional can help the family cope by examining its resources, including role structure, emotional stability, and previous experiences with stress.

Parental Reactions

Core Concept

Denial is a common parental reaction, especially during the initial stage of adjustment.

Denial.   Denial provides self-protection against painful realities. Parents may minimize the degree of disability or simply deny that any problem exists. They may close their minds to their child's limitations or explain their child's limitations by implying laziness, indifference, or lack of motivation. Denial can be both useless and destructive—useless because refusal to accept the reality of a child's disability does not make the child's differences disappear and destructive because it can impede the child's own acceptance of limitations and prevent necessary education and therapy.

Parental denial is frustrating to professionals. Parents may refuse to recognize the conditions for what they are; consequently, the needed supports and treatment frequently are delayed and sometimes never provided. Federal law requires parental consent before placement of a child in special education, so the child with mental retardation whose parents deny that the condition exists will be excluded from receiving the specialized instruction he or she may need. Denial also may deprive the child of necessary medical treatment, which only adds to the frustration of professionals endeavoring to help the family.

Professionals should always be aware of the extreme emotional stress placed on the family and realize that for the time being, this reaction may be the only one possible for the parents. With time, patience, and continued support, professionals eventually may help parents face the situation and begin making accommodations for the child in their family (Gallimore, Weisner, Bernheimer, Guthrie, & Nihira, 1993). Eventually, parents may realize that the birth of a child with retardation need not stigmatize their lives or cast any doubts on their integrity as adequate parents or human beings.

Core Concept

Parents may project blame for the child with mental retardation on others.

Projection of Blame. Another parental reaction is projection of blame. Targets are frequently physicians, whom the parents associate with considerable futility and agony. For example, blame often is directed at the allegedly incompetent obstetrician as follows:

> If only the doctors had taken better care of my wife (or me) before the baby was born, they would have known something was going wrong and could have prevented it.
> If only the doctor had not taken so long to get to the hospital, help would have been there early enough to keep something from happening.
> If they'd had enough sense not to use so much anesthesia . . .

Another allegedly incompetent physician is the pediatrician who did not properly attend to the child immediately after birth or who failed to treat an illness or injury adequately. Usually, this blame is not justified because the mental retardation is not directly correlated with incompetent medical care. However, parental hostility may be justified more frequently by inadequate and sometimes even improper counseling on the part of the physician. Although skilled in the medical aspects of their practice, physicians are often ill equipped to counsel parents; they know little about the resources available for the care and treatment of children with mental retardation. Physicians must be knowledgeable about community resources that are available, including other parents, educators, clergy, family counselors, and so forth. Parents may choose not to consult these individuals, but at the very least, they should be informed of their availability.

When mental retardation is evident and can be diagnosed at birth, it is usually the responsibility of the attending physician to inform the parents. Some may see the task of telling parents that their child has mental retardation as difficult, and physicians have been criticized for not assuming this professional responsibility in a sensitive, caring manner. The manner in which the physician counsels the parents may have a profound and long-lasting impact. Physicians cannot prevent the shock felt by parents as they learn of the child's disability, but they can lessen its impact. They can also provide parents with perspective and direction as they attempt to adjust their lives and make room for the child (Hardman et al., 1999).

School personnel are also open to criticism in their role of informing parents that their child has been evaluated and diagnosed as having mental retardation. Even if the counseling is carried out as professionally as can be expected by school personnel, frustrated parents still may use these individuals as scapegoats, projecting blame on them. School professionals most likely to receive the brunt of the projected blame from parents are former teachers. Parents may place the blame for the child's retardation on previous teachers for their supposed failure to teach the child properly. Once again, this blame may or may not be justified.

Core Concept

Common fears of parents are associated with having other children, loss of friends, a lifetime of care, and impact on the family unit.

Fear.   The unknown makes all of us anxious at one time or another. Anxiety, in turn, may generate fear. Parents of children with mental retardation face so many unknowns that fear is a natural and common reaction. Some of these fears may seem completely unwarranted. Yet they are very real to parents and must be acknowledged, listened to with sensitivity, and responded to appropriately. Until parents receive satisfactory information, these fears will persist. Unfortunately, answers to all parents' questions are usually not available, and anxiety persists. Some of the frequently asked questions are these:

What caused this disability, and if we choose to have other children, will they have mental retardation too?
How will our friends and relatives feel about us and the child?
Will we always have to take care of the child, or is independence possible someday?
What will this do to our family?
Who will take care of the child when we are no longer able?

Parents may lack knowledge and experience as they learn more about their child's condition; they need something on which to base their hopes or a means to control their fears.

Core Concept

When parents of children with mental retardation are unable to blame someone else, they may blame themselves.

Guilt.   Human nature generally dictates that when something goes wrong, the blame be attached somewhere. When parents of children with mental retardation are unable to blame someone else, they may blame themselves. They may look for and find something in their lives or their behavior that they believe is responsible. When people look hard enough, a seemingly logical reason can appear, causing them to feel guilt.

Guilt is insidious and debilitating. Assuming blame does not eliminate the disability, and intense feelings of guilt can erode parents' positive self-concept. The negative emotions of parents in a state of guilt are extremely difficult to dispel. Professionals working with parents who are experiencing feelings of guilt are most often successful when they support them in channeling their energies into more productive areas.

Core Concept

When parents realize that their child has mental retardation, they may react with grief or mourning.

Mourning or Grief.   Grief is a natural reaction to situations that bring extreme pain and disappointment. We all grieve when we lose something that we cherish or value. The birth of a child with mental retardation represents the loss of hope for a healthy son or daughter. Parents of an infant with a disability experience recurrent sorrow and frequent feelings of inadequacy that persist over time (Peterson, 1987). For some parents the grief process is chronic, and they may never adjust to the fact that their child has mental retardation. For others, the feeling of being victimized evolves into the view that they are a "survivor" of trauma (Affleck & Tennen, 1993).

The birth of a child with mental retardation represents the loss of the parents' positive self-image. To the parents, the event may seem more like a death. They may harbor death wishes toward the child, particularly when the child becomes burdensome and they wish to end their ordeal. In a few instances, parents institutionalize, immediately after birth, a child who is diagnosed as having mental retardation, announce that the child was stillborn, and even place an obituary notice in the newspaper. Some parents, preoccupied with thoughts of "when the child dies" or "if the child should die," unconsciously wish for the child's death. These parents may deny their death wishes if confronted, as they are unable to acknowledge these hidden desires on the conscious level. Other parents, however, are consciously aware of their death wishes and may or may not be willing to express these feelings publicly. More recently, however, a growing number of individuals have been willing to risk public censure by refusing to grant permission for surgery or medical treatment that would prolong the life of their child. Although such decisions raise many moral and ethical questions, only these parents know the true extent of the emotional, financial, and physical hardships they have had to endure. The difficult issue of who holds the responsibility for life-and-death decisions has yet to be resolved (see Chapter 13).

Core Concept

Parents may choose to isolate themselves because of their feelings of shame and guilt.

Withdrawal.   At times, we all want and need to be alone. We can be alone physically or have others around us and still feel isolated. We may choose to shut others out of our thoughts, giving us a kind of freedom to think by ourselves, rest, and meditate in our private world. Solitude can be therapeutic.

Although therapeutic in many instances, withdrawal is also potentially damaging. Parents may withdraw from friends, relatives, co-workers, or activities that may facilitate the healing process. By withdrawing, parents can construct a protective barrier or space and silence against outside pain, if not against the hurt inside. Staying away from social functions protects against "nosy" questions about the children and the family. By keeping away from restaurants and other public places, the family avoids critical eyes staring at the child who is different.

Core Concept

Parents may show rejection of the child through strong underexpectations of achievement, unrealistic goals, escape, and reaction formation.

Rejection.   Parental rejection has such a negative connotation that anyone who has been described as rejecting is frequently stereotyped as an incompetent parent and devoid of basic humanity. In everyday life, there are many instances between parents and children in which the child's behavioral patterns exceed the parents' tolerance level. Thus, if even nondisabled children can elicit negative reactions from their parents, it is easy to understand how a child with mental retardation can frequently cause such reactions. It is possible for this rejection to go to extremes. Parental rejection is expressed in four common ways:

1. *Strong underexpectations of achievement.* Parents so devalue the child that they minimize or ignore any positive attributes. The child often becomes aware of these parental attitudes, begins to have feelings of self-worthlessness, and behaves accordingly. This process is often referred to as a self-fulfilling prophecy.

2. *Setting unrealistic goals.* Parents sometimes set goals so unrealistically high that they are unattainable. When the child fails to reach these goals, parents justify their negative feelings and attitudes based on the child's limitations.

3. *Escape.* Another form of rejection may include desertion or running away. It may be quite open and obvious, as when a parent leaves the family and moves out of the home. Other types of desertion are more subtle: The parent is so occupied with various responsibilities that he or she has little, if any, time to be at home with the family. This could take the form of "demanding special projects at the office" or perhaps the requirements of "various responsibilities at church." Other parents place the child in a distant school or institution even if comparable facilities are available nearby. It is important to emphasize here that placement of a child into an institution is not necessarily equated with parental rejection.

4. *Reaction formation.* When parents deny negative feelings and publicly present completely opposite images, this may be classified as reaction formation. The parents' negative feelings run contrary to their conscious values, and they cannot accept themselves as anything but kind, loving, warm people. For example, parents who resent their child with mental retardation may frequently tell friends and relatives how much they love their child.

Many parents are in an untenable position when dealing with professionals. If they express honest feelings of not accepting their child, they are condemned as rejecting parents. If they profess genuine love for their child with mental retardation, they may be suspected of manifesting a reaction formation.

Core Concept

The final step in adjustment is acceptance of the child's disability, the child, and oneself.

Acceptance.   Acceptance is the final step in the sometimes long, difficult road to adjustment for the parent. Acceptance can develop in three areas: (a) acceptance that the child has a disability, (b) acceptance of the child as an individual, and (c) parents' acceptance of themselves. Acceptance of the child is a major and critical step in the healing and growing process. This step means recognizing that the child is an individual with feelings, wants, and needs like all other children. The child has the potential to enjoy life and to provide enjoyment to others. As each child with mental retardation grows into adolescence and adulthood, realistic and attainable goals can be set. The attainment of these goals can bring satisfaction, pride, and pleasure to both parents and child.

Parental acceptance of a child with mental retardation facilitates a healthy interaction between parent and child and promotes the child's development in many ways.

The process of reaching self-acceptance may be filled with pain, frustration, self-doubt, and ego-shattering experiences. Although some parents may never reach full acceptance, they can experience positive feelings as they attempt to move in that direction. Despite the hurts and debilitating experiences, parents can emerge with a firm conviction that the child is an individual worthy of respect, thus enhancing rather than diminishing the child's integrity. In such cases, the family is able to endure a major crisis and, in the process, grow into stronger, wiser, and more compassionate people (see "Her Life, My Life").

SUPPORTING THE FAMILY

Parents of children with mental retardation exhibit the same range of behavior as parents of nondisabled children. Most are well adjusted, but some may have varying social and intellectual deficiencies. Parents of children with mental retardation, however, differ from most parents in that they have an ongoing and extensive need for both formal and informal support networks.

Her Life, My Life

Roger Tulin

I was almost 29 that spring when I held my wife's head from behind her pillow and watched as our first baby's head appeared, full of thick hair. She was quiet, and to my astonishment, her eyes, still and steady, stared right into mine. As I held my new daughter against my shoulder and walked around the room, I felt peaceful and good. "You've got the jiggle already," a nurse said to me as I bounced ever so slightly up and down on the balls of my feet. "You can give her back now, Roger," she said. "You're going to have her for the next 18 years."

Last fall the 18 years were up, but our Claire didn't go off to college. Since 1977 I've been the father of a child with multiple disabilities.

Refusing to See

When Claire was an infant, we noticed that her body was loose and floppy. Benign congenital hypotonia, the doctors told us. It would improve in time, but she'd never be an Olympic athlete.

"Let me know when she takes her first steps and says her first words," the neurologist said. Claire finally walked at age two, and for the first years, I refused to believe anything was wrong that couldn't be fixed. Even as she fell farther behind, I clung to the belief that maturation would prevail and that our girl might even write poetry some day. Meanwhile, Claire made tiny, incremental steps as one developmental milestone after another passed us by.

There was joy, along with pain, in being Claire's father. We went sledding together, and she rode on my bike with me sitting behind. She loved walking, especially in the evening, and "night walks" became a special part of our lives, one that we still enjoy. I found within myself a capacity for patience and love I didn't know I had.

The Enigma

By the time Claire was eight years old, I had begun to accept the truth of my daughter's mental retardation—it would never go away. But what, I kept asking myself, does "retarded" really mean anyway? I knew that somewhere behind all Claire's difficulties was a thoughtful and sensitive person struggling to break through, a whole human being with thoughts and feelings.

When Claire was 10 years old, I took her to make a final visit to my grandmother in a nursing home. As we began the long drive home afterwards, Claire startled me by asking, "Dad, does she do anything in there except wait for people to come visit?" Instantly, my dutiful complacency was pierced. My daughter, not I, felt real compassion. A few hours later, we stopped at a rest area. I waited apprehensively, wondering if this time Claire would be able to find her way out of the women's room by herself. Between such extremes, I struggle to make sense of the enigma that is this child's life.

A Painful Turn

Much of Claire's painfully achieved progress was blown to pieces by the onset of temporal lobe epilepsy, at the age of 11. As we searched for the right combination of anti-convulsants, we watched our daughter grapple with the cruel interaction of mental retardation and a seizure disorder. For months, she didn't smile; inexplicably she began biting her skin and chewing her own hair. At 13, a combination of frustration and physiology brought on a full round of psychotic symptoms, not

continues on next page

continues from previous page

uncommon among children suffering from this disease. Claire seemed to respond only to inner voices, and her spoken words became impossible to understand. She became impulsively aggressive toward us and her younger sisters.

Slowly, the whole family began to deal with the reality that we could no longer meet Claire's needs at home. I stubbornly resisted the inevitable, grieving and afraid to let go. "You can't live your life driven by guilt," my wife hammered away at me. "It isn't fair to you or us." In the fall of 1990, Claire began life at a residential school and training center about an hour away from our home. Suddenly, there seemed to be an enormous amount of time—especially time to spend with our two younger daughters. Too often, they had lost out in an impossible juggle of my time and energy, and they knew it. My wife and I began learning to live together without having to focus most of our attention on our first child. Still, in the first several weeks after Claire's move, I felt lost and empty. I'm still learning to make my way forward in this newfound freedom; so much of my life had taken its meaning from hers.

Coming of Age

Claire is 19 now, a young woman with mental retardation. She lives in a group home only minutes away and visits home frequently. Her younger sisters show their love for her again; their resentment is in the past. Chronologically, Claire's childhood is over, and the only certainty is that she'll outlive her parents by thirty or forty years. Our greatest hope is that she can attain enough skills to work at a job someday.

In my life as Claire's father, I came of age as a man, saw myself in new ways, and learned to do things I never imagined I could do. The hopes I held so long and so stubbornly for Claire have not become reality—and that grief is part of my life. But the things I learned from being her father are also mine to nurture and keep. I try to share them now with the family that loves me.

And I try to use them sometimes myself.

Postscript: Roger Tulin lives with his wife, Marie, and his daughters, Gwen, 12, and May, 8, in an old farmhouse in Lexington, Massachusetts. His oldest daughter, Claire, 19, lives in a nearby group home. Roger has been a teacher, newspaper reporter, factory worker, roofer, and carpenter, but for the last ten years, he has worked as a lead machinist in a mold repair shop. He enjoys working on his house, playing folk guitar, and writing.

Source: Her Life, My Life by Roger Tulin, 1998, Kindering Center, National Fathers' Network, 16120 N.E. 8th Street, Bellevue, WA 98008-3937. Internet Address: www.fathersnetwork.org

Formal and Informal Support Networks

Core Concept

Families need government-sponsored services, as well as the assistance of an informal support network of family and friends.

Formal family supports are characterized by services provided by society (usually the government) and include special education services, health care, income maintenance, employment training and placement, and housing. These formal supports may extend into parent training and information centers, respite care, in-home assistance, and counseling services to help address the stresses of daily life, as well as planning for the future, which is a significant need for parents of all children with disabilities (Berry & Hardman, 1998; Dyson, 1993; Norton & Drew, 1994).

Informal supports extend beyond government-sponsored programs and include the natural supports provided by the extended family (e.g., grandparents), friends, and neighbors (McDonnell et al., 1995). Berry and Hardman (1998) suggested that natural supports "hold the key to stress reduction and positive coping for families because they enhance self-esteem and mastery through social support and community inclusion" (p. 91). Natural supports may include in-home assistance, house cleaning, and transportation from extended family members or friends. McDonnell et al. (1995) suggested that "the nature and type of support will be unique to the individuals involved, and be dependent on a mutual level of comfort in both seeking and providing acceptance" (p. 56).

Communication

Core Concept

Parents of children with mental retardation must have their needs and feelings recognized and understood by each other, friends, family, and professionals.

It is critical for parents to know they have the support of those who care about them. For professionals working with families, support implies recognition of each family member's individual needs (Patton, Beirne-Smith, & Payne, 1990). One critical need is to receive accurate information from professionals. Information should be presented in terms that parents can understand, rather than in what is often meaningless jargon. Parents often feel ambivalent when receiving information from professionals. Most parents want the truth in order to deal with their problems effectively. But they may have considerable difficulty dealing with the truth if it is too painful.

Unfortunately, in many cases both parents and professionals may not have the communication skills necessary for positive interaction. Too many professionals talk down to parents. They sometimes believe that parents lack sufficient experience or background to understand the information presented. This attitude can result in an interaction that is confusing and disappointing to all parties concerned. Occasionally, professionals even withhold pertinent information. Barash and Maury (1985) asked 33 parents of children with Down syndrome how they were informed about their child's condition. They found considerable variation from professional to professional in accuracy of information presented, when and how parents were told, and nature of future guidance. Professionals must remember that parents have the right to question information or decisions made by professionals that are inconsistent with family values (Berry & Hardman, 1998).

Parents often are concerned about the child's future development. They want to know how and when the child will develop and what the prognosis is for the future. Professionals may communicate ambivalence to parents, such as "we will worry about that later." If parents are confused by the counseling provided or believe the information to be unreliable, they may search on their own. In this search, they may find outdated material containing many misconceptions about their child's condition. Parents must have accurate information as early as possible to alleviate their anxiety and to give them the feeling that they are doing something to help.

Understanding the Causes of Mental Retardation

Core Concept

Parents' search for a cause is generally aimed in one of two directions: theological or medical.

When parents recognize and acknowledge the condition of their newly diagnosed child, they immediately may attempt to find the cause of the condition. Most often this search leads them in one of two directions—that is, for a theological or a medical explanation.

Religious Counseling and Theological Explanations. In times of crisis, people frequently turn to religion for comfort, security, and sanction. Some seek assurance that they are not to blame; others seek some help in picking up the "broken pieces of their lives." Wolfensberger and Kurtz (1969), however, found that in studies conducted during the 1960s, even religious parents of children with mental retardation found little guidance and comfort from their spiritual leaders. It remains a problem some 30 years later, given the widespread interpretation that mental retardation is primarily a medical problem. Clergy must have more current training and information if the misconceptions associated with the condition are to be overcome.

Mental retardation within a family unit may precipitate a theological crisis. The birth of a child with retardation can either weaken or strengthen religious beliefs, and the particular faith of the parents may affect their response to the event. Family acceptance of mental retardation may be a function of religious affiliation. Catholics consider redemption a continual process, so humanity continually experiences suffering for its sins. This does not imply that the advent of a particular child results from the sins of the parents but rather that it is an expiation for all humankind. Methodists believe that the child with a disability is a function of nature missing its mark. Mormons believe that individuals with mental retardation are part of the divine plan; their premortal existence was as whole spirits, and their presence on earth is merely temporal and for a short time, in comparison to eternity. They contend that when such children leave their earthly existence, they again assume a more perfect existence. Rabbis tend to assign no particular theological explanation, simply stating that the event occurred.

Explanations within specific denominations or religious groups may vary according to the theological interpretation of each religious leader. We wish only to point out that there are divergent theological views. Considering these divergent views, one can begin to understand why parental reactions differ with religious affiliation. Those who have no theological explanation may find acceptance far more difficult than those who are convinced that the child is part of a divine plan. Some devout parents view the child with mental retardation as a religious responsibility. Some even look on themselves as martyrs, ready to accept the responsibility as a God-given cross to be borne patiently and submissively.

Religious leaders need a grasp of the issues involved in counseling parents of children with mental retardation. It is important for religious leaders to conceptualize clearly the theological implications in their own minds. The distinct need is to formulate a plan for counseling parents in the light of the theological implications. Through this plan, the church may assist parents better to deal with feelings of anxiety and guilt. If religious institutions are to reflect the social conscience of society, they must undertake affirmative action to educate congregations about children with mental retardation and to provide effective programs for them (see "The Rose Fitzgerald Kennedy Program to Improve Catholic Religious Education for Children and Adults with Mental Retardation").

Medical Explanations. For many parents, it is the physician who first delivers the news that the child has mental retardation. In some cases-for example, Down syndrome or physical trauma-diagnosis is made at birth. In others, parents learn of the child's condition during the early childhood years or after formal schooling begins. Regardless of when the information is transmitted, medical counseling must be done with great skill to alleviate or minimize guilt feelings.

Generally, parents want a medical opinion on the nature of the child's condition, the prognosis for the child, and the possibility of having a second child with mental retardation. The odds, the risks, and the possible consequences should be clearly articulated by the professional. After the information is given, the decision of whether to have another child is rightfully that of the parents.

To provide comprehensive medical counseling and services to persons with mental retardation and their families, several considerations must be addressed:

1. The physician in community practice (e.g., general practitioner, pediatrician) must receive more medical training in the medical, psychological, and educational aspects of people with mental retardation.
2. Physicians must be more willing to treat patients with mental retardation for common illnesses, when the treatment is irrelevant to the patient's specific disability.
3. Physicians need not become specialists in specific disability areas but must have enough knowledge to refer the patient to an appropriate specialist when necessary.

The Rose Fitzgerald Kennedy Program to Improve Catholic Religious Education for Children and Adults with Mental Retardation

The Rose Fitzgerald Kennedy Program to Improve Catholic Education for Children and Adults with Mental Retardation was developed in 1996 from a grant through the Joseph P. Kennedy, Jr., Foundation and the Knights of Columbus. The purpose of the program is to help parents and Catholic religious educators understand more about the spiritual needs of children with mental retardation and provide a curriculum for teaching these individuals about the Catholic faith. It is used with children from ages 5 to 18 years of age and their families. The religious lessons parallel the same concepts that a nondisabled child would learn in a religious education program. Additionally, it can be used in a variety of religious settings and at home.

In preparing this curriculum, parents were asked to share their reflections on the importance of including the child with mental retardation in the life of the church. The following is an excerpt from a mother of a child who is mentally retarded:

> Children with mental retardation develop and learn more effectively through active participation. Spirituality and faith development are brought to a practical and meaningful level when the child is encouraged to act on their learned faith values. Active participation as an altar server, greeter, usher, lector, Eucharistic minister, member of the altar society and the choir, are wonderful ways for them to be involved in the celebration of the Mass. Our parish has several disabled children who are altar servers at Mass. There have been many positive comments from parishioners about how their presence on the altar is a witness of God's love for us. To prepare our children to play an active role in church, we as parents need to be assertive in making sure our disabled children are recognized for their talents and abili-

ties, not just for their disabilities. Some parishes have a parish advocate for people with disabilities who can help the child be placed where he can succeed and, most of all, feel good about being an important member of his church.

Many times the mentally disabled person has a very small circle of friends and family that provide for their emotional and social needs. The parish is the perfect atmosphere to develop a circle of support for your child. This can be developed by asking a small group of people with whom you are comfortable to meet and discuss ways to enhance and enrich the life of your disabled child. The parish advocate or someone else (not the parent) can facilitate the meeting. This group can find ways to fully include the child into the parish and provide a relationship that will expand their social circle. They can be involved in many outreach projects, such as sorting items for food, clothing, and gift drives, preparing meals for shut-ins, visiting the sick and elderly, decorating the church for holidays, working with the altar society, helping in the nursery, and many more projects. In any of these activities, it is always important to keep in mind their abilities and a level of support so that it becomes a meaningful experience for everyone. Parishioners from the "circle of support" can work with the parents in learning to be a mentor for the child. Many times, social outings will evolve out of their "circle of support," i.e., being invited to dinner, going to a ball game or movie. This is a "win-win" situation, because the disabled child and the mentor are able to grow from sharing these experiences together as they get to know one another. Working alongside a disabled person gives us the true sense of how we are all one in the Body of Christ. This is where we can see so clearly, whether we are priest, lay, or religious, that it is not our talents and abilities but the love we have for the Lord and each other that bonds us together and makes us equal in God's eyes. Sue

Source: The Rose Fitzgerald Kennedy Program to Improve Catholic Religious Education for Children and Adults with Mental Retardation, 1996, Pittsburgh, PA: Department for Persons with Disabilities, University of Pittsburgh. For more information on this program contact Grace T. Harding, M.S.Ed., Diocese of Pittsburgh, Department for Persons with Disabilities, 135 First Ave. Pittsburgh, PA 15222. Telephone: (412)456-3119.

4. Physicians must not expand their counseling role beyond medical matters but must be aware of and willing to refer the patient to other community resources (Hardman et al., 1999).

Searching for a Cure

Core Concept

When parents have accepted their child's condition, they usually seek out a "cure."

Once parents acknowledge that their child has mental retardation, they may immediately invest their energy in finding a "cure." Unfortunately, prospects for a complete cure are remote. However, when the mental retardation is a function of emotional problems or environmental deprivation, some remediation techniques may be prescribed (e.g., psychotherapy and environmental enrichment). If treatment begins early enough, some positive results are certainly possible.

In certain conditions, such as galactosemia or phenylketonuria, dietary controls can minimize the mental retardation. Physical therapy and speech therapy can improve functional level. Seldom, however, is it possible to "cure" the mental retardation.

Where financial resources permit, parents may take the child from one professional to another, hoping to receive the diagnosis they want to hear. During this process, it is necessary for professionals to help protect these parents from unscrupulous individuals who willingly provide programs of remediation at great expense, though with few, if any, positive results. When parents seek sanctions for questionable treatment, the most prudent approach is to refer them to professionals and other parents who are well known for the reliability of their judgments. Parents can be referred directly to such organizations as the AAMR, the ARC-A National Organization on Mental Retardation, or the Association for Persons with Severe Handicaps.

Searching for Help

Core Concept

Parent and professional organizations can provide valuable information and support to parents.

Many parents are in a state of confusion and find that professionals are often unable to give advice or to refer them to other resources beyond their own area of expertise. The physician is able to provide basic medical information; the school staff is a resource on educational matters. Each is limited, however, in its ability to provide information about other resources. One of the most comprehensive sources of information for families with a child who has retardation is the ARC-A National Organization on Mental Retardation. The membership of this organization comprises anyone interested in promoting the welfare of persons with mental retardation; the majority of the membership, however, consists of families with persons with mental retardation.

The ARC serves two very useful functions for parents. First, it helps families become aware that they are far from being the only ones in the world with their seemingly unique challenges. In the group, they find other parents who have experienced the same type of challenges they presently are experiencing and who can share with them the various methods they have used to cope. Second, these more experienced parents and the ARC professional staff also can give advice about various supports available for the child and the family.

If the community is so small that it has no local organization, parents can contact the office of the state ARC to obtain the necessary information and the location of the nearest local affiliate. Parents may contact the ARC at P.O. Box 6109, Arlington, TX 76005 (phone: 1-800-433-5255; e-mail: arc@metronet.com; internet address: www.TheArc.org/welcome.html).

Another helpful organization is TASH, an international advocacy association of people with disabilities, their family members, other advocates, and people who work in the disability field. TASH can be contacted at 29 W. Susquehanna Avenue, Suite 210, Baltimore, MD 21204 (phone: 1-410-828-8274; e-mail: info@TASH.org; internet address: www.tash.org). TASH works on behalf of people with severe disabilities to create more opportunities for them to learn in inclusive educational environments and actively participate in community life.

The community may have other resources besides TASH and ARC to assist parents. For example, some communities have organized "pilot parent programs" that assist parents who recently have given birth to a child with a disability or have learned of their child's disability. Pilot parents are a local group of parents who help other families with children who have a disability.

On the national scene are several federally funded advocacy programs for persons with a disability. These include the Disability Rights Education and Defense Fund, which was established to advance the civil rights of individuals with a disability through guiding and monitoring national public policy. The Developmental Disabilities and Bill of Rights Act of 1975 (Public Law 94-103) established a protection and advocacy system in every state for persons with a developmental disability. State protection and advocacy systems are authorized to pursue legal and administrative remedies to protect the rights of persons with developmental disabilities who are receiving education and treatment in a given state.

Maintenance of Family Functioning

Core Concept

A family with a child with mental retardation must be able to maintain typical functioning as nearly as possible.

Many challenges face the family with a child with mental retardation. First, parents may be so guilt ridden for having a child with retardation that they believe they must dedicate every moment of their lives to the child's welfare. These intense feelings of obligation may interfere with the parents' daily interactions with each other, with their children who are not disabled, and with their friends and relatives. Second, the additional financial burden of the child with mental retardation may reduce normal expenditures for recreation and other activities, as well as for basic necessities. Third, the challenges of care may be so acute that the parents are either unwilling or unable to find someone to look after the child while they engage in even minimal recreation or social activities.

The challenges just listed are not uncommon. Parents may need assistance to dissipate or at least minimize their guilt feelings. They may need some help to understand that the presence of a child with mental retardation need not destroy family relations. At times, however, parents become so intensely engrossed with care for the child that they become oblivious to their own needs and needs of other family members.

When the financial difficulties created by the birth of the child become so great that they interfere with other family and social activities, parents can be directed toward activities available at minimal or no cost. Various resources, including local social-services agencies or the ARC, can make respite care available for the child. Respite care provides temporary relief for families with a child living at home. The family can either leave the child with trained personnel in a community living setting for short periods of time or have someone come to the home and care for the child. These alternatives allow the parents to leave the child for short periods of time, knowing that he or she is receiving good care.

Singer and Irvin (1991) suggested that although respite care is among the most consistently requested services for families of children with disabilities, it is often the least available. Parents need relief time not only for day and evening care but also for extended vacations. Parents also need the option of being able to share responsibilities with other parents who may be more in tune with the routine and needs of the child with mental retardation.

The ability of the family to maintain some degree of socialization may be partly a function of how well extended family and neighbors accept the child.

Successful integration within the extended family and with neighbors may well be a function of teaching acceptance of the child. Although the child with mental retardation may create many additional challenges, life within the family unit must continue in a way that provides optimal opportunity to develop and maintain sound mental health for everyone.

Bennett (1986, pp. 50–52) advised parents about a balanced approach to rearing a child with disabilities:

- Get the best expert advice you can and use it.
- Develop realistic and specific goals for your child for both the present and the future.
- Don't continually "second guess" yourself or your mate.
- Spend a reasonable amount of time and effort working with your child.
- Reach out to other parents. (pp. 50–52)

Planning for the Future

Core Concept

One of parents' greatest concerns is what the future will hold for their child when they are no longer able or available to provide care.

A healthy family environment is very important for the child with mental retardation just as it is for all children.

A child with mental retardation attends public school until about age 22. At this age, though the individual may not function independently as an adult, the schools' responsibility ends. If employment, residential, medical, and recreational services are available, some direct support continues.

Parent concerns often focus on where and how their child's needs ultimately will be met. Parents often want to make necessary arrangements for continued support and focus on other matters through carefully planned provisions such as guardianship or trusts for their son or daughter with mental retardation. Parents interested in establishing guardianship or setting up a trust for their child usually can locate an attorney to help them.

THE NEEDS OF THE CHILD WITH MENTAL RETARDATION

 Core Concept

Children with mental retardation are more similar to their nondisabled peers than they are different from them.

Acceptance is a basic need of all human beings. Children with mental retardation are no different in this from anyone else. They need to be accepted as worthy individuals. Loss of self-esteem, feelings of inadequacy, and depression can make it difficult for parents to love a child. Physical stigma or lack of normal responsiveness also may delay the parents' attachment. The effects on the child can be devastating, and many children with mental retardation desperately seek someone with whom they can identify. With the inclusion of children with mental retardation into classes and schools with typical children, acceptance is even more crucial. By carefully educating a child's classmates and teachers about the child, fears of the unknown may be dispelled, leaving the way open for acceptance. The professional can and should be someone who exudes warmth and acceptance. By finding and capitalizing on the positive attributes of the child, professionals can assist parents in acknowledging the child's worth and can guide them toward acceptance.

 Core Concept

Every child with mental retardation can grow and develop.

Parents and professionals are responsible for providing the fertile environment and the proper atmosphere for a child to grow and develop. Parents need to provide children a wide variety of experiences even though they may be embarrassed and hypersensitive to what others may think of their child's public behavior. Unless children with mental retardation have the opportunity to participate in their community by going to malls, riding buses, and eating in restaurants, they will miss the critical experiences that all children should have for social development.

An important variable that affects adjustment is a balance of control within the child's environment. The child who is dependent solely on family members may develop an attitude of helplessness and a loss of self-identity. It is often far easier for a parent to dress a child with mental retardation, for example, than it is to teach the child to dress. Teaching may be a long and painful experience. When the child has learned to dress without help, however, another level of independence has been achieved, and self-esteem will improve. The other extreme is equally insidious. A child who completely controls and dominates the environment by overwhelming a too-patronizing family with unreasonable demands also fails to make an acceptable environmental adjustment. As the child learns to interact, participate, and accept responsibilities successfully in the family, these experiences can be transferred into the educational setting, peer group relationships, and other social arenas.

THE NEEDS OF SIBLINGS

Core Concept

The effect a child with mental retardation has on siblings is receiving increasing attention from professionals.

The needs of siblings of children with mental retardation change dramatically from childhood to the adult years. During childhood, siblings focus on such questions as "Why did this happen to my family?" "What will I say to my friends?" "Is the disability inherited?" "Is it contagious?" "Can my friend catch it?" "Will my children get it too?" During adulthood, sibling concerns center more on "Who is going to take care of my brother or sister?" "When my parents die, who will be responsible?" "Am I going to have to take care of my brother or sister all of my life?"

Griffiths and Unger (1994) found that a majority of siblings believe that families should be responsible for the care of their disabled members. Most indicated that they were "willing to assume future caregiving responsibilities for their brothers/sisters" (p. 225). In a longitudinal study of 140 families who had adults with mental retardation still living at home, Krauss, Seltzer, Gordon, and Friedman (1996) found that many siblings remained very actively involved with their brother or sister well into the adult years. These siblings had frequent contact with their brother or sister and were knowledgeable about their lives. In addition, they played a major role in their parents support network. Interestingly, about one in three of these siblings indicated that they planned to reside with their brother or sister at some point during adult life.

The reality is that sibling roles vary considerably depending on the attitudes and values of their parents, their own attitudes about responsibility, and proximity to their brother or sister. There are siblings who develop negative feelings very early in childhood, and carry these feelings through to adult life.

These siblings grew up resenting the time and attention parents gave to their disabled brother or sister, eventually becoming bitter and emotionally neglected adults. Such negative feelings often result in guilt that further isolates the individual from the primary family. Adult siblings, resentful of their brother or sister, may actively disengage themselves from parents and the disabled family member for long periods of time (Seligman, 1991).

Core Concept

Siblings who are not disabled often become neglected members of the family.

Siblings of children with mental retardation may be neglected for a number of reasons. Parents are often consumed with the responsibilities of caring for the child with mental retardation. Parents neglect their other children at times because they feel forced to devote all of their time to the child who is mentally retarded. Parents may neglect other children because they are attempting to escape from the entire family, which has become a threat to their self-esteem. They even may neglect a nondisabled child because they have come to believe that they are unfit as parents. Some children suffer simply because their parents cannot cope under any circumstance and are unable to give their children adequate attention. These children are often in desperate need of parental support. If they are unable to get the attention they need at home, they often try to attract it in socially unacceptable ways at home, at school, and in the community.

Resentment is a common reaction on the part of siblings. Although this reaction is typical, many parents and children who hold these feelings of resentment do not realize that such feelings are to be expected. It is important that parents and siblings be assisted in dealing with these feelings in an emotionally constructive manner.

Nondisabled children in the family may become angry because of the lack of personal attention to them and the parents' obvious favoritism toward the child with the mental retardation. Resentment may develop because the disability prevents the family from going on certain types of outings; because treatment, therapy, and special schooling place financial constraints on the family; and because the nondisabled child may have to assume unpleasant responsibilities, such as baby-sitting. The child even may wish for the other child's death, or at least that the sibling with mental retardation would just go away.

The sibling may have guilt feelings, sometimes because of negative feelings toward the child with mental retardation. Guilt feelings even may be present because the sibling feels fortunate enough to be "normal" while the other child with a disability is not.

Siblings may also feel fear. When they are younger, siblings may be fearful that they, too, may come to have mental retardation. As they get older, they may be afraid that they may have children with disabilities. They may be fearful th someday, when the parents are no longer able to provide care, they will have to assume responsibility for their brother or sister with retardation.

Siblings may be ashamed and embarrassed. They may be embarrassed to be seen in public with their sibling, embarrassed to tell their friends, or embarrassed to bring their friends home or to have a date pick them up at their home. It is understandable that a teenager may be reluctant to be picked up at home by a friend if the sibling with mental retardation is ill mannered and exhibits unpredictable behavior. As siblings with mental retardation become older, less attractive, and more difficult to control, they can be a much greater source of embarrassment. Older children, particularly in their adolescent years, become more cognizant of and easily influenced by peer approval. Because teenagers are often cruel in their remarks, siblings can become increasingly embarrassed as tactless remarks are made about a brother or sister with a disability.

In summary, siblings' needs often are overlooked. Careful guidance by parents and professional workers can lead to a healthy adjustment to the challenges created by the presence of a child with mental retardation.

NEW ISSUES AND FUTURE DIRECTIONS

Core Concept

The parent/professional partnership needs to be reinforced and expanded into the 21st century.

The field of mental retardation continues to experience dynamic change as the 21st century approaches. Educational, medical, and social services are expanding with new and innovative approaches. Such developments as inclusive education, fetal surgery, and supported employment are bringing about significant positive outcomes in the lives of people with mental retardation and their families. One issue, however, has remained unchanged over the years: the necessity to reinforce and expand the parent/professional partnership in meeting the individual needs of people with mental retardation. No one issue has received more lip service without achieving results, indicating that such a partnership is not truly valued by both professionals and parents. In the field of education, for example, active participation by parents in educational decision making continues to be inconsistent despite the mandate for parental involvement in IDEA.

A report from the National Council on Disability (NCD) (1995) also found mixed results relative to parental satisfaction and involvement in the IEP process. While some parents indicated that the process is effective and that they are engaged as an active member in decision making, others express considerable concern regarding barriers to parental participation. Powell and Graham (1996) summarized some of these concerns:

IDEA's provisions for parent-professional partnership are far from a reality for many families. True parent-professional partnerships seem to be atypical. In too many cases schools remain impregnable, mysterious places into which parents are allowed to venture for prescribed activities and sometimes only because of existing federal and state mandates. In many schools, parents are still viewed as uninvited guests whose participation is required, not welcomed (p. 607).

The evidence suggests that there are several barriers to parental participation. This evidence includes low parental attendance at IEP meetings, the scheduling of meetings at times that are inconvenient to parents, the use of educational jargon, a lack of adequate skills and available information for parents, an overall devaluing of parent input into the decision-making process, inadequate preparation of professionals to work with families, and time constraints (Powell & Graham, 1996; NCD, 1995). In regard to time constraints, the NCD reported that it is very difficult to accomplish the various IEP tasks in the time available. Silverstein, Springer, and Russo (1992) found that the average IEP meeting lasts about one hour. For many parents there is the concern that they will not be able to process the amount of information presented and make the appropriate decisions within this limited time frame.

The NCD report also suggested that the use of educational jargon and highly technical language by various education professionals was a barrier to full participation at IEP meetings. Language issues may become even more complex for parents from ethnic minority backgrounds. Research suggests that appropriate oral and written communication is critical to active involvement of minority parents in the education of students with disabilities (Harry, 1992; Harry, Allen, & McLaughlin, 1995). While federal law requires written communication to be in the parents native language, this is often not the case. Harry reports that important documents are sent home to parents in English, contain unfamiliar words, and are presented to parents with little or no feedback regarding their understanding of what has been written.

It is clearly time to reevaluate the nature of the parent/professional partnership and to move beyond rhetoric. Specific activities need to be explored that will maximize positive relationships. Positive parent/professional relationships are essential in the areas of (a) developing IEPs and adult service programs, (b) keeping parents informed about educational and community services, and (c) supporting organized parent advocacy (McDonnell et al., 1995). Organized parent advocacy moves beyond advancing personal interests to supporting change for a larger constituency of individuals, such as all people with mental retardation. The history of mental retardation is replete with examples of parent advocacy. Nearly all significant changes in services to people with retardation have occurred as a result of it. As such, it is imperative for professionals to continue to support and participate in this effort. Parent advocacy now and in the future is absolutely necessary if mental health professionals are to bring about services focusing on individual need and implement rapid systems change.

Core Questions

1. Discuss the stages in parents' adjustment to a child with mental retardation.
2. Discuss the common parental reactions to a child with mental retardation that have been addressed in this chapter.
3. In searching for a cause for their child's mental retardation, parents often seek either theological or medical explanations. Compare and contrast these two areas of explanation.
4. Identify some organizations that may help parents of children with mental retardation.
5. What are three challenges to maintaining normalized family functioning?
6. What are some basic needs of children with mental retardation?
7. What are some basic needs of siblings of children with mental retardation?
8. In what three areas is parent/professional collaboration essential?

Roundtable Discussion

In this chapter, you have learned about stages that parents progress through in dealing with a child who has mental retardation. These stages include awareness of the problem, recognition of the problem, searching for a cause, searching for a cure, and acceptance of the child. Review the discussion of these stages.

In your study group, organize a role-playing activity. Beginning with awareness and moving through acceptance, assign individuals to role-play the reactions and feelings of parents at each stage as they face the challenges of raising a child with mental retardation.

References

Affleck, G., & Tennen, H. (1993). Cognitive adaptation to adversity: Insights from parents of medically fragile infants. In A. P. Turnbull, J. M. Patterson, S. K. Behr, D. L. Murphy, D. L. Marguis, & M. J. Blue-Banning (Eds.), *Cognitive coping, families, and disability* (pp. 135–150). Baltimore: Paul H. Brookes.

Barash, A., & Maury, E. (1985). Giving the news about a child's disability. *Exceptional Parent, 15*(4), 32.

Bennett, C. (1986). Parenting a special child: How difficult is it? *Exceptional Parent, 16*(4), 50–52.

Berry, J., & Hardman, M. L. (1998). *Lifespan perspectives on the family and disability.* Boston: Allyn & Bacon.

Blacher, J. (1984). Sequential stages of parental adjustment to the birth of a child with handicaps: Fact or artifact? *Mental Retardation, 22*(2), 55–68.

Cleveland, M. (1980). Family adaptation to traumatic spinal cord injury: Response to crisis. *Family Therapy, 29*(4), 558–565.

Dyson, L. L. (1993). Response to the presence of a child with disabilities: Parental stress and family functioning over time. *American Journal on Mental Retardation, 98,* 207–218.

Gallimore, R., Weisner, T. S., Bernheimer, L. P., Guthrie, D., & Nihira, K. (1993). Family responses to young children with developmental delays: Accommodation activity in ecological and cultural context. *American Journal on Mental Retardation, 98,* 185–206.

Goldenberg, I., & Goldenberg, H. (1996). *Family therapy: An overview* (4th ed.). Pacific Grove, CA: Brooks/Cole.

Griffiths, D. L., & Unger, D. G. (1994, April). Views about planning for the future among parents and siblings of adults with mental retardation. *Family relations, 43,* 221–227.

Hardman, M. L., Drew, C. J., & Egan, M. W. (1999). *Human exceptionality: Society, school, and family* (6th ed.). Boston MA: Allyn & Bacon.

Harry, B. (1992). *Cultural diversity, families, and the special education system: Communication and empowerment.* New York: Teachers College Press.

Harry, B., Allen, N., & McLaughlin, M. (1995). Communication versus compliance: African-American parents involvement in special education. *Exceptional Children, 61*(4), 364–377.

Knoll, J. (1992). Being a family: The experience of raising a child with a disability or chronic illness. In V. J. Bradley, J. Knoll, & J. M. Agosta (Eds.), *Emerging issues in family support* (pp. 9–56). Washington, DC: American Association on Mental Retardation.

Krauss, M. W., Seltzer, M. M., Gordon, R., & Friedman, D. H. (1996, April). Binding ties: The roles of adult siblings of persons with mental retardation. *Mental Retardation, 34*(2), 83–93.

Kroth, R. L., & Edge, D. (1997). Strategies for communicating with parents and families of exceptional children. Denver, CO: Love.

Lamb, M. E. (1983). Fathers of exceptional children. In M. Seligman (Ed.), *The family with a handicapped child: Understanding and treatment.* New York: Grune & Stratton.

McDonnell, J. M., Hardman, M. L., McDonnell, A. P., & Kiefer-O'Donnell, R. (1995). *Introduction to persons with severe disabilities.* Needham Heights, MA: Allyn & Bacon.

National Council on Disability (NCD). (1995, May 9). Improving the implementation of the Individuals with Disabilities Education Act: Making schools work for all of America's children. Washington, DC: Author.

National Father's Network (1998). Kindering Center, National fathers' Network, 16120 N.E. 8th Street, Bellevue, WA 98008-3937. Internet Address: www.fathersnetwork.org.

Norton, P., & Drew, C. J. (1994). Autism and potential family stressors. *American Journal of Family Therapy, 22,* 68–77.

Patton, J. R., Beirne-Smith, M., & Payne, J. S. (1990). *Mental retardation* (3rd ed.). Upper Saddle River, NJ: Merrill/Prentice Hall.

Peterson, N. L. (1987). *Early intervention for handicapped and at-risk children: An introduction to early-childhood special education.* Denver, CO: Love.

Powell, T. H., & Graham, P. L. (1996). Parent-professional participation. In *National Council on Dis-*
ability, improving the implementation of the Individuals with Disabilities Education Act: Making schools work for all of America's children (supplement) (pp. 603–633). Washington, DC: Author.

The Rose Fitzgerald Kennedy Program to Improve Catholic Religious Education for Children and Adults with Mental Retardation. (1996). Pittsburgh, PA: Department for Persons with Disabilities, University of Pittsburgh.

Rosen, L. (1955). Selected aspects in the development of the mother's understanding of her mentally retarded child. *American Journal of Mental Deficiency, 59,* 522.

Seligman, M. (1991). Siblings of disabled brothers and sisters. In M. Seligman (Ed.), *The family with a handicapped child* (2nd ed.). Boston: Allyn & Bacon.

Seligman, M., & Darling, R. B. (1989). *Ordinary families, special children.* New York: Guilford Press.

Silverstein, J., Springer, J., & Russo, N. (1992). Involving parents in the special education process. In S. L. Christensen & J. C. Conoley (Eds.), *Home-school collaboration: Enhancing children's academic and social competence.* Silver Springs, MD: The National Association of School Psychologists.

Simpson, R. L. (1996). *Parents working with parents and families of exceptional children: Techniques for successful conferencing and collaboration* (3rd ed.). Austin, TX: Pro-Ed.

Singer, G. H. S., & Irvin, L. K. (1991). Supporting families of persons with severe disabilities: Emerging findings, practices, and questions. In L. H. Meyer, C. A. Peck, & L. Brown (Eds.), *Critical issues in the lives of people with severe disabilities* (pp. 271–312). Baltimore: Paul H. Brookes.

Turnbull, A. P., & Turnbull, H. R., III. (1990). *Families, professionals and exceptionality* (2nd ed.). Upper Saddle River, NJ: Merrill/Prentice Hall.

Willoughby, J. C., & Glidden, I. M. (1995). Fathers helping out: Shared child care and marital satisfaction of parents and children with disabilities. *American Journal on Mental Retardation, 99*(4), 399–406.

Wolfensberger, W., & Kurtz, R. A. (1969). Religious and pastoral counseling. In W. Wolfensberger & R. A. Kurtz (Eds.), *Management of the family of the mentally retarded.* Chicago: Follett.

Chapter 13
Social and Ethical Issues

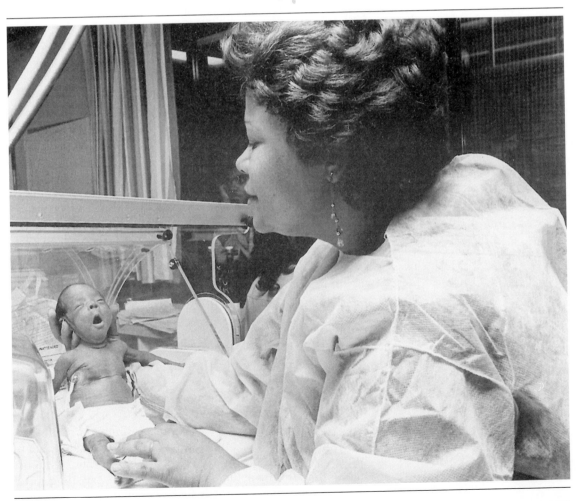

Core Concepts

- The complex social and ethical issues relating to mental retardation are often reduced to questions of individual versus societal rights.
- During the prenatal period, ethical questions usually focus on prevention by minimizing the probability that individuals with mental retardation will be born.
- During the early years of life, ethical issues pertaining to mental retardation are particularly troubling to many because they often deal with the life or death of a child with mental retardation.
- Social and ethical issues during the school years often relate both to society's responsibility and to the level of effort required to meet the educational and other treatment needs of the child with mental retardation.
- Social and ethical issues of the adult years once again pit the interests of society against the individual's rights. They often relate to adult functions such as marriage and reproduction.
- Research and professional ethics in mental retardation involve a wide variety of issues in which individual rights must be balanced against the need for scientific information and the complexities of appropriate treatment.

The complexity of mental retardation has become increasingly obvious as we have proceeded through this volume. Very few answers are simple; philosophies vary, and viewpoints and value systems often conflict. In this concluding chapter, we examine what is perhaps the most turbulent of all areas—social and ethical issues related to mental retardation.

Mental retardation has always been at the center of controversy relating to society's responsibilities for those with disabilities. Attitudes toward and treatment of individuals with mental retardation have always reflected the prevailing philosophies of human existence and human worth. These philosophies are the source of ethics, the rules that guide or govern conduct and define what is "good or bad."

During certain periods, some practices were unquestioned because they were accepted as being in harmony with the best interests of the human species and civilized society. Contemporary civilization, however, has publicly deplored such practices as euthanasia, or mercy killing, and has described the perpetrators as inhumane and barbaric. At the same time, many loudly denounced actions have quietly continued. Only in the last 25 years have public statements and examinations of these practices been forthcoming, breaking the silence on such social taboos. As public awareness has increased, many people have been shocked not only by the actions and conditions that exist but also by the realization that in many ways, this is a hypocritical society.

It is now our task to progress from shock to serious examination of fundamental values concerning what is right and important in this society and to determine the most effective means to achieve the desired outcomes. We must balance these considerations with our ability and willingness to expend limited societal resources. This chapter is one attempt at such examination.

BACKGROUND

Core Concept

The complex social and ethical issues relating to mental retardation are often reduced to questions of individual versus societal rights. ✿

It is important to explore society's philosophical foundations as we examine social and ethical issues related to mental retardation. Our daily activities seldom include any conscious consideration of philosophy, and in some quarters it has become fashionable to express indifference or even unfavorable attitudes about its place in contemporary civilization. Regardless of how we define philosophy, each of us operates on the basis of some set of guiding principles, whether explicit or implicit, that form a general code of ethics governing our behavior. And any reasonably consistent ethical code derives from a philosophy of life.

Two philosophic positions are important in our discussion of social and ethical issues related to mental retardation. These philosophies—utilitarianism and formalism—represent polarized viewpoints of the rights and worth of individuals in society. **Utilitarianism** holds that an individual's rights are limited to those granted by the larger society. **Formalism** rests on the notion that it is the individual who has basic rights and that those rights cannot be abrogated or curtailed by society—that is, the individual's rights supersede society's. Neither philosophy is workable in a complex society in its pure form. Strictly following utilitarianism leads to a tendency for the group with the greatest power to continue in power and often to expand that power by substantially limiting the rights of those with less power. Pure formalism is also problematic. As the rights of some are maintained, the rights of others are diminished. Where on the continuum between these two extremes can society operate comfortably? This is an enormously difficult question, but one that must be seriously addressed if professionals are to ensure individual rights without unduly taxing society in general.

One of the topics we discuss in this chapter—euthanasia—is defined in *Merriam Webster's Collegiate Dictionary* (10th ed.) as the act or practice of killing or permitting the death of hopelessly sick or injured individuals . . . for reasons of mercy." This topic, although not unknown to most people, initially was brought into the public eye nearly 25 years ago by the case of Karen Ann Quinlan, a 22-year-old New Jersey woman whose life was being maintained by means of an artificial support system. For nearly a full year from the time of her admission to the hospital in April 1975, she remained comatose, her life apparently wholly sustained by a respirator and tubal feeding. At the time of the New Jersey Supreme Court decision in March 1976, it was the opinion of all individuals involved that no medical procedures were available to facilitate her recovery and that termination of artificial support would result in almost immediate death. This case entered the courts because of a disagreement between Karen's family and the attending medical personnel. After much agony and soul searching, her parents had requested that the life-support system be terminated. Her physicians refused to take this action. To make a complex case even more difficult, after cessation of life support, Karen Ann Quinlan continued to survive in a comatose state. She died in June 1985, more than 10 years after she initially was admitted to the hospital. Although her death closed her story in one sense, the repercussions and issues raised by this case will continue for a very long time (see Jochemsen, 1998; Obernberger, 1997; Quirk, 1998; Wesley, 1993).

How often treatment is withheld and patients are allowed to die is not well documented on a general basis, although it has received considerable attention in the field of mental retardation (e.g., Wolfensberger, 1994). These and other such issues (e.g., assisted suicide) also are receiving increasing attention in broader scientific literature (Brief of the Attorney General in *Washington v. Glucksberg*, 1996; *McIver v. Krischer*, 1997; Oral arguments in *Vacco v. Quill*, 1997; Rosner, Rogatz, Lowenstein, & Risemberg, 1992; Weir, 1992). The regular occurrence of decisions "not to resuscitate," however, is commonly known among hospital personnel. The practice is sufficiently common that most hospitals use some type of "Code 90" sticker to indicate that the patient is to receive no intensive care or resuscitation.

The general topic of euthanasia warrants a great deal of attention. More directly related to our present area of inquiry, however, is the practice of euthanasia with individuals having mental retardation. Attention to this issue (at least in terms of published material) has focused most heavily on euthanasia with newborns who are or appear to have retardation at birth. This type of action usually involves a request on the part of the parents to withhold some routine surgical or medical treatment needed for the infant to survive. If the physician agrees, the newborn usually dies.

The practice of withholding treatment is far more widespread than most people realize. In the past, it was not typically open for public discussion (Berry & Hardman, 1998). Even 20 years ago, however, Robertson characterized it as "common practice for parents to request, and for physicians to agree, not to treat" infants with birth defects (1975, p. 214). Duff and Campbell (1973) investigated the background of 299 consecutive deaths that were recorded in a special-care nursery and found that 43 of them involved withholding of treatment. This figure represents over 14% of the sample studied. Euthanasia and withholding of treatment are topics that are now more openly discussed, although they remain controversial (Bopp & Coleson, 1997; Leiber, 1992; Lurie, Pheley, Miles, & Bannick-Mohrland, 1992; Reitman, 1996; Surman & Purtilo, 1992; Williams, 1991). Although one's initial reaction to the topic of euthanasia may be straightforward—that it is morally wrong—unfortunately, it is not quite that simple. The issue is rife with complexities from many perspectives that we will discuss more fully later in this chapter.

A concept that plays a significant role in societal dilemmas is known as competing equities—that is, as the rights of some individuals are emphasized, inevitably the rights of others are diminished. The issue of competing equities enters into several treatment controversies. Some contend vigorously that it makes little sense to expend the extraordinary resources necessary to maintain life support for a terminally ill patient when resources are so badly needed by others (e.g., Surman & Purtilo, 1992). It is argued that valuable resources such as expensive equipment and medical talent should be deployed to generate the greatest benefit to society. People with this utilitarian viewpoint would make big cuts in the resources available for citizens who are terminally ill or aged, or have mental retardation.

For others with a more "formalistic" point of view, there is a call for maximal effort to maintain life support for infants who have severe disabilities at birth. This position often is based on the infants' right to life, which from the formalist perspective cannot be abridged in any fashion by anyone. Competing equities are evident as one considers the potential conflict between the rights of the infants and the rights of the parents. Some have argued that the psychological, social, and economic burdens imposed by the care of a child with mental retardation are so extreme that parents should have the right to choose another alternative, particularly when extraordinary life-support measures are involved. Thus, the rights of parents and the rights of infants with disabilities present potentially conflicting situations without easy answers (McDonnell, Hardman, McDonnell, & Kiefer-O'Donnell, 1995).

It is evident from this brief overview that there are a myriad social and ethical issues that could be addressed in this chapter. The issues present complexities and controversies that defy simple solution. It is not the purpose of this chapter to present answers or to assume that one position is better than another. In most cases, the proponents on both sides are not only earnest in their viewpoints but also well armed with legitimate arguments to support their convictions.

THE LIFE CYCLE: ISSUES AND ETHICS

Although many ethical issues are not limited to a given age-group, some patterns relate to different stages of the life cycle. The rest of this chapter, therefore, is organized in a life cycle format. Discussions focus on prenatal ethics and issues and those particularly relevant to early childhood, the school years, and adulthood. Certain issues, such as competing equities, transcend life cycle stages and are examined as appropriate throughout the chapter.

Prenatal Issues and Ethics

Core Concept

During the prenatal period, ethical questions often focus on prevention by minimizing the probability that individuals with mental retardation will be born.

The prenatal period presents some uniquely difficult ethical questions. Because we are referring to the time before a child is born, we are addressing the prevention of mental retardation. Historically, the concept of preventing or eliminating mental retardation has been considered a very laudable goal. However, the means to achieve this goal (e.g., abortion, withholding treatment, or genetic screening) may be much more controversial.

Genetic Screening and Counseling. Previous chapters have addressed conditions associated with inherited traits or predispositions. Some of these are conditions in which the probability of occurrence increases because of family origin (e.g., Tay-Sachs disease). Others become more probable because of the age or condition of the parent(s) (e.g., Down syndrome). Many professionals believe that genetic screening and counseling should be routine when such high-risk situations exist. Although this is logical from the perspective of preventing mental retardation, various segments of the population object to this practice. Some view genetic screening and counseling as interference in individual rights and freedom to mate and reproduce by choice. These objections strike particularly sensitive chords when they relate to conditions associated with ethnic or family origins (e.g., sickle cell anemia, Tay-Sachs disease). It is understandable how such procedures could be viewed as discriminatory and aimed at reducing the reproduction of certain ethnic groups. Such an interpretation, however, goes far beyond the purpose typically defined and associated with genetic screening and counseling.

Genetic screening involves research that examines a population in search of certain genetic makeups that relate to disease or that may cause some disease or defect in offspring. Today, approximately 80% of all pregnant women undergo an ultrasound examination of their unborn baby between 16 and 24 weeks of pregnancy. The primary purpose of this examination is to identify birth defects. Because our present discussion focuses on the prenatal period, our immediate concern relates to the genetic causes of disease or defect. After genetic screening comes genetic counseling for the parents or potential parents. **Genetic counseling** includes providing information about the condition, the frequency with which it occurs (if possible, translated into the probability of occurrence in the situation at hand), and what behavioral and physical characteristics might be expected if it does occur (e.g., Wolf-Schein, 1992). All of these areas should be dealt with, including various reproductive options. The genetic counselor also must be prepared to answer all questions openly and completely for the parents to become informed about the problem they face (Wertz, 1992).

The fundamental purpose of screening and counseling is to ensure that parents or potential parents are thoroughly informed about the genetic disorder under consideration. It is not the counselor's task to make a decision for them. If the information provision and discussion approach is adhered to, the argument of discrimination and interference with individual rights is largely disarmed. It would seem that parents are even better prepared to exercise their rights if they are fully aware of the potential outcomes and options. As with most emotionally charged issues, however, this point of view does not prevent some from continuing to put forth arguments against genetic screening and counseling (see "The Perils of Human Genetics").

The Perils of Human Genetics

Why should we be concerned about the effects of human genetic research on social policy for people with disabilities? The reason for concern goes to the heart of genetic research. Everyone agrees that the product of human genetics research is genetic information about individuals and populations. The medical and epidemiological relevance of this information is obvious; but what about its social relevance?

Here we must be more careful since, at least potentially, genetic information can be the source for the most profound form of stigmatizing labeling people with disabilities has as yet experienced. For genetic information purports to tell us what someone is "really like," thereby relieving us of the need to look for signs, symptoms, or other overt characteristics. Human difference, when labeled genetically, opens the door to the most profound forms of stigmatization.

But is this possible consequence very likely to become actual? Researchers believe that a prudent concern is justified, since there are very powerful social forces which, if not checked, could increase the likelihood that genetic information will be sought and relied on in ways that are detrimental to the interests of people with disabilities.

In times of perceived restraint on social resources, policy makers will be driven to seek ways of predicting future costs. Genetic information is optimal for these purposes. If a health care policy analyst could have at her disposal accurate information about the prevalence of a variety of mental physical conditions in the population, then precise cost and resource projections could be made. If a specialist in income security policy could predict with great accuracy the number of people who will need income supports in the next fifty years, she would be able to integrate this policy into the general supply-side labor policy, with considerable savings.

Generally speaking, in social policy development, the ability to plan allows for overall cost reduction and rational resource allocation. People with disabilities, especially those with severe intellectual disabilities, have always been perceived to constitute a greater burden on social programs than others. In the absence of accommodation at the workplace, this perception is true, since without the prospect of meaningful employment, people with disabilities are forced to seek other sources of income.

Because of this feature of social policy, a more accurate, population-wide predictor of the number of people who can be deemed "unemployable" would be welcome by policy makers. With the increased availability of genetic information, these same policy makers will be pressured to improve the validity of their projection by encouraging more far-reaching genetic screening and testing. The more this information is used, the more entrenched it will become as the basis for identifying and classifying people, and the more likely people will be viewed in light of their inherent disabilities, rather than the actual abilities.

As well, the perceived need for more strictly applied eligibility criteria for disability benefits—income support, assistive devices, and special needs—could create a demand for genetic determinants of disability. Genetic testing could then join means testing as the de facto qualification for social supports. All of this demand will lead to the proliferation of genetic information.

More worrisome, though, is the pressure that has always existed in policy development to prevent costs where possible. "Costs" in this case are people, people with disabilities. With increasing availability of, and reliance upon, genetic information,

continues on next page

continues from previous page

we should see increased calls for "prevention" through genetic pre-selection. Genetically-based determinations of "low quality of life" already have an impact on the decisions of pregnant women whether to continue the gestation of "defective fetuses." With more genetic testing and screening available—even in the form of over-the-counter, self-testing kits—the more likely that pregnant women will be subtly pressured, through public opinion and professional advice, to decide to "prevent" a child with genetically-identifiable disabilities.

Given that there are legitimate concerns and fears about the effects of human genetic research on the wider domain of social policy, research is crucial in this area. The momentum of the Human Genome Project is, of course, unstoppable. What is needed is clear evidence of the effects scientific research and technological developments in human genetics has had and will likely have on social policy that directly affects the lives of people with disabilities (and indirectly affects the lives of all of us).

Source: From "The Perils of Human Genetics" by J. E. Bickenbach, Winter 1996, *Ethics and Intellectual Disabilities, 1*(2), 1-2.

Prenatal Assessment.   The prenatal development period presents other difficult ethical questions in addition to those already discussed. An immediate problem is assessment and resulting actions. There are many techniques that are currently available for prenatal assessment. Among them are amniocentesis, chorion biopsy, fetoscopy, and ultrasonography. In this area, as in genetic screening, significant strides in technological developments can present certain dilemmas.

Abortion.   What types of action might result from prenatal assessment? If assessment indicates that the fetus either has or is likely to have a defect, one alternative that might be considered is abortion. Perhaps no single topic receiving public attention is as controversial as abortion. Some factions contend vigorously that abortion is murder. This notion is based on the view that human life exists, with all of its pertinent rights and qualities, from the time of conception or shortly thereafter. On the other side of the issue is a substantial segment of the population that maintains, with equal vigor, that abortion should be an option for any woman under any circumstances. This viewpoint is based on the proposition that a woman has the right to be in control of her body and that being forced to continue an unwanted pregnancy violates that right.

As one approaches the abortion issue in relation to disabilities, the perspectives change. Some people hold fast to their blanket opposition to abortion, but their numbers are fewer when a fetus with a disability is at issue. Some who do not favor abortion in general by virtue of religious or personal philosophy are ready to accept it in the context of disabling conditions (see "Attitudes Toward Abortion"). In many cases, this shift in perspective is not limited to mental retardation but applies to any disabling condition (Wertz, Rosenfield, Janes, & Erbe, 1991).

The decision to abort a defective fetus obviously conflicts with the position that abortion should not be permitted under any circumstances. This opinion often arises from the belief that the fetus has a right to life that cannot be abridged

Attitudes Toward Abortion

In January 1993 (one day after the 20th anniversary of the *Roe v. Wade* decision), some 75,000 antiabortion protesters marched on Washington, D.C. The *Washington Post* (Warden, 1993) interviewed 742 randomly selected demonstrators on their attitudes toward abortion, and then compared the data with (1) a random sample of 881 abortion-rights demonstrators who marched on Washington in April 1992 and (2) a national random sample of 1,510 adults.

Source: From "Anatomy of a March" (p. A8) by S. Warden, January 23, 1993, *Washington Post.*

QUESTION: Should abortion be legal under each of the following circumstances:

(Shown: Percentage who said "yes.")

Question	Anti-abortion Marchers	Abortion-rights Marchers	National Sample
If the woman's life is in danger	35%	99%	91%
If the pregnancy is the result of rape or incest	9%	100%	86%
If the family cannot afford to have the child	1%	97%	49%
If the parents don't want another child	1%	95%	45%
If there is a chance that the child will be born deformed	2%	97%	73%

by anyone for any reason. Those who are more inclined to abort a defective fetus often argue that the quality of life for such an individual is likely to be so diminished that no one would choose to live under such circumstances. This argument, of course, puts them in the position of deciding what the fetus would or would not choose (a point the opposing faction is quick to emphasize). A further point of contention involves the effect of a child with mental retardation on the parents and siblings. In many cases, the immediate and continuing financial, psychological, and social burdens are extreme and detrimental to the family (Dyson, 1993; Gallimore, Weisner, Bernheimer, Guthrie, & Nihira, 1993; Nihira, Weisner, & Bernheimer, 1994). Those who favor abortion contend that parents should at least have the option to decide. The opposing view counters with the right of the unborn fetus to life regardless of the consequences for others.

This conflict is irreconcilable because the disagreement is so fundamental. Society is faced with competing equities that probably cannot be resolved to the satisfaction of both sides. More important, the conflict presents a very difficult dilemma for parents.

Ethical Issues During the Early Years

Core Concept

During the early years of life, ethical issues pertaining to mental retardation are particularly troubling to many because they often deal with the life or death of a child with mental retardation.

The ethical issues during the early childhood years (birth to five years of age) often involve agonizing dilemmas that have no easy or simple solutions. Each developmental period is critical to a child's overall growth process. The neonatal period (the first 2 months after birth) is our first focus for discussion.

The first half of the neonatal period is often described as the most dangerous time in a person's life. Many of the developmental processes that were under way before birth remain incomplete and are continuing at an extremely rapid rate. The infant is now without the protective environment provided by the mother's womb. Until a more complete arsenal of defenses develops, the baby is highly vulnerable to hazardous influences.

Euthanasia and Withholding Treatment.   The first few hours after birth and the first month of extrauterine life also represent a prime setting for one of the most controversial ethical issues relating to the life of an infant with a disability. During this period, the chances are greatest for withholding treatment from infants who are diagnosed as having mental retardation or other birth defects. This practice is often termed **euthanasia,** although there are some important distinctions between euthanasia and the decision "not to prolong life."

Ethical Issues.   It is not surprising that some important parallels exist between the ethical reasoning applied to abortion and that pertaining to decisions about postnatal survival of an infant. The diametrically opposed viewpoints on abortion, described earlier in this chapter, continue for issues of postnatal survival. Two arguments published more than 20 years ago vividly portray this point. The first, by Ramsey (1973), held that abortion should not be an option even when prenatal assessment indicates that the fetus has a severe defect or disease. In his view, any argument used to justify abortion could be used to support infanticide. Ramsey's argument was not based on the position that society would commit a given act. He was indicating that there is no distinct moral difference between infanticide and abortion; if society would not practice the former, then society should not practice the latter. Similar consistency is evident on the opposite side of the issue expressed by Joseph Fletcher (1973). He not only maintained that it is appropriate but also suggested a moral obligation to abort a defective fetus (*defective* is his terminology). Fletcher proposed that the same reasoning holds for the practice of euthanasia with defective infants. As would be expected, many philosophical positions fall between these two points of view.

In many situations, the decision is whether to prolong life rather than perform euthanasia. These two concepts have different meanings that may be very important from legal and moral standpoints. Euthanasia suggests mercy killing, or the beneficent termination of a life that might otherwise continue. Failure to prolong life suggests not artificially extending life that would naturally end. These differences, though subtle, clearly become part of the controversy.

Legal Issues.   From a legal standpoint, the distinction between euthanasia and the decision not to prolong life is the difference between acts and omissions. Euthanasia involves the act of terminating a life that would continue if the act were not committed. Not to prolong life, however, involves omission-the physician, by failing to act, permits death to occur. The legal view of omitting action depends on the relationship of the physician to the other person. If the individual is a patient who has a reasonable expectation that the physician will provide treatment, failure to do so is legally no different from acting to terminate a life. If the individual is not a patient, the physician is not legally bound to intercede in the same fashion. From a legal standpoint, the withholding of treatment and active euthanasia remain in flux and continue to be controversial (Fletcher, 1988; Glantz, 1988; Parry, 1990).

The absence of legal guidance regarding acts of omission seems particularly significant when viewed in the context of a newborn with mental retardation. Because an attending physician is usually present during and after birth, establishment of the infant's patient status is automatic. If the physician omits life-saving action for a patient who has a reasonable expectation of treatment, the law views this no differently from an act to terminate life. In practice, however, society has chosen to largely look the other way when decisions not to prolong life are made. "Do not resuscitate"—a phrase hardly uttered in public some 30 years ago—is more openly discussed and accepted in practice (Ebell, Smith, Seifert, & Plosinelli, 1990; Ventres, Nichter, Reed, & Frankel, 1992). This is particularly true in the case of disabled newborns.

The preceding discussion clearly illustrates a discrepancy between legal theory and case law pertaining to postnatal ethical issues. Should the theory be changed? If society has tacitly decided that selective euthanasia and decisions not to prolong life are acceptable, then one might wonder why formal statements (law) do not support the decision. As might be expected, this issue has been raised. More than 20 years ago, Duff and Campbell (1973) took the very strong position that the law should be changed, and this position has been echoed repeatedly since (e.g., Fletcher, 1988; Glantz, 1988). A majority of physicians, however, still do not favor legalizing euthanasia (Rosner et al., 1992).

The logic in favor of changing the law is perhaps deceptively simple when it is presented in relation to acceptable behavior. Some persuasive arguments can be made, however, against such change. One of the arguments against changing the laws is the extreme difficulty of developing legal standards that can be effectively put into practice. Legislation removing criminal liability for decisions to withhold treatment would probably be very narrow in its definitions. Those most reluctant to speak to these issues use such terms as *terribly diseased, tragically deformed,* and *hideously damaged.* But even if legislation with very strict and narrow criteria were developed, application of legal standards by society and the development of case law have a way of continuously expanding jurisdiction. Distinguishing between the clear cases and those that are less clear is done with great difficulty. Regardless of the care with which definitions are prepared, there will always be the "next hard case" that does not quite fit the description and requires professional judgment.

Topics such as abortion and euthanasia are discussed, examined, and practiced in ways that would have been viewed as clearly beyond the realm of possibility three decades ago. In some cases, technological advances have occurred that seem to have subtly governed philosophical changes. In other areas, it is not altogether clear what has fostered change, but one still finds ethical decisions being considered that previously would have been thought wholly impossible. Perhaps no other issue gives so much pause as postnatal ethical dilemmas.

Ethics and Decision Making.   As we examine our values in these very difficult topics, several immediate questions emerge regarding ethical dilemmas. How are such decisions made? Who makes such decisions and under what circumstances? For whom are these decisions made? We have offered some examination of the last question. In most cases, those who debate the ethical dilemmas are discussing infants who have extreme damage or defects at birth. But extreme and similarly descriptive words may be broadly defined and are subject to differing interpretations. How do these differing interpretations have meaning in the practical or real world? The classic Johns Hopkins case helps illustrate.

The Johns Hopkins Case.   In this case, which became public and received considerable attention in the early 1970s, substantial debate could transpire over the severity of the infants disability. The incident occurred at Johns Hopkins Hospital with a 2-day-old full-term male infant who had facial characteristics and other features suggesting Down syndrome. No cardiac abnormalities were evident, but the infant began vomiting shortly after birth. X-ray examination indicated duodenal atresia (a congenital absence or closure of a portion of the duodenum). Diamond (1977) specifically reviewed the Johns Hopkins case and examined the issues involved in medical intervention through surgical correction of the duodenal atresia. He indicated that the problem could be corrected, with a survival rate of 98%, and that mortality was higher for newborns with acute appendicitis than for this corrective procedure.

The intestinal obstruction could be surgically corrected with negligible risk. The infant reportedly had no additional complicating factors other than the clinical impression of Down syndrome. Is Down syndrome an example of an extremely disabling condition? This may be a debatable issue. Some would answer with a resounding yes. Others would not, noting the wide range of intellectual functioning for children with Down syndrome. The answer is not clear-cut, but the decision in the Johns Hopkins case was to withhold treatment. After discussion with the parents, surgical correction of the duodenal atresia was not performed, and all feeding and fluids were discontinued. Fifteen days later, the infant died of starvation and dehydration.

Many ethical issues are raised by the Johns Hopkins case. One can question the humaneness of permitting an infant to starve to death over a 15-day period. This is a particularly difficult question because the decision not to operate made it impossible for the infant to receive food and fluids in a normal manner. But the issue concerning the degree of disability represented by Down syndrome is equally provocative. It is questionable whether Down syndrome can be described as an extreme, a terrible, or a tragic disability. Some Down syndrome children reach a level of intellectual functioning classified as moderate or even mild mental retardation.

The possibility that infants with mild or moderate levels of retardation (e.g., using the 1994 APA DSM-IV classification scheme) are vulnerable to negative life management decisions raises serious concerns. This is particularly true in the context of some proposals to enact legislation authorizing selective euthanasia and withholding treatment. It is important to note that the application of legal standards by society and the development of case law tend to expand legal jurisdiction. Even in the absence of legal authorization, advancing technology frequently seems to desensitize society to encroachment on value structures. These tendencies should be considered carefully as society develops new values relative to ethical dilemmas. Will future life management decisions include children with mild disabilities? This may already be the case for visible disabilities such as Down syndrome. Will future decisions include the election of a particular gender on the part of parents? Perhaps only beautiful infants will receive favorable decisions. These suggestions are clearly repugnant, but some accept many practices that society once thought were wildly impossible. We wish to emphasize that we are not taking a position on ethical dilemmas. Instead, our intent is to provoke the most serious examination possible of the social and ethical issues related to such treatment alternatives with individuals who have mental retardation.

Decisions: Who and How?   The issues raised at the beginning of this section included how life management decisions are made, who makes such decisions, and under what circumstances. Neither the "how" nor the "why" question can be answered simply. Physicians' patients, when they are adults and mentally competent, have the right to be fully informed about proposed medical treatment. It is generally agreed that such patients then have the legal right to accept or reject that treatment and, in fact, to reject any treatment. When the patient is a minor, however, or not judged to be mentally competent, the decision process is vastly altered. In the case of infants with disabilities, parents have the right to informed consent but do not have sole decision-making prerogatives (Drew, Hardman, & Hart, 1996; McDonnell et al., 1995). When the parents' decision is at odds with the physician's, it is subject to legal review. Court cases represent the public review process. It is patently unacceptable for medical personnel to publicly reverse a parental decision to prolong life. Off the record, however, medical personnel do report cases in which unilateral (but not public) decisions are made to withhold treatment in certain circumstances.

Consent Issues.   The act of consent is not simple. Although *informed consent* is a term in popular usage, it is a misnomer. The AAMR determined that the issues surrounding consent were so important that it commissioned a special task force to examine the complexities of this topic. This effort resulted in publication of the AAMR *Consent Handbook* (Turnbull, 1977), which examined consent in detail and from the standpoints of both definition and application. This effort highlights the long-held view that individuals with mental retardation require special consideration and protection in areas pertaining to consent (Davis & Berkobien, 1994; Morris, Niederbuhl, & Mahr, 1993).

Although consent has specific meanings in a variety of contexts, the ramifications of consent often result in legal interpretations. This is certainly true in the current discussion. Three elements of consent must be considered: capacity, information, and voluntariness. For the most part, these three elements must be

Genetic counseling is an important resource for some couples as they consider starting a family.

present for effective consent. It is also important to realize that consent is seldom, if ever, permanent and may be withdrawn at almost any time. Generally, the act of withdrawing consent must also include the three elements.

The elements of consent are of particular importance in the context of ethical decision making with infants with disabilities. The first element—**capacity**—is defined in terms of three factors: (a) the person's age, (b) the person's competence, and (c) the particular situation. An infant does not have the legal or logical capacity to consent specifically on at least two of these factors. A person under the age of majority (generally 18 years) is legally incompetent to make certain decisions. Likewise, it is clear that an infant does not have the developed mental competence to understand and give consent. Thus, in terms of capacity, the parents, legal guardians, or other persons acting on behalf of the parents have the authority to consent for an infant. The issues involved in decision making generally for and by people having mental retardation are complex (McDonnell et al., 1995).

As addressed by Turnbull, the second element—**information**—also must receive careful consideration:

> The focus is on "what" information is given and "how" it is given since it must be effectively communicated (given and received) to be acted upon. The concern is with the fullness and effectiveness of the disclosure: is it designed to be fully understood, and is it fully understood? The burden of satisfying these two tests rests on the professional. (p. 8)

The last sentence of this quotation is particularly important in ethical decisions with newborns who have disabilities. Clearly, the giving or withholding of consent rests primarily with the parents, but in a sense, such decisions are the joint responsibility of parents and medical personnel. For effective information to be present, the physician must see that the information about the infant's condition is designed to be fully understood and that it is fully understood.

The third element—**voluntariness**—also has great importance. Although voluntariness may appear to be a simple concept, subtle influences in the process of giving or withholding consent make it far from simple. The person must give consent of his or her own free will, without pressure or coercion of any form from others. This requirement places even greater responsibilities on the physician. Information must be complete and without explicit or implicit inclusion of personal judgment. This guideline may be particularly difficult because physicians typically are viewed as authority figures by the lay public, and they certainly are not without their own feelings or beliefs in such situations. It also may be that parents are highly vulnerable to persuasion immediately after the birth of an infant with a disability.

Decisions regarding euthanasia or withholding treatment from infants with mental retardation or other disabilities are extremely complex and controversial. The preceding discussion has illustrated the agonies that these decisions involve and the stress that social values are under in such situations. Perhaps nowhere is the concept of competing equities so evident. The rights of the infant and the rights of the parents may be in direct conflict. Such conflict is not new to those who work with children who have mental retardation and their families. What may be unique is the stark realization that the decisions being made involve a degree of gravity that is totally unfamiliar to most people—the actual dispensing of life or death.

Other Issues.   The neonatal period and the remaining portion of the early years also represent a high-risk time for other actions involving an infant with mental retardation. If a child is identified as having mental retardation during this period, it is likely that a visible clinical syndrome is evident (e.g., Down syndrome) or that the extent of the disability is in the moderate to severe range. More often than not, a child with mild retardation with no physical characteristics associated with the disability will not be diagnosed with any degree of certainty until formal schooling begins. Parents of children with mild retardation may have some concerns about developmental delays, but these are often private concerns that remain in the back of their minds and are not discussed with professionals. Parents of children who are diagnosed with mental retardation during their early years, however, must address the issues of care and early education on a more immediate basis, which often raises ethical considerations that are emotionally laden and cause extraordinary stress.

Ethical Issues During the School Years

Core Concept

Social and ethical issues during the school years often relate both to society's responsibility and to the level of effort required to meet the needs of the child with mental retardation.

Some of the social and ethical issues that surface during the school years are similar to some discussed earlier in the chapter. Competing equities, consent, and placement issues are not limited to a particular age level. They can be observed in nearly all areas of services and supports for individuals with disabilities. The manner in which these issues emerge, however, alters considerably with different phases of the life cycle.

Educational Placement Issues.   The placement of children with mental retardation into educational settings raises both philosophical and practical questions of implementation. In earlier chapters, we examined educational programs for children and adolescents with mental retardation. From these discussions, it is clear that one placement alternative involves "pull-out programs." Such programs remove a child with mental retardation from the general education classroom and/or school and provide a program that is separate from the child's nondisabled peers. Examples of this type of placement include self-contained special education classes, special schools, and residential institutions. Earlier chapters noted that such placements exist as alternatives but should be viewed as existing on a continuum with others that involve specialized programming for the child within the educational mainstream. This view is not one that has prevailed historically.

Special classes and other pull-out programs for children with mental retardation have a long history. The first public school special classes in the United States were organized in 1896. Enrollment in such programs increased at a steady rate until recently. By 1922, more than 23,000 children were enrolled in special classes, and by 1958 this number had increased to more than 196,000. The increase in special classes for children with mental retardation was based on the belief that such placement was more beneficial than the general education classroom. Both the data and the logic supporting this as the sole approach to educating children with disabilities have been seriously questioned. According to current thinking, individuals with disabilities should be treated and educated as closely as possible to the natural settings of school, family, and community (Hardman, Drew, & Egan, 1999).

Much of the current approach to the education of children with disabilities has been captured in IDEA, discussed in earlier chapters. IDEA is an extremely complex piece of legislation that raises many questions and issues. One of these

Social issues may have placed each of these children at risk for different reasons.

relates specifically to the placement of children with disabilities into the least restrictive environment. This concept is very different from the logic that supported pull-out programs as the primary means for educating children with mental retardation. It emphasizes a continuum of placement alternatives and requires that education agencies develop procedures to ensure that children with disabilities are educated with nondisabled children to the maximum extent appropriate. The least-restrictive-placement provisions of IDEA allow special classes, separate schooling, or other removal of children with disabilities from the general educational environment as alternatives only when the child's disability is such that satisfactory education cannot be accomplished in general education classes even with the use of supplementary aids and services.

One of the issues raised by the least-restriction principle represents a somewhat fluid combination of competing equities and the formalism- utilitarianism philosophical conflict. As stated earlier, pure formalism presents a dilemma because as the rights of some are made more distinct, they impinge on others. The dilemma rests squarely on the philosophical questions raised by formalism in this complex society. When professionals make more distinct the legitimate rights to an appropriate education for some, this very act may impinge on the rights of others. The social value question at stake is at once simple and complex: Who sacrifices? Is it a matter of requiring that all be equally disadvantaged or all equally advantaged? Or do policymakers turn to a utilitarian philosophy in which an individual has only those rights granted by society at large (the privileged)? It may be possible for society to ensure an appropriate education for all children with mental retardation without significantly imposing a disadvantage on nondisabled children. This cannot be accomplished, however, without a cost, and society must determine whether it is willing to pay that cost. The least-restriction principle places a strain on societal values, for the question cannot go unanswered. And social structure is not accustomed to addressing such difficult questions in an orderly manner.

Appropriate Education Issues.   The language of IDEA raises many questions related to the school years. But one particular piece of the language is strikingly provocative. The term *appropriate education* is found in several parts of the legislation and connotes a qualitative description of educational programming. Placement and educational programs should be "appropriate" for the nature and degree of the disability. The terminology of *appropriate education* is often problematic from at least two standpoints. *Appropriate,* like many other adjectives, is a general term subject to a variety of definitions. Although this is characteristic of legislative language, the range of operational outcomes is as varied as the number of individuals responsible for implementation. This brings us to a second problem. IDEA is an intrusive piece of legislation. In some cases, professionals have been so engaged in responding to the law's major and obvious principles that the term *appropriate* has been largely ignored. This slight presents a significant dilemma because appropriateness of the educational program was a central reason prompting the legislation's enactment. In fact, appropriate education is a fundamental assumption that underlies the public's support for education in general. Some responses to the concepts of IDEA have seemed to ignore appropriateness to such an extent as to raise ethical questions. One such response involves a "paper compliance," in which efforts are concentrated more on making a child's program look appropriate on paper than on ensuring the actual appropriateness of the program. Although such situations existed in the past, they have become increasingly common with the advent of the federal legislation.

Paper compliance detracts from the effectiveness of instruction, the fundamental purpose of the legislation. It also brings into question the professional ethics of those who ensure it. Initial reaction to this type of compliance may be much like that suggested in the context of withholding medical treatment: It is unethical and should not be permitted. Whereas most would agree with this statement in principle, this problem is not susceptible to a simple solution.

One cannot excuse paper compliance, but it is easy to understand some of the reasons why it occurs. The public schools are not generally well equipped to implement IDEA on a widespread basis. It is a massive piece of legislation, which, if interpreted and implemented as intended, means immense changes in most school districts. In many cases, these changes require personnel and skills that are not currently available. Some of these resources might not be available for some time even if the schools had the money to afford them. From the perspective of those who are charged with the responsibility of implementation, the task often seems overwhelming. Once again, although we may not excuse or condone paper compliance, it is not difficult to see how it can happen.

Other factors add to the complex issue of providing "appropriate" instruction as defined in IDEA. The law is a prescriptive piece of federal legislation that from the viewpoint of many educators is being imposed on them by outsiders. Many elementary and secondary educators view the law as being imposed on them by special education. This has not exactly met with favorable reaction because one segment of the profession (and a smaller one, at that) is dictating what appropriate education is to another, larger segment of the profession. The outside imposition perspective also becomes evident because this is a federal law that, in part, dictates how education will be conducted at the state and local levels. This mandate raises the immediate question of whether the law is a case of federal intervention in states' rights.

Appropriate education, least restrictive placement, inclusion, competing equities, and states' rights are merely samples of the issues that complicate value questions related to the school years. Although the context has changed, the philosophical and operational differences are no more easily resolved than they were in the early years of the United States.

Ethical concerns have also arisen regarding specific procedures used in the education and treatment of children with disabilities. Behavioral principles have long been employed to achieve educational progress with children having mental retardation. In some cases, application of these principles has involved the use of punishment or aversive consequences to change inappropriate behavior.

Such techniques have received considerable attention as being both unethical and unnecessary (Butterfield, 1990; Mulick, 1990).

Aversive treatment creates a number of difficulties, including potential legal and ethical problems (Sherman, 1991). Additionally, such procedures are seen as restrictive in the sense that they are intrusive and do not represent contingencies that exist in the natural environment. This often makes it difficult for the person with mental retardation to generalize behavior learned to more natural settings where, for example, a time-out room does not exist. Thus, questions also arise concerning generalization and effectiveness of instruction, further highlighting the questionable propriety of aversive techniques (Bihm & Sigelman, 1991; Konarski, 1990). A variety of nonaversive approaches have been demonstrated as effective alternatives in recent years as concern has emerged regarding the ethical issues (e.g., Koegel, Koegel, & Dunlap, 1996; Koegel, Steibel, & Koegel, 1998; Korn & Hogan, 1992; Peine, Liu, Blakelock, & Jenson, 1991).

Consent Issues.   During the school years, parents must be actively involved in the decision process that results in changing the educational program for their child. In terms of our specific focus—the child with mental retardation—this process includes consent for assessment or eligibility, as well as any instructional changes that might occur as a result of such assessment.

To be effective, parental consent for all action, including assessment and programming, must include the three elements of capacity, information, and voluntariness. Consent is seldom, if ever, permanent and may be withdrawn at nearly any time. The educator attempting to obtain consent carries a heavy burden—just as the medical professional did earlier in our discussion—in terms of ensuring that the three elements of consent are present (Drew et al., 1996).

One element of consent that is altered somewhat in the context of the school years is capacity. For the most part, capacity to consent for the child having mental retardation remains with the parents. From a strictly legal standpoint, the capacity to consent does not rest with a child because of age (under the age of majority) and lack of mental competence to understand the nature and consequences of consent. Good practice, however, would suggest that a blanket assumption of incapacity throughout the school years is inappropriate. Specifically, older individuals with retardation (adolescents or young adults) who are functioning at a nearly normal level may be quite capable of participating in the consent process. Depending on the situation and the individual, they may be able to give consent directly or concurrently with a third party, such as the parents. Inclusion of a third party in consent is likely if the information is complex or the individual less capable. The burden of obtaining effective consent rests heavily with the professional, a situation that may create a certain amount of discomfort but that must prevail if the rights of individuals with retardation are to be adequately protected (Morris et al., 1993).

Ethical Issues During Adulthood

Core Concept

Social and ethical issues of the adult years once again pit the interests of society against the individual's rights. They often relate to adult functions such as marriage and reproduction.

Social and ethical issues surfacing during adulthood ring familiar from earlier discussions. Many of the principles, philosophical differences, and agonizing social questions remain relatively constant. As before, however, the stage of the life cycle alters the issues. Here we focus on those social and ethical issues that we hope will promote the most serious questioning on the part of the reader.

The emergence of certain social and ethical issues during the adult years is not surprising. Questions of marriage, reproduction, and sterilization become considerations during this part of the life cycle. As with most of the issues discussed in this chapter, these topics are highly controversial.

Sterilization Issues. Controversy regarding sterilization has a very long history. One way to approach the topic of sterilization is to examine how and why individuals with mental retardation receive different consideration from their peers without retardation (Kunjukrishnan & Varan, 1989). Both the historical controversy and the legal authority to sterilize people with mental retardation clearly indicate different consideration. For example, although voluntary sterilization of citizens without mental retardation is viewed mostly as an individual prerogative (a means of birth control), involuntary sterilization laws pertaining generally to these citizens are unheard of.

A variety of justifications have been advanced for sterilization of those with mental retardation (Elkins & Anderson, 1992; Kempton & Kahn, 1991). For the most part, these arguments can be summarized as those that hold sterilization to be in the best interests of (a) the society and state, (b) the individuals having mental retardation, and (c) the unborn children.

Many people express strong opposition to sterilization of individuals with mental retardation. Arguments on this side of the issue include (a) concern about the potential misuse of legal authority to sterilize, (b) some evidence that some of the prosterilization arguments do not consistently hold true, and (c) concern about the rights of the individual and the manner in which the process is undertaken. Each of these areas presents serious societal and legal issues that warrant examination.

The first prosterilization argument held that sterilization of individuals with mental retardation was in the best interest of society and the state. This proposition exemplifies, perhaps more clearly than any other issue, how the best interest of the state may come into conflict with rights of an individual. One very important basis for the "benefit to society and state" argument involves a reduction in the numbers of individuals with retardation. As such, it is another approach to preventing mental retardation. Proponents of this position point to the fact that such a reduction would decrease the number of citizens requiring extra services from society and would lessen the cost burden for such care on the state and the taxpayers. This argument is utilitarian; such savings, if they were to occur, could be redirected to those societal needs that might ultimately result in greater productive return to the general public.

One question immediately raised concerns the degree to which such a practice actually would result in reduced incidence of mental retardation. The answer is anything but obvious. If sterilization is viewed as preventing only the transmission of inferior or damaged genetic material, the reduction in incidence is quite minimal. Mental retardation that can be attributed directly to genetic causation represents a very small proportion of all cases. Furthermore, those individuals whose mental retardation can be attributed to genetic causes are more likely to be functioning at lower levels. For a number of reasons, one can make the case that such individuals are less likely to engage in procreation to begin with.

The difficulty with this entire line of reasoning becomes evident when one views the broad perspective of mental retardation. First, earlier sections of this volume examined the nature-versus-nurture controversy in considerable detail for effects on development of intelligence (and causes of mental retardation). It is clear from these earlier discussions that determination of environmental influences cannot be accomplished with great precision. It is also evident that the environment does have a significant role in causing mental retardation, particularly in the milder ranges. Therefore, sterilization is not solely focusing on the transmission of inferior genetic material.

One very strong influence in prosterilization arguments is society's apparent unwillingness to overrule the rights of individuals in favor of the rights of the larger society in any blanket fashion. One of the individual rights that seems to loom large in this regard is the right of procreation. As early as 1921, the importance of this individual right was noted in a legal interpretation of the Constitution. At this time, the Michigan attorney general issued an opinion, based on the Constitution, that held that the right to have and retain the power of procreation was second only to the right to life itself. It is generally accepted that such a fundamental individual right can be abrogated only on a voluntary basis by the individual involved. One then must ask how compulsory sterilization laws come to exist in certain states. Obviously, in these situations the state deemed that its interests superseded the rights of people with mental retardation.

Consent Issues.   Even voluntary sterilization of individuals with mental retardation presents some complex questions both conceptually and with regard to implementation (de Wit & Rajulton, 1991). The moment one considers a voluntary status with respect to sterilization, the question of consent must be addressed once again. The concept of consent in the context of sterilization presents some interesting implementation problems that we did encounter earlier.

Courts continue to play an important role in the lives of those with mental retardation.

The element of capacity was discussed earlier, with particular focus on the person's age and competence. A person under the age of majority is legally incompetent to make certain decisions. Because our main focus in this section is the adult years, age is not a consideration with regard to capacity. Competence, however, does become an issue. The basic question is whether an adult with retardation has the mental competence to understand sterilization and its implications. This question is unanswerable in a general sense. It would seem most logical to consider each case individually, depending on the person's level of functioning. But some would disagree vigorously. A decision concerning sterilization is so extraordinarily important and complex that many individuals of normal intelligence are perhaps not competent to comprehend its implications fully. Whereas this may be true for only certain individuals without mental retardation, it does seriously raise the competence issue when a person with mental retardation is involved. This in no way suggests, however, that the opinion of the person with mental retardation should be ignored.

The people to turn to for assistance in obtaining consent would seem, naturally, to be the parents or legal guardians of the individual. This has been the case in our earlier discussions of other procedures requiring consent. It is assumed that they will consider such decisions, with the best interests of their ward being the first and foremost concern. This may not, however, be a sound assumption with respect to sterilization, as we have noted before.

The noticeable tendency has been for the courts to intervene and review parental decisions regarding consent for sterilization. The court wishes to ensure that the individual's best interests are protected and are the sole determining factor influencing the sterilization decision. This aspiration presents a difficult dilemma, one that makes the consent process extremely complicated. Court intervention itself is complicated. To ensure objectivity, the court must hear information and arguments on both sides. This duality requires that advocates for both sides be present in court and be equally informed and articulate. It further requires that the arguments on both sides include all relevant information and that information presented be limited to the issues pertaining to the best interests of the individual. Presentation of information or arguments relating to either the state's or the parents' interests is not relevant.

This brief discussion represents only the tip of the iceberg in terms of the complex issues related to consent for sterilization. Although we began our examination with a focus on the element of capacity, the elements of information and voluntariness quickly became intertwined in the considerations. Our discussion demonstrates how issues can become extremely complicated as attempts are made to protect individuals' rights. It also raises other social questions that are not easily answered: Do the parents' rights and interests have no value? What about the interests of the state? The concept of competing equities becomes evident in situations in which the rights and interests of all parties are not in harmony. These are familiar questions, reminiscent of the extreme philosophical differences presented at the beginning of the chapter.

Marriage Issues.   Marriage issues are not as legally complicated as sterilization because an irreversible medical procedure is not involved. The overriding issues or questions in this area concern the existence of laws restricting marriage for individuals with retardation. Many states have laws restricting the right to marry for those identified as having mental retardation. One has to ask why these laws exist. Are these laws aimed at the protection of the individual, or are they basically for the protection of society?

We present this question in order to examine the issue. For some, the evidence is so compelling that objective examination of it is tantamount to ignoring how such laws came into existence. From a historical perspective, Wolfensberger (1975) discussed restrictive marriage laws as a part of society's need to prevent procreation by people with mental retardation. Credence for the perception certainly arises from the widespread negative attitudes toward sexual expression and marriage among people with mental retardation. Wolfensberger cited an 1895 bill passed by the Connecticut House of Representatives:

> Every man who shall carnally know any female under the age of
> forty-five years who is epileptic, imbecile, feeble-minded, or a pauper,

shall be imprisoned in the State prison not less than three years. Every man who is epileptic who shall carnally know any female under the age of forty-five years, and every female under the age of forty-five years who shall consent to be carnally known by any man who is epileptic, imbecile, or feeble-minded, shall be imprisoned in the State prison not less than three years. (p. 40)

It should be noted that a law to prohibit the marriage of people who are mentally ill and those having mental retardation was proposed at the national level in 1897 and received a great deal of support. One could interpret the above wording from either perspective (individual or societal protection) because specific mention of intent is absent. But there is little real question about intent.

It does seem that society's interests have been paramount, at least historically. Some of these old laws remain on the books. What about current legislation? Are current laws and efforts merely more carefully disguised attempts to protect the best interests of society, or are they really aimed at achieving some balance between the rights of individuals and the rights of the larger culture? Strong arguments can be made on both sides, and some limited research related to the topic appears periodically (e.g., Sundram & Stavis, 1994; Szivos & Griffiths, 1990).

The questions and issues discussed throughout this chapter are not pleasant topics. One might wish to avoid them, if possible. They are, however, social and ethical questions of great importance. These are issues that test the strength of societal fabric. We cannot ignore what seems to be the fundamental question, Are individuals with mental retardation considered subhuman, or at least less deserving of the rights of the rest of humanity?

RESEARCH AND PROFESSIONAL ETHICS IN MENTAL RETARDATION

Core Concept

Research and professional ethics in mental retardation involve a wide variety of issues in which individual rights must be balanced against the need for scientific information and the complexities of appropriate treatment.

The field of mental retardation has a clear link to ethical issues, as is evident from our foregoing discussion. People with mental retardation are in a high-risk category with respect to ethical vulnerability. They are among those who need special consideration and protection. This position places great responsibility on professionals working in the field as researchers and care providers.

To learn more about mental retardation, it is necessary to conduct research on individuals within the population. This necessity often raises concern because by virtue of investigating those with mental retardation, a researcher is in some ways invading their privacy and subjecting them to risk even though he or she might have the most honorable of intentions. To discover more effective methods of teaching, caring for, medicating, and otherwise treating these individuals, it is necessary to study them and to learn about their characteristics. Conducting research with people who are mentally retarded cannot be avoided in order to protect them and more effectively to provide treatment or intervention. In fact, some have held that it would be unethical not to conduct such research (e.g., Drew et al., 1996).

Conducting research with people who are mentally retarded while simultaneously protecting their rights as individuals requires constant vigilance. A careful balance must be struck between the behavioral scientist's need to invade and the individual subject's rights. For these people, special care must be taken in the areas of consent, privacy, and harm (Morris et al., 1993). Likewise, issues of deception (explicit lying to subjects, as well as omitting details about the study) remain controversial in mental retardation, as they do in all behavioral science (Howe & Dougherty, 1993; Wheeler, 1994). Certain medications and other treatments inherently pose some risk, and inappropriate applications may be harmful. All of these considerations make research on mental retardation challenging. Such safeguards as institutional review boards (sometimes known as human subjects committees) used by universities and other agencies to monitor research are vital to protecting subjects and to maintaining a balance between the needs of scientists and subjects' rights. Likewise, many professional associations and societies have ethics committees and codes of ethics to guide their members.

Research is not the only area in which professional ethics comes into play in the field of mental retardation. Schools, health-care centers, and other agencies must be careful to administer the most effective treatment possible while simultaneously remaining conscious of the rights of people with mental retardation. In some cases, the treatment administered may involve some risk, as is the case with some medications. Once again, people with mental retardation are at risk and more vulnerable than others who are not disabled. It is vital that professionals be adequately trained and qualified to administer the treatment being employed. Occasionally (we hope rarely), this does not happen because of personnel shortages, lack of knowledge, or carelessness. It is essential that government agencies, as well as parent and professional associations, remain vigilant to ensure the well-being of people with mental retardation.

NEW ISSUES AND FUTURE DIRECTIONS

Through seven editions, this volume has been based on the concept of human development. At this point in the text, the reader is well aware that from our perspective the life span begins at conception and terminates with death. These two boundaries of the life span-the very first and the very last phases-are stages where the future will witness the most dramatic ethical developments.

Earlier chapters examined the beginning of the life span, both in terms of normal development and for causes of mental retardation. In many respects, this early phase of the life cycle already presents society with extremely controversial ethical questions. We spoke of abortion, euthanasia, and withholding of treatment. Terminating pregnancy has been a known and practiced procedure for a very long time. Abortion, however, remains a volatile, controversial social question that continues to appear in the news and in the courts. It will continue to do so in the future. Euthanasia and withholding of treatment will continue, and they will become more acceptable as topics of public conversation. These topics will be important ethical issues in the future, and our observations suggest that they will appear more openly in the literature (see Hentoff, 1997; Wolfensberger, 1994). A variety of end-of-life dilemmas, such as assisted suicide, have become very visible in the public eye and will continue as issues for some time to come (e.g., Battin, 1991; Scofield, 1991).

Advances in medical technology are constantly presenting new and equally controversial topics for the first part of the life cycle. Geneticists are rapidly developing the capability to determine certain aspects of a person's genetic makeup through genetic engineering. This capability holds great potential for the prevention of those types of mental retardation that have known genetic causes. It also presents a serious question, however, that will emerge in the next wave of public awareness on such topics. To what degree is society ready to have some people determine the genetic makeup of others? This possibility certainly would represent a kind of ultimate control. Genetic engineering will clearly raise new ethical issues (see Bickenbach, 1996).

The last phase of the life cycle will also present challenging issues in the future for professionals in mental retardation. More than ever before, people with mental retardation are surviving to an older age and becoming part of the growing elderly population. Questions about how society will care for these people and how they will live in our communities are being raised now as ethical dilemmas (e.g., O'Brien, 1994). The issues of quality of life and dying with dignity will surface more publicly and test society's ability to understand the complete cycle of human development. As those with mental retardation are integrated into society, how they live and how they affect those around them will always raise an array of questions in between the beginning and end of the life cycle (Gallimore et al., 1993; Smith & Broughton, 1994; Sundram & Stavis, 1994). The future ethical issues in mental retardation will be many. We have only touched on some of the more controversial points. Those mentioned, at both ends of the life cycle, are truly life-and-death issues.

Core Questions

1. How do utilitarianism and formalism relate to individual and societal rights in dealing with mental retardation?
2. How do genetic counseling and abortion relate to prevention of mental retardation?
3. Some have taken the position that if nontreatment of certain infants is in violation of the law, then the law should be changed. How does this position fit with formalist philosophy, and how does it fit with utilitarianist philosophy? What are your views, and why do you believe as you do?

4. It appears that selective nontreatment of infants with disabilities is more common than the general public knows. Who should make these judgments, and which are life-and-death decisions? On what basis did you make your decision?

5. Special services for children with mental retardation often cost a great deal more than educational services for their peers without retardation. To what degree do you think parents of children without disabilities should be held responsible for the increased costs of educating children having mental retardation? On what basis do you believe as you do?

6. Sterilization of adults with mental retardation is often justified on the basis of the general welfare of society and the state. How might the best interests of the state and those of the individual be in conflict? Whose interests should prevail, and why?

7. How did early marriage laws related to people with mental retardation seem to place society's interests above those of the individual? Has this changed? Explain your reasoning in both cases.

8. How may scientific investigations aimed at improving the lot of those with mental retardation also be in conflict with their individual rights?

9. How does the interdisciplinary nature of the mental retardation field contribute to professional ethical difficulties?

Roundtable Discussion

Social and ethical issues related to mental retardation are complex and vary to some degree, depending on the life cycle period being considered. In many ways, however, these questions can be reduced to the fundamental questions of individual versus societal rights embodied in utilitarianism and formalism. These perspectives are found in various forms throughout the study of mental retardation.

In your study group or on your own, examine mental retardation, considering both individual and societal interests. Think in terms of prevention of mental retardation, abortion, withholding of treatment, provision of service, sterilization, and research. Where do you stand philosophically? Does your position shift, depending on age, topic, severity, or other bases? Do you feel comfortable with your position(s)? Why?

References

American Psychiatric Association (APA). (1994). *Diagnostic and statistical manual of mental disorders* (4th ed.). Washington, DC: Author.

Battin, M. P. (1991). Euthanasia: The way we do it, the way they do it. *Journal of Pain and Symptom Management, 6*(5), 298–305.

Berry, J., & Hardman, M. L. (1998). *Lifespan perspectives on the family and disability.* Boston: Allyn & Bacon.

Bickenbach, J. E. (1996, Winter). The perils of human genetics. *Ethics and Intellectual Disabilities, 1*(2), 1–2.

Bihm, E. M., & Sigelman, C. K. (1991). Effects of behavioral treatment, treatment setting, and client IQ on person perception. *Basic and Applied Social Psychology, 12*, 341–355.

Bopp, J., & Coleson, R. E. (1997). *Roe v. Wade* and the euthanasia debate. *Issues in Law and Medicine, 12*(4), 343–354.

Brief of the attorney general in *Washington v. Glucksberg* in the United States Supreme Court. (1996). *Issues in Law and Medicine, 12*(2), 275–294.

Butterfield, E. C. (1990). The compassion of distinguishing punishing behavioral treatment from aversive treatment. *American Journal on Mental Retardation, 95,* 137–142.

Davis, S., & Berkobien, R. (1994, August). *Meeting the needs and challenges of at-risk, two generation, elderly families.* Arlington, TX: The ARC-A National Organization Mental Retardation.

De Wit, M., & Rajulton, F. (1991). Voluntary sterilization among Canadian women. *Journal of Biosocial Science, 23,* 263–273.

Diamond, E. F. (1977). The deformed child's right to life. In D. J. Horan & D. Mall (Eds.), Death, dying, and euthanasia (pp. 127–138). Washington, DC: University Publications of America.

Drew, C. J., Hardman, M. L., & Hart, A. W. (1996). *Designing and conducting research in education and social science.* Needham Heights, MA: Allyn & Bacon.

Duff, R., & Campbell, A. (1973). Moral and ethical dilemmas in the special-care nursery. *New England Journal of Medicine, 289,* 890–894.

Dyson, L. L. (1993). Response to the presence of a child with disabilities: Parental stress and family functioning over time. *American Journal on Mental Retardation, 98,* 207–218.

Ebell, M. H., Smith, M. A., Seifert, G., & Plosinelli, K. (1990). The do-not-resuscitate order: Outpatient experience and decision-making preferences. *Journal of Family Practice, 31,* 630–634.

Elkins, T. E., & Anderson, H. F. (1992). Sterilization of persons with mental retardation. *Journal of the Association for Persons with Severe Handicaps, 17,* 19–26.

Fletcher, J. (1973). Ethics and euthanasia. In R. H. Williams (Ed.), *To live and to die: When, why, and how* (pp. 113–122). New York: Springer.

Fletcher, J. (1988). The courts and euthanasia. *Law, Medicine and Health Care, 15,* 223–230.

Gallimore, R., Weisner, T. S., Bernheimer, L. P., Guthrie, D., & Nihira, K. (1993). Family responses to young children with developmental delays: Accommodation activity in ecological and cultural context. *American Journal on Mental Retardation, 98,* 185–206.

Glantz, L. H. (1988). Withholding and withdrawing treatment: The role of the criminal law. *Law, Medicine and Health Care, 15,* 231–241.

Hardman, M. L., Drew, C. J., & Egan, M. W. (1999). *Human exceptionality: Society, school, and family* (6th ed.). Needham Heights, MA: Allyn & Bacon.

Hentoff, N. (1997). Not dead yet. In D. Podell (Ed.), *Perspectives* (pp. 18–19). Boulder, CO: Coursewise Publishing.

Hollander, R. (1989). Euthanasia and mental retardation: Suggesting the unthinkable. *Mental Retardation, 27,* 53–61.

Howe, K. R., & Dougherty, K. C. (1993). Ethics, institutional review boards, and the changing face of educational research. *Educational Researcher, 22*(9), 16–21.

Jochemsen, H. (1998). Dutch court decisions on nonvoluntary euthanasia critically reviewed. *Issues in Law and Medicine, 13*(4), 447–458.

Kempton, W., & Kahn, E. (1991). Sexuality and people with intellectual disabilities: A historical perspective. *Sexuality and Disability, 9*(2), 93–111.

Koegel, L. K., Koegel, R. L., & Dunlap, G. (Eds.). (1996). *Positive behavioral support: Including people with difficult behavior in the community.* Baltimore: Paul H. Brookes.

Koegel, L. K., Steibel, D., & Koegel, R. L. (1998). Reducing aggression in children with autism toward infant or toddler siblings. *Journal of the Association for Persons with Severe Handicaps, 23*(2), 111–118.

Konarski, E. A. (1990). Science as an ineffective white knight. *American Journal on Mental Retardation, 95,* 169–171.

Korn, J. H., & Hogan, K. (1992). Effect of incentives and aversiveness of treatment on willingness to participate in research. *Teaching of Psychology, 19,* 21–24.

Kunjukrishnan, R., & Varan, L. R. (1989). Interface between mental subnormality and law: A review. Psychiatric *Journal of the University of Ottawa, 14,* 439–452.

Leiber, M. J. (1992). Interactions between civil commitment and protective placement: An empirical assessment. *International Journal of Law and Psychiatry, 15,* 265–281.

Lurie, N., Pheley, A. M., Miles, S. H., & Bannick-Mohrland, S. (1992). Attitudes toward discussing life-sustaining treatments in extended care facility patients. *Journal of the American Geriatrics Society, 40,* 1205–1208.

McDonnell, J., Hardman, M., McDonnell, A., & Kiefer-O'Donnell, R. (1995). *Introduction to people* *with severe disabilities*. Needham Heights, MA: Allyn & Bacon.

McIver v. Krischer. (1997). *Issues in Law and Medicine, 12*(4), 385–389.

Morris, C. D., Niederbuhl, J. M., & Mahr, J. M. (1993). Determining the capability of individuals with mental retardation to give informed consent. *American Journal on Mental Retardation, 98,* 263–272.

Mulick, J. A. (1990). The ideology and science of punishment in mental retardation. *American Journal on Mental Retardation, 95,* 142–157.

Nihira, K., Weisner, T. S., & Bernheimer, L. P.(1994). Ecocultural assessment in families of children with developmental delays: Construct and concurrent validities. *American Journal on Mental Retardation, 98,* 551–566.

Obernberger, S. (1997). When love and abuse are not mutually exclusive: The need for government intervention. *Issues in Law and Medicine, 13*(4), 355–381.

O'Brien, J. (1994). Down stairs that are never your own: Supporting people with developmental disabilities in their own homes. *Mental Retardation, 32,* 1–6.

Oral arguments in Vacco v. Quill. (1997). *Issues in Law and Medicine, 12*(4), 417–439.

Parry, J. W. (1990). The court's role in decisionmaking involving incompetent refusals of life-sustaining care and psychiatric medications. *Mental and Physical Disability Law Reporter, 14,* 468–476.

Peine, H. A., Liu, L., Blakelock, H., & Jenson, W. R. (1991). The use of contingent water misting in the treatment of self-choking. *Journal of Behavior Therapy and Experimental Psychiatry, 22,* 225–231.

Quirk, P. (1998). Euthanasia in the Commonwealth of Australia. *Issues in Law and Medicine, 13*(4), 425–446.

Ramsey, P. (1973). Abortion. *Thomist, 37,* 174–226.

Reitman, J. S. (1996). The dilemma of "medical futility"—A "wisdom model" for decisionmaking. *Issues in Law and Medicine, 12*(3), 231–264.

Robertson, J. A. (1975). Involuntary euthanasia of defective newborns: A legal analysis. *Stanford Law Review, 27,* 213–269.

Rosner, F., Rogatz, P., Lowenstein, R., & Risemberg, H. M. (1992). Physician-assisted suicide. *New York State Journal of Medicine, 92,* 388–391.

Scofield, G. R. (1991). Privacy (or liberty) and assisted suicide. *Journal of Pain and Symptom Management, 6,* 280–288.

Sherman, R. A. (1991). Aversives, fundamental rights, and the courts. *Behavior Analyst, 14*(2), 197–206.

Smith, S. A., & Broughton, S. F. (1994). Competency to stand trial and criminal responsibility: An analysis in South Carolina. *Mental Retardation, 32,* 281–287.

Sundram, C. J., & Stavis, P. F. (1994). Sexuality and mental retardation: Unmet challenges. *Mental Retardation, 32,* 255–264.

Surman, O. S., & Purtilo, R. (1992). Reevaluation of organ transplantation criteria: Allocation of scarce resources to borderline candidates. *Psychosomatics, 33,* 202–212.

Szivos, S. E., & Griffiths, E. (1990). Group processes involved in coming to terms with a mentally retarded identity. *Mental Retardation, 28,* 333–341.

Turnbull, H. R., III. (Ed.). (1977). *Consent handbook*. Washington, DC: American Association on Mental Deficiency.

Ventres, W., Nichter, M., Reed, R., & Frankel, R. (1992). Do-not-resuscitate discussions: A qualitative analysis. *Family Practice Research Journal, 12*(2), 157–169.

Warden, S. (1993, January 23). Anatomy of a march. *Washington Post,* A8.

Weir, R. F. (1992). The morality of physician-assisted suicide. *Law, Medicine and Health Care, 20,* 116–126.

Wertz, D. C. (1992). Ethical and legal implications of the new genetics: Issues for discussion. *Social Science and Medicine, 35,* 495–505.

Wertz, D. C., Rosenfield, J. M., Janes, S. R., & Erbe, R. W. (1991). Attitudes toward abortion among parents of children with cystic fibrosis. *American Journal of Public Health, 81,* 992–996.

Wesley P. (1993). Dying safely. *Issues in Law and Medicine 8,* 467–483.

Wheeler, D. L. (1994). Obtaining informed consent. *The Chronicle of Higher Education, XL*(21), A8–A9, A16.

Williams, R. R. (1991). When suffering is unbearable: Physicians, assisted suicide, and euthanasia. *Journal of Palliative Care, 7*(2), 47–49.

Wolfensberger, W. (1975). *The origin and nature of our institutional models*. Syracuse, NY: Human Policy.

Wolfensberger, W. (1994). A personal interpretation of the mental retardation scene in light of the "signs of the times." *Mental Retardation, 32,* 19–33.

Wolf-Schein, E. G. (1992). On the association between the fragile X chromosome, mental handicap, and autistic disorder. *Developmental Disabilities Bulletin, 20,* 13–30.

Name Index

409

Subject Index